The History of Concord, Massachusetts

ALFRED SERENO HUDSON

The History of Concord, Massachusetts, A. Sereno Hudson
Jazzybee Verlag Jürgen Beck
86450 Altenmünster, Loschberg 9
Deutschland

ISBN: 9783849671808

www.jazzybee-verlag.de
admin@jazzybee-verlag.de

Printed by Createspace, North Charleston, SC, USA

CONTENTS:

PREFACE

The town of Concord is probably as attractive in historical features as any in this country. Its early connection with the American Revolution; its association with the life and works of Emerson, Hawthorne, Thoreau and other distinguished authors; and its having formerly been the County Seat of old Middlesex all contribute to make the place notable. It is thronged annually with thousands of visitors, some mere sightseers, some seeking inspiration from the shrines visited, some to say they have been to Concord.

The History of Concord written by Lemuel Shattuck and published in 1835, is not now easily obtainable. Only a few copies, if any, of the work of Charles H. Walcott, Esq., remain unsold; and the historical sketches of Rev. Grindall Reynolds, D. D., and the Hon. John S. Keyes were written for the Histories of Middlesex County, which are too bulky and expensive for common use.

Besides these standard works, nothing that we are aware of has been published of the town's consecutive annals, except occasional pamphlets and addresses. Because of these things we believe an available History may be desirable, and by the preparation of these pages we have sought to supply it.

The work is designed to be in two volumes; the first entitled Colonial Concord: the second, Provincial Concord.

Volume I includes the annals of the town from its origin in 1635, until 1692, at which time the Massachusetts Bay Colony became a Province, together with brief biographical sketches of the original grantees.

Volume II. will include the annals from 1692 through the Provincial period to the close of the Revolutionary war.

Volume I is divided into two parts. The first contains the story of the settlement setting forth the leading facts in the town's history, so far as known, to the year 1655.

In this portion of the work the writer has employed both fact and fiction; but in such a manner as to enable the reader easily to distinguish the one from the other. This method has been adopted because many of the early records were lost, and it is designed to supply the deficiency, as relates to manners and customs, by conjecture based on analogy as these were known to exist in other towns at the same time.

The second part is pure history. The facts are mainly given in chronological order and to a large extent set forth by copies of original records and ancient papers with references to the places where they are found.

A work on local history to be in the highest degree instructive should be more than a mere compilation of dates, statistics, and isolated facts, valuable only to antiquaries and genealogists. It should have such a background or setting of general history as will give the reader an intelligent understanding of the causes and results of the local events described.

For this reason, in instances where an occurrence is prominently connected with events in the country at large, the latter have been sufficiently described to show the relationship of one to the other.

No claim is made to great original research. The field of Concord history has been too carefully harvested in the past, to leave much opportunity for the gleaner to gather new sheaves, or to find much rich aftermath. We have collected our material from every available source whether of records, manuscript, publication or tradition.

1

We have avoided dogmatic assertion and have intended to state hypothetically whatever is doubtful or unsettled.

Prominent among the writers of local history from whom we have quoted are those of Lemuel Shattuck, Charles E. Walcott, Esq. Rev. Grindall Reynolds, D. D. Hon John S. Keyes, and Albert E. Wood. We have also received valuable suggestions from the late Alfred Hosmer, and are also indebted to the historian, Rev. G. M. Bodge, to the Littleton Historical Society, and others whose services have been kindly proffered and gratefully received.

That the work is free from errors it would be presumption to assert. No prudent writer of local history would make pretense to this. Neither do any who are charitably disposed and have had experience in the difficult work of the local annalist presume to judge the work of another from the standpoint of perfect accuracy. There are many subjects which will always be matters of doubt and controversy.

Evidence considered admissible by some might be rejected by others; and cases may occur when the evidence is considered about equal on either side.

This work has been written from the position of one who has great reverence for the religious faith of the fathers, and who recognizes in this faith a strong factor in whatever of greatness has accrued to us, as a Nation.

And if bringing out the facts, many of which are too little known, shall lead to a higher appreciation of the fathers and of the faith that made them what they were, one great object of the author will be accomplished.

A. S. H.

PART I. STORY OF THE SETTLEMENT OF CONCORD, MASS.

CHAPTER I.

A traveler's visit to an early homestead at Concord, Massachusetts — Scene at a Settler s fireside — Company expected—Strange sounds and sights talked about — Town Meeting topics discussed — Description of Concord in the present — Objects of Historic Interest — The North Bridge — Houses of the Revolutionary Period — The Wright Tavern — First Parish Meeting House—The Antiquarian House — Meriam 's Corner.

THE fire flickered and the sparks flew up the broad chimney, as a traveler sat on a fall evening before the half-burnt backlog, in Goodman Hartwell's snug farm-house in Concord town about two centuries and a half ago.

It was evident from the appearance of things that company was expected, for besides the usual oaken settle and chairs there were standing about sundry stools and a long, low bench. Presently a sound was heard at the door as if someone were fumbling for the latchstring, and as it opened several neighbors entered and also Goodmen Buttrick and Heald from the North quarter and Miles and Dakin from the South. A little later, Parson Peter Bulkeley arrived with the Gobble boys who had come from down by the river bay in an oxcart and having overtaken the minister had brought him along.

While waiting for others to come, various subjects were talked about, among which were some strange noises which Colonial Goody Dean said she "heerd near the buryin ground."

Some said they were made by an earthquake, others suggested a landslide, but these explanations did not satisfy Duty, who declared that "the sounds ware above the airth, not under it nor inside it. Besides," said she, "the milk has soured twice sence I heerd them so I think the cows heerd them too fur they feed there."

The matter being referred to the minister he said, after a moment's reflection, "Such things being unusual contain a lesson and should lead us to be circumspect and careful in our conduct." He was about to say more but was interrupted by a faint rap at the back door which was at the end of a low entry under the lean-to roof.

Goodman Hartwell snatched from the mantlepiece a save-all on which a short candle stub sputtered and going out soon returned with Goody Rice who had come across lots for an evening call. The newcomer created a fresh breeze of excitement for she confirmed what Duty had said of the queer noises, and also told about a strange creature which had several times been seen near the "great meadows," sometimes looking like a man and sometimes like a goat, but always vanishing when approached.

It was at once agreed that since the strange sight and sounds were at about the same time they might have the same cause, and as the matter was a serious one it was thought wise before considering it further to wait till others came in, "For," said Ensign Hosmer who had just entered, "there's some up our way who've heerd things, and I consait seen things too, and perhaps the creature is the 'specter wolf folks have talked of."

The further time of waiting was mostly occupied in talking over the condition of Dame Smeadley, who, Goodman Farwell who had just visited her said, was "low and languishing and much in need of the physic and paynes of the chirugeon."

When a sufficient number had come in to begin business all other subjects were soon dropped and the business of the evening was entered upon, which consisted of an informal talk about things that were to be considered at a coming town meeting, among which were matters connected with the cow commons, "the seating of the meeting house,"

and the making of some new rules relative to strangers, it having been noised about that one or two of these might become the town charge.

As each new comer entered he was introduced to the traveler, and when it was understood that he had journeyed all the way from Watertown to observe the customs, manners, and ways of doing things of the people at the Musketequid plantation, great interest was at once taken in him and a disposition was manifested to aid him in every way possible.

Among other marks of cordiality was the promptness with which they invited him to their "housen," offering the freedom and hospitality of their firesides and promising if he would set a time they would come for him.

The traveler appeared pleased, and afterwards in accepting their invitations, sat at many hearthstones listening to the sparks and gathering much of colonial lore and pioneer experience of the settlers of Concord.

Before narrating, however, what he heard and saw, we will speak of Concord as it is, and briefly outline its earlier history. Concord, Massachusetts, is in Middlesex County about twenty miles from Boston. It has a territorial area of about fifteen miles and a population of between five and six thousand. It is intersected from north to south by the New York, New Haven and Hartford railroad and from east to west by the Fitchburg division of the Boston and Maine. The Lexington branch of the latter road enters the town from the east, terminating at Concord Junction near the Massachusetts Reformatory. The trolley cars, also have found their way here, and rumble over the old roads and past ancient homesteads; and where once the farm boy drove his herd afield amid the quietness of nature, may now be seen strange vehicles, whose whizzing and whirring show plainly that Concord is not exempt from modern progress.

The Center or central village of Concord has a population of from two to three thousand and contains approximately five hundred private residences. It has no stores or shops beyond what are locally required; and more or less or its inhabitants are those who in retirement have sought here a restful retreat, or who, while doing business elsewhere, have made this their home. About midway of the central village is a small common or public square. In this square is a monument commemorative of the town's soldiers and sailors who died in the civil war. Near the corner of the Common to the easterly where the road turns towards the Battle Ground is the old County Court House where the District Court for central Middlesex holds its sessions. Southerly of the Court House is the Town House and on the opposite side to the westward is the old Registry of Deeds building used for county purposes when Concord was a shire town. To the northerly of the square is "The Colonial," a building associated with the Revolutionary war and the family of Henry Thoreau.

4

The places of interest in Concord are both historic and classic. Foremost among the former is the site of the old North Bridge about a half mile from the public square. By this spot several Provincial and British soldiers were killed April 19, 1775. The slain Americans were Capt. Isaac Davis and Abner Hosmer of the Acton Minute Men and the Statue of the Minute Man designed by Daniel C. French a Concord sculptor marks the spot on or near where they fell.

The English soldiers slain were two in number. They were under the immediate command of Lieut. Edward Thornton Gould and were of a detachment of three companies under the command of Capt. Lawrie.

The spot where these soldiers fell and the British stood when they began firing upon the Provincials just over the river is designated by a stone monument erected by the town in 1836. Near this monument by the sidewalk protected in part by a stonewall and in part by a simple chain fence are the graves of the two fallen Britons.

The locality of these monuments is called the "Battle Ground." The original historic bridge was long since swept away by a river flood, and the present one was erected for a memorial purpose.

A short distance from the lane leading to the bridge on the road toward Concord center is the old Jones house built in 1654, now the residence of John S. Keyes, Justice of the Central Middlesex District Court. In this house there lived at the time of the Concord fight Elisha Jones, an ardent patriot whose zeal was so demonstrative on the retreat of the British that his house was made a target of, and the accuracy of the Englishman's aim may still be seen by a bullet mark in the east end.

About a mile from the North Bridge stands the old Barrett house, the home in the Revolutionary period of Col. James Barrett who commanded a regiment of Middlesex militia.

To this place a detachment of Regulars were sent under Capt. Lawrence Parsons by Lieut.-Col. Smith, who with the main body of English soldiers were stationed at the central village. In the door yard of this house the Britons burned a parcel of Provincial cannon carriages and endeavored to discover and destroy other public property.

Various incidents are told of the doings of the Red Coats during their short stay about the house, and of the Provincials who sought to foil them. It is said of the aged mother of the Colonel that she would not seek for herself a place of safety when told that the British were coming, but preferred to remain saying, "I can't live long anyway and I'd rather stay and see that they don't burn down the house and barn."

As a soldier seized a trunk containing some pewter plates she pluckily exclaimed, "That is private property," upon which it was let alone. She also expostulated with a British officer who had laid hold of Stephen, her grandson, causing his release. When the hungry Britons asked for food she gave it saying, "We are commanded in the Bible to feed our enemies," and when offered money she said as she refused it, "It is the price of blood." In a field near the premises the provincials had concealed some muskets, and bullets were so disposed of in the house as to remain undiscovered, so that, all in all, Captain Parsons with his two companies of Regulars found but small compensation for his venturesome march. The Old Barrett house is about two miles north of Concord Center and is reached by the Lowell Road and the Barrett's Mill Road.

Near the Common or Public Square, and bearing a sign designating its historic importance is the "Wright Tavern" where it is asserted some of the English officers made their headquarters during their few hours sojourn in the town on April 19. Here, tradition says, Maj. John Pitcairn who commanded the British marines stirred his sugar and brandy saying as he did so, "In this way we will stir the blood of Yankees before night." This place was also the headquarters, or place of rendezvous, of the Concord Minute Men while awaiting on the morning of April 19, tidings of the advance of the English, and to this tavern Captain Smith and his company from Lincoln repaired and reported; so that it was within the course of a few hours the head center of two hostile forces who were to clash in battle on that fateful day. This tavern is very old. It was opened about 1747, by a militia captain named Ephraim Jones. In 1751, Jones sold the premises to Thomas Munroe formerly of Lexington, who continued the tavern business, and made the place, as Jones had done before him, a resort for the town officials on their days of public business, furnishing them with such refreshments as were demanded by the times and the special occasions.

About 1760, it came into the possession of Deacon Thomas Barrett, by a mortgage and was sold by him to Daniel Taylor. In 1775, Amos Wright became its proprietor, and although he kept an Inn there but a short period, it was long enough to give it a lasting name, for it has been known as the Wright Tavern ever since, notwithstanding it was sold in 1793, to Capt. Reuben Brown formerly of Sudbury.

Near the Wright Tavern on the south is the First Parish or Unitarian Meeting House, which stands on the site of one erected in 1712, where in 1774, the first Provincial Congress met, with John Hancock as President. The immediate predecessor of the present edifice after having been repeatedly remodeled was destroyed by fire April 12, 1900.

A few rods to the southerly, on the left going toward Lexington is the Antiquarian House, said to be one of the oldest buildings in Concord and formerly the home of Reuben Brown, a saddler. Here is now kept a collection of relics among which is the sword of Col. James Barrett, a gun of one of the English soldiers who fell at the North Bridge and a tobacco box of Maj. John Buttrick.

About a mile below the Antiquarian House on the Lexington road which was traveled by the English soldiers both in their advance and their retreat on April 19, is Meriam's Corner. Here was the first skirmish after the firing at the North Bridge, and the beginning of disaster to the retreating English, they having been attacked at this point by the Provincials who had crossed from the North Bridge over the "Great Fields" back of the Burying Ground, and also by companies from Reading, Chelmsford and Billerica.

A tablet suitably inscribed marks the spot of this memorable skirmish, and hard by, set back from the highway with its side upon the road to Bedford is the square antiquated dwelling house early occupied by the Meriams.

On one of its doors is the mark of a bullet received April 19th; and the brick oven and high mantle cupboard and corner beaufet are all indicative of the days of tallow candles and pewter plates.

On the east side of what is now Walden street at a place near the Congregational Trinitarian meeting house there stood on April 19, 1775, a store house in which some Provincial stores had been deposited by the Committee of Safety. These stores were saved from destruction by the English searching squad, by a ruse of the miller who had them in charge, who, placing his hands upon barrels of his own flour, said, "This is my flour. In the winter I grind my grain and in the spring I carry it to market."

The soldiers believing by this remark concerning his own flour that all the flour deposited there belonged to the miller departed saying, "We do not destroy private property."

CHAPTER II.

Places of Classic Interest — The "Old Manse" — Home of Ralph Waldo Emerson — The "Orchard House" — The "Wayside" Walden Pond— Thoreau's House — The Home of Frank B. Sanborn — Old Burying Grounds — Sleepy Hollow — Natural Objects.

THE places of classic interest in Concord are many and rare, for associated with its history both ancient and modern are men and women of world renown. Authors, poets, philosophers and jurists have contributed to the town's literary fame. The homes they once lived in are visited as shrines; and the paths once trodden by them are annually pressed by the footsteps of many who seek new inspiration by visiting the localities where these great men lived.

Probably the place of greatest interest is the "Old Manse." It is on the way to the "Battle Ground" and from its windows Rev. William Emerson witnessed the Concord Fight. Beneath its gray gables have lived a succession of the town's ministers; but what above everything else makes it distinguished is that it was for a time the home of Ralph Waldo Emerson and Nathaniel Hawthorne. Here the former wrote parts of his "Nature" and the latter "Mosses from an old Manse." It is about a half mile from Concord village standing back from the road amid a profusion of trees and shrubbery and has an air of antiquity and colonial comfort: The house was built for Rev. William Emerson in 1765.

The field between the "Old Manse" and the "Battle Ground" is supposed, on account of the many relics found there, to be the site of an Indian village.

Probably the object next in interest to the public is the house of Ralph Waldo Emerson. This like the birthplace of the bard of Avon is a place very dear to tourists. It is situated on the highway to Lexington and is easily distinguished by a cluster of pine trees which environ it. The house is of the colonial style of architecture, and of such pleasing proportions that it would be attractive to the passerby even were it not the home of the great essayist. It is now occupied by Miss Ellen Emerson, a daughter, and remains largely in its general outlook as when left by its former illustrious occupant.

The study which was on the first floor in one of the front rooms remains as when the great philosopher was alive, and the walks, the garden nooks, the home trees and such other objects as time, if let alone by man, leaves for years unchanged, are here much as in days of yore when Channing, Alcott, Hawthorne and Thoreau strolled among them.

Seldom, perhaps, in our land or in any land has a home been visited by more distinguished guests. From near and from far, from countries beyond the seas men have come to this spot and gone away bearing with them as an ample compensation the thought that they had visited the home of Emerson, walked in his footsteps, sat amid his trees and vines and heard the singing of birds and the humming of bees as he had heard them.

A quarter of a mile or more to the east on the left of the road is the "Orchard House". Here Bronson Alcott and his famous family lived; and here Louisa Alcott found material for "Little Women" and "Little Men" and several other of her notable books. In this house, Mr. Alcott founded the Concord School of Philosophy which was afterwards carried on in the small building at the rear.

Beyond the "Orchard House" is the "Wayside," another home of the Alcotts. It was sold by them in 1852 to Nathaniel Hawthorne who lived in it till his death, thus giving it double renown. The "tower room" at the rear was Hawthorne's study, and there he wrote "Tanglewood Tales" and "Our Old Home".

It is stated that the larches between the "Orchard House" and the "Wayside" were brought by Mr. Hawthorne from England. The place is now the residence of Mrs. Daniel Lothrop, who as Margaret Sidney wrote "Little Maid of Concord Town" and other books.

To the south of Concord center, distant a mile and a half over the fields and meadows toward the town of Lincoln is Walden Pond, made famous by the author, poet, and naturalist, Henry Thoreau. The pond is about a mile long and three miles in circumference. It is almost entirely surrounded by woods and has no visible inlet or outlet. Its waters are said to rise and fall but through what cause no one knows, for it is sometimes higher in dry than in wet seasons. Upon the northerly side of this pond Thoreau built a house which served him for a home for two years and two months. He moved into it in 1845, and it cost him, apart from the frame work, twenty-eight dollars and twelve and one half cents. The boarding was of material obtained from the house of a laborer. The frame was of timber cut and hewn by himself with a borrowed axe.

The building which was ten feet wide and fifteen feet long stood upon slightly rising ground about twenty rods from a small cove. It had a garret, a closet, a large window on each side, a door at the end and a brick fireplace. The land upon which it was situated was owned by Ralph Waldo Emerson who charged his tenant no rent. The site of the house is marked by a simple cairn made of stones placed there by tourists.

Not far from Thoreau's house was his bean field, where he raised one year "nine bushels and twelve quarts of beans" which he says he sold at a "pecuniary profit of eight dollars seventy-one and one-half cents."

As is the case with many forest lakes, Walden has its legend and as usual it relates to the Indians, who, as the story runs had displeased the Great Spirit by their profanity at a powwow, whereupon in place of a pleasant hill came a pond which took its name Walden from an old squaw who was the only survivor.

About this pond there lived several emancipated slaves left over from that period of New England history when the rum habit and human servitude were not considered inconsistent with a high standard of morality. Of these Thoreau mentioned Cato Ingraham who lived east of his "bean field, slave of Duncan Ingraham, Esq., Gentleman of Concord village;" and Zilpha, a colored woman who had a little house "where she spun linen for the towns-folk, making the Walden woods ring with her shrill singing." He also states, that on Blister's Hill down the road on the right lived Brister Freeman a "handy negro" slave of Squire Cummings and "Fenda his hospitable wife who told fortunes." Other habitants of the pond precinct mentioned in Thoreau's writings are one Breed whose hut he says was about the size of his own; and an Irishman, Hugh Quoil, whom rumor said had been a soldier at Waterloo, "Napoleon" as the writer continues, "going to St. Helena and Quoil to Walden woods."

Apart from its association with Henry Thoreau, Walden pond has attractions peculiarly its own. The waters are at times remarkably transparent partaking of the changeful sky tints, reflecting from the calm, clear depths the rich foliage upon its banks. In some places the adjacent ground slopes gradually forming a miniature beach where the bathers can walk out several feet, while in others it falls rapidly with a sharp, steep descent and the trees standing gracefully beside it give a very pleasing effect, so that all in all the variety of shore line affords the beholder very much the aspect of the famous Lake George in New York.

Walden pond may be reached from the Fitchburg R. R. station by a short walk down the track; or by carriage road down Thoreau street; or it may be reached from Monument Square by way of Main and Walden streets.

Among other localities especially associated with Henry Thoreau is the "landing place," a spot by the river near the South bridge, where he embarked on his trip for "A Week on the Concord and Merrimack Rivers," and to which repeated reference is made by him.

The birthplace of Thoreau is on the Virginia road, a somewhat disused way, opening from the Bedford road, and the house where he died is the third on the left before reaching the corner of Thoreau street as one goes up Main street. At the time of Thoreau's death the house was occupied by his family and afterward by Bronson Alcott and his daughter Louisa.

Just east of the South bridge with stone arches, on Elm street, is the home of Frank B. Sanborn, a well-known journalist and the biographer of Alcott, Thoreau, Channing, and John Brown. The house was for a time the home of William Ellery Channing, and to it men of letters have oft times repaired for literary and social converse.

Its distinguished owner and occupant became conspicuous in ante bellum days, by an attempt to kidnap him on an alleged order of the President of the United States Senate for contempt in not appearing before that body to be examined in the interest of the southern slave power. The scheme so far succeeded as to result in the capture of Mr. Sanborn under pretense of a lawful arrest but was soon foiled by the persistence and pluck of Mrs. Sanborn and the granting of a writ of habeas corpus by Judge E. Rockwood Hoar, then of the Massachusetts Supreme Judicial Court.

Mr. Sanborn was a friend of John Brown of Harper's Ferry renown, and through his influence the latter made a visit to Concord and lifted up his voice in behalf of freedom for the slave.

Next to the places made prominent by the Revolution and the objects and localities made famous by its distinguished men are its burying grounds. These places are of more than usual interest and few tourists leave the town without visiting them.

The one on the hill is supposed to be the oldest. Its exact age is not known but presumably it began as a church yard, for on a spot in the midst of it is supposed to have been built in 1635 or 1626 a little log meeting house; and it is altogether probable, as we shall subsequently state, that nearby contemporaneous with the erection of this first meeting house was the laying out of land, according to the old English custom for a place of burial. But be this as it may, the ground dates from about the beginning of the settlement and since then representatives of many generations have been buried there.

This yard contains fourteen or fifteen of the oldest gravestones in Concord, and more than two thirds of all the monuments and other grave markers bearing names of the original inhabitants of the town, are in this enclosure.

Upon these ancient tablets are the familiar names of Hosmer, Hartwell, Buttrick, Fletcher, Flint, Blood; also of Heald, Brooks, Wheate, Stow, Heywood, Temple, Taylor, Chandler, Clark, Minott and Melvin, — family names which, it will be observed as we pursue our narrative, are of men who were prominent in shaping the town's history. Besides the names, inscriptions and epitaphs in this yard have added to its interest. Conspicuous among them is one on the gravestone of the negro John Jack once a slave which is supposed to have been written by Daniel Bliss.

God wills us free; man wills us slaves.
I will as God wills; God's will be done.
Here lies the body of JOHN JACK
A native of Africa who died March 1773, aged about 60 years.
Tho' born in a land of slavery, He was born free.
Tho' he lived in a land of liberty, He lived a slave,
Till by his honest, tho' stolen, labors,
He acquired the source of slavery,
Which gave him his freedom;
Tho' not long before Death, the grand tyrant,
Gave him his final emancipation,
And set him on a footing with kings.
Tho' a slave to vice, He practised those virtues
Without which kings are but slaves.

Upon the summit of the hill within an altar tomb are the remains of Rev. Daniel Bliss, at one-time Pastor of the Concord church. Nearby is a tablet to the memory of the Rev. William Emerson. By the Catholic church, near Main and Bedford streets is a row of tombs in one of which repose the remains of the Rev. Ezra Ripley.

Space forbids a further notice of the names and exact place of sepulture of the honored dead. It is enough to say that the place is teeming with sacred associations of both the near and remote past; and as one looks up to it from the busy highway beneath, he may well feel it is a place unusual even in a town of exceptional interest.

The burying ground supposed to be second in age is on Main street a short distance west of the Bank. Tradition says that the land was given to the town for burial purposes by two maiden ladies. When it was opened for this purpose is not known; but it is designated in the records as existing as a burying ground as early as 1673.

The earliest stone is that of Thomas Hawthorne, who died November 17, 1697, and the next date found there is 1713. There are but few monuments and the stones are mostly slate. Prominent names on these stones are Hayward, Buss, Barrett, Miles, Potter, Stratton, Dakin, Jones, Davis, Prescott, Hubbard and Conant. Just east of this yard is the site of one of the town's old garrison houses.

"Sleepy Hollow" the latest cemetery in Concord is situated on the outskirts of the central village to the eastward, and a few minutes walk from the public square. The land was bought of the heirs of Reuben Brown in 1855. At its dedication the oration was delivered by Ralph Waldo Emerson, and an ode was sung which was written by Frank B. Sanborn.

11

The natural conformation is admirably suited for the purpose of a cemetery, and the locality was called Sleepy Hollow long before it was used as a place of burial. The first interment was in 1855. Here by the Ridge Path is the grave of Hawthorne marked by a simple stone bearing only his name. Just behind it is that of Thoreau, at the head of which is a common red stone, and near this is the grave of Emerson marked by a large piece of rock. In 1869 the town obtained a strip of land which united the New Hill burying ground with Sleepy Hollow.

The most notable natural object in Concord is the river. It takes its rise in Hopkinton and Westboro, and empties into the Merrimac at Lowell. Its original name is Musketequid, signifying in the Indian language grassy ground. It is about two hundred feet wide where it enters the town and three hundred where it leaves it. Its current is so slow as sometimes to be scarcely perceptible. Its meadows are broad and in places extend to woody uplands, fertile fields and pleasant secluded nooks, where grow the cranberry vine and the wild grape.

There are places of interest along the banks of this river in other towns as well as Concord; a few miles southwesterly in the town of Wayland is the Old Town Bridge of Sudbury over which the Indians under King Philip were driven in 1676. Nearby stands the late home of Lydia Maria Child, noted author and abolitionist. And on a tributary of this stream in the adjoining town of Sudbury stands the "Wayside Inn" made famous by Longfellow.

Other of the prominent natural features of Concord are three hills, Nashawtuc, Annusnuc and Punkatassett. These names are all of Indian origin. Nashawtuc is just west of the river, near the South bridge. At or near the foot of this hill was the wigwam of Tahattawan, and the squaw Sachem, two of the aboriginal owners of the Concord territory. At the southwesterly was the homestead of Major Simon Willard, the site of which is marked by a tablet. Annusnuc is at Concord Junction near the Massachusetts Reformatory. About this hill in the early days of the settlement was the "Hog-pen walk" a tract of land set apart by the original grantees for the pasture of swine.

On the plain land stretching to the southwesterly was held the famous State Muster by order of Gov. Nathaniel P. Banks, where in 1858 were encamped all the volunteer militia of Massachusetts.

Punkatasett is in the northeast part of Concord, about a mile from the North Bridge. It is conspicuous in Concord history as being the point of observation for the "embattled farmers" as they awaited events on the morning of April 19, 1775. Upon and about these hills there is a good outlook from which a large portion of the town can be seen and more or less of the winding river courses may be traced.

Fairhaven hill in the southwest part of the town overlooks Fairhaven pond, a tract of water or bay in Concord river having an area of about seventy-three acres. Brister's hill is beyond Walden pond near Lincoln. These latter places are frequently referred to in the works of Henry Thoreau.

Among the highlands which hardly attain hill proportions is the "Ridge" which skirts Concord center toward the east and south. This locality is of much historic interest as along the base of it was the "little strate strete", now a part of Lexington road along which the earliest house lots were laid out.

Upon the uplands to the rear were some of the first cornlands of the settlers, and from the more prominent points of this natural observatory they could look off upon their meadow lands which in those first years were the main means of sustenance for their livestock.

The Public Library building is of recent date being erected in 1873. It's situated at the junction of Sudbury road and Main street and stands upon or near, the spot where one of the town's old-time taverns early stood.

This Library is of especial interest because of what it contains of Concord authorship, having, besides the books that were written by Concord men and women, a valuable collection of the manuscripts from which the books were produced. There are also deposited here relics, pictures and pieces of sculpture relating to or made by Concord people. The Library is but a short walk from the public square and on the way to the Fitchburg Railroad station.

On the right hand side of Main street going westward and nearly opposite the Public Library is the house formerly occupied by the late Hon. Samuel Hoar. Here were born Hon. E. Rockwood Hoar, formerly a Judge of the Massachusetts Supreme Judicial Court and Attorney General in the Cabinet of President Grant, and Hon. George F. Hoar, United States Senator.

The portion of Main street from a point a little to the east of this place is of comparatively modern construction, the old road passing a little to the north of the present one, leaving the burying ground to the south of it.

The short strip of Main street between the Public Square and the beginning of Walden street was formerly in part the Mill Dam and was not used as a regularly laid out highway until almost within the memory of people now living.

The site of the first "Corn Mill" in Concord was here, at a spot just east of the Old Bank building. The pond which furnished the mill power extended from the dam southward.

The Trinitarian Church is upon, or near the site of Concord's first store which was kept by Robert Meriam, who had over a score of acres of land granted him in that locality.

The three-story dwelling house on the same side of Walden street, and next but one north of it, was long the only three-story house in Concord. It was built and owned by Duncan Ingraham, a wealthy merchant and father of Captain Ingraham of the United States Navy, who cleared the decks of his warship for action in the harbor of Smyrna, Turkey, in behalf of the Hungarian refugee, Martin Koszta, remarking, "Blood is thicker than water."

On the corner southwest of the Public Square, at the beginning of Main street was the Old Middlesex Hotel, where in the days when County Courts were held at Concord, many noted jurists were entertained.

Such is Concord in the present; and the foregoing are some of the objects and places much visited by the tourists, who on gala occasions and throughout the milder seasons throng into the town sightseeing, gathering souvenirs and pensively pondering upon the past.

CHAPTER III.

Origin of Settlement — Early Results — Erection of "Corn Mill" — Meeting House — Parsonage — Resumption of Traveler's Narrative — Coming from Watertown — First Conference with the Concord Colonists — Visit to the Home of William Hartwell — Indian Mission Service at Nashawtuc

THE earliest mention of this region was probably made by William Wood, in a book entitled "New England Prospects", a work supposed to be based upon his personal observation about 1633. An early description is also given by Johnson, in his "Wonder Working Providence of Sion's Savior in New England," published in 1654, in which the writer sets forth the Concord plantation as a place where the pioneers found hard fare and built their huts by leaning the rough logs against the hillside, which served the double purpose of a support and a chimney back.

The breaking of ground upon this plat for a permanent settlement was about 1635, when there arrived from England by way of Watertown, then Newtowne, which town, with Cambridge, then bounded Concord on the easterly, the other sides being bounded by an unclaimed wilderness, a company of colonists, under the direction of Rev. Peter Bulkeley, Elder John Jones, and probably Simon Willard, a merchant. Among the names of these colonists are some still familiar in Concord, which designate ancient and honored households, whose continuity with the distant past has never been broken by time's rude touch, and like faithful waymarks of history still chronicle by their suggestiveness what has made the old town great. Supplemental to such friendly services as borne by the living is that borne by the dead, and

"In that village on the hill,
Where never is sound of smithy or mill,"

the old-time tombstone, with its grime and its gray, and its quaint, weather-made defacement, stands representative of connecting links, as if, by a poor proxy like this, it could make the past and present, one.

That success attended the settlement is well attested by early results; and though the records of these results have been lost, so that for a half century and over not a sentence comes to us from the written page, save as we receive it from colonial sources, or in scraps and fragments of family documents, yet tradition, often true in its intent to preserve, and trustworthy even in matters of moment, speaks unmistakably of Concord's early town life. The earth and brush cabins soon gave way to substantial structures; the forest was felled along the plain land and the meadow margins; and a mill was erected "to grind the town's corn."

The spot selected for the mill was near what is now the Common, or public square, and the little stream upon which it was situated is known as "Mill Brook," though it is now so small as might lead one to doubt whether it ever had any mill power at all. But we should remember that not only do times and customs change, but nature changes also, and while the little brooklet that once ran a-roaring by the plain can still sing in the sweet strain of Tennyson, "And men may come and men may go, but I go on forever," yet it runs with a lessened current and speaks with a voice more subdued. Why it has become thus modest is not because it stands abashed at the busy human tide that trips over it, or because in many instances the traveler is all unconscious of its former worth and never stops to reflect that it once ground the

14

fathers' corn and furnished meal for the brown bread and pan dowdy; but its modesty is occasioned doubtless by a changed condition of surroundings.

It is considered probable by local historians that by the clearing up of the forests less water runs in some of the streams than formerly; and, probably, this is the case here; so that the Rev. Peter Bulkeley, for he it was who caused the erection of this mill, made no mistake, doubtless, when he gauged the capacity of this now miniature water power and concluded that it would suffice every purpose of a village grist mill.

But, conspicuous above everything else as marks of progress, were events of an ecclesiastical character. It was a usual condition of the colonial court in conferring a town grant that the grantees should maintain a gospel ministry, and pursuant to this important requisite the Concord inhabitants early erected a meeting house. The spot selected was on the summit of the ridgeway, near the burying ground, not far distant from the present public square.

The first structure was probably of logs; but this was soon succeeded by one of framework; for it was not in accordance with the customs of the forefathers to live in sealed houses while God's temples were neglected. Previously, however, to the building of the meeting house, and not far from the meadow margin a house was built for Minister Bulkeley. The site of this parsonage is on the present Lowell street a few steps from Monument Square and is modestly marked by a memorial tablet bearing the following record.

"Here, in the house of the Reverend Peter Bulkeley, first minister and one of the founders of this town, a bargain was made with the Squaw Sachem, the Sagamore Tahattawan and other Indians, who then sold their right in the six miles square called Concord to the English planters and gave them peaceful possession of the land, A. D. 1636."

This tablet has more than a passing interest to a reflective mind. It opens up by the suggestiveness of its simple inscription thoughts relating to over two centuries. Here, doubtless, if anywhere, centralized for a twelve month at least much that was political and religious, relating to the early land grant and its grantees. Here, doubtless, if in any place, was the cradle in which the township had its infancy, and as the little woodland municipality was nursed and grew strong, probably conference after conference was held here to consider matters relating to highways, bridges, and perhaps "cow commons" and "common planting fields;" for the minister in those days was not only the village high priest, but he had also a certain quasi magisterial jurisdiction, and by a generally recognized common law principle was "head center" of the settlement. As the parsonage was built prior to the meeting house, it is quite probable that the latter was here planned. Here, too, it may be, the church council was considered, which, July 5th, 1636, convened at Cambridge and organized the Concord church.

Other works of public convenience and necessity quickly followed. Roads were opened, bridges built, laws formulated; and the sunlight of civilized life was soon shining in the hitherto dark forest.

Such is an outline of some of the features of Concord, and of her early history. And now as we are about to leave the general for the particular, and consider character, processes, and events in detail, we will state that our plan is to suppose that we lived in that far away period, visited the settlers in their homes and sat by their fire-sides, and that the sparks were in part our oracles; also that we are living in the present when we are relating what we then saw and heard, together with some facts which occurred subsequently.

Assuming then that we are the traveler who two centuries and a half ago sat by the hearthstone of Goodman Hartwell on that fall evening, we will resume our narrative by saying, that we started from Watertown following the trail probably made by the first settlers, finding here and there what we suspected were sad traces of their toilsome journey, which Johnson has so dolorously described in his "Wonder-working Providence." On the upland was good traveling, but there were swamps and hard places which because of their wetness or stony nature, the forest fires of the Indians had not kept clear of underbrush, so that we were many times forced from our direct course and obliged to make long and painful detours. We traveled for a time by the "Old Connecticut Path", the ancient trail of the Nipnet Indians to the sea-board, and the same that was taken a few years previous by Rev. Messrs. Hooker and Stone on their way with a hundred people from Cambridge to Hartford, and which was traveled a little earlier by John Oldham of Pequod war fame. But, on arriving at the plain lands about the Charles river, near a stony brook, we veered northerly into a broken country, and after some hours emerged from the woods upon a sandy ridgeway where we found some squaws harvesting corn.

From our high point of observation we looked over a broad intervale threaded by a winding, sluggish stream, and we knew by this and by the houses on a little "strate strete" below us that we were in Concord.

Being a stranger to both place and people it mattered little whom we approached, or where we went, and as there were beyond the mill brook some people talking we joined them. Approaching, we found they were settlers and were talking English, but it was not such English as we hear to-day. In fact we found that here were brought together the dialects of Surrey, Kent, York and Bedfordshire. Goodman Buttrick, William Hartwell and James Hosmer were talking with Simon Willard the merchant, about a suitable place for a "cow common" because it had been represented to them that the cattle and goats roaming unrestrainedly through the "great meadows" much "damnified" the marsh red-top and lute grass, and that it would be better to have a place of common pasturage and "size it out" and have the income go to help pay the minister, rather than to risk any farther "indamnifying" by stray creatures.

As we introduced ourselves and disclosed our errand we were most cordially received and at once invited to their homes.

The first invitation was extended by William Hartwell, which we accepted; and it being near nightfall we were soon on our way to his house in the east quarter which we reached after a half hour's walk. Not long after our arrival we sat down at the supper table which was spread in a large kitchen before a great, open fire. After the meal and the returning of thanks, for Goodman Hartwell was a man of prayer, the men went to the barn to do the chores and the stranger was conducted to the front room to await the family and the arrival of the company who were to talk over town meeting. As it was no longer early evening, the work both indoors and out was done in a hurry and soon all were seated about the fireside as described in the opening chapter. And now to resume our narrative as there commenced, suffice it to say, the neighborhood gathering broke up to convene again at the parsonage two nights later. Meanwhile, particular care was to be taken in observing noises about the "buryin ground pastur" and as to tracks of the strange creature which Goody Rice saw.

16

Immediately after the company had departed we retired, for we were weary and the hour was late. Our sleeping apartment was large and unfinished, yet it had an air of comfort and its very commodiousness was of itself restful.

The night was a quiet one. Silence almost perfect pervaded everything, and our slumber was undisturbed save by the occasional hoot of an owl amid the pines which had been left near the house for a stormbreak and shade for the cattle.

As our visit to the Hartwells on this occasion was only for the night, it having been arranged with Timothy Wheeler at our interview with the settlers at Mill brook, to meet him at the village store the following day, and as we visited the Hartwell home later, we will defer any description of it for a subsequent chapter. About mid-afternoon of the next day we mounted an ox cart and behind a yoke of half broken bullocks started for the village, meeting Timothy Wheeler at the grocery according to previous arrangement.

As we were about starting for the home of our new host we learned that the Apostle, John Eliot, was to hold an Indian mission meeting that evening at the wigwam of Tahattawan near Nashawtuc, by candle light. Upon hearing this announcement, it at once occurred to us that here was an opportunity of learning something of Indian mission work, and of forming an acquaintance with its founder, Reverend John Eliot; so I asked Goodman Wheeler about the propriety of attending the proposed gathering. Our kind host immediately called back the swarthy messengers, who had just brought the announcement of the meeting, and upon my desire being made known, they invited me to go with them to Tahattawan's wigwam. It was not long before we were away, for although the distance was short it was approaching nightfall. Before starting, however, we called Goodman Wheeler aside to satisfy ourselves as to the safety of our proposed visit among the Indians, and to arrange about the time of making the visit to his home which had been so unexpectedly deferred. As to the first matter he informed us that we would be as safe with our Indian friends as with anyone; and with regard to the visit he said he would meet us at the coming town meeting when we would go home together.

CHAPTER IV.

Tahatawan's Wigwam — Supper Served by Squaws — Rev. John Eliot Preaching by Candlewood Light — Tribal Relations of the Musketequids — Stone Relics and Sites of Indian Villages — Spread of Christianity among the Concord Aborigines — Nashoba — Exile of Christian Indians to Deer Island— Humane Efforts of John Hoar in their behalf.

STARTING out from the village store we were soon in the forest. Our course was single file through a winding wood path to the meadow margin, and from there amid clustering cranberry vines, we proceeded to the river bank, where an Indian was waiting with a light canoe. As we passed through the woods we noticed along the way scarcely anything but tall timber trees, and these so scattered and so devoid of low branches that a man on horseback could easily ride between them. So singular was this circumstance that we afterwards inquired about it and were told that the woods were kept mainly clear of underbrush by the Indians, who, to facilitate the capture of game, annually set forest fires, and that this was done just before the fall rains. We stepped into the canoe, which was made of birch bark tied with thongs of deer skin and were soon afloat on the Musketequid and swiftly borne by the paddle strokes of Tahattawan to Nashawtuc.

The short river ride was made silently, for our friends were as mute as the grave, except that now and then a low murmuring went out from one of them, which, as it mingled faintly with the rising night wind — for it was now evening — and the strange whistling of the wings of a belated water fowl, were the only sounds save the splash of the water that we heard.

Soon we reached the large wigwam of Tahattawan near Nashawtuc and were ushered into the simple arcana of Nature's children, where all was new and surpassingly strange to us. In broken English we were presented to the head of the household and his daughters, of whom there were present Noonansquaw and Tahunsquaw, the latter of whom was the wife of Waban of Natick.

Although not invited to do so we sat down upon a low, rude platform upon which was a dressed skin of some wild animal, and silently observed the preparations for supper. Besides a "nokake" made of maize meal and baked in the ashes, they poured from a kettle into a rude wooden tray a stew or soup thickened with dried chestnut meal, and which consisted, as we were afterwards told, of dried alewives, several strings of which hung in a corner, and a few bones cut into small pieces. There was also in a smaller dish some substance that they called sic-qua-tash (succotash), which consisted of dried green corn and beans.

Supper over, we were glad enough to have our loneliness ended by the arrival of Messrs. Gookin and Eliot. It was not long before there entered several families from wigwams near, on both the upper and lower meadow and also several individuals from about the Assabet. The candlewood was soon lighted just outside the wigwam door, and the scene thereby revealed to us by these flambeaux was a weird and impressive one.

After a prayer in the Indian language Mr. Eliot addressed his swarthy audience in the same tongue, exhorting them, as our interpreter informed us, to beware of the evil influences of Hobbommoc (the devil), and to hold steadfast to the newly found Kiton (good spirit). Especially he advised them to beware of powwowing, and to have nothing to do with medicine men, whom he denounced as true children of Hobbommoc. At length, after another prayer in the Indian language, there arose the low sound of singing or chanting, in guttural, harsh, discordant tones; the effect was striking, for as the strains floated out over the moist meadows and up the woody slopes of Nashawtuc, not so much as the call of a night bird, not even the wind's moaning was heard, as a wild interlude to the words of the hymn.

At the close of the singing Mr. Bulkeley, who had accompanied Mr. Eliot, was asked to pray, and as the group kneeled on the matted leaves, such a petition went up from "Big Pray", as the lowly children of the Musketequid had rarely listened to. Slowly, reverently and peacefully, we were lifted heavenward by every sentence; and when he ceased we almost forgot we were on the earth.

At the conclusion of the evening services we were invited to remain all night, and as Major Gookin was proposing to do so, Mr. Eliot having gone home with Mr. Bulkeley, we accepted of our host's hospitality and were soon seated around the wigwam amid a little group consisting of Tahattawan's household.

As the flames flickered upward through the small aperture in the roof, we did not wonder so much at the copper colored complexion of the Indian, for every now and then the heavy night wind forced down the smoke, and an occasional rain drip on the coals made a close, thick atmosphere.

But the disagreeableness of an imperfect draught was soon remedied by Tahattawan, who, stepping to the door, dropped over it a coarse mat which was there pendent for this purpose, and which so completely closed the aperture that the smoke readily ascended; and as the sparks chased each other upward into the darkness, a strange feeling came over us and we almost wished that Goodman Wheeler had taken us home with him. Just then there entered the wigwam Major Gookin and Waban, the latter of whom could speak good English, having often acted as an interpreter and helper of Mr. Eliot in his mission work at Natick.

For an hour we sat conversing by the firelight and gained much interesting information concerning the aboriginal inhabitants of the Musketequid country and of their experience with the early settlers.

And now for a little time, exchanging fiction for fact, we will state some things about these Concord Indians that are matters of history.

Their tribal relations were with the Mystics, whose headquarters were at Medford. Their neighbors were the Pawtuckets, at Wameset (Lowell); the Ockoocagansetts at what is now (Marlboro), and the Natick Indians; the last three being probably related either to the Mystics or the Nipmucks.

The localities where the Indians lived are indicated by the presence of shells, arrow and spear heads and sometimes arrow chips, which are refuse material chipped from the stone when the arrow was made; also stone implements used for purposes of agriculture and cookery, and chisels, gouges, rude pestles or corn pounders. Some of the places where stone relics have been found, are the "Great fields" east of the center, the vicinity of "Egg Rock" not far from the "Hemlocks," about Fairhaven bay, on the south side of the river east of the "Old Manse," on the right of the river below Flint's bridge, the neighborhood of Spenser brook, and a place on the left bank of the river a little above the Fitchburg Railroad bridge where the river bends abruptly. At this latter point it is said, many bushels of shells have been found, and among them the remains of wild animals and parts of stone implements.

It is impossible to determine the exact number of Indians in the Musketequid country at the time of its settlement by the English. Probably the population was greatly reduced here as in other places along the Massachusetts Bay shores, by the pestilence that prevailed before the English occupation, so that very likely their villages were comparatively few and no more than small clusters of wigwams.

A portion or all of the Concord Indians, through the efforts of the Rev. John Eliot, who translated the bible into the language of the aborigines, early became converts to Christianity. These were gathered by Mr. Eliot and Major Daniel Gookin, into an Indian town or village named Nashoba, situated in what is now Littleton. The number of Indians thus gathered was about fifty-eight, representing ten families, only about twelve being able bodied men.

Nashoba was called by Major Gookin in his Historical collection the sixth praying Indian town. He states that, "The dimensions of this village were four miles square," that, "their ruler of late years was Ahatawance (Tahattawan), a pious man," and "their teacher is named John Thomas."

The petition for the establishment of this place is dated May 4, 1654 and was presented by Mr. Eliot. The Nashoba plantation began auspiciously and continued to prosper both in things temporal and spiritual until a war with the Mohawks, which resulted in its abandonment for a season, but as late as 1674, according to Gookin, it had become re-peopled and was in a "hopeful way to prosper."

There is ample opportunity for one to conjecture concerning the pleasant condition of things at the Nashoba plantation during the years immediately following its establishment.

As it was the custom of the Apostle Eliot to keep spiritual watch and ward over the native churches and to occasionally visit them for exhortation and conference, so we may suppose he did this one, and that more than once he journeyed from Roxbury to Nonantum (Newton) his first mission field, thence to Natick, and from there went on through the woods to Concord, visiting scattered wigwams by the way and the village at Cochituate pond (Wayland) and the home of Kato at Wigwam hill in Sudbury.

Upon his arrival at Concord, we may suppose that he made parochial visits among such of the Musketequid Indians as still lingered about their old haunts, faithful to the memory of their former firesides and the graves of their fathers. These visits completed, we may conjecture that the great Apostle passed on over the old Marlboro road, at that time perhaps a mere wood path trod mainly by the Occogoogansetts to Nashoba, bringing with him a benediction from their Bay brothers, and instructing them from the Up-Biblum (Indian bible.) But when Philip's war broke out the scene changed.

The Colonial communities everywhere became distrustful of all Indians, the praying Indians included, notwithstanding the evidence the latter were giving of continued loyalty, serving the colony faithfully whenever occasion required as spies, or as allies in the ranks of levied troops.

To such an extent did English distrust prevail that it was decided by the Colonial authorities to remove a portion or all of the Christian Indians to Deer island in Boston harbor, and the order was given and executed.

The details of this untimely closing of the Indian mission stations are sad to relate, and they remind one of the cruel treatment of the Acadians at Grand Pre, whose homes were broken in upon by the English and Colonial soldiers, and their families separated and cast forlorn upon a lone coast line extending from New England to Georgia.

Before the carrying out of this order, however, as related to the Indians at Nashoba, an attempt was made in their behalf which resulted in an order by the Colonial Court, that an arrangement be made by the Militia Committee and the selectmen of Concord that they be placed under the inspection of John Hoar of Concord, to see that they be kept employed for their maintenance and preserved from harm and the country made secure from them.

In pursuance of this arrangement, Mr. Hoar built a house for them near his own for their protection and comfort at night, and a workshop, in both of which they were under close surveillance.

The means thus provided by Mr. Hoar for the mutual protection of both the Indians and English were accomplishing their full purpose and would doubtless have continued to do so had it not been for an untoward interference with his plans, the account of which may be best presented by the following quotation from Gookin's "History of the Christian Indians."

"But some of the inhabitants of the town, being influenced with a spirit of animosity and distaste against all Indians, disrelished this settlement; and therefore privately sent to a Captain of the army, (Captain Mosely) that quartered his company not far off at that time, of whom they had experience, that he would not be backward to put in execution anything that tended to distress the praying Indians; for this was the same man that had formerly, without order, seized upon divers of the praying Indians at Marlborough, which brought much trouble and disquiet to the country of the Indians, and was a great occasion of their defection; as hath been above declared.

"This Captain accordingly came to Concord with a party of his men upon the Sabbath day, into the Meeting-house, where the people were convened to the worship of God.

And after the exercise was ended, he spake openly to the congregation to this effect: 'that he understood there were some heathen in the town, committed to one Hoare, which he was informed were a trouble and disquiet to them; therefore if they desired it he would remove them to Boston;' to which speech, most of the people being silent, except two or three that encouraged him, he took, as it seems, the silence of the rest for consent; and immediately after the assembly was dismissed, he went with three or four files of men, and a hundred or two of the people, men, women and children, at his heels, and marched away to Mr. Hoare's house and there demanded of him to see the Indians under his care. Hoare opened the door and showed them to him, and they were all numbered and found there; the Captain then said to Mr. Hoare, 'that he would leave a corporal and soldiers to secure them'; but Mr. Hoare answered, 'there was no need of that, for they were already secured, and were committed to him by order of the Council, and he would keep and secure them.' But yet the Captain left his corporal and soldiers there, who were abusive enough to the poor Indians by ill language.

The next morning the Captain came again to take the Indians and send them to Boston. But Mr. Hoare refused to deliver them, unless he showed him an order of the Council; but the Captain could show him no other but his commission to kill and destroy the enemy; but Mr. Hoare said, 'these were friends and under order.' But the

21

Captain would not be satisfied with his answer but commanded his corporal forthwith to break open the door and take the Indians all away, which was done accordingly; and some of the soldiers plundered the poor creatures of their shirts, shoes, dishes, and such other things as they could lay their hands upon, though the Captain commanded the contrary. They were all brought to Charlestown with a guard of twenty men. And the Captain wrote a letter to the General Court, then sitting, giving them an account of his action.

"This thing was very offensive to the Council, that a private Captain should (without commission or some express order) do an act so contradictory to their former orders; and the Governor and several others spake of it at a conference with the deputies at the General Court.

"The Deputies seemed generally to agree to the reason of the Magistrates in this matter; yet notwithstanding, the Captain (who appeared in Court shortly after upon another occasion), met with no rebuke for this high irregularity and arbitrary action. To conclude this matter, those poor Indians, about fifty-eight of them of all sorts, were sent down to Deer Island, there to pass into the furnace of affliction with their brethren and countrymen. But all their corn and other provision sufficient to maintain them for six months, was lost at Concord; and all their other necessaries, except what the soldiers had plundered. And the poor Indians got very little or nothing of what they lost, but it was squandered away, lost by the removal of Mr. Hoare and other means, so that they were necessitated to live upon clams, as the others did, with some little corn provided at the charge of the 'Honorable Corporation for the Indians,' residing in London. Besides, Mr. Hoare lost all his building and other cost, which he had provided for the entertainment and employment of those Indians; which was considerable." This was in February, 1675-6. Only a few Indians returned to Nashoba after the exile.

Such was the melancholy ending of the mission at Nashoba, in which more or less of the Musketequid Indians were gathered together in Christian fellowship. It is the old, oft repeated story of the supremacy of the strong over the weak and the power of evil to destroy in a few days what it took many years to construct.

There is also seen in this sad episode of Indian history something of the transmuting power of the gospel, in that while others of the aboriginal tribes were filled with vengeful hate toward the white men and giving way to the powerful persuasions of King Philip of Pokanoket to pillage the fields, to burn dwelling places, and to murder or capture the inhabitants in defense of their ancient hearthstones and hunting grounds, the Christian Indians stood fast in their new faith and proved firm friends of the English.

William Tahattawan, brother of John the Chieftain, although among those who were exiled to Deer Island, served as a faithful guide of Major Savage, a Colonial officer.

Thomas Doublet or Nepanet, another of the Nashoba Indians did good service in procuring the release of Mrs. Rowlandson, who was captured at Lancaster; and when Captain Wadsworth and his command were destroyed at Green hill, Sudbury, the Christian Indians brought from Deer Island were the first to search the battle ground and help bury the slain, weeping, it is said, when they saw their prostrate forms.

Upon these things history has not greatly enlarged; and while the multitudinous records of the misdeeds and evil practices of the pagan Indians have been preserved, the true, the noble, the honorable acts of the Christian Indians may have been too much overlooked, Christianity thereby losing a merited tribute.

After a while the conversation flagged, the fire burned low, and two or three of those who had been sitting on the ground with their hands clasped around their ankles and their heads dropped upon their knees withdrew, flung themselves upon the couches and pulled up the bear skins.

As Major Gookin suggested that we also retire, we did so, and soon all was silent save the pelting of the storm on the bark covering and a slight splashing of the river waves against the canoe.

As the strange surroundings were not conducive to the soundest slumber we awoke. Once we heard the howling of a wolf not far distant. Now and then there was the jerky bark of a fox, and toward morning a bear poked his head under the rush mat hanging at the doorway, and we caught a glimpse of his long, slender snout, but he quickly withdrew when he sniffed the scent of fire.

CHAPTER V.

Duck Hunting — River Scenery — Beaver Dam — Indian Granary — Sweating Pit — Mysterious Sight upon the Meadows — Arrival at the Manse.

AT length the morning came and the inmates of the wigwam arose; thoughtless of toilet or bath, they swung the kettle over the coals as on the night previous, and threw into it a little maize meal, to which was added a couple of slices of dried pompion, and a small handful of ground nuts. Not desiring to stop for breakfast, we thanked our kind hosts for their hospitality, and upon invitation of Mr. Gookin stepped into a canoe and were paddled across the stream by Waban.

Upon stepping ashore we at once entered a path by the meadow side, which we were told would take us to Parson Bulkeley's house, when we met Goodmen Humphrey Barrett and George Hayward, each carrying a gun with a long slender barrel and a short stock. We recognized them at once having met them the day previous at the village store. They informed us that they were going up the river duck hunting and would be glad of our company.

Being desirous of learning something about the river and its meadows and the game that frequented them, the invitation was accepted with hearty thanks. Before going, however, we went to the parsonage to inform the minister of our change of plan and get some breakfast, also to borrow a fowling piece as Humphrey Barrett said the minister had a good one.

A half hour and we were back and afloat, gliding along by willow clumps and water brush, starting now and then a solitary bittern or musquash and pushing our way mid such a profusion of lily pads and fragrant blossoms as half concealed the river's channel.

As we moved slowly up the stream past Nashawtuc and the South bridge, we were as much in the wilderness as if midway between Concord and Watertown, for the trees approached the meadow bank on each side, and but for the smoke from various chimneys near the Ridgeway, and the sight of a clearing by Major Willard's at the bridge, we might for the moment have forgotten that there was a settlement at Musketequid. The scenery was beautiful.

The trees were touched with a tint such as Nature in her best mood only produces after the first fall frosts. The sky was blue, and such a blue as is seen after an autumnal storm and when the very cloudlessness causes it to be called a "weather breeder." Afar over the woodland were occasional traces of white smoke indicating scattered Indian encampments; while circling high over all were here and there large flocks of wild water fowl, some of which after wheeling gracefully over the meadows, at length settled on the stream. So many times they did this and so numerous were the birds that we got many good shots.

Having passed Fairhaven bay we noticed a small stream that suggested trout, and as we had fishing tackle which Parson Bulkeley had also loaned us and moreover were a little reluctant to accompany our friends further, since they were intending to go as far as Gulf brook to hunt for other game, we requested to be allowed to land that we might fish and look about till their return.

After stepping ashore, we strolled inland by a small stream, fishing as we went, and now and then capturing one of its speckled inhabitants, until we discovered a miniature mill dam, which much surprised us. The dam was about five feet high and well braced, and the thin waterfall that slid over it upon the green moss beneath made a soft, pleasant murmur. Not a creature was visible, and so peaceful was the scene that we involuntarily stopped at the first glimpse of it. And it was well we did, for had we not, we should have lost an interesting spectacle. We had come upon a beaver dam, which the settlers, even with their laudable greed for beaver skins, had overlooked. As we crept through the alders and tangled junipers for a safe point to observe from, we found ourselves in a well-worn path, which was doubtless made by wild animals as they watched the little colony, to make it their prey. For half an hour we observed the doings about this beaver dam from a distance, and then in order to observe it more particularly, we advanced nearer. In an instant, there was a sound as if a hundred beaver tails had slapped concertedly upon the pond, and almost simultaneously silence reigned, broken only by the soft splash of the waterfall and the whistling wing of a wood duck which sought its haunt in a neighboring oak. The tocsin had sounded and the clan was gone. Well knowing that further study of the beaver there was impossible, we concluded to make a fire and cook some trout and see if perchance the sparks would say anything about them.

As we saw the day previous at Goodman Hartwell's that we could start a blaze with the flint lock of our fowling piece, we quickly whipped out some tow wadding, and placing it over the powder pan, pulled the trigger.

The sparks caught, and the tow was ablaze, and nursing the feeble flame with some dry moss we soon had a good lire and were listening to what the sparks said about the beavers. We learned that at one time they were quite plentiful in the Musketequid region and that certain localities were named after them, as Beaver hole, Beaver meadows, Beaver pond, and Beaver brook; we learned also that they were much sought after in trade and that a company was early formed to traffic in them, and that Simon Willard was at the head of it; we learned, furthermore, that the Indians valued the fur next to wampum; that it was a rude standard of value; that court fines were sometimes paid in them; and that they were good if taken in any month with an R in it.

At length the sparks ceased, and as our trout were about broiled, having before listening placed two of nearly a pound weight upon a couple of spits, the largest, which weighed about three pounds, having been reserved for Parson Bulkeley, we dined sitting upon the moss among the birds.

We had hoped and expected from what we had heard to obtain a few salmon and some shad, but our expectations proved groundless, and showed our ignorance of history; for although these fishes are abundant in the spawning season at the falls, yet at other times they are not numerous.

However, we had no cause to complain, for there was no dearth of other things that were desirable. The woods were full of brown nuts, rich river grapes hung in clusters beside the meadows, the ruffed grouse made the woods resound with their whirring flights, and several wild turkeys crossed our path. We now concluded to steer straight through the woods to Fairhaven, where the boat was to stop for us; so, putting up our fishing tackle and carefully extinguishing the fire, for we had heard that the colonial court had passed a law forbidding the Indians setting fires in the woods in the fall season, from the great danger of their spreading, we struck off due east from the dam and soon found ourselves in a sunny upland which indented the forest like a small estuary in a sea of grass.

As we emerged from the low birches on the wood's border we saw not far from us two Indians, and near them what looked like a large earth oven or a half underground tomb. One of the Indians was sitting at an aperture at the bottom and the other was at the top pouring down something, while from the lower aperture steam was rapidly issuing, nearly enveloping the man who sat near it. Curiosity prompting our approach we soon found that here was an Indian "sweating pit," such as we were informed might be connected with every well-appointed wigwam of a Sagamore (subordinate chief). Within the pit was a small stone heap, which had been previously heated, and the man at the door was a patient, who was receiving treatment, while the zealous head of the sanitarium sat at the summit pouring in water for the purpose of generating steam.

In broken English everything was explained to us, both about the process and the cure; and then the Indian, looking at our game, inquired of our day's hunt, while we in turn, by our inquiries concerning their hunting, drew forth much interesting information. Among other things we learned that they seldom stocked up with game until late fall, because, having no salt, they relied mainly upon the weather as a preservative.

As the subject of food was before us and the Sagamore noticed that our queries were quite particular, he asked us to visit his granary, which was another low earth mound of about the dimensions of the sweating pit. We accepted the invitation. The Indian pulled away some short poles, which he said were placed there to keep off bears, and we leaned over and peeked in. Stored snug in every cranny were eatables of various kinds, and in such quantities as might well explode every theory of Indian improvidence.

There were small pompions (pumpkins), some acorns, walnuts, a parcel of ground nuts, several strings of dried shad, some split salmon, a stack of alewives, a pile of raccoon skins (tanned), a huge heap of corn, and three honey combs. The corn he said his squaw raised, and that the whole plot upon which it was planted was broken up by her with a stone hoe. He afterwards showed us a specimen of the hoe, which was a sharp stone fastened to a handle with a sapling withe. The nuts were gathered jointly, and the fish were taken by himself, it being no part of a woman's task to take game, she doing wigwam work or being a field hand. After this last interesting information our noble friend, for such he appeared to be notwithstanding his low estimate of a squaw's sphere, inquired after "Big Pray," as he recognized the parson's fowling piece, and requested us to take a salmon to him. Upon our assurance that we would gladly do so, he thrust down into his underground storehouse a sapling pole with a spearpoint, the same, he said, which he thrust into it when it was captured, and brought up a ten pound fish, which he deftly rolled and wound with a willow twig for convenient conveyance. By this time the other Indian, who evidently was much recuperated by his late treatment, brought pipes; not being a smoker, we refused them, yet the act showed such friendliness that we ventured to inquire further about their hunting habits. We learned that the great hunt of the year came in late autumn, and at a time when a warm, hazy atmosphere made animate nature unusually astir. In other words, it was intended to be the last warm spell of fall, when the game captured would keep, and from this fact we were not slow in inferring that here was the true origin of Indian summer, and that whenever such a "spell" comes, if sufficiently late, it might be so called. We did not visit the wigwam, well knowing there was probably nothing new there; besides, the shadows were lengthening by the birches and the long lines of wild duck, which are more active toward evening, announced that nightfall was near: so, while the steam was still issuing from the "sweating pit," we bade the Indians good-bye. At the bay we found Goodmen Hayward and Barrett, and in the boat were several turkeys and a small deer, the latter shot not far from "Gulf brook."

But a step and we were in; and down the Musketequid we glided, through the bay, past the hill; and soon on the banks of the south meadow we saw the lights of several wigwam fires. The night was dark and it began to rain, for the storm presaged by the morning "weather breeder" had set in, and swift clouds from the southerly gave a threatening prospect. It was not long before there loomed a light from Tahattawan's wigwam at Nashawtuc, which was quite welcome, as it showed we were nearing home. But we were not to reach it quite as soon as we thought, for scarcely had we passed the precincts of this last point, when, of; sudden, Goodman Barrett dropped his paddle and almost fell, as with a shriek he uttered something about "a sight."

Quickly starting up, for we had crouched low to avoid the storm, we saw "the sight," which consisted of a small luminous ball just over the meadow, slowly moving and only a few rods ahead of us. Gently shoving the boat towards the bank beside some water brush we lay low and quietly waited. It was not long before the strange light vanished, but so thoroughly aroused were we to the danger of encountering a spook if we proceeded, that we concluded to remain where we were until the apparition, if such it was, had settled itself. While we sat with bated breath by the water brush various conjectures were made as to the cause of the strange "visitation," as our friends called it, and Goodman Hay ward ventured the suggestion that "as near as he could make out it was over the 'mort stone' near the Cart bridge by the 'Carsey,' and he had heerd it was a bad sign to set a 'cops' down anywhere after it was started, and this was done with John Heald's 'cops' when they stopped the bier at the 'mort stone' to keep the 'buryin' cloth on."

But Goodman Barrett did not think so, "for," he said, "Mort stones wus made on purpose to set copses on when the bearers got tired of carryin 'em: besides, John wus everybody's friend, and it wus not likely that his sperit would haunt the medder-land." As for myself, I did not know. I had heard somewhere and sometime of strange lights called "Will-o'-the-wisp," but I had never seen one and was not sure, so I kept still; and as Goodmen Barrett and Hayward thought we had better leave the boat and go to the manse across-lots, I acceded, and we were soon ashore.

It was but a short walk that took us from the landing place to a point where we got a glimpse of the friendly light gleaming out of the little manse window, and, perhaps, the distance appeared less because of our haste, for as the darkness deepened and the pelting storm increased, we hardly looked backward or sideways, except to take a furtive glance toward the "mort stone" when we crossed the mill dam. On arriving indoors, however, all was cheerful.

Our wet doublets (thick, sleeveless jackets), were thrown aside, and having dried our clothes by the welcome blaze of Parson Bulkeley's bright fire, we were soon seated upon the oaken settle regaling ourselves with a posset (porringer) of hulled maize and goat's milk, in pleasant anticipation of a proposed talk on the town meeting, which was to take place on the morrow.

In preparation for the neighbors who were to convene for the evening's conference, the parson had brought in an extra settle from the room adjoining and placed an armchair at the hearth's corner

CHAPTER VI.

Informal Talk Preparatory to Town Meeting — The Apparition — Exodus of Concord Settlers to Connecticut — Statement of Rev. Cotton Mather — Effect of the Exodus on the Laity — The Town Meeting.

IN the short space of time before the first arrival not much was said of the ordinary day's happenings, for all the talk was on the episode closing.

That we had seen something strange no one doubted, but, it was said, "sich things have been observed before," and that this was similar to that seen by Goody Bateman at "Cedar Croft" and by Prudence Ball up at the "bend." That it prognosticated evil, however, was not thought probable by the Parson, to whom all looked in this matter, as in every other, for sound counsel and safe solutions, because on other similar occasions nothing had happened out of the ordinary, except that shortly after Goody Bateman's discovery the Pequod war broke out; but there were other signs about that time, such as sounds over the trees, and the pale flashings of a luminous night mist, and a sickly look of the sun, which latter, however, some were venturesome enough to assert was caused by a dry spell. With these various conjectures as to the cause, the subject was dismissed after a few practical remarks by the pastor about the proper way of improving all strange and inexplicable phenomena.

When the company had assembled we saw that not all were present whom history informs us were early at the plantation. Among those absent were Elder John Jones, Goodman Middlebrook, two of the Wheelers, and some others. Both personal interest and curiosity prompted us to inquire the cause of this; but as Goodman Hayward when on the boat had intimated that some families had gone away and that there had been discord in the new township, we kept still, thinking that when the sparks snapped they might tell us. But as there was just then burning on the back log only some small split spruce which came from the Parson's mill meadow swamp, the sparks could say nothing about it.

Presently someone brought in an armful of cleft chestnut, which we were informed was cut at Simon Willard's at Nashawtuc and came from a clump of trees in his clearing, beneath which the faithful pastor and his beloved parishioner, Mr. Willard, had often held sweet but sad converse on town affairs. As the wood was thrown on the "cob irons" and began to crackle and glow, while Jude Farwell puffed at it lustily with a small pair of buff colored bellows, we knew we should soon hear something, since it is characteristic of chestnut-wood to snap freely. Nor were we wrong in our conjecture, for as the coals brightened the sparks snapped, and we eagerly caught the following: There had been an exodus and a sad one. Some of the original grantees had died. Mary, the wife of James Hosmer, was buried December 3, 1641; Joseph Meriam died January, 1640; and Jane, the wife of Timothy Wheeler, died in December, 1642. But other causes besides death had broken the ranks. Several had returned to old England; some had gone to settlements near the sea; and in October, 1644, about one-eighth part of the Concord colony followed Elder John Jones to Fairfield, Conn. Of course, curiosity was aroused to know the cause of this last removal; but as before intimated, we surmised that the subject might be a delicate one, and that some present might be sensitive to any inquiries we might make concerning it.

But soon the sparks snapped out more vigorously than ever, and the inference from them was very direct and clear that it was not alone the "badness and wetness of the meadows" or the "poverty and meanness of the soil" that caused all the trouble, but an inharmonious mixture of too much ruling Elder with a proper amount of teaching Elder; so that it was difficult to tell where the authority of the latter began and that of the former ended. This position of the sparks was confirmed in our minds by Cotton Mather, author of the "Magnolia," who stated that "difficulties arose between the minister and people at Concord, which were settled by calling a council after the abdication of one of them," that is, one of the ecclesiastics; and, also, "that upon Mr. Bulkeley's pressing a piece of charity disagreeable to the will of the ruling Elder there was occasioned an unhappy discord in the church of Concord," and the same thing is also implied in a letter of Rev. Peter Bulkeley to Rev. Thomas Shepherd of Cambridge, in which he asks his opinion as to the relative power of the ruling Elder and the pastor; and also in a letter of Mr. Bulkeley to Cotton Mather, when he hints about "The evil of the times we live in, and what mischief one lofty spirit that has reputation for understanding can do among the weak."

When the sparks from Mr. Willard's cleft chestnut burned low we hardly expected to learn anything of the effect of this ecclesiastical broil on the laity; but just then Robert Fletcher threw on the fire a stick of well-seasoned pine, which we were told was cut and hauled for the minister from trees growing by the highway on the "strate strete" by the "housen," where a large share of the original settlers lived, and under which many conversations had been held. Upon this, we expected to obtain just the information we desired; and as the fire flashed and the sparks merrily snapped up the chimney flue, we learned that the ecclesiastical disturbance had a depressing effect on the laity financially; so that some refused to pay their proportion of the public charges; and a council called to consider matters had advised the clergy to be content with what they got, since the burden on the people was heavy. From these statements we inferred that, though the minister's salary was only about £70 annually and this to be paid partly in country produce, yet, for the people to be taxed in addition for a supernumerary, was thought too grievous.

We also inferred this from the fact that in 1645 Lieutenant Simon Willard was excused from attendance as deputy to the General Court, and was supposed to go home to cheer up the people; and from the fact that about the same time the Court passed an order forbidding any person leaving the townships of Concord, Sudbury, and Dedham except by permission of the selectmen; and that the Concord citizens be exempt from the payment of certain rates for three years; only directing that they still exercise in the train band.

As the various topics talked of were considered in the town meeting on the day following, we will not refer to them until that meeting is described. It is sufficient to say that while this preliminary conference in some of its features might correspond to the modern caucus, yet in others it did not, for there were no objectionable politics whatever, neither was there anything representative of two parties; but it was only an informal neighborhood gathering, designed to expedite matters at the coming meeting. What was talked about was an admixture of social, ecclesiastical and civil interests, showing plainly a quasi-connection of church and state, and best designated, it may be, as a New England theocracy, where the old maxim, "Vox populi est vox Dei," was reversed and made to read, "Vox Dei est vox populi." When the conference broke up the room was soon vacated. There was no lingering for a last word of senseless small talk, but soon all was still except for the clink of the tongs on the andirons as Parson Bulkeley heaped the brands on the back log and tenderly covered them with ashes. The storm beat on the diamond-shaped window panes; a fox barked near the out-buildings, while from afar, beyond the meadows near where the "sight" appeared, came the deep baying of Simon Willard's two house dogs. We picked up the brown "betty," and carefully carrying it so as not to spill any of the grease, we bade the Parson good night and went to our room. We found it an unplastered one, opening into the lean-to garret, upon whose roof the autumn rain was falling pleasantly.

To describe an old-time town meeting at Concord as it occurred in the remote past is a difficult and delicate task, since the records of each session for about the first half century of the settlement were probably destroyed, as before stated, in the destruction of Major Simon Willard's house by fire. But if we assume that Concord had customs in common with other colonial towns, and make conjectures based on analogy, we may suggest what may have taken place in a town meeting at Concord about 1655. Let it be understood, then, that though the following narration is in part fictitious, yet, like much of the foregoing, it is designed with due reference to such matters of tradition and record as have come to us, to set forth the character of a people and the customs and usages of an age long since vanished. The next morning we arose bright and early.

The sunlight streamed into the manse windows and stretched across the mill meadows, giving assurance that the storm had subsided. As it was our purpose to note everything about the settlement, while breakfast was being prepared we walked out to look over the premises. The house was not by any means an uncomfortable one, for though it was low and plainly built, yet it was snug and fairly commodious. The chimney was of stone, with clay mortar; the outside was covered with "clayboards" (clapboards), so called because they were fastened to the clay daubing of the walls, and the roof was thatched with meadow "blue joint."

As we strolled abroad beyond the meeting house and over the Ridgeway we came to one of the "common planting fields," where many pumpkins still remained ungathered, and now and then scattered on the ground was a long, full ear of maize, showing the value of fish as a fertilizer, and also that though the Indians had tilled this same field long before the English purchased it, the soil was still strong. At the farther end of the enclosure we saw a red deer timidly browsing among the weeds for stray corn, while skulking along the outskirts of the adjacent woods was a lank wolf. Upon seeing the wolf we were reminded that it might be breakfast time and made haste to return, crossing over the burying ground to the street, this being nearer than the way we came and farther from the wolf.

We were shortly at the manse door and seated at the table. The morning meal consisted of toast made of goat's milk and journey (johnny) cake, so-called from the ease of making and its adaptation to people journeying. The toast was served from a tureen, which had been placed in an iron chaffing dish with coals in it, this useful article having been brought into requisition to keep the breakfast warm till our return. The trenchers (plates) were of pewter, and beside each was a beaker of water. There was also some apple mose which the fruit of a few apple trees the first in the settlement had afforded, and this, with some cranberry tarts made with rye crust, completed the meal. After breakfast the Parson returned thanks and taking the well-worn Bible from a shelf read a portion of it, then kneeling and with hands reverently clasped upon its dark leathern lids, offered upon that altar in the wilderness a worship that was far more than form. After prayer he exchanged his light outer garment for a red "doublet," and went to the barn to fodder his stock. We accompanied him, conversing on various practical matters, among which was the value of meadow grass, and our conclusions were that notwithstanding what some have said about its worthlessness, it nevertheless was quite serviceable, and that without it perhaps the settlers' cattle would have starved. The weather also was considered, and about this we concluded it was no colder in Concord than elsewhere, especially if we could credit the statements of good Cotton Mather, that in Salem it was so cold that sap forced out of the wood by the fire in the middle, froze simultaneously at both ends.

After the chores were done, which were few, for the parson had but two cows, we returned to the manse and soon went to the meeting house where the town's business was to be transacted pursuant to a warrant previously posted on the door, and also upon a "publishing post" by the wayside.

As we entered the low, rectangular structure, almost severely plain in its appliances, and with no chimney, steeple, or porch, we saw at a glance that we could learn nothing from the sparks about the political management of the municipality as it related to the past, for there was no fireplace. We reverentially removed our hats and seated ourselves in one of the hard, pen-like pews before the communion table, behind which the moderator afterward stationed himself; and while waiting for the session to open we talked with Ensign Meriam as to the methods by which town affairs were conducted.

Our conversation on this subject was soon interrupted by the arrival of "Clark" Willard with the "town books;" whereupon by motion of Goodman Potter, Ensign Hosmer took the chair and the session began. Parson Bulkeley was asked to pray, the "clark's" records were read and "silentiously" approved, and business commenced. We soon saw that the principles of parliamentary usage differed but little from those of the present, though there were some quaint variations in terminology. If a measure was passed without opposition it was said to be passed by a "silentious" vote. In some instances "it was resoluted," and so recorded, but generally, acts were passed by a "majer vote" or by a division of voters, and the record might read "by a clere vote." The resolutions and measures adopted ranged all the way from the appropriation of twenty shillings to pay for the "diet" of the deputy to the Colonial Court, to the requisition of a receipt from Abimeleck Bateman for the ninepence paid for publicly whipping a stranger for disorderly drunkenness, and for the sixpence paid for placing a persistent Sabbath breaker in the stocks.

Among the officers chosen were selectmen, commissioners of rates, highway surveyors, tythingmen, fence viewers, and a "dark." Among the appointments was that of a person to procure a "branding iron" for marking horses, a person to take care of the town's stock of ammunition; a person to beat a drum to call people to meeting on Sundays and lecture days, and to sweep and keep clean the meeting house; a committee to establish rules for cutting wood on the "commons"; a person to look after and repair the watch house; and George Fowler was appointed to "breed salt petre" in some out-house used for poultry. Mr. Simon Willard was allowed to sell wine and "strong water," and was to exercise the "train band."

Among things "ordered" were that "all persons who shall cut down trees within half a mile of the meeting house shall cut them up within three months;" (This order was perhaps to prevent forest fires.) that "any persons who neglect to attend town meeting, they having been properly warned, shall pay a fine of two shillings, and if they leave before the close they shall be fined the same;" and that "the chief trees shall be left standing by the highway as shelter for the cattle from the heat."

Among the appropriations were "ten shillings to pay Sergeant Scotchford for warning suspicious persons out of town," they being liable to become a public charge; "ten shillings to purchase a new buryin' cloth to cover up copses;" "twenty shillings to set two mort stones between the Blood farms (Carlisle) and the buryin' ground;" "eight shillings to set stakes by the causeways, for the use of travelers at high water"; "five shillings to be paid Goodman Woods for mending the pound, besides half the receipts for impounding stray cattle the ensuing year;" "three shillings to purchase a padlock for the stocks;" and "five pounds for paying the board of poor people to such as would take them at the lowest bid, they to have good and sufficient diet and suitable clothing."

After the meeting broke up but little was said, for the cool shadows at the close of that early October day sent each householder hurrying home "to cover up things," as Goodman Woods said there would be a hard frost up his way. The meeting was adjourned without date, for Lieutenant Willard did not know of anything that should call them together until Michaelmas.

CHAPTER VII.

Scene by the Way side—Home of Timothy Wheeler— Evening Talk by the Fireplace— Statements of John Scotchford—Cause of the Settlement of Concord.

ACCORDING to previous arrangement, no sooner was the meeting over than we started with Timothy Wheeler for his home. This visit we considered quite a privilege, inasmuch as having seen the easier side of a settler's life at the manse, we greatly wished to see the other side in the quiet homestead of an outlying farm: moreover, we had heard of Goody Wheeler's "apple mose" and "sweet conserve," and knew that we would receive there more than an average of Concord comforts, besides a chance of listening to some good stories from her consort, since Timothy, as he was called by the town folks, was acquainted with everybody from the "nine acres" to the "lower medders," and knew many strange incidents of settlers' life by the Musketequid.

As we left the meeting house there passed us a drove of cattle composed of cows, calves, and several oxen, which we were informed were the property of various owners who were pasturing them on the common feeding field. Not caring to be too inquisitive at the outset, for we knew there would be much to inquire about, we asked no questions on the subject, but by the data obtained from the sparks and elsewhere we inferred that there was a daily herding of these animals, and that it was done by each householder in turn collecting them in the morning and returning them to the barnyard at evening; and if we are right in the above inference we may well wait for a moment at the next bar-way while we reflect upon a custom that has such pleasing and pastoral relations. The farm boy driving home the cows has long been a favorite subject for the painter, and justly so, but is it hardly comparable in its picturesque suggestiveness with the bringing home of that little lone herd from the broad meadow lands and the sunny hillsides to the snug straw thatched barns of the Concord husbandmen?

We can almost conceive of the scene, as at sunsetting by the woodside pathway is heard the tinkling sound of the bell wether and the deep clank, clonk of the cow bell, and the familiar, breezy call of the tired herdsman, all of which are as welcome to the waiting milkman and maid as were the notes of the post horn in the days of stage travel to the old-time tavern-keeper.

The natural concomitant of all this was the dropping of the barnyard bars while Flora, Brindle and Bess, good stock from Surrey and Kent, stepped over them, and the rest of the drove moved to their own stalls further on.

And the children, for they are there in this true backwoods nursery, little Cerinthy, Hannah and Hope, Jonathan, Jesse and Abiather, are all on hand with their porringers, each to be served first.

We were not long in reaching Timothy's house, which was a plain structure with a stout frame roughly boarded with thick planks set upright inside, both for finish and for defense from attacks of the Northern and Eastern Indians. Within the building, things differed from those at Parson Bulkeley's, for the Parson was more than well-to-do; he was for the times wealthy, and things at the manse were somewhat in accord with his estate. The chimney was a massive one placed near the middle of the house, and up the broad flue over the fire-place was a large "lug" of green walnut that extended from ledge to ledge and which Timothy told us might last for several months, but with a liability if left too long, of burning through. This "lug" was used in place of a crane, which came later, and upon it were suspended "hooks and trammels"; below were a pair of andirons, before which was a broad, flaring hearth; . above the fireplace was a mantel piece, and upon it a pair of candle-snuffers, a tinder box and a "save-all"; the latter article being a small candle stick with an upright pin proceeding from the center and used for impaling partly spent candles when too short for the common candle stick. Squashes, sage, and savory were also there, while overall were a couple of firearms resting peacefully upon wooden pegs.

As we entered the house Goody Wheeler met us with a cheery look and we soon felt at home. The evening meal which was awaiting our arrival was laid on a small pine table without leaves, and though every dish was unpretentious, yet there was a display of neatness and taste which at once convinced us of the good sense of Timothy's consort.

The food consisted of johnny cake, a trencher of apple slump, and pumpkin pie with a rye crust. There was also on a narrow side board or adjustable shelf hinged to the wall and upheld in horizontal position by a single stake, or leg, the remnant of a boiled dinner, but no potatoes; the absence of the latter being accounted for by the fact that potatoes were as yet but little grown by the settlers, being regarded by some at that time as unlit for food. For drink there was home brewed beer either made from barley malted at the village malt house or from malt bought by the ball.

It is needless to say that town meeting had made us hungry, and for a half hour we showed our appreciation of this simple farm fare. Supper over, the food that remained was removed to the buttery in a "varder," a utensil made for the purpose, and the dishes after being washed were placed in the "dresser," a triangular shaped closet in one corner of the room.

The kitchen work being completed a trundle bed was drawn out from under the high bed for little Cerinthy and Charity: and then Goody Wheeler joined her husband and myself who were sitting by the fireside.

Hardly were we fairly seated and engaged in conversation concerning Timothy's crops, and methods of husbandry, when here was a pull at the latch string, and in walked Goodman John Scotchford, whom we met at town meeting, and who had come over with his wife Susanna for an evenings talk. Their arrival was timely, for we had ascertained in a conversation held with him at the meeting house that he was of the company that arrived at Concord the first fall, and was therefore conversant with the settlers' earliest experience the first year, and also knew something of their antecedents in England; some of which things we could hardly have expected to ascertain from Timothy Wheeler, since he did not join the Concord colony until 1639.

It was not long before we were conversing on these subjects, and soon obtained facts which taken in conjunction with what the sparks had deposed in other places led us to infer that the Concord grantees, whether of the company first arriving or those who soon followed, were mostly Englishmen, and that they came to America not as worldly minded adventurers but rather as sturdy Puritans; so that it is by no false nomenclature that we speak of the Puritan pilgrims of Concord, and assert that their early homes by the Musketequid were in every sense shrines of the truth, where liberty loving devotees burned incense. That these pilgrims founded the township at a sacrifice can scarcely be doubted; for was it not that which John Scotchford told

34

us? and did not the sparks snap vigorously and even the cob irons suddenly redden with an additional glow as he described his home beyond seas?

Most surely, there could be no mistaking on this point; for, although the wind blew bleakly outside and occasionally crept down the chimney with a melancholy wail, giving an unwonted brightness to the back log, yet not half so bright was it as the picture given by him of his far, English birthplace. But the more pathetic part of his narration was that relating to his leaving home; and here he became agitated and appeared to live again that part of his life which he thought the saddest. He spoke of the prayers and the parting at his parents' threshold, and the words of blessing at the garden gate.

At this point in the narrative the sparks stopped snapping and the coals were fast fading into an ashen hue, giving the room a somber appearance; moreover, John acted as if he did not care to talk further, but sat silently gazing upon the changeful embers as though he saw images in them; while Susanna sighed heavily like one thinking of things far distant. Presently, Timothy Wheeler arose and threw upon the fire a few chips, whereupon John began slowly pacing the room.

As for ourselves we did not care to say anything. It was a time for thought. The facts stated had been impressive, and John's manner was so demonstrative that it needed nothing farther from anyone to convince us of the cause of the Puritans' exodus to America; and that the inhabitants in the lone hamlet at Concord became pilgrims for things not of earth. Moreover, the spell that had overtaken John was upon us also; we saw specters in the air and weird pictures. Sprites danced down the great chimney flue and perched on the sooty lug bar; the candle flared; its spent wick sputtered and the last spark ceased to twinkle; the back log broke and half buried itself in the ashes; and it was twice night in Timothy Wheeler's domicile,— the night of nature and the night of the past.

Meekly bowing to the inevitable, as we always mean to, we immediately mused on the apostrophe of the poet Lowell to the great monarch whose realm we had invaded: "O realm of silence and of swart eclipse, The shapes that haunt thy gloom Make signs to us and move thy withered lips Across the gulf of doom; Yet all their sound and motion Bring no more freight to us than wraiths of ships On the mirage's ocean."

The silence had continued till it began to be quite uncomfortable, when the chips last thrown upon the coals became suddenly ignited, and as the flames roared up the chimney the sprites followed them, and when the hindermost leaped over the lug stick there was a sharp whine from the dog Towser as if making sympathetic response to the sad narration.

The noise of Towser awoke Charity and little Cerinthy, whose deep and peaceful breathing had been one of the pleasant features of the evening. As Cerinthy climbed out of the trundle bed and ran to Goody Wheeler, saying she was lonesome, it occurred to us to inquire something about child life in the earlier days of the Concord colony. This we did, and learned among other things that some of the settlers who arrived early brought with them several children, and that the families were generally large, as the Hartwells, Willards and some of the Wheelers, although this was not the case with our friend Timothy, for we had ascertained in the course of our conversation that Cerinthy and Charity were not their own children, but they had taken them into their home from a household that was somewhat straightened in means.

As the subject of child life was being discussed we noticed that the ears of little Charity were evidently open to all that was being said and thought it might be in poor taste to continue our interrogatories farther concerning this matter. We were not compelled, however, to leave the topic here, for no sooner had our talk upon it ceased, than Timothy took from the wood box and threw against the chimney back a handful of pine cones, which he informed us the children had gathered in the warm fall days for winter kindling. Immediately, these inflammable objects became ablaze, and as they crackled the sparks snapped and struck out until all moved back from the hearth's edge lest they be burned by them.

CHAPTER VIII.

Continued Account of Colonial Child Life—Synopsis of Events the First Tear at the Musketequid Settlement — Purchase of Territory from the Indians — Plan of the Township — Names of the Original Grantees — Description of the Journey from Water town to Concord.

HERE was an opportunity, for not only were we in the way to get at the indoor experience of the children, but also to know something of their prattle and play and their little duties outside; so while the rest were talking together about an expected visit from Parson Bulkeley to catechize their households, we sat quietly listening as the sparks spoke, and the following is what we learned.

Before the birth of a child preparation was made for a jubilee dinner or supper to be held a few weeks after the child was born, at which the nurse and others were invited, and what was called "grooming" beer and "grooming" cake were prepared for this occasion weeks beforehand. On the Sunday next after the birth the babe was taken to the meeting house for baptism, and it mattered not about the weather, for the "chrisom" child was to undergo the rite even if ice had to be broken in the "christening bowl."

It was usually carried in the arms of the midwife and was attired in a "bearing cloth" or "christening blanket" made of linen and woven by hand, and when at the altar it was placed in the arms of the father. The little children in early times were usually clothed with the best the householder could afford. An important article of dress for church service, whether in summer or winter, was a low necked and short sleeved shirt, and its head was covered with a "bigger" or cap.

The first time a babe was moved from the room it was carried upstairs with silver or gold in its hand to bring wealth and to cause it always to rise in the world. It also had scarlet laid upon its head to keep it from harm.

Among the prescriptions for children's ailments was "snailwater"; a concoction of garden snails, earth worms, rue, agrimony, barberry bark, bear's foot, and betony. The snails were to be washed in small beer and bruised in a stone mortar and then mixed with the crushed earth worms.

To facilitate teething, babes sometimes wore anodyne necklaces; and one old writer recommends for teething, milk pottage, "flummery," and warm beer. The children were early sent to what were called "Dame schools," where they were taught among other rudiments of knowledge, to sew, knit, spin, and weave.

The "boughten" luxuries of the boys and girls were not many nor great. We hear of "lemon pil candy," and "angelica candy," and "carraway comfits"; but confections were probably only the things of an occasional holiday, and even then not to be practically thought of by the average child. Amusements of an intellectual nature were quite as few, there being little perhaps of an amusing character until the appearance of the "Mother Goose Melodies."

Some of the books of the period are the following :—the titles of which we conclude could not have been very attractive, notwithstanding Cotton Mather said in his election sermon before the governor and council in 1685, "The youth of this country are verrie sharp and early ripe in their capacities."—"A Looking Glass for Children," "The Life of Mary Paddock, Who Died at the Age of Nine," "A Particular

Account of Some Extraordinary Pious Motions and Devout Exercises Observed of Late in Many Children of Siberia."

But notwithstanding the paucity of amusements and gala days caused by the severity of the times, child nature would assert itself and mirth and many making could not be suppressed. It found expression at the corn huskings, apple bees, and quiltings, and whenever the older folks gathered of an evening in a neighborly way the children were present, and seated on stools in the back part of the room, listened to stories of forest adventure and village gossip, and shared with their elders the pop-corn, apples and cider, or cracked nuts all by themselves near the oven's mouth, while they may have made many an innocent caricature of some quaint individual. Even in their work they found play. If they kept the blackbirds from the corn there was many a skip, and jump, and gleeful halloo. If they drove afield the herds and flocks there was the bird's nest that they visited and the brook in which they waded or swam.

If they went on errands there were the berries by the wayside, and the squirrel, woodchuck and coons. They had access to the purple wild grapes, and the brown nuts of the woods. The field flowers they could see at their best, and they had an appetite for anything eatable. With such pleasures they were satisfied.

"Learn to Obey" and little "Hate-evil" could frolic and romp as much as they pleased when sent to the "close" to call the men folks, and nothing could prevent Welcome Wheat from waiting at the bar-way before dropping the rails until she heard the familiar co, co, co, from Mindwell Dean, as he coaxed his herd from an adjacent pasture in order to drive their droves home together.

In these homes the families were usually large, and there was the companionship of near ages, and the crude playthings served as did the same cradle for each new comer.

It mattered not if Helpful Hunt and prattling Patience Potter, and the twins, Thomas and Haggai Hay ward, could not go with a "ha-penny" to Robert Meriam's grocery for a "carraway comfit" or a stick of "angelica candy," for their happiness did not depend on these things. Moreover, their mothers made marmalade, and "quidonies," and "typocias," and sometimes when they had company there was the "sack posset" made of sack, ale, cream, and eggs, which even baby Jane sometimes sipped from the "pap spoon." There was the sweet "pumpkin bread" and the occasional sweet cake of "guinny wheat." Furthermore, at the "Dame schools" there was doubtless no little of fun, and of that merriment which school life always finds no matter how staid or strict the environment, and we may easily conjecture that at one of these early Concord kindergartens while Dame Dakin had stepped to the kitchen to get a noggin of hot "mumm" (a fat ale made of oat meal and malt) "to stay her stomach," Fidelity Flint and Honorbright Hartwell have crept to the "noon mark" to see how near it is to dinner time.

As it was getting late we concluded to retire, and upon making known our intention, Timothy Wheeler slipped from the candlestick the spent candle and placed it upon a save-all, saying, "It will more than last till you git to bed." He did not know, however, that to retire from the hearth side was not to retire to our couch, but that there was to be a review of what had been said by John Scotchford and a noting of it.

And now let us pause in our story and briefly consider some events that are matters of record, together with what may have been some of the scenes, incidents and processes in connection with the beginning of the settlement of Concord.

As has been stated, several families in the fall of 1635 went from Watertown to a spot by the Musketequid river to establish a township. The territory was purchased of the Indians and was surrounded on all sides by their land. A part of the price was paid in "wampum-peage, hatchets, Hows, knives, cotton cloth, and shirts." It is stated that an agreement to sell the land, or the actual sale of it, was made at the house of Rev. Peter Bulkeley.

The deed was early lost and never recovered, but there is ample evidence that it was duly executed and delivered. Tradition states that the bargain was made under an oaktree called Jethro's tree, and that the tree stood at a spot just in front of the site of the old Middlesex hotel at the southwesterly end of Concord square.

On Sept. 2, 1635, the tract was granted by the act of the Colonial Court, as was customary, and was to be, according to Governor Winthrop, "6 myles of land square." The name Concord may have been given it from the harmony early existing among the grantees. The deed of conveyance was probably signed by those who made the agreement to sell, among whom were the squaw Sachem, Tahattawan; Muttanktuckes, Nimrod and others, according to various depositions, and we believe it not improbable that the others referred to, were Kato, a former Indian owner of the Sudbury plantation, Jehojakim, Majus, Musqua, some of the Speen family, Musquamog, Bohew, Boman, Nepanum, and Wenneto.

No plan of the territory acquired by the first purchase is known to have ever been made, but it is supposed that the township was surveyed and laid out by Major Simon Willard. It has been stated that the tract was to be three miles north, south, east and west, that the house lot of Rev. Peter Bulkeley was its geographical center, and that it included among its natural advantages six mill privileges, seven ponds and more than nine miles of river course.

Stone bounds were set at the corners of the township, and tradition has pointed out the place of some of them. In process of time other land acquisitions were added to the original grant, notably among which were Concord village (Acton), and the Blood farm (Carlisle).

The names of all the settlers who had reached the place of settlement by 1635 and 1636 is uncertain but a part of them are Rev. Peter Bulkeley, Elder John Jones, Hayward, Heald, Fletcher; William and Thomas Bateman, Hosmer, Potter, Ball, Rice, Hartwell, Meriam, Judson, Griffin, George, Joseph and Obadiah Wheeler and John Scotchford. Peter Bulkeley came from Wodell, Bedfordshire county, England; James Hosmer from Hockhurst in Kent, John Heald from Berwick in Northumberland, William Buttrick from Kingston on Thames in Surrey, John Ball from Wiltshire, and the Wheelers, according to tradition, from Wales.

The names of settlers who arrived at Concord between 1635-6 and 1640 are Thomas Flint from Matlock, William Hunt from Yorkshire, Ephraim Thomas and Timothy Wheeler, whom tradition says came from Wales; Thomas Brooks from London, Jonathan Mitchell from Yorkshire, Stow, Blood, Brown, Andrews, Atkinson, Barrett, Billings, Miles, Smeadley, Squire, Underwood, Burr, Draper, Farwell, Chandler, Gobble, Fox and probably Middlebrook, Odell and Fuller.

Some of the larger estates of these settlers are estimated as follows: Peter Bulkeley, £6000; Thomas Flint, £4000; William and Thomas Bateman, £348, George Hayward, £500; William Hunt, £596. James Blood and Thomas Stow were large real estate owners. There is no evidence that these families lived together before their arrival in America; neither have we any evidence that the settlement was planned in England.

The journey to the Musketequid country was doubtless an arduous one and attended with peril, as we may infer from the following account given by the writer Edward Johnson in his "Wonder working Providence of Zion's Savior."

"Sometimes passing through the thickets, where their hands are forced to break way for their bodies' passage, and their feet clambering over the crossed trees, which when they missed they sink into an uncertain bottom in water, and wade up to their knees, tumbling sometimes higher and sometimes lower. Wearied with this toil, they at the end of this meet with scorching plains, yet not so plain but that the ragged bushes scratch their legs fouly, even to wearing their stockings to their bare skin in two or three hours. If they are not otherwise well defended with boots or buskins, their flesh will be torn, — some of them being forced to pass on without further provision, have had the blood trickle down at every step. And in time of summer, the sun cast such a reflecting heat from the sweet fern, whose scent is so very strong, that some herewith have been very near fainting, altho very able bodies to endure much travel. And this not to be indured for one day, but for many; and verily did not the Lord encourage their natural parts with hopes of a new and strange discovery, expecting every hour to see some rare sight never seen before, they were not able to hold out and break through. * * * After some days spent in search, toiling in the daytime, as formerly said, like true Jacob they rest them on the rocks where the night takes them. Their short repast is some small pittance of bread, if it holds out; but as for drink they have plenty, the country being well watered in all places that are yet found out. Their further hardship is to travel, sometimes they know not whither, bewildered indeed without sight of sun, their compass miscarrying in crowding through the bushes. They sadly search up and down for a known way, the Indian paths being not above one foot broad, so that a man may travel many days and never find one. * * * This intricate work no whit daunted these resolved servants of Christ to go on with the work in hand, but lying in the open air while the watery clouds pour down all the night season, and sometimes the driving snow desolving on their backs, they keep their wet clothes warm with continued fire till the renewed morning gives fresh opportunity of further travel."

This account may perhaps relate to the journeys of various companies who went at different seasons to the proposed new plantation, rather than to any one journey made by explorers or permanent settlers. The language is strong and may have been designed to convey for substance a general instead of a detailed description.

Captain Edward Johnson was one of the prominent founders of Woburn and a good man. He wrote about the settlement of other New England towns also; and doubtless obtained much of his information from conversations with their inhabitants.

The goods of the settlers were conveyed to Concord in teams which were impressed by order of the Colonial Court; as indicated by the following record, dated Sept. 2, 1635: "It is ordered that there shall be a Plantation at Musketequid, and that there shall be six miles square to belong to it, and that the inhabitants thereof shall have three years immunities from all public charges except trainings. Further, that when any that shall plant there shall have occasion of carrying of goods thither, they shall repair to two of the next magistrates where the teams are, who shall have power for a year to press draughts at reasonable rates to be paid by the owners of the goods to transport their goods thither at seasonable times. And the name of the place is changed, and henceforth to be called Concord."

The preparation for the departure from Watertown into the wilderness was doubtless short; for the settlers would have but few household articles to take with them; but the scene at the departure was probably an interesting one.

We may conjecture that foremost in the procession were several outriders, who were for watch and ward lest the train be attacked by hostile Indians, for as yet the settlers did not know the friendly character of the natives. Between the wagons and the vanguard were, naturally, the cattle, sheep, goats and swine, upon whose safety so much depended. Lastly, and accompanied probably by some of the more lusty of the company as a rear guard, we may suppose rode reverentially and anxiously, Rev. Peter Bulkeley and Elder John Jones.

As there were no roads nor bridges, fording places were to be sought, for crossing the streams; swamps were to be avoided by a circuitous path, and fodder for the animals was either to be carried or obtained from the tufts of wild wood grass or from occasional open spaces in the forest.

As more than one day was consumed in making the journey, at night everything was to be carefully guarded, and, let the weather be what it might, there was no shelter but an improvised one of tree branches or that of some projecting rock or friendly windfall.

No welcome of any kind awaited their arrival, but instead, "Bleak Nature's desolation wraps them round, Eternal forests, and unyielding earth, And savage men, who through the thickets peer, With vengeful arrow."

The only sounds that greeted them were of the wilderness. The eagle screamed over the pines by the ridgeway, and from the vast meadow wastes came the deep booming of the lone bittern. Down the gentle defiles, which after a lapse of two centuries have become such pleasant places, danced the dim shadows of an early twilight, and long before the day was done the wild beast began his nightly prowling with dismal cry and suspicious skulk.

But there are other things which may have lent their influence to make the arrival a forbidding one. There was in the nature of the Massachusetts Bay settlers an element of superstition which was easily aroused, and there were conditions in the country about Concord suited to call it forth to an unusual degree; ponds with lonely environments, from which the loons wild and pathetic cry as it pealed over the woodland might be mistaken for the spirit of some unavenged victim of Indian hate; dark recesses by the meadow border, upon which the night bird descended with whistling wing, making sounds which to unaccustomed ears might be mistaken for voices unearthly; dark, evergreen groves by the hillside; tangled and vine webbed archways beneath which were the imprints of unknown animals, or of strange moccasined feet; fresh coals on abandoned hearthstones, suggestive of someone living, and perhaps somewhere listening and watching; all these things and others it may be of like nature awaited the settlers.

41

CHAPTER IX.

Character of the First Houses — Food, Clothing., Occupation — Preparations for Cold Weather — The Setting in of Winter— Trials and Amusements — The Coming of Spring — Scenes Along the Musketequid.

THE first work that presented itself was that of providing themselves shelter; in doing this they seized upon every advantage. They laid out their stinted house lots at the foot of the ridgeway before spoken of, thinking, it may be that the bank to the northerly would prove a friendly wind break, and that the southerly slope would catch the slant beams of the winter's sun. But the expected advantage had its drawback, for old Boreas strode ruthlessly down the little "strate strete" and knocked loudly at their cabin doors, while the snow swept by his besom from the "great fields" above, fell unexpectedly over the bank, and only awaited the springtime to melt and flood their dwellings.

The first houses were thinly scattered from what is now Concord square to "Meriam's corner." They were constructed by the driving or setting of upright stakes or logs at the foot of the hill, and the placing thereon of stringers or poles, which, resting on the sloping ground formed a roof admitting of a room beneath, by the removal of the earth. The roof poles were covered with sods, or brushwood thatched with grass. The fireplaces were against the bank; and for light, the door may have served a partial purpose, supplemented by one or two small apertures, closing with slides or filled with oiled paper. It is stated that these structures were only designed for a temporary purpose, and made to the end that when kindly spring opened they could provide things more durable. It is said, however, that even the first winter Parson Bulkeley had provided for him a frame house.

As to the food supply, we may make no mistake in supposing that it was scant in quantity and altogether unsuitable for either hard work or good health; for commercial relations with other places were few, and but little corn could be obtained from the natives. Besides, there was inconvenience in the preparation of what food material they had. Corn may have had to be ground after the Indian fashion of pounding it with a pestle in a mortar of wood or stone, or if a few families were fortunate enough to own a "querne", before the erection of the "Bulkeley grist mill", and also in seasons of drought afterward, they may have been put to the hardship of grinding their corn by hand.

We may also believe that the clothing was unsuited to the climate, for, doubtless, they wore the garments they brought with them across the ocean, and the change from the equable temperature of England to the inconstant climate of Massachusetts Bay, and the encountering of the malarial exhalations and damp meadow mists of the Musketequid, together with the snowfalls and floods that go with great forest growths in an unreclaimed country, would naturally result in much suffering. If we may believe the writer, Johnson, some of the people were at times only partially clad in anything, for, he states, that "at the first, many of the people in the season of frost and snow went barefooted and barelegged." The same writer says that "some of their cattle, for which they paid five and twenty pounds a cow, died," and, also, that "for want of wheat, barley and rye, the Indian meal proved a sore affliction to some stomachs."

The late autumnal days following the arrival were busy ones. There was much to be done before the setting in of a winter which to the settlers was all untried, and whose severity at its mildest might if unprepared to meet it subject them to hardship.

Besides the building and banking up of their houses, a supply of food and fuel was to be provided; shelter was to be made for the cattle, and fodder laid by for them when they could no longer feed upon the brown meadows nor browse upon the brushwood. To perform these tasks was not easy; the forest being of the "first growth," as it was termed when no woodman's axe had been used upon it, would not readily fall before the rude implements that were used for wood-cutting in those days; and the tall blue-joint, the juiceless lute grass, the "pipes" and the "flags" had all lost some of their summer sweetness, and were tough and woody, and in some places standing half high in water.

Furthermore, the time for gathering these was short. Any week, any day, might bring the snow, and any night the ground might freeze, so that not so much as a fence post could be set. The summer birds had all flown, and the late stragglers from the north flew low down, as if laden with an apprehension that they were late. The leaves had fallen, and the wind blew through the bare branches with a melancholy wail, and rustled coldly through the coarse sedge in the runways; while in the morning, thin ice covered the meadow lands, all betokening the near approach of cold weather, and admonishing the settler to make haste in preparing for it; perhaps, too, predisposing him to homesickness, and causing solicitude for things ahead.

What was thus indicated soon occurred. The last honk of the gray wild goose was heard over the bay at the river bend, as if croaking back a note of disappointment, at not finding open water in which to rest itself. The dusky duck, the hardiest and latest of the wild waterfowl that frequents the rivers and ponds about Concord, had days before taken its departure because the water was frozen; and nothing remained of the bird kind but a flock of querulous robins, which still lingered about the swamp near the mill brook, as if to discover what the strangers were there for, and to finish eating a few alder berries.

Soon, "announced by all the trumpets of the sky," and prognosticated by bird and beast, the snow came. It filled up the paths and dropped heavily upon the cabin roofs and lodged gloomily upon the drooping tree branches.

Easy access with the outer world was closed, and the colonists were left to themselves, with wild animals and wild men in a wild wood, with no promise of any visitors before spring, except the winds and the storm clouds. But, although thus exposed to the hardships of the wilderness we may well conjecture that they were not idle, for there was much that could be done in the winter season by way of preparation for the spring. Seed was to be obtained of the natives; spots suitable for planting it were to be selected; and fencing stuff was to be split out; for the forest had plenty of marauders ready to break into the planting fields and claim the crops. Besides these things, there were farming tools to be made, daily chores to be done, and divers contrivances to be adopted, whereby the settlers might adjust themselves to their new circumstances.

As to just how that first winter was passed, and what were the painful and pleasurable details of each family's experience, we have no certain knowledge. The records do not inform us, tradition gives no hint of it, and we have no faithful Bradford's Journal, as concerning the planters of Plymouth, to lift the curtain and let in the light. The writer Johnson informs us, in a general way, that they suffered from exposure, from fear, and from a lack of many necessary things; while, as to things specific and personal, he is mostly silent.

But, although left to conjecture, we may, perhaps, fairly assume that there was both tragedy and comedy on that strange stage of human action, and that of the former class death came, and that a grave was opened in the town's first burial place that winter. That such was the case is probable, for although there were in the first arrival the names of only about a dozen heads of households that have come down to us, yet these may represent several scores of individuals, as wives, children and servants, besides stragglers, who are sometimes found attendant upon adventurous undertakings, as in the case of the Plymouth plantation, where there were several persons not signers of the original compact, and of whom posterity has had small reason to be proud.

The severity of the climate, the scant accommodation for warmth and shelter, the stinted food supply,— all these would naturally superinduce disease and perhaps death, to reckon nothing upon casualties arising from special exposure, accident, and a variety of other causes and mishaps incident to life in a new country. The first monument to bear record to a death in Concord is that of Joseph Meriam. It stands in the old hill burial ground where for two hundred and twenty-six years it has faithfully borne the following inscription: "Joseph Meriam, aged 47 years. Died the 20 of April, 1677;"

It is a simple tombstone, unpretentious and time-worn; but a special interest is attached to it in that it has for so many years stood as a sentinel between the known and unknown of Concord's dead. It is on the line of demarkation, beyond which, no tombstone deposeth and none durst venture. What names of persons who may have died the first winter would be inscribed on other tombstones, had all of those whose bodies resting in "that thick peopled ground" had a stone to bear record of them, none can declare; but, there is large opportunity to conjecture that some would be there, and for the following reasons, if for no other.

It is supposed that the earliest meeting house at Concord was built on what now might be called the hill burial place, within a year or two or perhaps three of the first arrival; for it is stated, that by its first recorded vote, Feb. 5, 1636, the town decided that the meeting house "stand neare the brook in the east side of Goodman Judson's lott;" and tradition has always located that spot in or near the old burying ground. As a church organization at Concord was not effected till April 6, 1637, there may have been a little delay in erecting the meeting house; it being deemed, perhaps, less consequential to have a church building before the family going into it was constituted.

But, however this may be, the query naturally arises, why was this spot selected for a meeting house? It was not adjacent to the parsonage, for tradition fixes the site of that, as we have seen, on the present Lowell street; neither was it most accessible to all the houses. It was not there, as we believe, for a defensive purpose, for, with exceptional amity existing between the white and the red men, there was no necessity of placing the meeting house on the top of a hill for the purpose of better watch and ward; we conclude, therefore, it was built there because about that spot was their burial place, and because the settlers decided that God's house should be upon God's acre. If this be true, then death may have occurred the first year.

44

In the few years next following 1635, some few records of deaths have come down to us. These may be found together with a list of births in what have been termed "the Boston Records." The earliest date of a death in this list is 1639, and the record is as follows: "Richard Harvy had two daughters burried 1638, Margaret his wife dyed 1639." The day and the month of the births and deaths in this list is given in the quaint method of the period.

The occurrence of any comedy amid circumstances of so grave a character as existed the first winter, it may be hard to conceive of, but human nature will usually assert itself, even among adverse surroundings, so we believe it did here.

There were, doubtless, many accidents and incidents where mirth and even hilarity found vent. There were old songs to be sung, old stories to be told and jokes to be cracked; strange customs were to be inaugurated, queer costumes to be worn, and things to be done quite different from anything done in old England; for instance, bullocks or kine harnessed tandem to suit the narrow wood path; coon skincaps instead of Puritan hats, loose leggins in place of boots, and first attempts at wearing snowshoes. As for events of a humorous nature, it might be hard to avoid them. For instance, a person lost in the woods at Nashoba, and led home with a sprained ankle by a couple of squaws; another dropping his doublet when treed by a bear, which doublet was instantly devoured because made of goatskin with the hair on; and still another starting from Beaver pond with a string of fish, and sowing them by the way as he ran homeward because he heard wolves following him. Many such like things may have occurred to excite merriment, and as they were recited about the evening fireside when the wind blew and the snow drifted, why should they not laugh; they were men and women such as we are, and although called Puritans, they were not too pure to do what Providence designed them to do, and Providence designed them to laugh sometimes.

Their practices were far from being what some have represented. They did not carry firearms to kill harmless savages, neither did they sell them firewater for a six pence to buy powder and shot to shoot them with. They did not go to meeting on Sunday to learn about Divine decrees, which would lead them to leave duties undone during the week, nor to act in a manner inconsistent with the fullest exercise of a free will. But they were rational agents of the Almighty to help colonize a new country; and how well they did it history tells.

As to what was done in the long evenings we can only guess. There were few books, no papers, and as yet little or no material for spinning or knitting; neither was there much corn to be shelled; no apples to be pared, and no pumpkins to be cut and sliced. The men might do some coarse carpentry, perhaps, also some rough shoemaking from green hides, and it may be, turn a hand to some small coopering or rude basket making; so, for the most part there was tediousness, lightened by the thought that winter would not always last, and spring would come bringing brighter things.

And spring did come. The settlers soon saw signs that winter was on the wane. The sun rose higher and shone brighter. The days grew longer and longer; and at length spring burst upon them with a novelty known only to such as have colonized a new country. Indeed it was as if they were introduced into a veritable wonderland; every day was a new revelation. Some bird came from the south; some insect spread

45

its wings and chirped at them; some animal crawled from its winter hiding place; and these were for the most part unlike what they had ever seen before.

In the floral world also there were surprises. Along the meadows, by the brookside, in the springy places, were the marsh marigolds; in the "pine dark glen" and along the hillside were the star flower and the ferns; while in the runways and by the rivulets a variety of violets lifted their modest heads as if to welcome them. Amid this scene of animate beauty there also awaited the settlers a melody, which was as new to the ear as these were to the eye; the lark whistled from a tall tree between the river and the ridgeway; the song sparrow sang sweetly by the wayside; a score or more of gay warblers twittered and trilled in the brushwood; and the robins which were so complaining the autumn before, no longer stood aloof with discordant note and shy presence, but acted as if desirous of being neighborly.

But the scene of greatest change, it may be, was along the course of the Musketequid and by the ponds; all of which from the setting in of the cold weather till now had been as silent as the fishes that swarmed within them. The icy covering that closed over them in November had remained unbroken until March, during which time but little of animate life had been audible or visible; while the cone-shaped nests of the musquash might, by their look of abandonment, have made the landscape look even more desolate.

But now, all was changed. From Nashawtuc to Punkatassett, life appeared. The air was alive with wild water fowl: the wood duck and teal flew low down as if seeking nesting places, while, high above them, the "cloud cleaving geese" sent down their harsh, querulous honk, as if to say such places were too tame for them. Upon the soft grass of the meadow uplands the snipe stopped in his zigzag flight to find a feeding ground; the sheldrake oiled herself contentedly on a hassock; while in the reedy coves by the river bend the returning bittern sent forth his booming note no longer lonely, admonishing the settlers to "mend fence."

But of more interest than anything else was the wealth of meadow grass giving promise of plenty of hay. And this promise proved true, for Johnson informs us that the settlers along the river had not only hay sufficient for their own cattle but took in cattle from other towns.

There was no time, however, for idle enjoyment; opportunities were passing which would not return for another twelve months, and they should be promptly improved.

CHAPTER X.

Capture of Fish — Breakfast Table of Timothy Wheeler — Morning Walk Through the Woods — Visit at the Simon Willard Homestead— Historic Sketch of Major Simon Willard — Description of Colonial Farm Houses — Domestic Products.

THE first thing to be done was to capture fish, which were to be used for food and fertilization. In the long winter evenings the settlers doubtless obtained from the Indians a knowledge of the best methods of maize culture; that it should be planted in the month of green leaves at a time when the oak leaf was the size of a mouse's ear or a squirrel's paw, and that each hill should contain an alewife. They also learned how and when the alewives were to be captured. The fish were already ascending the Musketequid and pushing their way up the north and south branches for spawning purposes, and the season would soon be over. The Indians were gathering in their harvest, working by day with a scoop net at the wier, and at night watching with a flaming flambeau in one hand, and a long sapling with a stone point in the other, ready to capture the fish as it swam in sight. We can conjecture that the English were not far behind, and that there was soon seen starting from every house on the "little strate strete" a man with a basket, or two men carrying a basket between them, suspended from a stout pole on their shoulders. Soon there came in sight perhaps John Meriam, from the corner, with a clumsy cart of spokeless wheels drawn by a bullock, in which were some scoop nets, and several spears, and sundry other articles. As he stopped before the house of William Judson, near the burying ground, perhaps Goody Judson brought out a basket in which was some boiled venison, a dish of samp and a large pone cake. Truth Temple may have come soon after, with a half cheese. We infer that the fishing season was a lively one. The fishing places were famous resorts; and about them the Indians were accustomed to gather by families and by clans for feasting and for tribal greetings. Another early work of importance was that of fencing; as, however, this subject properly belongs to that of land allotments and the common planting fields we will leave it to be considered later.

Such was the commencement of the colonization of Concord, and such we conceive may have been some of the scenes incident to it. The cause of the colonization it is unnecessary to further consider. Every circumstance as well as record and tradition assert it to have been at the dictation of duty, and a desire to reach a place, remote though it might be, where they could worship God as a spirit in spirit and in truth.

"What sought they thus afar Bright jewels of the mine?
The wealth of seas? the spoils of war?
They sought a faith's pure shrine."
And the shrine of truth which they sought, they kept.

Through all the vicissitudes that followed them, of the wilderness, of church dissensions, and divers other difficulties and dangers, they always adhered to their noble intent and righteous endeavor. No wonder that the sons of such sires have added greatly to the world's worth, that their homes are Meccas which many a pilgrim visits, and that about their burial places are ever the fresh imprints of pilgrim footsteps.

But the bright disk of the harvest moon was now fast descending over the distant Wachuset mountain, and, long ago, the candle in the save-all had sputtered and gone out, leaving us in the darkness with our thoughts, which like the gray embers on the now cold hearthstone had about spent their vitality, for we were weary; we had seen, and heard, and thought so much, it was a relief that the sparks had spoken no farther, so, lest the sprites reappear we retired. A moment, and the rising wind rattled rudely the loose window frame; another, it dropped down the chimney with a low, weird sigh, the next we were asleep.

At an early hour in the morning we were astir, and, descending the narrow stairway, we perceived a savory smell of fried flitch (a strip of smoked pork) which was all the more satisfactory inasmuch as the light living at the manse, while all sufficient for parsonage purposes, had proved inadequate for our more active pursuits. Hardly was our simple toilet completed in the "back room", (for it was there that everybody washed) when a horn was blown, and, soon after, we were all seated at the breakfast table devouring with appreciative appetites the morning meal.

This meal consisted in addition to the aforesaid flitch, of the remnant of a pan dowdy which, though made the day previous, had been so banked with hot ashes in the brick oven that this delicious dish of quartered apple cooked in a rich cream crust was still hot. As steam issued from every crevice in the crisp covering, and as Goody Wheeler stirred a rich sauce to spread over it, we felt that farm fare after all had its advantages.

We would state in passing, that meeting the hired man led us to inquire of Goodman Wheeler what he paid him, to which he replied, "Ten and six a week and his diet."

The meal ended, and the settle hitched back, for some of us had sat on it while eating, Goodman Wheeler took from the stand a small Bible, thoroughly time stained and finger worn, and having read a long chapter from the book of Judges invoked the Divine blessing with great fervor. In his reading there were oral interpolations of an expository as well as hortatory character, and in his prayer nothing was omitted that was practical, he being especially earnest in his petition for his pastor and the king of England.

When they arose, for all knelt in Timothy Wheeler's domicile even to little Cerinthy and Charity, all was bustle, getting in readiness for the day's work.

Timothy had planned for the hired man and chore boy to go to the south meadow for some sedge, while he went with two of his neighbors to cut corn. The two neighbors we ascertained were swapping work with him, Timothy to work a like time for them a little later; a custom much prevailing in that period, not only as related to work, but to other commodities; as, for example, if one householder killed a hog, neighbors would borrow of it and the piece would be returned when a like animal was slaughtered by them. In the present instance Timothy Wheeler was harvesting corn for his annual husking, which he said was to take place the following week.

But, beside the haste occasioned by the husking, he was pressed for time in other ways; one of which was that it was his custom on a "growing moon" to kill his hogs, in order, as he stated, to prevent a shrinkage of the pork.

He informed us that this principle likewise applied to other things, as the planting of garden seeds; they doing much better if planted on the moon's increase.

Other signs he was about speaking of when the hired man came with the "hay riggin'," and inquired whether he should take the sedge from the stack by the meadow border or from that on the river brink; and upon being instructed to take it from the latter, we inferred that even after the September storms, the broad meadows would admit of the hauling of hay over them, something not always possible at the present time.

We had now, as we believed, learned all we could from a short tarry with Timothy Wheeler, and grateful for his hospitality proffered payment. This he refused; and, as if the obligation was on the other side, remarked that he would "call it square" if we would come to his husking; at the same time promising that if we would do so and stop overnight he would tell us more about "signs and sich," for, continued he, "I've seen a good many in my day and some's sartin to tarn true."

Nothing could have suited us better, so, with a promise to accept his invitation we parted, steering for Major Simon Willard's, a lad leading the way. The walk through the woods was a wonderful one, for everything was massive, primitive, and grand. There was no underbrush to impede our progress, and the tall tree trunks towering upwards with their branches expanding in the upper air and sunlight, like things of beauty as they were, formed a safe hiding place for the pigeons and crows, which almost constantly cooed and cawed over us. So impressive was the spectacle, and so reverent our feelings, that we instantly recalled the words of Bryant in his "Forest Hymn:"

"Father! Thy hand
Hath reared these venerable columns. Thou
Didst weave this verdant roof. Thou didst look down
Upon the naked earth; and, forthwith rose
All these fair ranks of trees. They in Thy sun
Budded, and shook their green leaves in Thy breeze,
And shot towards heaven. The century living crow
Whose birth was in their tops, grew old and died
Among their branches, till, at last, they stood,
As now they stand, massy, and tall, and dark, —
Fit shrine for humble worshipper to hold
Communion with his Maker!"

To such an extent did the gigantic trees interrupt our direct passage that we felt convinced that the primitive wood paths led the traveler a much longer distance from place to place than if he walked direct as the bee flies.

Beneath the oaks was a profusion of acorn mast, and in the precincts of farm houses were swine busily crunching it; the custom of the settlers being to feed them in this way until the time for fattening. In one place several Indian women were picking hickory nuts, while at the foot of the tree were a couple of papooses cunningly clad in musquash skins.

We crossed the South branch of the river at the cart bridge near the upper meadows, and, following a path along the upland, where the purple grape and rich alder berry mingled alike their fragrance and their beauty to make the walk a delight, we soon saw the smoke wreaths of Major Willard's farm house. The very surroundings of the place were at once suggestive of the large heartedness of the owner, and of an estate of a more than well-to-do farmer of the times. There was upon the premises besides the ordinary buildings a smoke house; and the sweet odor of smoldering corn cobs and green hickory wood that came from it reminded us of the juicy flitch at Timothy Wheeler's breakfast table.

There was also a small barn for the storage of corn, which was set upon posts to protect the contents from squirrels and rats, and loosely boarded to let in the air. Not far away was a shed for beaver pelts, which the sparks informed us at the beaver dam Mr. Willard traded in.

Approaching the premises, Mr. Willard saw and hastened to meet us, accompanied by two large Kentish mastiffs; and as we grasped the hand of this well-known merchant of the Musketequid region we felt as we had heard that he was much of a man.

And here it may be in place to relate a little of his history. Simon Willard came to America from Kent county, England, and was at Cambridge, Massachusetts, as early as 1634. While in this country he formed an acquaintance with Rev. Peter Bulkeley and joined with him in the purchase of the tract of territory now Concord, going there as a colonist and becoming a prominent and potential factor in its settlement. Mr. Willard was a man of affairs as well as a person of means, being versed in matters of both a civic and military character. About 1660, he went to Lancaster, and in 1672, to Groton, and in these townships there are still traditions, and records, and ancient landmarks showing the impress of his personality. In that dart of the town of Harvard, once Lancaster, near the northern border, is still pointed out the site of a garrison house which he erected; and in the town of Ayer, formerly . a part of Groton, is a large land tract once his property.

On May 21, 1658, Simon Willard had conveyed to him five hundred acres of land "on the south side of a river that runneth from Nashua to Merrimack between Lancaster and Groton, and in satisfaction of a debt of £44 due from John, Sagamore of Pawtucket."

The land was laid out in 1659, by Thomas Noyes, and is situated in the present town of Ayer, about Nonacoicus brook. Major Willard commanded forces in King Philip's war, and was long identified with the Massachusetts Bay Colony militia in times of peace. He married for his first wife Mercy Sharp, and for his second and third, two sisters of President Dunster of Harvard college, and he had seventeen children, descendants of whom are widely scattered throughout the land. The old Willard house at Concord was standing, it is stated, until the last quarter century, when it was destroyed by fire. It was situated at the foot of Nashawtuc and the site is now marked by a tablet, not far from the first south bridge.

As we walked to the house, Mr. Willard said some very pleasant things about our late host, Goodman Wheeler, and about the Concord families generally, who, he said had come to a strange country for conscience sake: and as we reached the doorstep he said if we would remain over the coming Sunday, which would be the next day, he would take us to meeting, where we could see them in their worship.

Here was an opportunity of observing still another phase of the settlers' life, and of hearing a sermon from the Rev. Peter Bulkeley, so we gladly accepted the invitation; whereupon Mr. Willard, who had waited for our answer, pulled the latch string and we walked in, meeting Madam Willard in the entry way.

It is unnecessary to give a detailed description of Major Willard's house, for it was modest, considering the competency of its owner, and although more capacious, yet in other respects not unlike many others of the period.

We will, however, describe the average farm house of the times, though in doing so we may subject ourselves to adverse criticism by running counter to pet theories of log cabins, of gambrel roofed manor houses with picturesque accompaniments, and various architectural features suggestive of ghosts, goblins, and witch lore. — The early frame houses were rectangular in shape and of a severe simplicity. In about the middle was a large chimney having several flues, which afforded a fireplace to each room. There was usually a commodious cellar which seldom "froze" it being a part of the farmer's fall work to "bank it up;" and so even was its temperature that vegetables kept in it the year round.

The larger of these houses commonly contained four square rooms on the ground floor, and the smaller ones at least two: and to the latter was often attached an ell or a "lean-to" containing the kitchen. The roof was either gambrel or gable, the latter being the more common. The fireplaces were amply large enough to contain four-foot sticks; and the hearths which were made sometimes of stone and sometimes of brick extended well out into the room. Beside the fireplace in the kitchen was a brick oven.

The floors were made of the widest boards obtainable, and as they shrank and became worn, large seams and knots were visible. The framework was massive, a large beam extending across the top of the rooms, with stout, upright timbers at each corner supporting the roof plates, while above all, directly under the saddle boards, was a triangular "king piece" large enough for the sill of a modern house.

Inside the outer boarding thick upright plank were sometimes placed, to make a bullet-proof protection in case of Indian attack. Sometimes, for greater security bricks were used instead of plank, especially in garrison houses, and occasionally there was a projection of the upper story over the lower one, in which were small port holes.

Such were the houses of the seventeenth century. Here and there might have been a miniature manor house, where some attempt was made at architectural display, as in the case of some well-to-do squire, whose official position, together with an income of a hundred pounds a year invested in mortgages, gave him some personal prominence; but such instances were rare, and we have nowhere found in the Concord colony anything indicative of a desire for undue display in architecture; nor should we expect it. The characteristics of the times were the natural outgrowth of a reaction from the vain glory of mere externals. Character was the test of personal worth. Scholarship and culture found easy combination in Massachusetts with that rugged manual labor which wrenched from a sterile environment some of the world's best results. If the Bulkeleys, and Flints, and Bloods, and some others were, after the standard of the times, men of means, we may believe that they used their means wisely and for the common weal, rather than for the establishment of great estates; and so it was that their garrison houses were their castles; their sanctuaries were their manor houses; and that the sites of these are to the present generation more impressive by far than would be the remains of "High raised battlements or labored mounds, Thick walls or moated gate."

CHAPTER XI.

Domestic Products — Reminiscent Effect of Madam Willard's Dutch cheese — Conversation upon Colonial Drinking Customs — Clerk of the Writs — Legal Fees — Furnishings of Early Farm Houses; Lighting Appliances, Table Ware, Fireplace Utensils, Room Decorations — Class Distinctions.

ALTHOUGH we have abstained from giving a detailed description of the Willard house let us suppose that we examined the inside so far as to note the use and furnishing of some of the rooms.

We first went to the cellar, and there found such produce as by mid-October had been placed in store for the winter. There were carrots, parsnips, onions and cabbages, but no potatoes, turnips taking their place. Several small cider casks were in sight, which showed that the New England beverage of later times was not wholly unknown even then. We were informed, however, on this subject, that but little cider was used at that time, partly because apple trees were not abundant, and partly because the means of its manufacture were limited. Some people, we were told, made it by pounding the fruit in a wooden mortar, and pressing the juice out through a basket; all of which indicate how hard the human family will work to obtain what it ought not to have. There were several well filled meat tubs, and a barrel of soft soap, the latter of which, Mrs. Willard said, was made of clear beef tallow and lye of her own leaching.

There was an absence of dairy products, which, as we shall presently notice, were upstairs, except a number of unusually large firkins filled with butter, which the Major said was soon to be shipped to England in exchange for a Durham cow, which he was intending to import in order to improve his stock.

But what attracted our attention as much as anything were the great arches at the chimney base, which indicated the immense brickwork in the building. We could now understand how so many large fireplaces could be afforded; for the two arches that formed the foundation of the chimney were rooms of themselves. They were furnished with shelves like a pantry. Upon the shelves were sundry jars of conserve, jelly and sauce, also several brown cream pots, the contents of some of which, Madam Willard informed us, were pickles, "hog's head cheese," and mincemeat prepared especially for "company pies." On the stone floor of one of the arches we noticed several jugs and a couple of demijohns, reminding us of modern "bottled goods," so called. We thought best to make no inquiries concerning these, so passed them silently by and went upstairs. We first visited the garret, this we found to be a place of storage, in which among other things were the following articles: A beehive, cranberry rake, and sausage filler, some candle molds, an old foot stove, a warming pan, a pair of steelyards, a large bread trough (used for mixing sausage meat), a pair of snowshoes, a bunch of birch brooms, a flax hatchel, a lot of butternuts, a bag of dried mullein stalks, a cow bell, and an old tin lantern full of small holes to let the light out. There was also a pillow bier filled with feathers, several bunches of sage, betony, and summer savory, a pair of sheep shears, an old cheese basket, and a box of hogs' bristles for waxed ends.

From the garret we descended to the room used for dairy products. By this time Madam Willard had joined us, and as we stood admiring some yellow butter which had just been taken from a "dash churn" and made into balls, she pointed with pride to her cheeses. As the cheeses varied in appearance we ventured to ask the difference whereupon she replied, "There is a name for each kind there is the "new milk," the "skim milk," and the "four meal" cheese; those in the corner are the "sage" cheeses, and that half one on the table is a "Dutch" cheese.

As the Dutch cheese with its snowy whiteness had slightly crumbled, we tasted it; instantly a strange feeling came over us, and our mind became reminiscent. That slight morsel had proved to us like the evening bells to the poet Moore, which, as he expressed it, brought to mind "His home and youth and that sweet time When first he heard their tuneful chime."

For an instant we stood gazing at those simple fragments, mutely wondering how they could occasion such mischief; for mischief surely it was to be sent so summarily into the great kingdom of the past, from which returning we could take nothing away. But in that kingdom we evidently were, for spread before us were its rarest treasures. There was another old farmhouse with its "lean-to" roof, and the cows and the pasture bars; there were the lilacs and the lilies by the garden wall; the broad, low, stone door step; the smiling supper table, so delightful to the eye of the hungry school boy; the thick, golden ginger-bread, and the Dutch cheese that mother made.

As we stood reflecting upon the curious predicament in which we so suddenly found ourselves, it occurred to us that here was a mental mirage, when by the simple suggestiveness it may be of a sight, a sound, an odor or a taste, memory casts upon the screen of our perceptive faculties experiences and scenes long vanished. Wordsworth may have felt the same when he said: "To me the meanest flower that blows can give Thoughts that do often lie too deep for tears."

So inappreciable was the time occupied by all this, that Madam Willard hardly noticed anything unusual, and just then, a call came from below summoning her to the turnstile to talk with Mercy Miles of "Nine Acres" about a marriage that was to take place at her house. Surely, thought we, this is an opportune circumstance, for we can again taste of the cheese; we did so, but to no purpose; the enchantment was gone; and we were left to content ourselves with recalling another verse of Wordsworth where he said:

"The thoughts of our past years in me doth breed
Perpetual benedictions ....
Which neither restlessness nor mad endeavor,
Nor man nor boy,
Nor all that is at enmity with joy
Can utterly abolish or destroy."

Finding that we could no longer revel in our own early history, we wished we could have followed our hostess to the turnstile, as by so doing we might have been invited to the wedding; but at that moment she returned, saying smilingly, that the couple whose intentions had been published the preceding Sunday were to be united in matrimony the next week by Mr. Flint, whom the Court had appointed to join persons in marriage, and that we were invited to be present.

Greatly pleased at being the recipients of so great a privilege, for this was another scene we had much desired to witness among the settlers, we forgot the mirage and went down stairs, where we were met by Major Willard with a glass of cordial, saying as he offered it that it was an extra brand. It was with no little embarrassment that we excused ourselves, being a total abstainer, for we were fearful of being misunderstood; but out apprehensions proved groundless, for Mr. Willard informed us that he appreciated our position, and considered it the correct one to take where it was possible; "but," said he, "The Concord climate requires sperit."

He then took occasion to inform us about the drinking habits of the community. Before doing this, however, the doughty Major dashed off a beaker to our health, saying, as he smacked his lips and set the decanter on the dresser, that what he had just drunk was pure liquor from old Kent, and that he considered it superior to any other in the colony, not excepting a cordial that he once drank at a consociation of clergymen held in Boston at the Governor's house, at which the Mathers were present. A regard for our health having been thus expressed, the Major continued his dissertation on alcoholic liquors by assuring us that in addition to the climatic requirements, there were certain times and occasions when "sperit" was very essential, as at raisings, huskings, log rollings, and apple bees; also, in haying, hoeing, harvesting, and getting up wood. It was a sine qua non at military elections, and training days, and ordination occasions; at funerals, weddings, and house warmings; when sheep were to be sheared, hogs to be slaughtered, or any extra work to be done. Travelers and teamsters he thought should have it, and those who watched with the sick, and sat up with "copses," but especially was it to be used in winter to keep the cold out, and in summer to keep it in. "The only trouble," said the Major, "is that some abuse it, and that good sperit is so scurce." He informed us that fermented liquors were more commonly used than the distilled, because the latter were more expensive and limited in quantity, while the former were within reach of everyone.

The beer was made from malted barley. The process of malting was to cover the grain with a few inches of earth for a few days, until it was well sprouted, and then remove it to the mash tub.

At the close of our conversation on the subject of colonial drinking customs, we came to the conclusion that there were in those times many deplorable instances of gross drunkenness; that alcohol was as destructive then as it is now, and that the same stock excuses were made for the use of it.

Conversation now turned upon desultory subjects, when the Major was summoned to the "beaver house" to appraise some pelts just brought from Nashoba by Nepanet, which he wanted to exchange for a kettle and some beads.

Being left to ourselves we looked around and seeing on the table a worn book upon whose cover was written "Town Book," we quickly opened it. Here indeed was a source of information most desirable; for in addition to the minutes of public meetings, was a list of births, deaths, and marriages, down to 1654, which Simon Willard had entered as "Clark of the Writs." And here it may be observed, that in addition to the duty of recording and returning to the colonial authorities the vital statistics of the township, Mr. Willard was empowered to "end small causes" or to "hold court;" his jurisdiction amounting to that of a miniature municipal court or trial justice; and thus judicially empowered he could issue writs, order "mesne process," and make petty decrees, having for fees as follows: replevin, 2nd.; attachment, 3rd.; bonds, 4th. On Mr. Willard's return from the beaver house, dinner was in readiness, and we entered the large "room of all work" or the "living room" and sat down to a meal which did ample justice to the large heartedness of our host.

It may be proper here to describe the dinner and its appurtenances, in order that we may note any difference between the way of living in the home of the average settler and that of the more well-to-do trader or merchant.

The table was set in what was known as the "living room." In this room was the occasional use of the flax and spinning wheel; and the "picking over" of small farm produce, as cranberries or beans on a winter evening or wet day; and where apples and pumpkins were sliced and strung for drying; where also the family usually sat, and the loom was sometimes "set up," and the itinerant shoemaker "whipped the cat," in his usual round of repairing. Above the table which had leaves was the clumsy "candle beam," constructed by the crossing of two slim scantlings, and an attaching of them by a perpendicular one to the beam in the ceiling, making a fixture for lighting purposes corresponding to the modern chandelier.

We noticed that the candles in the beam sockets were of an olive color, and, on subsequent examination, we discovered by their fragrance that the material was in part bayberry tallow. The chairs about the table had high backs and were similar in every way to the specimens of old furniture seen sometimes in modern houses, and which are said to have been brought to this country by "two brothers" (seldom more than three) in the "Mayflower" or "Ajax" or "Kingfisher," ships of quite too small tonnage for bulky cargoes. These particular chairs were said to have come over in the ship "Confidence" from Southampton, John Jobson master, of CC tons burden. As there was an utter absence of "stools" and "forms" such as we had seen at Timothy Wheeler's, we inferred that chairs were indicative of "forehandedness." On the "dresser" shelves also were many such articles as are exhibited at the present day as souvenirs of the colonial period.

Among the articles on the lower shelf was a set of metallic plates or a "charger of pewter," as it was called; a "milk ewer," "sugar basin," "butter boat" and "pickle boat," all brightly burnished. On the middle shelf there was a "mint stand," a "pottle" for milk holding a couple of quarts or thereabouts, also a "losset," "twifflers," two dainty "wine tasters," and a coarse glass decanter. The upper shelf contained a row of "beakers" (later called tumblers, perhaps because of the tumbling sometimes caused by their contents), and a few "caudle spoons."

We did not care to inquire what were the contents of the demijohns and jugs in the closet under the dresser shelves, so can give no certain information concernnig them; but we inferred, from what we 'had seen in the cellar arch, that here were the middle means for the easy distribution of such "schnapps," "cordials," and "strong water" as the Willards made use of.

The fireplace furnishings were, likewise, in strong contrast with those at the Wheeler farmhouse; those being wholly of plain iron, while these were ornamental. The dog irons, shovel and tongs were surmounted by brass, and brightly polished, showing fidelity in the hired help. Instead of the usual "lug bar" up the chimney there was a "crane," the first, it was said, that came into Concord; and above the fireplace was a long "clavel," over which was a string of peppers and "braids" of choice seed corn. In one corner of the room, the most remote from the smoke of the fireplace, and upon wooden pegs in the corner post, were the sword and leathern belt which Simon Willard wore when he "exercised the train band;" and hard by these, against the wall, in a plain, pine frame, unpainted, was the commission from the King of England making him major in the Bay Colony militia, a commission of much distinction and recently obtained. This was the only attempt at mural decoration, with the exception of a small picture of the martyrdom of John Rogers and a profile of Parson Peter Bulkeley.

Such was the furnishing of Major Willard's "living room." It was simple and for the most part serviceable. But although there was nothing sumptuous for style or substance, we could detect as we thought, on the part both of Mr. Willard and his wife, a faint consciousness of mild gentility, insomuch that we half concluded that the New England colonists, notwithstanding their avowed aversion to all class distinctions of the Old World, had much respect to rank, and some small desire for modest display.

But lest our conclusion be an untenable one, and based on superficial observation, we hitched up to the hearth's edge to hear from the sparks, dinner being not quite ready, and Madam Willard and a servant being engaged removing the food from the brick oven.

It was well that we did so, for the sparks informed us that human nature is usually the same everywhere in spite of all attempts to suppress it, and that the Willards on account of their modesty only partially represented the colonial families of wealth in their style of living. In fact these oracles of the fireside informed us that the principles of caste were slightly recognized in every New England community, whether of the village, hamlet, or crossroads.

But money was not alone the basis of distinction; it was position as well. The selectmen had prominent seats assigned them in the places of worship, as did other conspicuous personages, while the poor people and the servants took seats in the rear, or occupied benches in the gallery, thus making the colonial meeting house a "house of lords" as well as a "house of commons."

Madam Willard had directed the servant to "set the chairs up," so we left the sparks and sat down to the table, the servants sitting at one at the same time in the kitchen, it not being necessary for them to serve since there was no hot drink and all the eatables were on the table.

The Major in doing the honors of the table helped us most bountifully, believing, perhaps, as did all of his ilk, that brawn is born of good living. The first course, or "meat vittles," as they called it, consisted of a juicy roast from a beeve fattened on the upland pasturage of the Musketequid, and a plump piece of pickled salmon taken the April previous at the "lower meadow falls," with a mint sauce additionally seasoned with savory and thyme.

For desert, we had hot rye cakes mixed with fresh buttermilk, marmalade that smacked of wild river grapes, and sweet conserve which consisted of successive layers of sugar and rose leaves, but the crowning piece was the pumpkin pie; and here there was such an exhibition of old-time cooking as we had heard spoken of but had never before tasted.

CHAPTER XII

Talk at Nashawtuc — Fire of Candle Wood— Nantatucket —Municipal management at Musket equid — Division of Concord into "quarters" — Limits and Inhabitants — Committee on rules regulating Highways and Bridges — Location of Homesteads— Early Roads.

DINNER over, and a little post prandial conversation, we repaired to a sunny slope at Nashawtuc, and there, seated on a log, talked until the slant shadows of the hillside extended far beyond the river confluence at "Egg Rock," and the evening meadow mist enabled us to trace the windings of the Musketequid far down towards Punkattassett.

During the latter part of the afternoon the wind blew from the east, making the atmosphere damp and chilly, and as Mr. Willard had with him a "flint, steel and tinder box," which articles he stated he seldom went without, being much in the woods engaged in surveying, we concluded to start a fire. At once suiting the action to the thought we gathered some light kindling, and placing about it a little dry moss, a spark was struck and the material was ablaze. The fire was the more agreeable because we hoped to obtain from the sparks some information additional to what Mr. Willard might give, for we felt that perhaps the Major would hesitate to speak freely of events and matters in which he himself had been a chief actor.

But we were by no means positive that the sparks would give anything supplemental to his statements, since we were sitting under his own timber trees, from whose ancient tops the very fuel we were then using had fallen, and we were well aware that nothing would work against Simon Willard's wishes if he made them known.

Besides, those sparks could not if they would depose about some things, for, although Nashawtuc overlooked much of the broad alluvial area between the river and the ridgeway, and about the hog pen walk at Annusnuc; yet its highest point did not overlook every precinct, and there was many a settler beyond Flint's pond and over against Punkattassett, and across the "great fields" to the easterly, that it could not look down upon.

Every obstacle, however, was soon unexpectedly removed, for, as we were about seating ourselves on a log which we had just rolled before our fire, Nantatucket whose wigwam was just below us, the same Indian who years later deposed about the first Concord land deal, was seen coming along the hill path, having upon his back a bundle of candle wood, which in broken English he stated he had gathered from a clearing below the ridgeway, where some of the Hartwells, Bakers, and Healds lived.

For the sake of the sparks we begged some of the candle wood designing if need be to cast it occasionally on our fire, thereby, perhaps, to supplement Major Willard's statements. Nor, as it happened, was this all the advantage that accrued to us from the arrival of Nantatucket; for, as he sat with us for fully a half hour smoking his pipe and talking, he greatly confirmed our supposition as to the early friendship existing between the Indians and English at Concord. He reiterated what Tahattawan had told when we sat in his wigwam on the evening of the Apostle Eliot's visit. With a native eloquence and true sincerity, he said that a mat was always spread by the settler's hearthside for any belated wanderer of the woods who might wish to occupy it, and the subjects of "Big Pray" (Parson Bulkeley) always extended to those of the Squaw Sachem and her sagamores every needed hospitality, whether of their snug cabin homes during the week or of their meeting house where they worshiped their "Kiton" on a Sunday.

Nor was this all the good the English had done them; the dreaded Maquas (Mohawks) had ceased to visit them, and no longer was their dreaded war cry heard as a death knell along the meadows and over the midlands of the Musketequid; but peace prevailed, and the protection sought by the English in building their garrison houses, of which we had been informed there were several, was from predatory bands that might come from the East and North. After this statement, Nantatucket sat for a time quietly smoking his long-stemmed pipe, then suddenly arose and exclaimed that he saw the canoe of Nepanum just coming around the bend below the fording place, and as they had arranged to go a spearing together on the Assabet that evening he would leave us.

Upon the departure of Nantatucket, Mr. Willard and myself engaged in conversation concerning the municipal management of the Concord colony in its incipient stages; and the information which we have obtained from all sources upon this subject is the following, which we give as the substance of history on this subject.

In 1654, the town was divided into three parts designated "quarters." These were known as the "North," "South" and "East" quarters, and the following are approximately their territorial limits.

The North quarter contained the land north of the "Great river" to the Assabet, including most of that about Annusnuc (Concord Junction). The term "Great river" or "Concord river" was applied to that portion of the Musketequid below the confluence at Egg Rock. In this quarter were the following families: Heald, Barrett, Temple, Jones, Brown, Hunt, Buttrick, Flint, Blood, Smedley and Bateman.

The South quarter contained the land south and southwest of Mill brook, a small stream crossing the road near Concord square at the center to the southerly limit of the North quarter with the exception of three families. The following are the names of householders living in this quarter: Dean, Potter, Buss, Heywood, Hayward, Gobble, Woodhouse, Wheeler, Billings, Bulkeley, Stratten, Wigley, Dakin, Miles, Hosmer, Scotchford, and Wood.

The East quarter comprised the area between a line extending to the eastward from Concord Center toward Lexington to the great river, with the exception of a small tract between the latter limit and the old training field. In this ward were the families of Wheeler, Fletcher, Rice, Meriam, Brooks, Fox, Hartwell, Ball, Farwell, Taylor, Baker, Wheat, and Flint.

The following is supposed to be a verbatim copy of the report of the committee appointed to execute rules and to regulate affairs relating to highways and bridges, and the subjoined are the committees, and the date of the report: "The limits of each quarter (are) as followeth: "The north quarter by their familyes are from the north part of the training place to the great river and all to the north sid thereof.

"The east quarter by their familyes are from Henry Farwels all eastward with Thomas Brooke, Ensign Wheeler, Robert Meriom, Georg Meriom, John Adams, Richard Rice. The south quarter hy their familyes are all on the south and south west sid of the brooke except those before acsprest with Luke Potter, George Heaward, Mikel Wood and Thomas Dane, Signers Simon Willard, Robert Merion, Thomas

Brooks, Thomas Wheeler, James Blood, Georg Wheeler, Georg Heaward, Thomas Bateman and John Smedly.

"The date of report 7th of the 1st mo 1654."

It would be a matter of interest indeed could all the homesteads early established in their various quarters and by their several families be identified or located.

This however would be impossible, for time, seldom friendly to the perpetuity of even the most enduring monuments, easily brushes aside many of the frail landmarks such as "A small tree by the brook," "A pine stump by a stone heap," "A red oak sapling by a fox's burrow," "Two short logs one of them with the bark stripped and abutting John Smith's brush fence." But apart from the uncertain and transitory nature of some landmarks and boundary lines, to trace original homesteads would be difficult, because there prevailed at an early period among the grantees a desire for change, the result of which was that a land lot acquired one day might be exchanged the next, so that if an original house site could be identified, to determine the original ownership of the land might be impossible.

But, furthermore, some early families at Concord, as before noticed, did not long remain there, for like gold hunters they sought new fields in hopes of betterment.

They put their names on record and staked out lots but selling and leaving them the lots were thereafter identified with new owners. Moreover, families died out leaving no issue, their names ceased to be heard among the living, and were read only upon the mossy surface of their tombstones; their homesteads went to waste, their firesides were dismantled, and their cold hearthstones might form material for pasture walls.

Such are some of the processes by which change has been busy at Concord, and whereby old paths have been made to designate new ownership.

What all these changes have been we are unable to state, but many of them have been given by the historian Walcott, and it would doubtless be a difficult task to attempt gleaning anything valuable after him. But notwithstanding there have been many changes, it can, nevertheless, be said with safety that some families kept their homesteads from the first and passed them on to their posterity with little if any break in the old paternal boundary lines. So was it for over two centuries with the Hartwells, and to a certain extent with the Buttricks, Barretts, Miles, Healds, Dakins, Browns, Balls, Bakers, Hunts, Flints, Meriams, Brooks, some of the Wheelers, and a few others, most of which have long been associated with the original homesteads or with certain localities.

At the time of a division of the town of Concord into quarters, measures were adopted for the making and maintenance of highways and bridges. Commissioners for this work were appointed and the following were the names in the first list: "East quarter, Ensign Wheeler and William Hartwell. North quarter, John Smedley and Thomas Bateman. South quarter, George Wheeler, James Hosmer, George Hayward and Sergent Buss." Each quarter was to make its rules and assess "rates," and in order to limit liability against the entire town, it was enacted that all damages arising from defective highways should fall upon the quarter where it was incurred.

As to where all the original highways were, and whither they went we cannot state, for like the sites of old homesteads, they have in many instances become obliterated. Some, however, are still in use, and some that are not in use may to some extent be traced by record or tradition.

Mr. Albert E. Wood, a civil engineer of Concord, and well acquainted with the topography of the town states that "Until the Bay road was built, which was a good while after the town was settled, there was no way to get to Concord except by the Virginia road." This road, according to the same writer, was reached by way of Middle street, Lexington, which latter road he believes is the one followed by the early settlers as they journeyed from Watertown into the wilderness at Musketequid. This road, the same writer thinks, was laid out perhaps by a company of explorers who went forward and pioneered a path preparatory to the going forth of the Concord Colonists.

The course pursued in order to reach this road Mr. Wood conjectures was as follows: — "starting from Watertown, and going northerly through what is now Waverley, almost to East Lexington; then bearing off to the left, and passing through the entire length of Lexington, by what is now called Middle Street, to the Lincoln line; then turning a little to the right, so as to avoid Hobbs' Brook, upon a road which tradition declares to be very old, and crossing the present Lexington Road, coming by the Virginia Road to Concord."

As a matter of course the "strate strete" or the road along the ridgeway from the public square to Meriam's corner is one of the oldest streets, since houses were erected upon it as before stated about 1635. Of this highway an early record says, "The highway under the hill through the Towne is to be foure Rodes broad." Other old roads are the Woburn road, whose course was through the East quarter and toward the Shawsheen district (Bedford), the Watertown road in the South quarter of date 1638, the Sudbury road through the South quarter of the same date, the Billerica road from the Lexington road at Meriam's corner, 1660, or before; the Groton road (North quarter), 1699; and the "Old Marlboro road" and the road to Lancaster. The origin of some of these is only a matter of conjecture. As a rule it is safe to conclude that they were started for communication with some point of importance, as a fording or fishing place, or an extensive land grant, or • to find outlet into some leading thoroughfare. The ancient highway was usually a development from a blazed bridle path to a rude drift or cart way, and thence to the "county," or, as sometimes it was termed, "great road." Their widths range from the Indian trail, which Johnson states was "one foot broad," to a road from four to forty rods; the latter being the width of a highway early laid out through the town of Sudbury.

One object of so much apparently superfluous space was, doubtless, to pre-empt the timber trees along the way for public purposes. In the formal or official laying out of the early roads it is not improbable that drift ways and paths that were private property were sometimes subsidized, so that what the record designates as "the laying out of a new way" or "a way", may have been only the formal appropriation or public recognition of an old one; an instance of which may be the laying out of the Groton road over the North bridge in 1699, when, as we are informed, the roads of the North quarter were reconstructed or relocated.

It is probable, also, that in the formal laying out of the early roads old Indian paths were utilized. Such might naturally be the case with the road to Sudbury. Between the latter town and Concord there doubtless was considerable communication, before the coming of the English, carried on by the aboriginal inhabitants of these as well as of other towns. The Indians at Natick and Nonantum,

60

Kato and his family whose home was at "Wigwam hill" (Goodman's), in Sudbury, the natives dwelling in the vicinity of Cochituate pond, near the head of which was a fort and fishing place (Saxonville), all would know the most feasible route to the Musketequid and follow it, and the English would naturally take advantage of this in laying out their own roads. So it might have been with the "Old Marlboro road;" perhaps it was the shortest course through the domain of Tantamous (Maynard) to Occogoogansett (Marlboro). The road to Lancaster or "the road that goeth to Nashaway" might have been the nearest way to Nashoba (Littleton), and many times may have been pressed by the soft moccasin of Nepanum before it was trodden by an Englishman. The road to Woburn may have been the trail to the home of the Squaw-Sachem at Mystic (Medford) and to the Shawhine fishing ground; the one to the northerly, at the Blood farm (Carlisle), may have been the trail to Pawtucket Falls (Lowell); that to Watertown may have found outlet at Weston, then Watertown, in the "Old Connecticut Path," which ran into the interior of the Nipnet country toward the Indian village of Maguncook (Ashland), and to places beyond these; to all of which villages the tribal relations of the Musketequid Indians probably extended. Of the later and lesser highways of Concord, whether in use or disuse, we will say but little.

CHAPTER XIII.

Sites of Ancient Highways — Their Reminiscent Character — Vestiges of Old Homesteads — Earth Dents — Traces of Old "Tavern Stand"— Shoemaker's Shop, Laborer s Cottages, The Dame School.

BEFORE leaving the subject of old and disused highways, let us consider some suggestions that come to us; for as we remember that they were once well-worn thoroughfares of the fathers, and the avenues of public intercourse, they furnish food for much thought. To begin with, the very tracing of them is interesting to one possessed of an antiquary taste, or who is a lover of Nature, for there may be frequent and pleasant surprises.

It may be a rare flower whose presence was detected by its fragrance, and as the eager explorer thrusts away the blackberry vines to examine it more closely, or to pluck it as a trophy, he may discover the crank of an old hand mill last turned by Goody Gobble and left stranded when the tide of travel went out. As he pursues his way, which in its devious course at one time takes him through meadows green and pastures pleasant or along merry brooksides, and at another leads him a tangled and tiresome chase through woodlands wild and up and down defiles that are shadowy and deep, he may at length find himself seated by a fox's den with no living object in sight except a few ferns and blueberry bushes, while within easy reach is the rusty nozzle of a blacksmith's bellows last used at the Village forge.

But perhaps the greatest attractiveness of the old and disused highways is in the suggestiveness of the house sites upon them. Indeed, it may be by the aid of the mounds and earth dents that mark them, that the entire course of an obsolete way can be traced; for although in many cases they are matters of record, yet so remotely were they traveled that Nature has quite claimed them, and in some instances so covered them with trees and grasses that it may be said they have reverted to the original owners by "prescriptive right." But the house sites may betray them, and to ferret out these sites and sit beside them; to muse upon their possible or probable history; or to search for some significant object that will break the spell of their mystery and give hint as to who lived there may be as interesting as to trace the roads themselves.

And in some cases it is quite as difficult, for time is never friendly to relics of any kind, and Nature strives energetically and promptly to cover the scars that are made upon her, as is clearly seen by the incoming of vegetation even upon a sandy railroad embankment.

Notwithstanding, however, all efforts to the contrary, man's work long defies Nature's best attempts to obliterate it, and if no traditions or records of the Colonial age were extant, it might perhaps be distinguished by the things now and then discovered in the moldering debris, where stood the old farm house, the barn, and the rude work shop.

Among the tell-tale objects of a durable character are cellar walls, old door stones, bits of metal broken from miscellaneous culinary articles, and crumbling brick work; while in the vegetable world and quite as lasting in their perennial upspringings are "gill run over the ground," patches of plantain, a few clumps of catnip, the red sorrel struggling among a few sickly lilies, a stunted lilac, a rose bush or two, an ancient pear tree, and perhaps as indestructible as anything, the yellow tufted cypress, and old maid's pinks.

But let us consider more closely the subject of house sites, and as we do so let us at times leave the realm of actuality, and as we stand by these wayside souvenirs, while not overstepping the possible and perhaps the probable, consider some old time customs and superstitions, and modes of living and of dress: and in this manner, it may be, feast our fancy upon the fictitious counterparts of what occurred in the half forgotten long ago.

That depression, about which are the fragments of old bricks with the blackened mortar still upon them, marks the spot where was born and died an "old inhabitant" who was foremost in town affairs. The path to his door now covered with "mouse's ear" was trodden much, because everybody respected him and he kept open house for the country side. In the intercolonial wars he and his son fought side by side, and when the war was over both came back. At length the old man died; the son left the farm, the road went into disuse, the house to decay, and this is the last of it. If you listen at the early twilight just as the witch hour comes in you may hear something, for that ghostly looking poplar whose leaves tremble so may be sheltering some sprites who will tell the history of that house, which history may be that intemperance had to do with its loss and decay; the moral of which is that in every place and among every people alcohol is destructive rather than constructive.

Near that leek covered ledge by the barberry bush may have been an old-time tavern stand. The sign that swung before it said: "Entertainment for man and beast," and the landlord's license was "to sell strong water." In the accomplishment of these objects, the keeper of this "Ordinary"

was much assisted as well by the villagers as by the occasional traveler, in that some of the former were always ready for the latter to "stand treat," and it may not be too much to suppose that more than one stone on the wall opposite has been surreptitiously thrust upon the "steelyards" and weighed, and afterwards returned to its place, in order to insure a safe bet on its weight for the drinks, which bet was made with some unsuspecting teamster.

The usual village loiterer was there also, tempted by the odor of the tap room, and with an eager expectation that he would be benefited by its scant leakage, if he now and then groomed a teamster's horse or made the hostler's bed in the "bunk."

Soldiers sometimes stopped there on their way to or from "Old Ti" and Crown Point, and swapped stories, and talked of the war; and the neighboring farmers of a winter evening or a wet day sat before the fireside in the bar room and smoked their cob pipes and talked crops, taking good care to leave with the landlord no more than their good will when they went away, for a nine pence with them was stronger than appetite; as money usually came hard in those days, and to make both ends meet was a matter of economy and close management.

By the bushy lane where that large boulder is encircled by the low savin bush as if to save it from the encroachments of all larger vegetation, may have stood the shop of a shoemaker. There, bits of old leather, curled and wrinkled by long exposure to sun and weather, show that this son of Crispin was a careful craftsman, for those stitches that grin and glisten are well set, and the shrunken awl holes even yet show their shapeliness. There by that burdock is the remnant of a "tongue boot." The leg is stiched to the instep leather in a well-rounded seam, which indicates that the ancient shoemaker had regard to both stoutness and symmetry.

In a barn that stood back of this building the minute men drilled, and on winter evenings the yeomanry met there and went through the "manual of arms" with their mittens on, while the cows lowed in the stalls and longingly looked to the haymow in the wish that a loose lock might be thrown them.

Beyond the road-bend on the rising ground and half concealed by that hazel clump, may have stood the cottage of a laborer who worked for "four and sixpence" a day "making it fair weather." Near that bush was his garden, where he worked at early evening and of a stormy day. Here and there a few turf bound herbs as sage and rue still disclose it, and if time has not been too relentless, the fragrance of a few grass pinks or the flash of a sweet williams blossom may reach you. In the adjacent bog by that cone shaped musquash's nest he cut his peat, and the straggling hop vines that vainly strive to entwine themselves about that wild cherry tree are the poor remnants of once productive vines which the laborer relied upon to "work his beer."

Just beside the runway there by the bank, was a "Dame school," which we will suppose was kept by Goody Dorothea Dean in the northwest chamber of her sister's husband's farm house, the parents of each pupil sent to her paying six pence a week for tuition, she having her rent free. Here, we will suppose that the good dame taught year after year, and sang the same old song of addition, subtraction, multiplication and division, as the winter snows came and the spring suns melted them away, until her life became as dry and methodical as the simple rules with which she dealt, and every hue of her once fair face was faded, and there was little left to tell of the former freshness which once made her a favorite among the village beaux.

It was not hard work that had shriveled the fair features of Goody Dean, although she did everything that was required of her, and was a painstaking little body, doing her duty in every detail and to the last moment by the "noon mark;" but the humdrum of her experience was what wore on her, for it was day after day the same thing without special incident or episode, except now and then the entrance of some new comer, who, although too young to enter even the simple curriculum of a Dame school, had been sent by an overworked mother in order to make one less child to be under foot in the cheese-room. This monotony was not peculiar to the school of Dorothea Dean, for this school taught in the northwest chamber of her sister's husband's house was as good as any of the Dame schools. But education was at a low ebb in that period. The financial circumstances of the colonists were straightened. An intense conservation prevailed and only the practical was then popular. As they could do without grammar better than they could do without corn they raised corn. As their meeting house educated in matters religious, and much secular knowledge was not considered essential, they let the latter take care of itself, and were fairly content if they could read, write, and "cast accounts" in whole numbers, as mathematics were then styled.

So it was that Goody Dean and her Dame school were up to date, and her pupils were abreast of the times; and although both were in the doldrums of the days of a juiceless pedagogy, yet neither expected anything better nor looked beyond what that northwest chamber afforded.

The mistress went her simple round of duties day by day with a punctiliousness that was commendable and in exact accord with the staid circumstances that surrounded her.

Her work was to a large extent manual, and that of her pupils was formal and imitative. There were quills to be sharpened, rules to be written, and learned by rote, and recited, courtesies to be taught and carefully practiced, instruction in sewing to be given, and the children to be kept quiet on the tripod or made to sit straight on the backless bench.

Nothing very progressive could under the circumstances be expected in these schools, either on the part of the teacher or the taught, for time, a very important factor with the settler, had an allotted limit with each scholar. So if perchance some exceptionally ambitious and precocious youth got so far in arithmetic as to "enter fractions," and in grammar as to "parse" in some old copy of "Paradise Lost" borrowed of the Parson, his ambition might suffer speedy curtailment, for just then might come planting, hoeing, haying, or harvesting, in which all the little folks could be serviceable, and so although the term went on, away hied one after another to their several homes, leaving the Dame with a loss of their sixpence a week, to await their return after an interval of weeks or months.

But notwithstanding the drudgery of the Dame school with its absence of attractive text books, and its dry methods and its arbitrary rules, the children loved Dame Dean and would do almost anything for her. They respected her next to the minister and magistrate, and many were the little tokens of affectionate regard sometimes seen on her coarse desk in the corner, in the shape of sprigs of "southern wood", or "goose's tongue," or wild roses, or early fruits, so it may be said that the pupils of the Dame school, in what we will call district number two, to make matters more natural, though the district was never numbered that we know of, were as good and contented as any could be who were similarly situated.

But children were human in those days as well as these, and it is no wonder if they sometimes got tired and as they sat of a long drawn afternoon watching the wasps buzzing on the ceiling, or craning their necks over the high window stools to get a look at the fresh, green earth, and as they thought of the sweet flags by the water courses, and the tender checker-bush by the pasture lane, and the strawberries among the meadow rocks, it is no wonder that in their well wishes for themselves and their school mistress, there should come into their immature minds the innocent hope that as the dear old Dame had long sharpened their quills, so there might be somebody to sharpen quills for her.

And their little wishes were at length gratified. One day — it was a bright and cloudless one — when the tanager's wing flashed in the forest, and the frogs peeped loudly in the marsh stubble, and the dimpling waters of mill brook lapped lovingly the cowslip roots just below the Parson's sedge meadow, and looked up to the yellow blossoms as if impatient to become a part of them, someone rapped at the door, and upon its being opened there stood the familiar form of Farmer Fletcher, who lived just beyond that hollow in the highway yonder where those purple grackles are perched on the willow tops.

He was dressed in his best, having upon his head the "castor hat" which his father Jedediah left him in his last will and testament, and for his other attire, he had on a steel blue duffel coat and a white fustian waistcoat sitting low down on a pair of short and stinted pantaloons that just reached the tops of a pair of start ups, or high boots. The sleeves of his duffel coat were made short in order to display a pair of loose fitting "muffeteers" or "wristers" that extended well down to his sheepskin gloves.

Dame Dean went softly to the door and as she stood with her diminutive yet comely form facing the tall, stalwart frame of Farmer Fletcher, the contrast between them was striking: but not more striking in their forms than in their dress, for, not having expected a caller, as none except the minister and the tithing-men were supposed to visit the Dame school, she was attired in her every day dress, which so far as the fashion of it went, might befit any woman of the middle classes who was dressed for the work or leisure of an afternoon, except that her garments were of a little finer fabric and finish perhaps, because she was a school mistress. Her hair was neatly ruffed upon each side and kept in position by a pin plucked from a thorn bush, while dangling delicately over her left ear was a thin, lone curl. The front hair was brushed straight back between the ruffs and queued behind against a high comb.

She wore a sacque slightly decorated with faded "inkle," a kind of tape braid used in embroidery, both the fabric of the sacque and trimming showing that it had seen its best days before being worn in the school room. Beneath the sacque, and just disclosing itself through an unclasped hook and eye, was the edge of a "murry" colored waist, while thrown above these upper garments and resting tastefully upon them with a "set" that was without wrinkle or pucker, was a fringed "whittle" or Holland neck cloth. For lower garments there was an overskirt of "calimanco" which was caught up at the bottom to avoid the dust of the floor, and thus exposing an inch or two of a green linsey woolsey petticoat with a sage gray binding.

It was indeed a heap of clothing of faded gay colors for such a little body, but it showed how well kept were the garments of the middle classes in those days, and how things passed down by will, or inheritance, or as heirlooms to be worn by successive generations, each in its turn holding them in trust as it were, to be transferred to others if not worn out by themselves.

Farmer Fletcher smiled at the little school teacher as she appeared at the door and bowed low with his whole body; the bend being from his broad shoulders down to his well-rounded calves, which were swathed in close fitting cloth socks, and just apparent between his breeches and startups. The whole motion made by him described a half circle, and the hat which by this time he was holding in his hand almost touched the well sanded floor. The salute was responded to by the little school mistress in a manner as gentle as it was given, and the courtesy which she returned was such that her fragile form dropped gracefully and without a perceptible curve in her whole body, until it was only about half as high as that of her gallant caller who now had recovered his wonted uprightness; and her clinging linsey woolsey petticoat with its sage colored binding completely covered the dainty slippers, and coyly wrinkled on the coarse floor boards. Farmer Fletcher followed up the response by continuing to smile the sweet smile that was upon his countenance when he entered, and while all this was going on, the interested school children noted this practical observance of the "proprieties" which had often been taught them theoretically by their fond teacher, but which seldom had been illustrated by such a perfect object lesson, not even when on one occasion the minister met the tithing-men.

The school closed early that afternoon, much earlier than usual, and the scholars hardly knew why, and wondered, as with hop, skip, and jump they went through the nearer pasture bars into the lane to catch butterflies. Dorothea and Daniel repaired to a sunny bank by the woodside in the dingle you see in the distance, and there seating themselves with all proper decorum engaged in conversation.

Farmer Fletcher inquired with considerable apparent solicitude, though with an air of partial absent-mindedness, after the Widow Fox, whose condition of late had been feeble and languishing, and whose case was "made mention of" in a "note put up" the last Sunday at the meeting house. They talked of the news from the sea-board, and the fresh arrivals in the Bay. Especially animated was their conversation about the startling rumor of a stranger who had recently come into town, who had rashly proposed that the town buy a carriage "to carry copses to the grave in." The more exciting topic, however, before the final one, was the notable discussion that was going on from the Blood farm to the Nine acres as to whether the minister was not too much of a "legal preacher," that is whether he was not dwelling unduly in his discourses, on the "covenant of works" to the disparagement of the "covenant of grace."

Whether or not this last subject was too dry, or whether Daniel felt that the afternoon was passing, and was apprehensive that further delay might defeat the main object of his visit we cannot say, since the only sparks here available depose nothing; but so it was, that as soon as he had shifted his position to get out of the sun, which in its low descent now shone full in his face, giving to it a worried look, Farmer Fletcher said, hesitatingly, "Dorothea, art thou not tired of the Dame school?" for he used a scripture form of language, "and hast thou not taught long enough? and wouldst thou not change if thou couldst? for thou couldst if thou wouldst, and I have come to talk with thee about it, Dorothea." No matter of record has been made of Goody Dean's reply neither has tradition informed us about it, but from whatever facts are obtainable we infer that she informed him in substance, that since life with her had long been reduced to its lowest terms and she was wearied with whole numbers, if it would greatly add to his pleasures and much multiply his joys she was willing to divide with him her heart if he would share with her his home; for that she believed in so doing there would be nothing subtracted from their sum of happiness.

Just then a thrush sang in the brushwood, and an owl, which for the last half hour had haunted Farmer Fletcher by its dismal hooting, flew away, and the sun shone on the clouds above, giving them a rosy red hue, while a couple of song sparrows that had for a short time previous been chirping and twittering in the brushwood, flew out into the open and airily alighted on the spray of a hazel bush and sat swaying and singing, while Daniel and Dorothea looked and listened.

As the mists began to gather, and the grass was getting damp, Farmer Fletcher and Dame Dean arose and walked lovingly down the dewy pathway into the common highway and then and there arranged for the wedding, which, because of her position as a school mistress, they decided to have in the meeting house if it were allowed them.

But we will get back to the highway and only say further about the Dame school, that it soon closed, and as the husband of Goody Dean's sister did not care longer to keep open house for the school children, since then as now, they trod on the grass, Dorothea had no successor there. The farm was finally sold piecemeal, and as the house was old, it went into disuse, decayed, and fell but that is the site of it.

CHAPTER XIV.

The Haunted House — Casting of the Tarn Ball— The "Witch Call" — Adventurous Search for an Apparition — Explanations Relative to Houses said to be Haunted.

NEAR that barberry bush stood a haunted house which was shunned by the children and even the rough wood choppers. There the yarn ball was cast as a ghost test, and Ike Bateman went for a witch-call, but he failed to obtain it because at the very moment of success, when the spun yarn refused further to unwind, he dropped it and fled as if forgetful of what he was there for. He said afterwards that he heard the "call," and although his testimony stood alone almost everybody believed it.

Let us, since Ike failed, suppose we make the test for ourselves, if so be, by a little eavesdropping or espionage, of such as hold in mortmain old estates, we may discover the real sound and sentiment of the "witch call" and the color and shape of an old-time apparition.

In order to do this, let us suppose we visited the spot for this purpose, when the house was standing, with a ball of woolen spun yarn in our hand, a sprig of witch hazel in our hat and a horseshoe saddled upon our forearm to keep any inhabitant of that once human dwelling place from coming too near. We did not go alone, we did not dare to, lest when the spun yarn caught we should scamper away as others had done, without waiting for the dreaded yet desired "witch call." So we went, myself and Simeon Buss, for Sim said, "He'd go ef I'd go," and that "he'd gone afore but was afraid to."

We went at an hour which for our purpose was considered a timely one, for it was the hour of twilight; a time when lovers get together, and the birds twitter and trill their sweet good nights, and the sprites commence their escapadings, and the late loiterer from the village grocery quickens his footsteps and furtively looks behind him to see if his own shadow is following him.

On approaching the house we involuntarily shrank back at beholding its dark outline on the wood's edge, and half wished we had not started. But we kept on and espying near the doorway a low lilac shrub crept under it and listened among its stunted sprouts to see if the coast was clear in which to operate. As no spirit was astir Sim fumbled for the spun yarn, and by a dexterous thrust passed it through a hole in the broken door and began to pull the end he held in his hand.

Before doing this, however, he shoved the horseshoe higher up towards his shoulder blades. It was a good cast he had made, for the spun yarn was clear and it was not until the ball was half unwound that it ceased further to "pay out." As it stopped we were startled, for Sim said there was a jerk, and we felt as if communication had commenced with another world. If the ball had stopped unwinding much sooner it ought not to have surprised us, for Sim had taken pains to make it sensitive by boiling it in a strong concoction of "witch broth," which was made of several ingredients, conspicuous among which were wild herbs gathered at midnight in a thunder storm, and at a time when the moon was on the wane, and the tide had turned; besides these, was a small sprig of betony plucked at a grewsome spot known as the "Devil's wallow."

Here was a crisis, the moment had come when we could retreat as others had done, or remain and hear the "witch call." Having resolved upon the latter course, for that was what we had come for, we looked well to the horseshoe, and also cast away the witch hazel sprig, for we felt as if the spell was strong enough, and crouching lower among the lilac sprouts awaited the "call," hoping that if it was to come at all it would come soon, though rather hoping it would not come at all, and fully resolved in our cramped condition not to wait long.

But there was no delay, for while we listened there came a low sound, at first scarcely audible, and hardly to be distinguished from the soft sighing of a gentle breeze, for the wind had arisen, and cold, grey clouds were scudding over the moon's disc. Soon the noise grew louder, with various quavers and modulations and at length broke with the expulsory force of a pistol shot; at the same instant two forms from a broken window casement dashed by us and disappeared in some currant bushes just beyond, the fruit of which, it was commonly said, the witches claimed, and were accustomed to pick of an evening after the moon was up; so that no one in the neighborhood dared touch it.

Moreover, it was stated that Sofy Smedley, and Cinthy Billings, she that was Goody Taylor before she married, belated in gathering "yarbs" in "medicine medder," as they were making their way homeward just at nightfall, saw two strangers picking the currants in their aprons.

Not knowing but that the witches would return, and in consideration of our cramped condition, we thought it might be wise not to stay longer among the lilac sprouts but to get out into the open and view things from a longer range; just then however matters adjusted themselves, for the objects crawled out into the moonlight and as they frisked and gamboled and were joined by two others we discovered that they were cats, and were convinced beyond peradventure that the sights, sounds and jerks on the spun yarn were now fully explained. Instantly our courage returned and we concluded to explore the premises. Crawling from our hiding place we entered the house, started a fire, and finding a half-burnt candle, we lighted it. In order that we might make the most of the sparks we went for fuel into the door-yard and gathered a few fragments of broken branches, which had fallen from a ghostly looking sycamore tree, believing that it had stood there ever since the house was built. Upon the hearth was a heap of crumbled mortar and chimney dust and soot and a few fragments of old bricks which half covered the dog irons. As the flames crept up the chimney there fell upon the fire several swallows' nests which looked as ancient as the house, and the smoke set to twittering the inmates of new nests.

Taking the nearly spent candle we impaled it upon a pointed stick and started for the garret. The stairs creaked as we ascended, and when we reached the place which in ordinary times is studiously shunned by the small boy after nightfall, there whizzed by us through the shattered window a couple of owls with such a screech as might be considered a cry of vengeance on those who had molested

"Their ancient solitary reign."

There were no rats, for their was nothing for them to eat; but hard up against the chimney and reclining upon it, in a way that on an exceptionally tempestuous night when the wind blew through the long windowless garret it might sway and tremble on the bricks with a distinctiveness that could be heard outside, was an old tin kitchen used for baking before a fireplace. Here also we saw at a glance was another of the would-be "witch calls" and the source of inexplicable sounds. Returning, we resolved to go into the outbuildings; one of which was an old carriage shed just opposite the room in which we had made a fire, and a few yards distant. Passing over the intervening space with some slight trepidation, we opened the door and passed in; but instantly, we slammed it together again and started back more affrighted, if possible, than when we were in the lilac sprouts, for plainly before us in the back part of the building was a white form, motionless, yet distinct and upright, and Sim averred, with one hand beckoning us.

In less time than it takes to tell it we fled into the pasture; but, as we glanced behind us to see how much we had the start of the ghost, we chanced to observe that although the door was shut, there was upon it the exact counterpart of what we had seen inside, and that it conformed exactly to the tall, narrow window frame opposite the fireplace. As we stood wondering and reasoning, Sim and I, the figure grew fainter and fainter, and at last disappeared. Not wishing to be too precipitate in our conclusions, since through our coolness we had succeeded so well before, we resolved to return to the house and make bold to investigate the cause which we strongly surmised. Cautiously retracing our steps, we saw that the firelight no longer shone through the window. We opened the shed door again — all was dark within. To make sure that our reasoning was correct we replenished the fire that had gone out on the hearth, and when the bright flame streamed up the chimney we went out, and there on the shed door was the same shaft of light, lacking the beckoning hand. Everything was now fully explained; the light from the blazing hearth shining through the window, had, on opening the shed door, passed into a dense atmosphere that had long been confined there, and striking the boards on the back side of the building, had been reflected back to us with magical effect; and a loosened clapboard dangling on the side of the window and gently swayed by the wind had caused the appearance to Sim's excited imagination of a beckoning hand.

After the satisfactory clearing up of the mystery we heaped fresh fuel upon the hearth and shoving up before it a huge stick we sat down upon it. Sim took from his pocket the stub of a cob pipe and began to smoke, saying, "Strange I'd forgot to smoke afore," showing, to one who knew Sim Buss, his complete absorption in the night's adventures. It was near midnight. The moon, which for the last hour had struggled through gathering clouds and only at intervals shown itself, was now wholly hidden.

The wind wailed through every knot hole and every now and then the cellar door opened in spite of all our efforts to keep it closed with a weaver's beam. Cheered however by the thought that we had done a good work and accomplished what a couple of generations had not done in the solution of a neighborhood mystery, we were content to wait a while, if perchance the sparks, fanned by the gusty blasts as they dropped down the chimney or as they came from the damp old cellar when the door blew open, might volunteer some information that would be of interest; and we threw upon the fire an old dresser shelf upon which doubtless had stood the beakers and decanters from which the former inhabitants had drank, Sim said the sparks fairly turned blue. However this may have been, they snapped as if they were eager to speak, and the following, in substance, is what they and we ourselves have to say concerning haunted houses in general and this one in particular: as a rule, houses said to be haunted were those that nobody cared for. Having fallen into disuse, they came under the ban of suspicion, and became a prey to every whimsical and superstitiously inclined person who might start a story about them, which might, or might not have a foundation in fact. The farmer's boy returning late from the village store from a desire for a little cheap notoriety could say that he "saw a sight," and it might be that he did see something. Tramps or as they were called "old walkabouts" might rendezvous there, and their firelight gleaming out of a dark evening would be an unusual sight to the passerby; or, it might be, the rising or the setting moon, throwing its slant beams through vacant chambers and seen from certain positions by timid persons, might give rise to strange stories. In neighborhoods where there was a readiness to believe such things, it would take but little to convince the credulous.

A lonesome environment, doubtless, had much to do with these beginnings, for houses said to be haunted might be in sparsely settled districts or near the edge of a wood, or perhaps in close proximity to a place where tradition hints about a tragedy having sometime taken place. Sometimes stories may have started because of the questionable history of a former occupant, and, in an early period when each knew everybody's business, anything secretive on the part of a family was amply sufficient to give rise to a suggestiveness of wrong doing; and when a house became unoccupied without a sufficiently known cause, this might be due occasion for suspicion.

In the present case let us suppose there were various conjectures as to the cause, none of which were fairly settled upon. No one knew of anything that had actually happened there, although various events had occurred in Concord of a grewsome character, the actors in which might have been at this house. Years ago, it was said, some pirates from the Spanish Main were in the vicinity for the purpose of concealing their treasures. They were lavish of their money, even to recklessness, and cast about their "pieces of eight" as if they were of little value.

Dark hints were thrown out that this house was their headquarters, and that about its hearth they held high carnival and drank heavily of wine. Not long after they left, strange stories were afloat. It was even said that people had been seen at night through the windows handling coin.

And some went so far as to assert that "pieces of eight" had been picked up about the premises, and that when an attempt had been made to pass them in trade they would vanish, leaving the hand empty. It was also asserted that, on dark, snowy nights the house would rock like a ship, and that at such times there had been heard a shrill sound, as of a boatswain's whistle piping the pirates to meet for a carousal. Another thing alleged of the building was that some reckless Provincial soldiers lodged there for a night, and reveled in the spoils brought from a campaign at the North, and that a portion of the spoil left over was placed in charge of the Devil, who doled it out, long years afterwards, as the shades of some of the soldiers revisited the spot to celebrate the anniversary of that night's dark debauch.

But to return to the old disused highways. It is asked, who at the present time are occupying them? If you look and listen you may discover. That partridge is one occupant whose whirring flight through the birches so startled you. It had a nest near that rock, and in the spring time its mate drummed on that lichen covered log which was a portion of the roof tree over Seth Farwell's cottage.

The fox nightly skulks over the wheel ruts once pressed by the farmer's wagon, the doctor's sulky and the minister's chaise, yes, and by the town hearse also, as it carried the mortal remains of the former owners of these vehicles to their "last, long home" on the hill.

The young of the wild rabbits play at twilight by the door stone of old Samuel Smedley's cottage, and scratch their fur upon the remnant of that forlorn rose bush nearby, from which a bud was plucked by Matilda Mitchel to bedeck her "bonnie brown hair" when she wedded Billy Ball.

Besides the ancient and disused roads of Concord, there are summer lanes, and winter woodways that are beautiful in their season; and over these we would delight to ramble and listen to the birds, or falling of nuts, or catch the flash of the fall flowers if it were autumn. But as it is history that we are after, we will leave the lanes to the cows and the winter ways to the woodchoppers, and proceed to the subject of bridges, which are properly a part of the highways.

CHAPTER XV.

Bridges—Their Associations — Rules for the care of Concord Bridges — The Historic "Old North Bridge" — Its Environment — Graves of British Soldiers — The South Bridge — Its Successors — Other Bridges.

THE subject of bridges is usually an interesting one, whether considered by historian, novelist or poet. Its associations are with the rippling, or rushing, or still water courses, and the human tide of travel that goes over them. We are accustomed to picture them with rustic accompaniments, as the boy with his fishpole, barefooted and bareheaded, or with a broadbrimmed hat, a truant from school, perhaps, or a runaway from farm chores. Or, perchance, the scene may be laid within sound of the boatman's oar, or the splash of the water fowl, and near a tree embowered cottage, where, smiling in the sunlight, are pleasant gardens with geraniums, roses, and pinks. The causeway approaching the country bridge is also attractive, with its willow clumps, the singing of blackbirds upon them, and the buzzing of bees of a bright May morning in the furzy blossoms. All seasons are alike at the ancient bridge, and even in the desolation of bleak December, when all other objects are clad in snowy white, the bridge is usually bare and in the road-bed over it may be seen the mother earth reminding us that she has not quite forgotten us.

But there is a difference in bridges, and the interest that attaches to one may be unlike that of any other. One bridge is conspicuous because of its natural environment, resting peacefully beneath an archway of vines, where, low drooping, are the purple grapes and wild clematis blossoms, while beneath are the dimpling waters of a still, clear stream moving between banks fringed with blue joint and meadow queen. Another may be historic, and although shorn of every other attractiveness, yet to stand beside it and think of what has passed over it and of its eventful past, is soul-stirring. On the Musketequid and one of its branches two bridges at least possess this latter characteristic. One met the advance westerly of the British empire led by King George the Third, the other the advance easterly of King Philip of Pokanoket about a century before, when with one thousand of his best warriors, he strove to pass this same river at Sudbury over the "Old Town Bridge" in his raid toward the seaboard. As before stated, rules were made concerning bridges, upon a division of the town into quarters in 1654, and in order to obtain an equable adjustment of their maintenance it was then enacted that the following regulations should prevail: The East quarter was to care for all the bridges in its own precinct and contribute three pounds toward supporting those in the North quarter.

The South quarter was to maintain it? own bridges, and also care for the Darby bridge in the North quarter; while with the foregoing assistance, the North quarter was to look after its own bridges. Among the oldest bridges here referred to are the North and South bridges. These two bridges and their successors have long been associated with Concord history, and with the coming and going of nearly a half score of generations of men. The floods from many storms have beaten about them and have sometimes swept over them, occasionally carrying them wholly away or in part dismantling them or causing the authorities to weight them temporarily, or to chain them to the near willow clumps, lest they go up stream or downstream, as the setting of the waters might choose to carry them; for the Musketequid and its south branch are fickle streams, and have the peculiar trait of moving both ways. Probably the sluggish current of this river has done more damage to its bridges by its lifting than by its propulsive energy; for though never in a hurry, yet when there is a freshet, it lingers upon the broad meadows as if it liked to, and as if loath to leave their quiet precincts. At such times the current may actually set backward, as when the floods of waters fed by a hundred rivulets and especially by the occasionally fierce current of the North branch or Assabet meet the main body at Egg rock. So it is that one or more of the South bridges have been fairly lifted from their abutments and carried up stream. The exact date of the erection of these two bridges we cannot state. Before they were built the river and its branches were forded or ferried by the use of canoes.

The stream farther up at Sudbury was early crossed by a boat paddled or "poled" by Thomas Noyes, for which he received two pence a passenger. Before the construction of the North bridge there was a fordway just below the mouth of Mill Brook. The fordway over the North Bridge is said to have been situated at the "old Hosmer place." Probably the shoal spots used by the English for crossing had been used by the Indians time out of mind.

It may be said to be characteristic of a part of the bridges over the Musketequid that they abutted on one side against a bank, or were built near it, which was done doubtless to avoid the construction of a causeway only on one side. So it was with the old town bridge at Wayland; so also with the North and South bridges at Concord. But to be more specific, let us notice first the North bridge, since this is the most famous of them all. This bridge, situated in the North quarter, is the historic "Old North bridge." Just when it was erected no one knows, but it was after the erection of the South bridge. Probably the first structure was a rude one and was washed away, and it is not unlikely that it was the same with the second one, since in 1660 three new bridges were constructed in the town of Concord, these taking the place of those referred to in the highway regulations in 1654. The road or trail that it accommodated was doubtless the one leading to the Blood farm, the territory of the Groton township, and the Pawtucket fishing grounds. But besides accommodating these places there were other and cogent reasons for a substantial crossing at this point. It would be a way to the outlying timber lands and to the rich pasturage and meadow crops on the other side of the river. To reach all these, a fording place, a ferry, and hay scow would hardly suffice at all seasons. There were floods that remained for weeks, there were times when the ice was forming and breaking, and weeks when, if the waters were open, they were too cold for even cattle to wade through. It is no wonder then if some evening the neighbors gathered about the fireside of Parson Bulkeley, and talked over the feasibility of building a narrow foot bridge near the fording place by Mill Brook that would suffice through the next summer and fall, after which time they would turn out and have a "bridge bee,"

each bringing his stick of timber, or stringer, or whatever part might have been allotted him; and so perhaps it was that a bridge went up near Goodman Buttrick's outlying land. The first structure was perhaps clumsily constructed, low set, and at times wholly submerged. It was probably made of logs roughhewn, resting on coarse abutments, and if swept away could be easily replaced. The second, we may suppose, was more elaborately constructed; for the settlers usually made progress in their public works, and so improvement continued, we may believe, until the construction of the historic "North," which the pictures represent to be slightly arched, stoutly framed, and spanning the stream upon several rows of strong upright posts. The

74

approach to the bridge over the meadow land was by a low causeway, along which stakes or stones were set to guide the traveler at high water. At the time of the "Concord fight," rough stones may have taken the place of stakes, for it is said that Captain Isaac Davis, when shot, fell upon one of them before his body rested upon the ground. The last historic "North bridge" floated downstream in a freshet, and as the road which it had served was discontinued, the North bridge was never rebuilt, for its late successor, which is there in part for a souvenir purpose, cannot properly be called its lineal descendant or take its name. But though the structure is demolished, its name and its memories will remain forever; and every pilgrim who visits the site of it will naturally glance backward into the past for an imaginary glimpse of those grim old timbers which were hewn by the fathers and pressed by the feet of the patriots as they pursued the retreating foe on April 19, 1775. The rude cut of this bridge made by Messrs. Doolittle and Earle gives a perspective which is far from satisfactory, but as it is the only one taken at the time now extant, it is tolerated; but the natural surroundings have not all changed, and some of them are the same as on that beautiful spring morning when the grain waved on the fall-sown fields.

On the site of the "Old North bridge" is the present one, which might be properly called the memorial bridge. Opposite to it on the west bank is the minute man, and a few rods to the westerly is an apple tree which approximately marks the spot where Capt. Isaac Davis of the Acton minute men fell. The old causeway to the upland is nearly obliterated, it being grass-grown and hardly perceptible above the meadow land. On the easterly side of the bridge site is the battle monument. Beyond the river up the hill side is the ancient Buttrick estate, and nearby is the place where the militia and minute men were drawn up in consultation and stood looking down upon the lone guard of Lieut. Thornton at the bridge. Near the river bank to the easterly repose the remains of several slain Britons, the first of England's dead in that great struggle in which she fell out of favor with America and lost a continent. Their graves are guarded by a stone wall and simple chain fence. The pine trees chant their elegy, and the winding river in its gentle flow or when in flood time its waters beat against the nearer bank utter sweeter voices about their graves than stranger tongues could sound. So it matters not what fortune or adverse fate has given or denied to the conquered or the conqueror, for time has dealt alike with each and with the bridge that is associated with them.

"The foe long since in silence slept;
Alike the conqueror silent sleeps;
And time the ruined bridge has swept
Down the dark stream which seaward creeps."

Toward the village is the old manse, and but for the shrubbery it would be in view of the scene just described. To the easterly is the "lane" and the ridge, and the great fields over which the continentals ran to head off" the British. For years silence reigned about the notable neighborhood of the North bridge, and the place was practically deserted, except as the infrequent pilgrim or the town folks on a gala day or people from the surrounding country side visited it. At length the scene changed, the battle monument was erected, then the memorial bridge and the statue of the minute man; and since 1875, in pleasant seasons, this place of monuments has become the Mecca of multitudes, and it may be said all roads lead to it.

Next in importance of the ancient bridges is the South bridge. This was situated at the westerly of Concord Center and crossed the south branch of the Musketequid a little to the easterly of Nashawtuc not far from the present South bridge near the Fitchburg railroad. This is supposed to be the first bridge erected over the river and is said to be situated at a point of land below Joseph Barrett's Esq., by "Lees hill" (Shattuck). It was washed away in 1665, and its successor was built the year after on the site of the present South bridge. At the least a half dozen bridges have been erected at this spot, and one of them was washed away and floated up stream by the backwaters of the North branch as they rushed downwards in a time of freshet and found easier egress above than below. Before the erection of a bridge at this place the river was probably forded not far away. The "Darby" or "Derby" bridge was over the Assabet at the present Concord Junction and named doubtless from its proximity to the Derby estate. As the fall of this stream is rapid compared with that of the Concord river proper, less casualties would probably occur to its bridges; since when the current is sluggish the pressure may be greater. As to when it was built we have no knowledge; but probably it was nearly coeval with the "South," as both might to an extent subserve the same purpose in affording an outlet into the western wilderness. As in 1660, a new bridge was erected here, the presumption is that the first was built much sooner.

As to the other ancient bridges erected after the date of these, Shattuck says of them as follows: "The bridge by Captain Hunt's was first built about 1792; that by Dr. Ripley's in 1793; those at the turnpike in 1802; and that beyond Deacon Hubbard's in 1802."

At one time the town was allowed twenty pounds towards defraying bridge expenses, and later, thirty pounds. There were several lesser bridges at this time, which crossed the smaller streams, but of these it is hardly necessary to speak, except to state that a principal one crossed Mill Brook by the mill dam on Haywood street, and has been known as "Fort bridge" and "Potter's bridge," the former name being derived, doubtless, from its proximity to one of the garrison houses, and the latter from the owner of the adjacent lands.

CHAPTER XVI.

A Sunday with the Settlers — Walk to church — Description of the meeting House— The Service— Colonial Church Edifices — Quaint Accompaniments— Early Ecclesiastical Objects, Customs and Influences — Their Value — Succession of Concord Meeting Houses.

IT was early twilight when we closed our conversation concerning the municipal management of affairs at Concord: and the log upon which we were sitting was already dampened by the dews that were gathering about Nashawtuc, when a horn sounded from the Willard farm-house informing us that supper was ready.

We slowly descended the hillside, talking as we went, and when we reached the bar way just behind the first barn for there were two of them, we saw gleaming through the bushes the bright firelight of the kitchen hearth, and heard the sound of children's voices as they trooped ahead of the hired men with their pails full of milk. Soon we were seated at the supper table, upon which were several dishes of a savory odor steaming hot, a beef soup highly seasoned, a samp cake, and succotash made of dried green beans and dried green corn which Madame Willard said were just as good as when picked. The absence of pastry led us to infer that even among the well-to-do in those days, instead of the luxuries of modern times the table was supplied by the more healthful diet direct from the pastures and fields.

After supper we sat down for a quiet time all by ourselves, for the children had gone with their mother for a last glance at the catechumenal exercise of the coming Sunday, and the major was summoned to the "beaver house" by a squaw, who wanted some beads and a piece of dimity, giving as a reason for coming so late in the week to barter that she wanted the articles for her pappoose to wear next day at Big Pray's meeting. The Major demurred very emphatically at "this way of doing things after sundown Saturday night." His words were very suggestive, and not being fully persuaded what they meant, it suddenly occurred to us to throw upon the fire some pieces of knotty, pine stumps, which Mr. Willard informed us his hired men that very day had hauled from in front of the meeting house, the trees that grew upon them having been cut years before when the ground was cleared.

As the pitch stewed from the fat splinters the sparks flashed, and since we were alone we heard every word; and long before these remnants of the grand old woods that once crowned the hilltop, where stood the first forest sanctuary of old Concord, were reduced to ashes, we had reached valuable conclusions about the ecclesiastical customs and social, moral, and religious observances of the inhabitants, some of which we will give now and others later in their order.

It was a practice of the people in colonial times to close the work of the week about sundown Saturday night; the gate was shut down at the mill; the door was closed at the store; the children put away their play-things; and all this in preparation for holy time. When the Sunday dawned all secular labor was suspended, works of necessity and mercy alone excepted, and a close construction was placed upon the meaning and nature of these; even the stranger who stopped at the tavern was supposed to tarry till Monday; and if he attempted to resume his journey sooner, he might be detained by the landlord, who perhaps was a tithing-man. Within the domicile was a like strict observance of sabbath sanctity. The house was put in order, the food prepared, the Sunday clothing carefully inspected and laid out, and everything was done that could be done on the preceding day to prevent the necessity of work. As the evening wore on, various topics were talked about, and it was not until the clock in the corner struck ten, a late hour for colonial times, that we went to bed.

The morning dawned bright and rosy; and as we looked out and saw the sun rising over the ridgeway, where stood the little meeting house in which we were that day to worship, a feeling of unwonted restfulness came over us. The air was still. There was no sound of hammer or axe, and no stroke of distant threshing flail; but silence prevailed everywhere; the wayside warblers had all gone, and the birds of passage which still lingered about the willows and in the pasture lane gave utterance to no note of farewell either to the passing autumn, or to the generous farm folks among whom they loitered. Upon the river course a soft mist rested peacefully, while beyond the upper meadows by the bay there floated a light, fleecy cloud so soft and still, it appeared to sleep. Upon such a scene the Sabbath dawned; and it was as if Nature was already in her own sanctuary at worship, and it only remained for man to join with her to make the worship of the world complete. As we stood admiring the prospect and half in wonder at the change that had been made in a few years, a call came from below summoning us to the breakfast table. We were reluctant to respond, for the feast of soul that was spread before us was we felt far better than any that could be afforded to the body, however delicious it might be.

But being a guest we went down, and shortly after found ourselves with a great zest partaking of beans and brown bread baked in a brick oven, both of which were of that tint and exquisite flavor which only comes with slow cooking and a soft heat. Breakfast over and devotions ended, for the Major was a good churchman in his way, we went to the meeting house, Mrs. Willard leading the way, followed by the younger children led by the elder daughters, Mary and Abovehope, and a couple of servants. In passing the bridge over the south branch the stillness was broken by the beating of a drum; this we were told was to call people to meeting, and that that the "saxton" had twenty shillings a year for "beating the drum Sundays and lecture days," and for sweeping out the meeting house, besides being exempt from "minister rates."

As we entered the little "Strate strete" at the foot of the hill, we saw several families which had come from a distance, among whom were the Hartwells, Brookses, Meriams and Rices, from the direction of the Shawshine, the Bakers and Flints from beyond the pond southerly, and the Bloods, Buttricks and Healds from the North quarter.

The dress was simple, but better than that worn on week days, and we saw that great care was taken to keep it so; for we observed that all the children and several of the adults stopped before ascending the hill and put on their shoes, which they had carried in their hands; but the most noticeable of anything was that all the men carried firearms.

We had read in books that the settlers in those days carried muskets to meeting to shoot Indians with, yet we did not expect to see it at Concord, but here they were, each man with his weapon with the exception of the old men, for almost every age was represented in this procession of churchgoers.

We inquired about these firearms and were informed that they were carried to meeting at Concord in conformity to a law of the land which required it; but they only carried them to shoot wolves with in case they met any, and never as a protection against the Musketequid Indians.

We felt much better after hearing this, for we had heard and read so much about English hate, and Indian hostility, and had seen so little discrimination made between the Indians of different localities, that we were not quite sure we were safe on Sundays if we were on week days, notwithstanding what Nantatucket told us. As we drew near the meeting house the minister arrived, and entering, all followed him. The drum stopped beating and all was still save the occasional note of a belated wood thrush, and the soft foot. Colonial steps of a slow pacing sentinel left outside to conform to custom and law.

It was evening; and amid the meadow mists by Nashawtuc we repaired to a quiet spot to review the scenes, sermons, and events of the day.

Having made the foregoing statements concerning church and church-going at Concord in Colonial days from a fictitious stand point, let us now consider the matter historically, and present facts.

The first meeting houses of the country were without chimneys or glass windows. They had four plain rectangular sides, and the crevices between the logs were filled with clay. The roof was low and covered with thatch.

Their immediate successors were made of sawn material and had a truncated pyramidal roof. Sometimes the roof was crowned with a belfry, and sometimes a small tower was erected nearby, which contained the bell, and in some cases the town's stock of ammunition, and the burial appliances it may be, as the bier and pall or "burying cloth."

The third meeting house in the succession came into use in the eighteenth century, and was more elaborate, having a projecting porch with a steeple upon it.

It is probable that the Concord colony conformed to the customs of the period in church building, and that its first meeting house was like that of other towns. Let us suppose such to be the case and conceive of its earliest house of worship as standing somewhere near the summit of the hill in the old burying ground, at a spot which overlooked the first street. It was reached, we will conjecture, by several narrow and winding wood paths—one from the direction of the manse, one from over the great fields to give a short cut across lots to the Bakers and Flints; one running southwesterly around the millpond and across the brook, to accommodate the Mileses, whose canoe was moored snugly by the upper meadows after having brought them over the river. The walls of the structure, if like some others of the period, consisted of layers of logs, the bark hewn roughly on the upper and under sides, the crevices being filled with clay. It had perhaps a low, gable roof, and was devoid of any attempt to distinguish it from other buildings by means of a cupola or dormer windows, or even a weather vane. To erect a structure better than this at the beginning of the settlement would doubtless have been difficult; for there were no saw mills, the nails were hand wrought, and carpenter tools were few and clumsy.

Here it may be surmised, that since tradition says the first meeting house was used for a score and a half of years, it is possible, if not probable, that there has been a mistake about the identity of it, and that there were two buildings during that time; the first perhaps not such as they would call a meeting house, it being so short lived and poorly built, and designed only to serve for two or three years, and to be superseded by one with more churchly characteristics.

This supposition may commend itself from the following considerations; first, because of the early date at which it was ordered that a meeting house should be built, which was nearly contemporaneous with the first steps taken in the settlement; second, because it was the custom of the colonists of other towns to build for the time being merely; third, the fact that so long a time as thirty years has been assigned for the length of service of the first meeting house when we think it improbable that a single dwelling place in Concord constructed during the first one or two years, stood very long after the existence of mills made sawn material possible; fourth, the structure that would suffice for a congregation of the first few years would hardly be large enough for that of thirty years later, notwithstanding the shrinkage in 1644, caused by the departure of Elder Jones and his company for Connecticut.

The timber trees used for the first meeting house were doubtless those nearest at hand; so that the designation by record or tradition of this or that lot as "the meeting house lot," we believe has reference to the land from which the timber for some subsequent meeting house was taken. This supposition is more plausible, since it was an object to early clear the space about the meeting house of trees, to prevent forest fires from endangering the building.

Probably the first structure was an unslightly one, for impatience to get into it would render the builders regardless of the element of beauty; as in the case of their little log cabins by the bank they only sought a slim shelter from the cold and storm for a season, so now with their church home, if they had a place for a few benches, a communion table, and a plain pulpit, they were content, for it would be a meeting house and in conformity to the order of the court. The logs may have projected at the corners unequally like the rails of a Virginia fence or the rafters of a Swiss cottage; the long coarse thatching may have drooped irregularly below the eaves line, leaving a loose and ragged edge which almost shaded the small apertures called windows; while about the crevices may have been here and there an ugly stain as the rain washed out the clay filling or the sun baked it until it cracked and crumbled.

As Providence smiled on the plantation, and times grew better, other houses of worship were constructed, whose succession is as follows, according to history.

The order for the first meeting house was in 1635, and it was ordered that it "stande on the hill near the brook opposite Goodman Judson's lott." In 1667, it was ordered that a new meeting house be built "to stand between the present house and Deacon Jarvis." This second or third meeting house, whichever it may have been was nearly square and had a gallery. The lower floor had a few pews and the remaining space was filled with seats.

The roof was ornamented with four projections on the sides, resembling, it is stated, Lutheran windows, or gable ends with a window in each. In the center of the roof was a turret or cupola, in which was a bell. On the spire was a vane, bearing date 1973, the probable time when the building was finished.

In 1710, arrangements were made after several town meetings for the erection of a new house of worship. It was to be 60 feet long, 50 wide and 28 high; it had no pews until sometime after it was completed, and when they were put in, it was only by special vote of the town as a favor to certain distinguished persons. There were two galleries and no porch or turret. It was finished in 1712, and cost 608 pounds. In 1749, pews were placed around the lower floor and a few in the lower gallery. On Jan. 31, 1790, the town voted to repair the meeting house, making it 72 feet long, 50 feet wide and 28 feet high, with an addition of three porches, a spire 90 feet high, square pews along the wall on the lower floor and in the gallery. It was dedicated Jan. 24, 1792, and Rev. Dr. Ripley preached the sermon. The first "church going bell" at Concord was placed upon a tree. About 1696, it was broken and sent to England for repairs. In 1700, it was placed in the belfry.

About the meeting house at an early date were various quaint objects, prominent among which was a "horse block," a pillory, stocks, a publishing post and whipping post, and sometimes a cage. The horse block was of stone or logs and was used by church goers who went horseback for mounting and dismounting and was especially serviceable to the women who rode behind the men on a seat called a "pillion." A fine horse block was early procured and paid for by the women of Concord, each contributing one pound of butter.

The pillory and stocks were for penal purposes; the former intended to keep the arms and head of the culprit in a constrained position while he remained standing; the latter to confine the feet and hands when sitting. The whipping post was where the law breaker received lashes publicly administered. The cage was for the confinement of evil doers for a short time where all could look upon them.

The publishing post was used as a bulletin board; and there might have been seen all kinds of legitimate notices, such as colonial orders, intentions of marriage, rules regarding Sabbath observance, town warrants, etc.

A reason for using the meeting house and its near precincts for giving publicity to events and orders may have been, that everyone if able bodied was supposed to go there in conformity to law, and custom, and individual desire; and perhaps from this fact has arisen the maxim of English jurisprudence, that ignorance of law excuses no one, in that as everyone was expected to go where the law was promulgated, therefore there could be no ignorance of it. The precincts of the meeting house were also sometimes the place to which the heads of wolves were brought when bounties were to be paid for them; the order being that they should be either "nayled to the meeting house" or to a tree near it, and hence, here and there might sometimes be seen these grim objects suggestive of both the peril and prowess of the pioneers.

From the foregoing facts, together with others to be observed, it may be safe to infer that the Puritan's place of public worship was not the most dreary spot possible, but on the contrary the most interesting in the settlement.

As it was often the town's geographical center, so about it was centralized whatever was in a wholesome manner enlivening, recreating, and agreeable. The people there obtained the latest news; there they exchanged neighborly salutations, made familiar inquiries, and took a fresh start physically, morally, and spiritually.

Neither was the meeting house and its precincts lonely and unvisited between Sundays. There were the, meetings on "lecture days," the occasional military elections, the town's civic gatherings, and miscellaneous or incidental assemblages. In short, the meeting house with its grounds was the people's trysting place, where a community of interest was recognized, and where everything that the settlement stood for was represented.

From such facts we may easily conclude that all was not constraint about the church-going customs of the early New Englanders, and that there was much besides the ecclesiastical associated with their houses of worship. The average colonist went to meeting because he wanted to, and because there was pleasure in it; not merely through a sense of stern duty. His meeting house was his church home, and he could say of it with a sincerity that was softened by the sweetest endearment —

"I love thy church, O God!
Her walls before thee stand,
Dear as the apple of thine eye.
And graven on thy hand.
Beyond my highest joy
I prize her heavenly ways,
Her sweet communion, solemn vows,
Her hymns of love and praise."

He looked forward to the recreation of the holy Sabbath and its sanctuary privileges with glad and expectant longings, and his hard, secular life was sweetened by its services.

In short, about those homely altars where burned the incense of a fervent faith, the worshiper of the lone, wide-spreading, and stilly woods found his flesh and spirit refreshed and refurnished; and it was because he drank at such fountains that the greatness of the generations following was made possible. Because of these things the locality of the meeting house was attractive, and its exercises were popular; and if the "blue laws," so called, that are sometimes so alluringly spoken of were needed, it was largely for the laggard and thriftless, and had the same significance to that class as did the whipping post, the pillory, and the stocks.

Having considered the meeting house, let us next notice how people got to it. The greater part went on foot, no distance being deemed too great if within the township, or about its border. A half-dozen miles was a small matter to a person who could travel a score of miles on foot with a sack of corn on his back. In Concord and towns adjoining, in many cases miles separated the worshiper from the meeting house; and often the way lay through swamps and at times partially submerged causeways. But nothing daunted, they pushed their way through or over these obstacles unflinchingly. For the conveyance of the women and children and aged people anything, available was used, — clumsy ox sleds or carts, hay wagons, and the saddle and pillion. In the latter mode of conveyance the "ride and tie" system prevailed. This method was for one or two to start on horseback and another or others to follow on foot, and when the former had ridden a piece they would dismount, tie the horse to a tree, and when the latter came up they in like manner would ride a distance and then dismount, tie the horse and walk on; and so parties would ride and walk alternately till they reached the meeting house.

In the matter of dress, care was exercised then as well as now. The fathers were far from being slouchy in their attire. Moreover, what might be the silly promptings of pride in the present, might then have been the promptings of duty, for such was the reverence for sacred things that nothing was thought too good for the meeting house, and it might have been considered sacrilege to go in a shabby garb, if something better were possible; thus what in one age may be a virtue, in another may be a vice. The material of the women's dress was all the way from a sleazy dimity to costly calamanco. The men, according to their ability might wear a coat of match, or a jacket of rough woolen frieze with dornex breeches of a coarse linen similar to canvas. So the pendulum swung then as now; nor will it cease, it may be, until society settles upon the golden mean, that they are the best dressed who are attired in clothing that is the most comfortable and the least noticeable and have means with which to obtain it.

Within the meeting house all was plain and simple. At first there were no pews whatever; but in process of time there was now and then one put in by permission at the expense of the occupant.

The "seating of the meeting house" was a very consequential affair and was to be done with such delicacy that the sensitive nature of no one could be injured, and each one would have a position suited to his rank and station.

The deacons had sittings near the pulpit, and if there was an elder a proper place was assigned him next to the preacher. The minister's family was to have seats at the front, and if there were magistrates, they and their families and also the selectmen and their families were to be provided for in a way that would magnify their office. A "seating committee" was chosen regularly, and because there might be heart burnings incident to the faithful performance of their functions, the office was unpopular; which shows that one elective office at least has gone a begging.

The men and women sat in different seats; also the boys and girls. Near the minister's seat was the "saxton's," where that faithful custodian of the meeting house sat in readiness to respond to any call, and to turn the hour glass; not, perhaps, that the preacher might be reminded when to close the sermon, but to know how long to continue it.

Above the pulpit and just over the minister when he was speaking, was a "sounding board," placed there for projecting the voice. It was either round or square and several feet in area and held in position by an iron rod extending from the ceiling above. In some places it was customary for the congregation to wait at the door until the clergyman arrived and to enter just after him. In others it was the custom to enter just before him, and at his coming in at the door to rise and remain standing till he was seated in the pulpit, a form somewhat similar to the present court custom when the justice enters.

After service began it was the rule that no one should go out until the close except in case of necessity; and so closely was this rule adhered to that one or more tithing men were stationed at the door to enforce it.

The service was usually quite lengthy, sometimes continuing from half-past nine till twelve; this time however was not all taken up with prayer and preaching. Besides the usual preliminary exercises there were others that were occasional. Before the long prayer "notes" were "put up," such as, "Betsey Bateman desires prayers that the death of her husband may be sanctified to her;" "Daniel Darby desires to express gratitude for a great deliverance from danger;" "Abiathar Brown desires prayers that he may recover from sickness." Marriage intentions were also proclaimed at this time, and the "Chrisom" service had place. The scripture reading was accompanied by expository comments; and the singing of psalms was preceded by "lining off," or the reading of a couple of lines at a time for the congregation to sing.

From the foregoing facts we infer that statements indicating that the clergymen of those days prayed an hour and preached two or three is an exaggeration. For if the meeting began at half-past nine, and we see not how it could have begun earlier on an average the year through, considering the long distance which many of the worshipers came with their slow cattle or on foot, and the necessary farm chores that preceded the journey, how, we ask, with all the miscellaneous matters and scripture reading and with elaborate expositions, psalm lining, and slow singing, and a prayer to close with, could so long a time have been devoted to the sermon? Moreover, the sermons themselves which are extant may be evidence to the contrary, as may be also the character of those who wrote them. The clerical profession of early New England was a learned one; it conformed well to the economics of the times and the desires of its constituents, and the product of it as seen in the present is indicative of its prudence, its piety and its sound common sense.

There was an intermission of about an hour between the services on Sunday, during which time some of the congregation went to the tavern, some to the neighboring houses, and some of the noon houses; which were small structures erected by private parties for this express purpose. These noon houses had fireplaces and were supplied with a barrel or two of cider, it may be, and utensils for warming their lunch.

As there was no means of heating the meeting house, various expedients were resorted to: among the most common of which were the foot stoves, small receptacles for holding coals. These were filled when taken from home and at noon were replenished at the noon house.

They were placed at the feet of the older people, and about them the little children could warm their fingers. They also tended to take the chilliness from the house, which being low and well filled, and with few windows, afforded more comfort than would be thought possible.

Wolf skin bags were attached to some of the pews or benches to put the feet in; and dogs were also taken to church for the purpose of keeping the feet warm. Indeed, to such an extent did this latter custom prevail that a law was passed prohibiting it. Whether this was done because the animals imparted so much comfort as to induce drowsiness in the listeners, or because the dogs sometimes made themselves heard in protest when too much pressure was brought to bear on them, the sparks do not depose.

As a means of maintaining order, tithing men or tenth men were appointed, so called because one was appointed for every ten families. These tithing men were each equipped with a long staff having at one end something with which to "rap up" unruly boys; and at the other end a delicately adjusted fox tail with which to tickle the faces of the staid dames and thoughtless daughters when regardless of the sermon. Besides these staves of office there were set up in conspicuous places about the room tithing men's sticks ready to be used if occasion required. Nor were these all the means for the conservation of good order, for there was sometimes placed midway of the audience a "culprit's seat," where might be seen sometimes a mischievous person bearing a paper upon which was inscribed the nature of his misdemeanor.

Outside the meeting house peace and tranquility were secured by means as systematic and grim. It was an early law of the colony that a fourth part of the "trayne band" was to go to church armed. A regular sentry was posted outside with an equipment regulated by law, which in some instances was a coat "basted with cotton wool" to ward off bullets, a "corslet" to cover the body, a "gorget" to guard the throat, and "tasses" to cover the thighs. Each sentinel was to carry a "bastard musket with a snap chance," "a full musket" or a barrel with a matchlock, or some other efficient firearm.

Such were the surroundings; and such were some of the scenes witnessed within and without the meeting house of "ye olden times," and we believe they are sufficient to convince anyone that the colonial meeting house and what went with it were far from being prosy; and that the times that produced them and the people whom they served were not doltish nor given to objectionable tranquility.

We do not affirm that all the foregoing practices were observed at Concord, nor in any one of the colonial towns; customs differed with communities, and each of these had their peculiar church cults, according as these were brought from the old country, or created by circumstances, or by contact with a neighboring borough; but if even a portion of them prevailed in a given township, it was enough to impart to it an activity and an air of sprightliness which would naturally prevent any social stagnation and make the life of the Puritan far from being staid or "slow-going."

We believe the foregoing facts also indicate that the olden times were more intense than we are wont to suppose; and that the secular strenuousness of the present has only taken the place of a spiritual strenuousness in the past. As in the natural world the same elements take different forms, so in society the energy of one age may be exerted in such a manner that the people of another age do not recognize it.

Society being largely conventional, it may be only by the discovery of the motive or the inspection of the mainspring of the machinery that enables us to make right estimates of an era and its actors. So when we measure the men and women of whom we have been speaking by what their meeting houses meant, we find them intensely active, and living in a period that demanded intense activity. Each person was a storage battery of spiritual force, and the electricity of thought, purpose and action was generated at the great "power house" of the church, of which the meeting house was the symbol.

Before we conclude our observations on the old-time meeting houses, let us notice their place in history. They were the beginnings of our national greatness and unprecedented progress. This we believe to be preeminently the case with regard to matters civic and educational. The colonial meeting house was the town house. The minister was for the town, and the town elected and maintained him.

Minister's rates were assessed by the same process and paid with the same cheerfulness as others; and indeed they might have been a standard for the making up of all other rates.

The first polling place was beside the pulpit. The contribution box might have been the first ballot box. On the communion table the town clerk made the town records. On the meeting house door were posted the town warrants and town "orders." Attendance at church on Sundays might relate to eligibility to town office. It was the meeting house and what it represented that made the minute man, and with it may be associated his whole history; for to its pulpit he looked for his encouragement, to its Bible he looked for his authority in resisting oppression, and to its belfry or the powder house of its precincts he repaired for his ammunition.

The foregoing statements are amply sustained by a variety and profusion of simple facts which the records and traditions of many New England townships attest to, and Concord bears her full share of the testimony; and there are circumstances which can only be construed as showing through a long period a oneness to her ecclesiastical and civic affairs. The records inform us that the order for building the first meeting house was passed Feb. 5, 1636, when the affairs of colonization were largely under the leadership of Rev. Peter Bulkeley. The substance of the records concerning the building of the second or third meeting house of date Jan. 27, 1668, is that Capt. Timothy Wheeler, Joseph Wheeler and John Smedley were constituted a committee to make a contract for a meeting house; and that in 1672, the selectmen were directed "to see if the contract was completed." The building erected about this date stood on the town's common land at a spot on or near the site of the present Unitarian church, or what is known as the "First Parish Church." In this meeting house, which it is stated had the characteristics of one erected at Hingham, Mass., in 1681, the town meetings were held until as late as 1712, after which time the deliberations of the church were held in the new building, and those of the town were held in the old one.

In 1719, the town voted to build a house for its "town meetings" and court sessions, the latter having been held for ten years previous in the old meeting house.

Oct. 11, 1774, an adjourned meeting of the First Provincial Congress was held in this meeting house.

March 22, 1775, the Second Provincial Congress also met there. The same year the military companies met there to listen to a sermon by Rev. William Emerson.

In 1776, the commencement exercises of Harvard College were held there.

Such is a partial epitome of events connected with the succession of early meeting houses which have stood on or about the site of the "First Parish Meeting House," and they substantiate the foregoing statements and bear out our conclusions concerning the mission of the modest colonial meeting house.

Moreover its natural environment was as picturesque as its history is romantic. On the one side was the bluff or ridgeway, safe sheltering from storms that swept from the easterly, upon whose peaceful but stinted summit sleep what is mortal of the faithful church founders, and at whose foot was the little street which ran just past the church doorway, once traveled by the second Bulkeley, Estabrook, Whiting, Bliss, the famous Whitefield, Emerson, Ripley, and Reynolds; and also by Hancock, Adams, Otis and others world renowned, whose voices were once heard within the meeting house walls soundly denouncing the "king's orders," and imploringly appealing to the people to resist them.

At the northwesterly was a small portion of the "town's common land, "where once stood the "Jethro" or "bell tree," underneath which, as tradition declares, an agreement was made for a sale of the township for "beads, wampum, hoes" and other commodities, in the presence of grave sagamores and mystical witnesses, with dark, wizard-like looks and strange movements. In that direction was the "town pound" and a snug garrison house, and perhaps the "tanyard" of one of Concord's first artisans, to whom the town early granted land to encourage his trade. To the northwesterly also was the mill and the brook, its fresh meadows opening downward in pleasant vistas towards the manse. To the westerly was the wilderness and a road leading into it, with smiling homesteads alongside; while to the southwesterly and southerly and half skirted in that direction by a drift way upon which stood one of Concord's first grocery stores was the mill pond, forest fringed and newly made, reflecting back from cool shadows the gnarled oaks and tall pines, and the lesser shrubbery of bending bilberry bushes and elder and willow clumps, and whose friendly waters withal came so close to the meeting house as almost to wash its sills;

so that in 1672, the selectmen were instructed to adopt measures "to keep out the waters of Mill brook, which encroached on the common and wore it away."

Such to an extent was the scene, and thus varied were the objects of beauty and of interest that surrounded the first in succession of these meeting houses, when Parson Edward Bulkeley and Deacon Griffin entered the portal of the new edifice, perhaps on a bright morning in the year 1672, to see if everything was in readiness to hold the first service there.

But even more might be said of it; for were it our province to speak of things modern we would pause and make mention of the illustrious gatherings that have convened about this ancient church site at the occasional funeral services of the "mighty dead"; for as statesmen, orators and distinguished preachers, philanthropists, philosophers, poets and jurists have spoken and worshipped within the walls of the structures that stood there, so their mortal remains have been borne from there; and more than once has the world's great grief been manifest in the sad and solemn requiems and notable eulogies that have been sung and spoken there; and so long as this ancient church site is associated with these its renown is secure, for their's were of the "few immortal names that were not born to die."

That the early meeting house stood for the educational interests of the colony needs no reiteration. It was at these places and by means of the ministers, that many of the people acquired even the little knowledge that they possessed during that period of New England history that has been called "the dark age." This period, which was between the passing away of the original grantees and the coming of the second generation following, was approximately from 1675 to 1725. That the settlers were friendly to education during this period goes without saying, notwithstanding towns were sometimes fined for not providing proper school privileges. They loved and demanded a learned Gospel ministry. They welcomed the catecumenical exercises; and that they improved themselves with books when they had them and when the pastor loaned them from his meager library indicates what might have been their literary status "Had fortune frowned not on their humble birth." Moreover, the people loved their long sermons, doubtless, and the long prayers, for by them their spiritual and intellectual natures were fed. But the settlers were many of them poor, schoolmasters and schoolmistresses were scarce; life was a scramble for bread, a fight to make both ends meet; and when the immigrant settler who came to this country with a fair education had passed away, then the dark age came; many signed their names with a mark, many could not read, and there was a lamentable lack of learning generally. But the meeting houses by their ministers kept brightly burning a lamp of knowledge when others had gone out. The long and elaborate discourses were educators; good language was encouraged. In short, a high intellectual standard was kept before the people, and the desire for better things was fostered by frequent contact of the parishioner with his pastor. Let not then too much credit be ascribed to "the little red schoolhouse," for the little log meeting house was before it; and but for the latter, the former might never have been. So let us in ascribing "honor to whom honor is due" leave a large place for the New England meeting house, which made "giants in those days," and which made the minute men who came later, and was the beginning of our present greatness. And let us, like those who founded them, say with a whole-souled sincerity, "I was glad when they said unto me, let us go up to the house of the Lord."

CHAPTER XVII.

Visit to the Home of Goodman George Heywood— Talk with Miller William Buss— Ramble about the Mill Pond—Flint's Pond—History of the Bulkeley Grist Mill — Succession of Millers — Stroll about Concord Center — Description of the Mill Pond.

THE next morning we arose about sunrise, and after breakfast and family prayers, started with one of the hired men who was going to mill, for the house of George Heywood. We went in an ox cart, and as the bullocks were but imperfectly "broken" we were bounced and jolted over many remnants of old roots and through sloughy places, insomuch that we concluded that the highway work of those days consisted mainly in shoveling snowdrifts, and keeping the wheel ruts from the constant encroachment of the shrubbery, and the casting of brushwood into the wet places to prevent miring.

As we entered the village, for we will call it such, although it was "only a collection of housen," as miller Buss told us, Goodman Heywood met us at the bar way, for there were gates and bars at the head of lanes which it was the common law should be kept closed, and with a smile and voice as bright and breezy as the day, bade us good morning, and insisted upon our taking a second breakfast.

Hospitality in those days was the rule and not the exception, and "stay to dinner," or "stay to supper," or "stop overnight" was only a natural accompaniment of one's coming, and everywhere expected as a matter of course.

As Goodman Heywood had an important town matter to look after he excused himself for the forenoon, and we went into the mill which was nearby, where we found the miller standing by the meal trough in the midst of a score or more of bags of unground maize. Entering into conversation, we found that the task of grinding the town's corn was not easy; "For," said the miller, "we've got but one run of stone and slow at that;" "but," he continued, "we have ter try, for folks fetch their grists here from far and near; some come clean from the Nashaway, some from farms nigh Nashoba, some from beyond Shawshine, and there's a few towards Sudbry and up agin Malbry."

After inquiring as to how they brought their grist, we found that those who had horses threw the sacks over their backs, that some brought them in ox carts or on sleds, some in wheelbarrows, and a few on their backs; even though coming sometimes from miles away. At times, he stated, they "stayed over" or started home late at night and this, it might be, in cold or stormy weather, or in deep snow, so great at times was the stress for meal. He did not tell us about his "toll rates," neither did we ask him, knowing as we did that there had been several misunderstandings about this matter, both in relation to himself and his predecessors.

Having learned what we could from the genial miller and growing weary of the noise of the mill machinery, we resolved to ramble about the pond to discover anything that might be of service in describing the central village of Concord town as it was about the middle of the 17th century.

Leaving the Mill dam we passed the "pound," and keeping on the side of the pond next to the "Strate strete" and going just back of the site of the "First Parish Church," we found ourselves on the swamp lands to the eastward, which but for a dry October would have been damp.

After walking a considerable distance in the brushwood, occasionally through the openings, catching a glimpse of the pines on the ridgeway, we reached the "Bay road," where a bridge of loosely laid logs crossed Mill brook on a level with the roadbed. Hard by was the house of Goodman Meriam, beside which was a snug barn and sheep shed and a couple of barley stacks. Near the barley stacks was a threshing floor consisting of logs, square hewn and closely set, where with slim walnut flails fastened with eel skin, Goodman Meriam and a neighbor, Nathaniel Ball were threshing, while the plump barley grains were bounding briskly all about them. Thinking it uncivil not to call, we halted; as we did so the men, flails in hand, came to meet us and greeted us with a right hearty cordiality, and the rest of the household consisting of his wife and several children appeared in the doorway.

On leaving Goodman Meriam's dooryard we rambled over the fields in a southwesterly direction and soon came to a ditch. At first we thought it might be one of the ditches that the early settlers used for fencing, but upon following it a short distance we came upon a body of water, perhaps as charming as ever traveler beheld. It was completely surrounded by woods and tinted with a blue as beautiful as that of the sky that bent over it. We knew where we were, for Major Willard had spoken to us of Flint's pond, which on the modern maps is called "Forest lake," and said that it received its name from Esquire Thomas Flint, who owned all the territory since occupied by the village of Lincoln center.

The discovery of the pond explained the presence of the ditch; for we at once concluded that this ditch, which in the "records" is repeatedly referred to as "the gutter," was the means of conducting the water from Flint's pond to the Mill brook, in order to raise the water in the Mill pond whenever needed.

We did not long remain at Flint's pond, beautiful though it was, but soon retraced our steps to the Mill brook and followed its course till we came to the head of the Mill pond where we sat down upon a log which had been lifted at high water upon a hassock of coarse grass, and listened to the multitudinous voices which, strangely mingling with the deep bass of the distant mill, made a strange medley.

The day was beautiful; the sky cloudless; and the soft south wind which had set in with the sunrise was just beginning to tone down the crisp atmosphere and make it enjoyable. The foliage was at its best, for but few leaves had fallen and every branch and spray was painted with those perfect colors which art cannot imitate; and as the yellow birches and crimson maples flashed their tints among the dark evergreens, it was as if the wood nymphs had lighted the torches and were awaiting guests. And the guests were there; for while we sat meditating in wonder, a couple of kingfishers sprang their rattle just over us, and as one dashed into the water and came up with what looked like a trout, we concluded that the small mill stream, before its waters were made to work, was a "trout brook" that once went rollicking riverward as free as the wind, notwithstanding the level country through which it passed.

In a shallow cove among some lily pads were a doe and two fawns, while beyond, under some hemlocks in the flags a flock of dusky ducks was riding at anchor and keeping at an aristocratic distance from three diminutive teal, which lingered later than was their wont in Concord waters because of the mildness of the Fall. As the air was still cool in spite of the south wind, and the frost sparkled on the bilberry bushes, we decided to make a fire to warm our fingers and see if anything could be learned in addition to what we already knew relative to the ponds the mill, and the adjacent hamlet. Accordingly, we started in search of some drift wood from the pond shore, well knowing that the sparks from this if from anything would be prolific of information. With this fuel, a little moss, and a flint and steel which Major Willard had lent us, we made a blaze.

Soon the flames crackled and the sparks snapped merrily; and the story stripped of all that is fictitious is as follows: The little brook which was early crossed by "Fort bridge" or "Potter's bridge," and now runs through the culvert at "Hasting's Corner," and by the Bank, has the distinction of first serving the town of Concord for mill purposes; and except for its presence, there might have been no Concord center where it is, but its location might have been determined by some other stream. A "corn mill," as these places were once called, was considered indispensable to a new township. Like an army, the settler should keep near his base of supplies, and a mill house with a good water power was his commissariat. The usual order was a mill, a meeting house, and an "ordinary," or a public place of entertainment for man and beast.

The miller was an important personage, next to the tavern keeper, and both made good material for selectmen and militia officers. The mill was a place for news or a kind of village exchange. There the farmer learned patience as his grist slowly fell into the mill trough, or as he waited his turn, or was told to come the next day or the day after. There he compared crops and made bargains.

Perhaps, also, it was there he learned as much about colonial law and provincial politics as at any place except the meeting house; for people came "to mill" from far away, bringing not only their bags of corn and barley but tidings of accident, adventure and the rise and fall of market rates at the seaboard.

The first mill in Concord was erected by Rev. Peter Bulkeley, or with his money; which circumstance, were there no other, would show that Mr. Bulkeley was a "man of means"; for mill machinery was costly and doubtless much of it, together with the mill wright who put it up came from "below." Probably the mill was never "run" by its original owner but was leased; for we find that as early as 1639 it was in charge of William Fuller, who the records state, was fined £3 for abuse in over-tolling."

The first mill was doubtless small and stood on or near the site of the brick building by the old Bank. In consideration of building the mill, or as a gratuity, Mr. Bulkeley was allowed a tract of thirty acres upon which his house and mill stood, lying between the pond and the river. He was also granted the right to raise the water of the brook "to a perpendicular height of four feet and ten inches from the bottom of the mill trough," and of digging clay on the common for making repairs on the dam; franchises akin in principle to those accorded to early mill builders in other places; and the small amount allotted may indicate that landed possessions were not lavishly bestowed upon any one, nor as a rule, conveyed without value received.

Timber trees, pasturage, planting places and hay on meadow lands, whether they were public or private property, were jealously guarded, and whether the common lands were "sized" or divided, or conveyed as a gratuity, or perquisite, it was in a manner that established no unsafe precedent.

How many years the Bulkeley mill continued to grind the "town's corn" we were not told, but there was a long succession of millers. Among them were some of the town's staunchest citizens; and if the records show that in one or two instances there was a deviation from what was conventional or statutory, all the circumstances not being disclosed, we may not be able to judge fairly, since there might have been mitigating facts; for example, William Fuller may have properly set up in defense by way of "justification and avoidance" that morally the laborer is worthy of his hire, whether legally so or not, and that at times the mill did not pay; for when there was a scarcity of water in the pond, or too much back water in the brook, it was slow grinding, and he perhaps took it upon himself to adjust prices, and so likewise when in 1665, William Buss was warned by Constable Thomas Brooks "to answer for his want of scales and weights in his mill," he may have pleaded inability to purchase them. The year previous, the Heywood mill was established, and perhaps competition had commenced, and business may have been done on too small a margin to make "up to date" appliances profitable; we were not there, the sparks say nothing, and we can be charitable. Moreover, so far as Buss is concerned, presumption is greatly in his favor; for when he kept tavern in 1664, at about the spot where the town library now stands, he wished to be excused from selling strong drink, and he was considered by the selectmen a most suitable person for a licensed innkeeper.

That Mr. Bulkeley retained ownership of the mill for many years is indicated by the fact that after his death, which occurred March 5, 1659, a controversy arose concerning the mill' between his widow, Grace Chetwood, and the citizens of Concord, and the matter was investigated by the Colonial Court, one result of which was a conclusion that the contract between Mr. Bulkeley and the town of Concord had been loosely drawn.

About 1666, Captain Timothy Wheeler, who lived in the house of Mr. Bulkeley, became owner of the mill, and he left it by will to his daughter, Rebecca Minot; and her husband, James, operated it for many years. The building which now stands on Main street by the brook near the bank is in the succession of these ancient mills. It has been supposed by some that it may have been built by Captain Timothy Wheeler, but no record nor reliable tradition gives any certain information of its age. It is very old but that it existed earlier than the first quarter of the 18th century is considered improbable.

But long ago the rumbling of the old mill ceased; and the water of the mill brook released from its useful bondage once more went dancing downwards as wild and unrestrained as when the settlers first saw it. The pond shrank back into its original channel, and the flags and clover blossoms upon its grassy border, looked laughingly down into it as if glad to be brought back to their old playground. Today, nature and art are both there; tomorrow it may be only art.

It was nearly high noon when we started on our return to the village, which we reached in time for dinner. The meal was served in accordance with the hospitality of the times. In the early afternoon and after a conversation with Goodman Heywood, in which he spoke of his plan for the erection of a saw mill, we proposed a stroll over the village, to the end that we might better describe at some future time the mill pond, the village roads, and the homes of the inhabitants.

As good fortune would have it we were left to go alone; for just as we were about starting, John, the eldest son, stepped in and said that the Gobble boys down at the "Bay" (Fairhaven) had sent for his father to come and weigh some tar, which article we infer was a commodity in early times in Concord, and that sometimes there was trespassing in order to obtain it, as the Sudbury records inform us that in 1661, the town appointed men "to agree with Robert Porctor of Concord about his trespass

91

of burning up our pines for making tar." Having obtained all necessary instructions we went forth, and by sunsetting had gathered many facts and formed many theories relative to the village, the mill and the ways of the inhabitants; but lest our observation may have been too limited, and being a visitor, we had been shown only the best side of things, we will relate only what conforms with history.

First, we will describe the mill pond. From the height of the dam, and various records relating to the flowage of water in its vicinity, together with the "lay of the land," we may fairly conjecture what was its shape and size and trace its outline on at least three sides. The north side was bounded by the dam, which probably extended from the mill house to a point a little east of Mill brook where it crosses the present Main street. From the dam on the east side it followed the upland until it shoaled up near the crossing on Heywood street, and lost itself among the meadows, then swamp grounds, in the direction of Meriam's corner. On the west it had a similar contour.

Beginning at the mill, it followed the general direction of the present Walden street, and keeping well within the upland as it variously sloped, made a curved shore nearly corresponding to the one opposite.

That this outline is fairly correct, may be indicated by traces of ancient water lines detected in excavations for building purposes; and also from the records of town action relating to early riparian rights. A pond of this description and situated amid such scenery as Concord center may then have possessed was doubtless exceptionably beautiful. Not only would such a sheet of water pent up in the woodland solitude of itself be charming, but we infer there were objects accompanying it that would make it doubly so. Among these was the abruptly rising ridgeway a few rods to the eastward, its crest crowned with ancient oaks and dark pines, and its slope variously indented with gentle hollows; at its foot the "little strate strete" curving gracefully, its sides fenced by snipped saplings and along which were small wood-colored cabins with prim door yards, where in summer might have been seen busy housewives deftly twirling the flax reel or tethering some pet animal, or sitting, it may be at noonday in the cooling shade, or in the autumn attending the drying of their sliced "pompion" or whisking the wasps from their spread huckleberries, or snatching from the night damp their half cured herbs. Moreover, there might have been seen standing separate and far out in the water a few maples and pines left there when the pond was filled, the perching place of fish hawks and crows, conspicuous landmarks and a general outlook for all birds; further up there might have been a fording place for cattle, used before the building of a bridge at Potter's lane, where of a spring morning might have been seen the farm boy following the cows or a tired teamster watering his oxen, while wading at divers points along the pond's margin and feeding among the lilies and pickerel weed and brushing flies, may have been seen animals both domestic and wild.

But not the least of its attractions perhaps were its dark, rich reflections which were to be seen on every side except that of the dam and the shallow water on the south. These reflections may have been of objects rarely seen in the vicinity at the present, for in process of time there have doubtless disappeared from the precincts of Concord center rare plants and grasses and shrubbery that once were there.

There may have been on the banks among the lesser shrubbery both the yellow and black birch, the "sweet scented saxifrage" and the red osier, and the spoonwood or mountain laurel, as it is now called, purple and white azaleas, and the pink rhodora of which one of Concord's poets has so beautifully written, alder, elder, and wild holly, with their sprinkling of bright berries to give sprightliness.

Among the trees there may have been the white and the red spruce, and perhaps the bass, the horn beam, and false elm. Peeping out from beneath and looking over the pond's edge as if laughing at their own loveliness may have been rare flowers, as the trumpet weed, the buck bean and the fringed gentian; the painted cup may have also presented itself, and rare orchids, the mountain rice, and the flowering dogwood, all of which have been found in the vicinity in later times. That the mill pond did justice to this gentle company we cannot doubt, and that the scene afforded on its surface on a calm, clear day would be a gorgeous one is as little questionable.

But not the sights alone but the sounds also naturally made this spot a restful one, and such as they only could expect to find who are willing to penetrate a wilderness and pioneer under old time condition, where everything is wild and primitive. There might have been the monotonous sound at stated intervals of the church drum; the oft recurring roaring of the "rolling dam" when the rain had filled the pond to an overflow; the mournful call of a distrained animal from the usually empty town pound, reminding its owner to pay a shilling and rescue it; the dull rumble of the mill stones and jolt of the clumsy water wheel; the slow, measured jog, jog, of the farm horse, and the harsh rattle of the farm wagon, as they moved over the rough roads; now and then might have been heard the strokes of a distant threshing flail, or the echo of a cheery halloo, or the dropping of some pasture bars; and now and then may have come to the ear the sweet strains of psalm singing, or the imploring accents of prayer; these with the multitudinous voices of Nature might enter into the sounds of that little lone hamlet. In such a place and amid such a scene was born Concord's first village. Perhaps in part from its peaceful aspect the town took its name, and if so we may conjecture that the mill pond not only located the hamlet, but also christened it. Such a conclusion may by no means be unwarranted. Large things are often occasioned by small ones; and though the latter may be lost or forgotten, and only live in their effects, so may it not be that the presence of this pond, which was a factor so important in the success of the settlement, and the beauty of its environment, together with the tranquility of the town's inhabitants all suggested the name of Concord, and hastened the approach of its "chrisom" hour.

Before however leaving the subject of the mill pond, additional mention should be made of its upper limit, which we stated shoaled up and was lost in the direction of Meriam's corner. How far it ran in that direction may never be known unless by actual survey, since the nature of the country is such as to hardly disclose it. Doubtless it spread with a shallow depth to the vicinity of Love lane or Hawthorne street. Near here at the time of the Concord colonization was a beaver dam, which may indicate that about this place the brook had more than its usual fall; and if so, perhaps here was the pond's upper terminus. But there is no visible sign by which to determine it, neither is there anything to indicate that a portion of the present rich tillage and productive garden lands were formerly overflowed. The fields stretch themselves in the distance and vanish; the blackbird sings and safely builds its nest there; the dew sparkles on the buttercups in the morning, and in the evening the perfume of a thousand flowers makes fragrant the atmosphere, while tired nature rests all unconscious of the great change of two and a half centuries.

93

CHAPTER XVIII.

Description of Village at Concord Center in Early Times — Streets— House Lots — Robert Meriam's Store — Street Scene — Tavern — Landlord William Buss— Rules and Regulations of Ordinaries— Old Time Taverns at Concord.

WITH a knowledge of the shape and site of the mill pond the way is open for a description of the first village of Concord as it may have existed a score of years after the town's settlement. And here, as of other matters prior to the period of preserved public record, much is left to be learned by sitting at old firesides and listening to the sparks. But tradition concerning the village roads, and recorded data concerning house lots reaches so far back as to enable us correctly to locate some of them.

The earliest street was the "Strate strete" or the "Little Strate strete" by the ridgeway which began or ended at the town's common land, now the public square, and may have extended as a lane, now Lowell street, to Parson Bulkeley's, and possibly to the river meadow.

From the "Strate strete" at the "Common," as we will call the public square, a narrow causeway crossed at the mill dam, coming out on the west side of it near the old Bank building. This causeway at the time of the Revolutionary war and for years afterward was only a few feet wide and was used as a mill path and a short way connecting both portions of the village.

A principal or main street ran between the mill dam and the South bridge, the latter then near Nashawtuc. It was very crooked and in its short course partially described the letter S twice made. Beginning at the mill dam it passed to the northwesterly around the town's second burying ground, and after running a few rods bent southerly almost to the site of the present Main street. It then turned northwesterly and after running a few rods again bore to the southerly, and passing the great elms on the present Frederick Hudson place crossed at the corner of Main and Thoreau streets, as these are now, and running diagonally toward the southwest, curved at a point across the Fitchburg railroad just beyond the section house, and by the agricultural grounds, leaving a small "heater" piece, now owned by the Boston and Maine R. R. corporation, and thence proceeding northwesterly, ran in a direction approximately parallel to the first few rods from the assumed point of beginning by the mill dam.

The third street, as we will term it, was on or about the site of the present Walden street, and was made it may be, for the two-fold purpose of accommodating the house lots that lay along the west side of the millpond, and also to meet Potter's lane, unless perchance the latter was made to meet this. The "Strate strete" may have early extended or branched off beyond the present Public square in the direction of the North bridge.

Along these roads were the early homes, and because they were there the roads were there. It was here a house and there a house and a path between them. The path, being much traveled by the neighbors and by the cattle, at length became a well-recognized public way and in time, by an extension of it, became a county road.

In endeavoring to locate the first house lots along these roads, we can perhaps do no better than to take for our authority the historian, Walcott, whose painstaking researches have been so valuable in the locating of Concord's early estates.

On the "Strate strete" near the common was the house lot of Thomas Dane, which consisted of six and one-half acres, and extended from burial hill to the mill pond; Luke Potter's lot of six and one-half acres was situated on both sides of Potter's lane (Heywood street). Following the Bay road in an easterly direction there were house lots as follows, occupying both sides of the road and extending to the mill brook: John Farwell, twelve acres; Thomas Wheeler, Sr., thirteen acres; Moses Wheat, sixteen acres (Staples place). East of Wheat's on the north side of the road, was the house lot of William Baker, then the lot of William Fletcher, fifteen acres. This lot ran to the brook and was afterward purchased by Nathaniel Stow; and near it was a lot owned by Peter Bulkeley, Esquire. Then followed the lot of Thomas Burgess, ten acres; Francis Fletcher, eight acres; Edward Wright, ten acres; Eliphalet Fox, eight acres: Nathaniel Ball, thirteen acres; William Hartwell, nine acres; John Hartwell ten acres; William Taylor, eight and three-quarter acres; and beyond these to the eastward were lots of Caleb and Joshua Brooke, Christopher Wooley and Richard Rice.

John Meriam had one and one-half acres at the corner of the Bay road on the south and the Billerica road on the west. Joseph Dane and Thomas Pellet occupied one homestead on the Billerica road.

South of the mill pond, house lots were laid out from what is now Main street by the mill-dam to the almshouse, running to the pond or brook on the north and extending toward the southwest to about Thoreau street. By the mill-dam and nearly opposite the Bank. George Wheeler had eleven acres, near which was Joshua Wheeler's lot of fourteen acres. Robert Meriam had twenty-six acres about the Trinitarian church site. The came John Wheeler's lot of ten and one-half acres (Nathan B. Stow's) Lieut. Joseph Wheeler, twenty acres (George Everett's); George Meriam, thirty acres (the Bartlett place); Nathaniel Billings, six acres (Nathan Derby's); Samuel Stratton, twenty-four acres (the almshouse).

On or near Main street James Smedley had a lot of eighteen and one-half acres north of and adjacent to the burying ground. Going to the westward was John Heywood's lot of four acres, near the burying ground. Then came the lot of William Buss, seven acres. Farther westerly, and beyond the South branch of the river was the house lot of Michael Wood, and later of William Buss, and as has been mentioned, the homestead of Major Simon Willard.

These are the names of some of the people who lived in this first village of Concord, and such the location of their house-lots. That these are all is not to be supposed, for probably about the beginning of the settlement and while under the restraint of a colonial law, which for prudential reasons allowed no one to establish a homestead beyond a certain distance from the meeting-house, all of the colonists had homes in the "middle of the town; and if perchance by an actual survey of the premises about the meeting house, the mill, and the pond basin, spaces of territory should be found which neither record nor tradition has assigned to early householders, we may nevertheless suppose they were owned and occupied by someone, and that there was but little public land in the vicinity.

By colonial custom so far as we have ascertained, the town's common land, with the exception of its burial places and its pound, its house of worship, and ministerial reservations, and it may be a small parcel here and there for some general use, — as for a gravel pit, a training field, or fence bote or bridge bote, — was largely outlying.

But the little hamlet was not only well peopled and provided with homes; it also had its store, and tavern, and doubtless its smithy; for it was in accordance with town usage to give encouragement to the useful artisan to "set up his trade among them," although we know not who it was in Concord at this time who had "set up" a forge.

The village store was situated at or about the spot where the present Trinitarian church stands and was kept by Robert Meriam. We are not to suppose however that he kept it in a building separate from his dwelling house for as was not uncommon we believe in the case of storekeeping in the olden time, he may have kept it in an L, or in a room of the house where he lived.

And now for a little space laying aside matters of fact, let us suppose that on a mild October afternoon in the first half of the seventeenth century, Betsey Burgess and Goody Fox descended the ridgeway by a narrow, winding path that led from the meeting house hill, up among the early graves, and passing over the mill dam by a rickety crossing made of slabs, which were laid along the splash boards for a short cut to the mill from the "Strate strete," entered the village store to converse with Concord's first store keeper about the purchase of some "sweetening" for preserving some barberries, which they had just gathered, and to see if he would take in exchange a little spun yarn and some cheese. They found the village store-keeper away, he having gone to Boston for his stock of winter goods. But Goodwife Meriam knew the price list as well as her husband and informed them that she would take the yarn and the cheese, although to take the latter was a little venturesome, since it would be so long before her husband went to Boston again that it might not keep.

While the women were waiting, someone was seen coming through Potter's lane, who by his look and step was evidently a stranger. Goodman Luke Potter undoubtedly thought so too, for he was looking down the lane from his dooryard, shading his eyes from the rays of the setting sun and apparently starting to follow him. Presently the traveler came up, stopped at the store and inquired for the tavern. Goody Meriam directed him to turn to the left just past Goodman Wheeler's house, then keep on a bit, following the road bend, and he would soon see Sergeant William Buss's Ordinary.

After being directed, the traveler sat down on the doorstep as if too weary to go even this distance before resting himself, saying as he did so that he had come from Boston that day and started at sun-rising. Soon there gathered about him a group of villagers, for the news had spread that a stranger was there, each to inquire of events "further down," of the prices, the newly-arrived ships, and what folks were doing in the lower towns.

As Luke Potter came up, the traveler was just relating something about the late Anabaptist disturbance, and what the prospect was of future peacefulness among the churches.

After further conversation concerning ecclesiastical matters, and a little inquiry after the progress of the new township, the traveler arose to leave. Before he started, Goodwife Meriam gave him a posset of warm milk, dipped fresh from a pailful that the hired man was carrying past, and with an expression of thankfulness and well wishes, the stranger started for the Ordinary.

The coast clear, for the villagers scattered when the man went away, Goodwife Meriam informed the two women that although in the Boston price-list, molasses, as quoted by the late visitor, to be sold in "country pay at country prices," was a little higher than at the Concord grocery store, and although the price of cheese had gone down somewhat, yet she would stand by the price just named by her, at the same time informing them that it was her husband's practice to sell as he bought, and that as for the cheese, she would wait, and split any possible rise or fall of it and thus divide between them any risk.

But to return to facts, let us next consider the village tavern. This was situated near the spot where the present Public Library stands, and was kept by Sergeant William Buss, who was we conclude, as before stated, a most estimable citizen, not desiring even in those times to sell "strong water;" for he asked the selectmen to exempt him from so doing when they gave him an inn license.

The sparks do not inform us just where Landlord Buss drew the liquor line. Perhaps between the fermented and the distilled, but however that might be, we believe this much at least, that he had a regard for the public weal and that the selectmen who sustained him in his extreme position and who considered him, notwithstanding his radical attitude, a most suitable person for the place were also interested in the public well-being.

There is also suggested by the stand taken by Landlord Buss, a query as to whether the many and perhaps too easily made representations in modern times of a gross indulgence, and of the prevalence of a lax sentiment on the part of the fathers as to the uses of alcoholic beverages is correct; for if so, then in case Concord was fairly represented by Sergeant Buss and the selectmen, it was evidently in advance of the average town.

To the end that we may know more about old-time taverns, let us suppose that we followed to the Buss tavern the traveler from Boston, who we represented as stopping at the store and inquiring for an ordinary.

As we approached, we met at the doorway Goodwife Anne Buss, who was watching a large flock of domestic fowls picking the barley grains which she had just scattered.

She addressed us with the term Mr., which showed that while in accosting strangers there was an absence of the formality of later years, here was nevertheless shown them marked respect, since it was only when special recognition of one's social standing was intended, that the term Mr. was used, as in the case of a minister, or a magistrate, or perhaps a schoolmaster, or one whose circumstances might entitle him to be considered wealthy, or a "gentleman" after the old-time signification of the term.

Passing through the bar-room we entered the large kitchen. The supper table was set, upon which was placed only average farm fare with the addition of "plum cake," a commodity which was also sold at the bar and was, it may be, a substitute for modern confections.

Supper ended, we returned to the bar-room; and there with a company of villagers, in chairs tipped back against the chimney bricks, and the coarse boards of the "bunk," and the high bar, we sat and talked till the small hours of the night. We will not repeat all that was said as it would take too long, but we will tell it in part.

In the first place we will relate about the traveler just referred to. He said he started that morning from the "King's Arms" tavern at the head of Dock square and stopped at the "King's Head" to obtain the latest marine news, well knowing there would be inquiries as he went inland about the most recent ship arrivals. He crossed by ferry to Charlestown and called at the "Three Cranes."

The only incident that occurred on his journey to Concord was the meeting of Robert Meriam about half-way down, and the assisting to stay up his heavy load of country produce with some willow withes, it having sagged sideways in jolting over the rough road. The stranger's business as he disclosed it was to obtain samples of iron ore said to be deposited in the region of the Assabet, and this with a view of locating a forge there.

While the conversation was going on several more villagers dropped in, among whom was Goodman Heywood who was out looking for us; and the conversation turned on current events, especially on what was going on "down below," as Boston was then called.

In the meantime we were looking around the room and noting its contents. On one side was a bar upon which were a couple of toddy sticks and several tumblers.

On the opposite side was the bunk for the hired man to sleep in, that he might be in readiness for night patronage.

Upon wooden pegs along the horizontal framework of the room, and the upright timbers, were several powder horns, an old saddle, a grain sickle, a measuring stick, a pair of sheep shears, a small mash-tub and sieve, a string of spigots, a pair of saddlebags, two muskets, and a couple of cowbells.

Behind the bar was a small closet in which were kept a few cordials, such as were considered necessary for funerals, weddings, or other notable occasions; but we noticed there was no fastening on it, neither was there a lock on the outer door of the bar-room, though it opened directly on the road, indicating a prevailing honesty in the neighborhood and in the traveling public. Above the mantle-piece were several braids of sweet corn, and onions, between which was a rude cut of Governor Winthrop, and of an English warship.

For a while, the conversation was upon occurrences at Boston; and among other events spoken of was the then recent great fire, and the burning by the public executioner in the market-place of some books written by two persons purporting to be witnesses and prophets of Jesus Christ.

The calling of Rev. John Mayo to be the pastor of Boston's second church, then lately formed, was also discussed, and the execution of Mary Parsons, accused of witchcraft, which although a little stale as news, was a subject still much talked of.

It was very noticeable during the evening that everything was well ordered, and that there was no profanity, nor coarse, ribald remarks, nor anything else inconsistent with good breeding. We inquired if in other ordinaries the conduct and conversation of those frequenting them was thus circumspect; and were informed that they were in general, and that the laws concerning them encouraged it.

We will now pause in our story to give the following facts about old time taverns.

Taverns were early considered a necessity, and hence were established by law. They were usually under the sanction and surveillance of the town officials, who had power to grant, limit, or revoke an innholder's license, either as a victualler or a seller of drinks. The keeper of the public house usually went by the title of landlord, which was often abbreviated to "lan'urd."

The ancient hostelry often had a suggestive or picturesque name, which was symbolized by some object upon a sign which swung before it. Some of the early names of Boston taverns were the "Three Mariners," the "Ship Tavern," the "Red Lion" and the "Castle Tavern." In the vicinity of Concord were the "Red Horse Tavern" (Wayside Inn), Sudbury, and the "Inn of the Golden Balls" (Jones's Tavern, where the spy John Howe stopped in 1775), Weston.

The keeper of the ordinary might be a deacon, a military officer, a civil official, or a "Deputy to the General Court." His house was a convenient place for convocations, important or unimportant; and there might be held in it a parish meeting, a military election, a council of clergymen, a ten-shilling referee case, or an assessors' talk.

So important was the ordinary, that its affairs, such as the establishment of prices, the limitation of patronage, and the quality and quantity of goods to be sold were regulated by colonial law. In order to discourage the use of strong drink at these places, it was enacted about 1634 by the Colonial Court that not over one pence per quart should be charged for ale purchased out of meal times. It was also ordered that not more than a penny a drink should be charged for any beverage. This was done to make the business of dram-selling unprofitable. At another time it was enacted by law that every inn-keeper should sell good beer, lest a traveler for want of it might purchase wine.

A law was passed at an early date, by which a person who might be appointed for the purpose could join a drinking company at a tavern, and countermand any order made by it for a drink, in case he believed any were drinking too much, and who could also direct how much liquor could be drunk.

At an early period the law also undertook to discourage certain amusements at inns which were supposed to be deleterious, and dancing was prohibited there even upon marriage occasions.

At one time no tavern keeper was allowed to permit guests to remain at his house drinking or tippling in a loose or idle way. In 1664, a penalty was enacted for rude singing at inns. The court also undertook at one time to decide how much a man might drink without being considered drunk; and the Plymouth Colony lawmakers decided that a man was drunk, when because of strong drink he lisped, or staggered, or vomited. In 1634, the taking of tobacco at inns was forbidden.

The following are some of the prices charged at ordinaries. In 1634, the price of a meal was six pence. In 1779, in a town adjacent to Concord it was decided that "A mug of West India flip should cost 15 pence.

A mug of New England flip should cost 12 pence.
A good dinner should cost 20 pence.
A common dinner should cost 12 pence.
Breakfast and supper, each, should cost 15 pence.
Lodging should cost 4 pence."

These rates may have been higher than usual because of war times.

How long Sergeant William Buss kept the village ordinary is not known, but he was keeping it as early at least as 1660; and since there is no record of any prior innholder at Concord, it may be that he was there much sooner pursuing the business of a tavern-keeper in a small way furnishing meals and lodgings, while Major Simon Willard, who was licensed to sell "strong water," acted as the village tapster.

In the first century of its settlement, Concord had several taverns. In 1666, John Hayward kept one on the main street. Later, the "Black Horse Tavern" was well known to the traveling public, although this may have been identical with the foregoing. The "Wright Tavern" was established in 1747 and kept open as a public house until the War of the Revolution. Of another tavern in this vicinity Hon. John S. Keyes states: "Previous to the Revolution Ephraim Jones kept a tavern at the west end of the main street burying ground in a large roomy house that had grown by various additions, perhaps from that of John Hayward. The site of this, now the fine lawn of Colonel R. F. Barrett's residence, was close to the old wooden jail, and feeding the prisoners was part of the tavern-keeper's business."

It doubtless not infrequently occurred in early times, that tavern-keeping was evolved from some other occupation or was carried on with it. The process might be first farming, and an occasional entertainment of travelers and then a full-fledged inn. Public patronage being scant, one could hardly afford to give much time to it. There was comparatively little communication of place with place, when public entertainment was required. Moreover, parties journeying or teaming often took their food with them, and stopping wherever overtaken by noon or night, refreshed themselves from the lunch box without regard to form. Indeed, this was in accord with the conventional method. Anything then was fashionable, that was matter of honest economy, and the landlord deducted from his bill of charges the price of bread and cheese in his patron's victual basket, as a matter of course.

It was a late hour when the company about the bar-room fireplace broke up, and as we left Landlord Buss and bade him good-night, it was with regret that our acquaintance should be so brief and our stay so short at an old-time tavern, and there came forcibly to our minds the words of Shenstone:

"Whoe'er has travelled life's dull round,
Where'er his stages may have been,
May sigh to think that he has found
His warmest welcome at an inn."

Along the willows that spread themselves by the wayside we walked to our host's quiet home, where, after listening for a little time to the monotonous roaring of the rolling dam, and thinking of the strangeness of the surroundings, we fell asleep, and slumbered undisturbed until the soft sunlight came streaming into the east window, and awakened us just in season to salute the miller as he was going to open the mill house.

CHAPTER XIX.

The New England Village — Its Origin and Equipment — The Village Doctor — His Medicines and Charges — Early Physicians of Concord: Read, Prescott, Minot, Hey wood — The Village Magistrate — Condition of Colonial Jurisprudence — First Lawyer at Concord — History of John Hoar.

BEFORE leaving the subject of the primitive village of Concord, a few words relative to early New England village life may be appropriate and may suggest some practical lessons, since from it influences have gone forth that have been happily formative, and since about it cluster associations pleasant to contemplate. In these villages was centralized the life of the communities called townships, and from them radiated what little of fashion or style of living was recognized, where the tendency was for every man to be a law unto himself. In the village, if anywhere were supposed to be "up to date" methods; there if at all was an acknowledged leadership.

It was also a sort of local exchange or market place. As it came in contact more frequently with the traveling public it was supposed to possess the latest news, and as there were held all the convocations, it was considered a privileged place to dwell in. In short, it may be true that the early village was to the remainder of the town what the city has since become to the country generally, in so far at least as relates to the tendency of the latter to imitate the former and to rely upon it for outside news, conventionalities and artificial commodities.

The earliest inland villages of the Massachusetts Bay Colony were created by necessity; inasmuch as the court compelled the first settlers to keep within a circumscribed area; as soon however as restraint was removed, a portion of them bounded away, as if their nature was more centrifugal than centripetal. After bounding off they again centralized; the result of which was the formation of new villages which became the centers of new towns. That this tendency affected the people of Concord in common with those of other places is indicated by the establishment of the various villages which became the nucleuses of prospective townships, as that of Concord village (Acton), the Blood farms (Carlisle), the Flint estate (Lincoln). There was left however, in almost every instance, about the first spot of settlement, a faithful home guard of houses that never forsook it, and which by common consent was ever historically considered "the middle of the town," whether the geographical center or not. Exceptions there are, notable among which are Londonderry, N. H., Groton, and Sudbury of this state. It is true that a village was sometimes deflected slightly from its original site, but it seldom went far, and like a stream the waters of which change but the identity of whose channel is not disputed, so the first "middle of a town" usually keeps its prestige as the original center.

In the equipment of the early village there was a completeness which assured to every inhabitant all that was necessary for a comfortable living. There was the doctor, the squire or justice of the peace who was sometimes a lawyer, a blacksmith, shoemaker, carpenter, wheelwright, and sometimes a gunsmith, tailor, tanner, brewer and cooper these, with a store, tavern, meeting house, and school, constituted the mechanical, mercantile and professional make-up of the average village. The representatives of these several crafts and callings made or kept in stock everything essential to personal attire, and house and farm furnishing; in short, to life and death, to birth and burial.

The doctor acted as druggist and obtained his herbs from his own garden or from the neighboring fields and forest. Some of these herbs were black hellebore, great bryony root, clown's all-heal, jalap, scammony and snake root. He obtained his leeches from the pond. His pills, powders and other compounds he prepared with mortar and pestle. He rode horseback with saddle bags in which he carried his medicines; and there was usually about him a strong odor of the "study," as he called his office. In this "study" and arrayed on shelves were various jars, vials, and crude instruments for cupping, surgery, and extracting teeth; for he was dentist as well as doctor. Some early practitioners, supposed to be skilled in surgery, were styled "chirurgions," and sometimes served as barbers as well as bone setters, in which case they were sometimes called "barber surgeons."

Among the earlier remedies prescribed were "A Wild Catt's skin on ye place grieved;" this for pain in the heart or limbs; and charcoal made from burnt toads as a preventive of small-pox and fevers. Cotton Mather mentions the efficacy of a dead hand for scattering wens; he also speaks of the healing virtue of sow bugs. Prescription: "Half a pound putt 'em alive into a quart or two of wine; dose — two ounces taken twice a day." Such remedies were in accord with the practice of physicians in England at that day; for it is stated that there was forced upon Charles the Second when upon his deathbed a volatile salt extracted from human skulls. Almost, if not quite, within the memory of the present generation, in a town adjacent to Concord, pills made from ashes obtained from burning a human heart have repeatedly been administered as a cure for consumption.

The price charged for medical service may be seen from the following bill charged to the town of Sudbury by its physician in 1755: "For medicine and attendance for the French Neutrals from Nova Scotia.

"1755, Dec. 11 — To Sundry Medicines for French young woman— 27 — To Do for girl 6d.

1756, Mar. 22— To Sundry Medicines and Journey in the night west side the River—0—5—8.

To Sundry Medicines Journey west side 0—4—0."

The doctor was careful about his attire; and is described as going forth, when not on horseback, in a sulky or calash dressed in a long coat with full skirts above a low-setting waist-coat; his small clothes met at the knees silken stockings which were secured with brightly burnished buckles.

He wore a cocked hat above a powdered wig. It was conducive to his success to be a man of wealth or influence.

He obtained his knowledge of medicine by riding with an old physician; and though he might only brush off his horse or pound his herbs, he could obtain a license and practice medicine. The indications are that the town of Concord was more favored in its physicians than most towns, in that for the most part they were educated men.

The following are some of the physicians of Concord in the first century: Dr. Philip Read, who, the historian Wolcott says, wrote himself: "Physition," married the daughter of Richard Rice and settled in the east part of the town. He practiced in Cambridge, Watertown and Sudbury. In 1670, he was fined twenty pounds because he compared Rev. Peter Bulkeley as a preacher with the Rev. Joseph Estabrook in a manner which was thought to be unwarranted.

Dr. Jonathan Prescott, who was born Apr. 5, 1677, and died Oct. 28, 1729. His epitaph says of him: "A gentleman of virtue and merit. An accomplished physition but excelling in chirurgery. Of uncommon sagacity, penetration and success in practice, and so of very extensive service."

Dr. Joseph Lee, born in Concord Oct. 16, 1680; died Oct. 5, 1736. He lived on the estate formerly occupied by Joseph Barrett, Esq.

Dr. Alexander Cummings, who came to Concord about 1726.

Dr. John Prescott, who was a son of Dr. Jonathan Prescott. He was greatly esteemed for his professional skill.

Dr. James Minot who was at Concord about 1680 and died Sept. 2, 1735. Shattuck says: "He practiced physic." His epitaph states among other things: "Excelling Grammarian. Enriched with the Gift of Prayer and Preaching. A Commanding Officer. A Physician of Great Value." Shattuck also says he married Rebecca, daughter of Timothy Wheeler, and lived on the estate left by his father-in-law near Capt. Stacy's. They had ten children, the eighth and ninth being twins and named Love and Mercy.

Dr. Able Prescott, who was a brother of John Prescott was born April 7th, 1718, and died October 24, 1805. His practice at Concord was large and extended to adjoining towns. He lived, says Shattuck, in a house formerly occupied by Capt. Moore.

Dr. Abiel Heywood who was a son of Jonathan Heywood and began practice in Concord in 1790. He was prominent not only as a physician, but as a citizen, being appointed as a justice of the peace, a special judge of the court of common pleas and an associate justice of the court of assistants.

As it is not our design to publish the more modern history we pause here in our list of distinguished names, observing as we do so, that in the medical as well as in the legal profession, as we shall see, Concord in later times has had associated with it names that are illustrious not only locally but in history at large.

The early magistrate was a justice of the peace, but not usually an "attorney at law" after the modern acceptance of the term. He was authority in legal matters, a conveyancer, settled estates and was sometimes "appointed to join persons in marriage."

He wrote wills and read them on the return from the grave after a funeral. He was a legal advisor and was looked up to as a man next to the minister. The very early magistrates are to be distinguished from those who came later; for the law was but poorly represented by practitioners in Massachusetts as far down as into the Provincial period. Even the judges were not all learned, and any person though a layman could plead in the courts without a license; for licenses setting forth one's competence were not then issued. Common law pleadings were ignored through ignorance and there were few or no specific statutes on the subject of practice. Court sessions were many of them farces and the jury system was not infrequently a mere mockery. In short there was little to correspond to the exact and orderly manner of conducting the courts at the present day. It is said that Judge Lynde, who was appointed to the Superior Court in 1712, was the first judge trained for the bench. History also informs us that English barristers who had been fitted for that profession found little favor in this country, because here any one might plead the cause of another.

In process of time however the light of greater learning shone upon both the bench and bar; and it may perhaps be said with truthfulness that the progress of medicine from a low art to a masterful science is no more pronounced than the strides forward in the profession of law. In passing, it may be proper to state, that the low condition of the barrister's calling was not due wholly to the absence of any desire for litigation, for dissention and the spirit of strife were then it may be more rife than now, and cases were commenced and continued in bitterness that today perhaps would be settled by easy compromise; all of which shows that a learned legal profession tends to discourage rather than promote law suits.

The first lawyer whom we hear of as being a practitioner at Concord is John Hoar. As his character was somewhat unique and perhaps sometimes picturesque and as he was connected with an important event in King Philip's Indian war, we will give more than a passing mention of him.

John Hoar, tradition states, was the son of a wealthy banker of London, who came to Boston where it is supposed he died not later than about the middle of the 17th century, his wife, Joanna, dying at Braintree about 1661. He was, the youngest of five children and we first hear of him in Scituate, where he "bore arms" as early as 1643.

While in Scituate he owned land on the west side of Musquashcut pond, which land in 1658, adjoined the farm of Gen. Cudworth. That John Hoar practiced law before going to Concord is indicated by the fact that while in Scituate he not only actively engaged in town business, but drew legal documents for the people, as deeds, bonds, etc.

His father's family was substantial and gifted, as is shown in the career of John, Jr., in the marriage of his daughters and in the appointment of his son Leonard to the presidency of Harvard College.

While John Hoar was at Concord he owned over three hundred acres of land situated beyond the Assabet river and near Annursnuc in the west part of the town. The greater part of this property he conveyed about 1671, to Edward Wright, and received as a consideration land in the East quarter and also "all the right, title and interest which Edward Wright of Concord aforesaid, husbandman, has or shall have in and to certain houses, lands and hereditaments, etc.," in the Lordship of a Castle in the county of Warwick in the kingdom of England. As a lawyer he was distinguished for bold and independent action and his outspoken opinions sometimes got him into trouble. His conduct in defending the Christian Indians and protesting against their unjustifiable exile to Deer island in Boston harbor in 1675-6, furnishes strong ground for the supposition that his purposes were philanthropic, and that he would assert them even if persecuted therefor.

The following is an abstract of Leonard Hoar's will: "To daughter Bridget £200 at 21 or nonage with her mother's consent. To my brother Daniel, whose real and perpetual kindness I can never remunerate, my stone signet and my watch. To my dear brother John a black suit.

To my dear sisters Flint and Quinsey each a black serge gown. To Cousin Josiah Flint out of my Library, Rouanelli Bibleotheca. To my Cousin Noah Newman, Aquina's sermons, and to them both the use of books of mine to return them on demand, my medical writings to my wife's custody, till some of my kindred addicted to those studies shall desire them, and especially John Hoar's or any other of my brothers or sisters' sons and grandsons."

It had been arranged that upon leaving the home of Goodman Heywood we should return to William Hartwell's to finish our visit; and as he had sent us word the day previous that he would meet us at the mill we were there early.

We found Miller Buss quite busy that morning tending the "bolter," a rude sifting wheel that was separating the bran from some guinea wheat; and also looking after the corn grist that was slowly jolting from the hopper.

Not caring to interrupt the miller, we strolled out by the willows and reviewed the events of the previous day and also recalled the facts which our late host had given us concerning his family history.

As the Heywood family is a conspicuous one in the history of Concord, we will leave our story for a little time to give some facts relating to it.

Shattuck says of the Hay ward family: "The name has been written Heaward, Heywood and Howard, and although several now (1835) Dear the last name; they all originated from a common ancestor. Heywood is a distinct name. George Hayward came here in 1635; died March 29, 1671; his wife died in 1693; estate £506; children, Mary, married Richard Griffin; John, Joseph, Sarah, Hannah, Simeon, George, and perhaps others." The same writer says of the Heywood family: "John was here before 1659; married Rebecca Atkinson in 1656 and had John and Benoni. His wife died in 1665 and he married again Mary Simonds. He died Jan. 11, 1707." John Heywood was the ancestor in this country of distinguished descendants. John, Jr., was an early deacon in the Concord church, and one of his sons, Samuel, who married Elizabeth Hubbard in 1710, was a deacon and town clerk. John Heywood, Sr., died Jan. 2, 1718, and Samuel, Oct. 28, 1750.

The only records preserved among the vital statistics of Concord down to 1654, relating to the name as spelled either way are the following: "John the sonne of George Hey ward was borne 20-10-1640. Joseph the sonne of George Heyward was born the 26-1-1643. Sara the daughter of Georg & Mary Heywood (this it is said should be Hayward) borne 22-3-1645. Hannath the daughter of George & Mary Hayward the 20-2-1647. Simon the sonne of George & Mary Hayward the 22d-11-1648."

The historian Walcott states; "The location of the first house lots of George Hayward and Michael Wood I have been unable to fix but am inclined to believe that they were on the north and west sides of the Common."

"George Hayward at an early date sold his house, barn and land near the mill pond to Mr. Bulkeley and built a house and corn mill at the southwest. John Heywood bought Thomas Dakin's house and barn."

In 1676, John Heywood was a constable, and in 167- the selectmen requested that John Heywood might be allowed "to keep a house of entertainment for strangers for nights' lodgings, beer and sider," and two years later "John Haywood ordinary keeper at Concord renewed his license" and was allowed "to retaile strong water to travellers & sick persons upon giving bond."

As we left the village it was with regret that we could stay no longer, for its sweet savor and its pleasant people made us reluctant to depart, notwithstanding our desire to visit other places. When however we saw the cheery countenance of Goodman

William Hartwell we bounded buoyantly on the ox cart with the cleverness of an athlete, for the farm fare was beginning to make us feel boyish.

He had been to mill the week before and the pond being low he had left his grist: he was now taking it home together with some belonging to his neighbors, and the bags piled high behind us formed a back: but as we rode on a "dead ex" and the East quarter road was stumpy it was at a slow pace and with much jolting that we got over the ground.

So uneven was the way that one of the bags fell off and the string becoming untied the contents were spilled. As the meal lay strewn over the road, the importance of this staple commodity to the people of Concord in the earlier stages of its settlement was suggested, and when Goodman Hartwell was reseated we plied him with questions concerning the corn crop. Since corn culture was of considerable consequence to the New England colonists we will pause in our story and state a few facts relating to it as we have found them in record or history.

To an extent the early corn fields were cultivated by neighborhoods and were termed "common planting fields." A tract of land was set apart and the work of tilling it apportioned to a certain number of the inhabitants living near; but the principle upon which the planters proceeded in the work we have not ascertained. It might have varied. Perhaps in some case's the fence was made in common, and each man had space assigned him in the enclosure proportionate to his original investment in the town's territory; this space he may have cultivated and had exclusive ownership of the crop. In another case all might have shared equally in the work and in the crop: but as to the manner of distribution of the corn and the fodder in the latter case and where and when it took place, we know not. Some of the planting places were old Indian fields, which had long been used, some were virgin soil which had been newly cleared and burnt over. Tradition or record have located some of these fields in Concord, Shattuck describes them as "The Great-fields extending from the Great meadows on the North to the Boston road on the South and down the river considerably into the present limit of Bedford, and up the river beyond Deacon Hubbard's and the extensive tract between the two rivers contained large quantities of open land, which bore some resemblance to the prairies of the western country. These plains were annually burned or dug over for the purpose of hunting and the rude culture of corn."

It is perhaps hardly to be supposed that more than a comparatively small portion of the above described territory was used for planting purposes either by the Indians or whites at any one time, but that here or there small patches such as were most available were selected for cultivation. The following is a record concerning the "common planting fields" as late as 1672 and is given as one of seventeen articles of instruction to the selectmen of Concord, of whom William Hartwell was one: "7— To take order that all come fields be sufficiently fenced in season — the crane field and brick'll field especially."

"8—that incougement be given for the destruction of blackbirds and jays."

A paper dated March 1st, 1690-91, which was signed by forty-one persons who were owners of the "Great Fields," contained an agreement that these fields should be enclosed with one fence and cultivated upon equitable conditions. The soil of these fields was at first largely broken up by hoes and of this and the use of corn by the settlers, Johnson in his "Wonder Working Providence" wrote as follows in 1654:

"Standing stoutly to their labors and tare up the roots and bushes which the first yeare bears them a very thin crop till the soard of the earth be rotten and therefore they have been forced to cut their bread very thin for a long season * * * but the Lord is pleased to provide for them a great store of fish in the spring time and especially Alewives about the bigness of a herring.

Many thousands of these they used to put under their Indian corn which they plant in hill five foot assunder, which assuredly when the Lord created this corn he had a speacell eye to supply these his peoples wants with — ordinary five or six grains doth produce six hundred." That Indian corn was the main staple is evident from what Johnson still farther states: "The want of English graine, wheate, barley and rie proved a sore affliction to some stomaks, who could not live upon Indian bread and water, yet were they compelled to till cattell increased and the plows could but goe."

The corn fields had many enemies both beasts and birds; more prominent among the former being perhaps the bear, raccoon, wolf and squirrel. The bear may have been attracted by the sugar in the corn; the wolf dug for the alewives; the raccoon relished the young and tender kernels, and in its maturer stages the squirrel sought it to lay away for winter use. The birds that partook of the crop were principally the crows, jays and blackbirds.

The Colonial towns passed laws for the protection of the cornfields. An order in a town adjacent to Concord was as follows dated 1651: "That whoso shall take pains by nets, guns, line or otherwise to destroy common offensive blackbirds * * * shall be paid for every dozen of heads that are brought to any public town meeting six pence in the next town rate."

In 1654, in the same town it was enacted that a person who killed a woodpecker or jay might receive one penny, for killing a fox within the town's precincts one shilling and six pence, and for a wolf ten shillings.

Laws were passed early by the towns with regard to the fencing of these cornfields. Fence viewers or surveyors were appointed who among other things, were to judge of the sufficiency in case of damage and difference; and the time was sometimes specified at which the fence must be cared for. In one instance mention is made "of good rails well set three feet and one-half high or otherwise good hedge well staked or such fences as would be an equivalent; the fences to be attended to by April 1st if the frost give leave if not ten days' after."

It was also ordered by the same town that all the fences that were in general fields should be shut up by the tenth of May "or else to forfeit for every rod unfenced five shillings." Ditches were sometimes made use of for fencing purposes; and there are now or were until recently in territory about Concord vestiges of old ditches upon uplands where ditches for draining purposes were unnecessary. It is not improbable that upon the ditch banks stakes were set for additional protection.

But notwithstanding the difficulties attendant upon corn culture, there remained for the farmer rich results and he was greatly cheered as he patiently plodded through the long, warm days of May and June, seeding, weeding and hilling as he thought of the plenteous October harvest, of its merry huskings and of well filled bins.

CHAPTER XX.

Goodman Baker s Husking Party — Colonial Corn Fields — Invitations — Culinary Preparations — Red Ears — Social Sports — Fireside Talk of the Old Folks — Sign Seen by Bet fey Billings — Origin of New England witchcraft — Recital of Strange Event by Simeon Slowgo—Story of Tilly Temple — The Surprise — Early Judicial Attitude Toward Witchcraft — Efforts of the Clergy for its Abolition.

AS these huskings were great occasions let us suppose that we attended one of them, and that the following description fairly represents one of these Fall festivals.

It is in the East quarter, and the Great fields lie warm in the dry October atmosphere. Partridges in full flocks are shyly basking on their outskirts, and occasionally a red deer ranges by the fence side as if furtively to snatch a stray stalk. The plaintive call of the quail is here and there heard, coaxing together its scared brood, which has become scattered by the swoop of a hen hawk. Over the meadows the ducks fly. Nuts drop in the woods. Upon the nearer tree-tops the crows caw as if prematurely lamenting the loss of their feeding grounds, and the falling foliage of a thousand forest trees announces that the time has come for the For several days the farmer has been busily at work gathering in those concomitants of the corn fields, which in his estimation almost as surely go with them as the husk with the corn. There were the stooks of tall, tasseled ingathering of the stalks, as fragrant when he cut them as flowers on a June morning, and which have stood for weeks at the sides and corners of the field like kind sentinels to guard things within it; the plump pumpkins with bright, golden rinds giving promise of many pies; and the dry bean heaps whose pods bursting with their grinning contents bespeak the Saturday supper and Sunday breakfast.

Besides these things that grew in and about the planting field there were divers loads of white turnips, called also English turnips whose green, outspreading leaves and purple tops were still untinged by the frost, and which profusely scattered throughout the whole cornfield indicated how well the ground was utilized.

Several days before the one appointed for the husking party, the corn had been cut and laid between the rows, and from thence it had been thrown upon various teams from the neighboring barns, which deposited it in Goodman Baker's yard, where we will suppose the husking was to occur, and from which place the fodder and its rich fruitage could be distributed.

Invitations to the party had been sent hither and yon throughout the town, and from every direction on the night appointed the people gathered. From the immediate vicinity there came the Rices, Foxes, Fletchers, Taylors and Brookes, also the Meriams, Wheats, Farwells and Balls.

From the north quarter there came the Hunts, Temples, Jonses and Browns; the Barretts from the neighborhood of Punkatassett; the Buttricks from near the bridge; the Hosmers from their pleasant homestead to the westward and the Batemans from about the pond. From the south quarter were the Hosmers, Deans, Potters and Dakins, the Woodhouse family, the Bulkeleys, Strattons, Billingses, Wigleys, and Woodses; the Mileses and Wheelers were there from the Nine Acres; the Gobbles from the river bay; and the Flint farms and Blood farms and the territory about Concord village all had their representatives at this Fall festival.

As each dismounted from saddle or pillion or jumped from the ox cart or "hay riggin'," the animals were fastened to a row of stakes which had been set behind the buildings for the purpose.

For weeks, Goodman Baker knowing that his place had been selected for the husking had been alive to all the requirements of the coming occasion, and his home had been a busy hive of willing and enthusiastic workers for many evenings since the early frost began crisping and curling the corn leaves. The woods had been scoured for game, and the clink clonk of the mortar had been a familiar sound for many evenings, while good wife Baker and the boys pounded cloves and coriander seed, caraway, savory and sage, that all might be in readiness when the merry "mixing time" came, and the rich sauces and gravies were to be prepared.

Several mornings previous to the day appointed for the husking the large brick oven had been made ablaze, and by mid-forenoon was well filled with loaves and puddings and pies.

The broad boards of every floor had been scoured and sanded, and everything not to be used had been set aside from the old garret whither the modest might flee to avoid the forfeit upon the finding of a red ear, to the shelves in the arch of the cellar, to which the elders might resort to sample Goodman Baker's choice cordials.

When the day came, everything was ready. The cider barrel had been "hossed up" in the dooryard, beside a bountiful pile of "eating apples." The corn heap had been pierced here and there with pitch-forks and stout poles upon which to fasten the tin lanterns, and sundry milking stools and logs had been arranged at convenient intervals as seats for the huskers.

The evening began with steady work, which was mainly performed by the younger and more nimble of the party.

Back in the shadows sat the grave old men comparing the year's crop with former ones and wondering why the present is so different from the past in many things.

As the pile perceptibly diminished the work began to flag, and as the boys saw the end of it they grew mischievous. It was not long however before the work was broken in upon by the discovery of a red ear which was found by Sam Smeadley. No sooner was it seen than a flurry set in and each person braced himself for what was to follow; some ran, but more stood their ground, and if any escaped the person was chased till caught and the forfeit paid.

Many were the red ears found during the evening, but whether kind nature had favored the common planting fields of the East quarter with an unusual number, or the boys had surreptitiously brought them from other places we cannot say, but that husking party was long remembered, and the old men said, over their cider mugs, that "for red ears Farmer Baker's husking was the beater."

In two or three hours the husking was finished and the supper was eaten; the young people repaired to the chambers to engage in games, and the elders, grouped about the sitting room fire, talked of olden times and reviewed the leading events since the settlement started, and told who had come and who had gone.

In consequence of a remark made by Betsey Billings about a sign which she said she saw in the sparks, conversation turned upon the subject of the supernatural; and personal experiences of a curious nature were related, some of which but for the good character of the narrators and the tendency of the times might have been doubted.

It is true society had not reached that state of credulity and fanatical frenzy which existed toward the last of the century, and there had been but few instances of witch trials in this country; but the belief in witchcraft and devil dealing had already set in and supposed alliances with evil agencies were not uncommon; so that the conversation of the plain people of this East quarter husking party was only representative of a sentiment too generally prevailing; and when, in order to catch every syllable of old Wigley, when he described what he saw and heard on a late evening while passing the three graves at Witch end, the people leaned toward him lest they miss something, they only expressed the common avidity for grewsome subjects.

It may be well here to consider how this came about and the responsible cause of it. This tendency of the times was not born but brought here.

The colonists have been too often and too harshly criticized for things which, although they fostered, they did not originate. There was more than old furniture and curious bric-a-brac from far off manor houses, and heirlooms of ancient date, and traditions of heraldry confirmed by antique coats of arms, that came to these shores in the "Harpers," the "Halcyons" and the "Hopes," ships and brigs of good repute and wise masters; there were superstitions, and false conceptions of demonology, and dismal beliefs in possible alliance with "familiars." These existed, though in embryo, and were ready to develop on easy occasion; and easy occasions were frequent. The soil of New England was a congenial one. The dark forests, the wild morasses, the lone pond shores, the long and deserted ocean beaches, the crumbling and scrawny ledges where lurked suspicious shadows, these all with the voices of the wilderness were like deft and dutiful nursery maids or over indulgent foster parents quick to promote what had better been prevented. But these conditions and agencies would never have produced spontaneously the grewsome beliefs and practices that so deeply and darkly stained the closing decades of the 17th century.

What was then developed was but an imitation of what many times over had occurred in Old England, and although British writers may still turn in their study of witchcraft to this continent, and notwithstanding the town of Salem may still be the synonym for, and suggestive of, all that is classic on the subject, yet not Salem nor the combined boroughs of the entire country can show a record of court cruelty on account of witch conviction in any way comparable with the English tribunals.

The colonists came to America as pupils from an ancient school, and they practiced here what they had been taught to believe elsewhere. It is not to be wondered at then if Delilah Dean thought her churn was bewitched because the cows browsed in Betsey Balcom's back yard, since Bess was considered a witch. But it might be wondered at had not Goody Dean's grandfather informed her that on one occasion in old Yorkshire the kine had come home with dry udders because the woman who lived on the hillside by his master's manor house had cursed the herd and said it should go barren. Again, why should not Sol. Stratton say he saw something, and everybody believe what he said, when old Smithson, Sol's uncle, had frequently told him and all the people also that when he lived on the Dorset downs in the Old Country he was warned not to gather fagots from the bewitched hedgerow lest the smoke tarnish whatever it touch.

After the company had listened to the recital of several strange things by old Simson Slowgo as to what he had seen in his day before coming to Concord, for he was late there, having but recently come from down country to follow the trade of an itinerant shoemaker, they turned their conversation to things about home. Several spoke of unusual appearances recently seen near the river, which, by the description, were similar to the one seen by Goodmen Heywood and Barrett on the evening of our excursion on Parson Bulkeley's boat.

One incident that especially interested the company was told by Jeduthan Jones, Squire Flint's hired man, an outlander who had gotten into town without anyone being responsible for him; but as Jed had proved good help he was allowed to stay, although it was said "his word should be taken with a leetle keer." The incident was about a strange creature that he saw down at Cranberry Crossing by the brick kiln. The company at once recognized in the animal what was known as the spectral wolf which it was asserted was the "familiar" of Sarah Doubleday, an old grandam who once lived at Bogbottom.

This beast had prowled all over Concord, carrying away shoats and calves, and even milking cows. So exceptional was his nature that the usual means of thwarting witches were in his case unavailing; and when Bray Wilmot, a Welshman, nailed a couple of horseshoes over his henhouse he lost not only his hens but the shoes; the latter having been wrenched off, as was supposed, by the spectral wolf, which, by the "disportation" of Sarah, had been made immune from either enchantment by horseshoes or harm from silver shot; moreover the mystery was increased upon finding the horseshoes later, on Jake Flin's old mare, an animal that some said was as much bewitched as the wolf, since it had been seen in various lone localities under suspicious circumstances.

It proved a surprise to hear from the spectral animal, for he had not been seen, it was said, since Lemuel Loker over at Sudbury tried to shoot it and by mistake hit Jake Flin. Lem had lost several pullets and a couple of cocks and naturally laid it to the white wolf, as he was sometimes called, for it was supposed he could take all colors.

After this last loss, it was stated by those present, for Lemuel was not there, as he lived out of town, that he delivered himself of some very strong language, so strong that his wife rebuked him; and with great emphasis he declared that he "would capter that wolf ef it cost him suthin, pervided he could do it at a safe distance, for he didn't care to deal with Sarah with bare hands." "So," continued Hilkiah Heald who was relating it, "Lem sliced up an old spoon, it was a silver one, and arter breakin' it up inter bits and rounding 'em over, he put a pooty stiff charge of powder in his snaphance and the bits over it, and then lay down behind the lalock bushes and waited. Well, about midnight Lem heered suthin and fired at it and it fell, and as he went to look at it he found he had shot Jake Flin. He hadn't injured him much, for Jake's coat, which was made of wolf skin, kept the shot out, but he was terribly scared and somewhat jarred, and when asked how it happened that he was there, Jake said he was out arter the specter wolf which had jest stole his fowls. When Lem saw the coat he didn't wonder much at his mistake, for he said it looked for the whole world like the wolf which he got a glimpse of round the corner when he lost the horseshoes."

It is unnecessary to state that after the shooting of Jake Flin by Lem Loker the people of Concord were no longer pestered by the spectral wolf, for Jacob Flin left the poultry business.

After the narration of incidents, the methods of detecting witches was discussed, and the making discovery of such as practiced the black arts or were allied with "familiars."

One way suggested was to ascertain if any relative had ever been suspected of being a witch. Another was to look for the "witch mark," which might be a mole or any irregular growth, or perhaps some slight deformity, not enough or itself to be a mark but only as taken with other things. To accuse one of dealing with the devil and receiving in response no denial was suspicious and to do one harm by well-known witch methods was a bad symptom.

When it came to stories of apparitions such as were supposed to stalk about ancient burial places it was noticeable that those who were sitting in the back part of the room hitched nearer to the fireside. Someone also got up and closed the cellar door, which a few moments before had sprung open without anyone knowing the reason, for Goodwife Baker said she knew she buttoned it when she brought up the last pail of cider.

As the subject of apparitions was talked about each speaker grew somewhat subdued in his manner of narration, and the hearers bunched together as if the last handful of chips that was thrown on the back log did not sufficiently warm them.

Just as the group were in the midst of a story told by Tilly Temple, in which she was relating how Peg Willoughby, a new comer, concocted a mixture of dragon leaf and swamp adder root with which she tried to charm Felix Fox's cows in order that she might stealthily milk them, and how, in order to prevent it Felix consulted an old grandam down at the slough, a large lug bar which had long been braced across the chimney ledges, but not lately used, because the Bakers had a crane, having become weakened by the unusual fires of the husking party, suddenly dropped, bearing with it a couple of jib cakes, a hook and a dislodged brick. In its fall it struck upon a dish kettle hanging on the crane half full of water, and upsetting it emptied its contents upon the glowing back-log which, being struck by the falling lug bar, rolled down upon the cider pail and upset it.

A dense cloud of hissing steam and flying ashes quickly filled the apartment and shrieks issued from every quarter.

The two dogs, Fleck and Towser at the same time set up a cry, the one a long howl, the other several sharp whines and for a moment it was as if Peg Willoughby's witch broth had been poured down the chimney, which some thought was the case. The tumult being heard in the chamber above, where the games were going on, brought down the young people, who only added to the confusion.

When order was restored it was found that no serious damage had been done, except the spotting of several calamanco gowns.

Goodman Bateman said he "guessed he'd go as the hour was getting a little late and he had got to ride clean over the river to the North part and pooty nigh the spot where Sim Slowgo saw the wolf." Upon this suggestion Pete Potter surprised the company by saying he was certain it was late, for, said he, "I have tamed that hour glass nigh agin five times sence the moon passed the quarter mark on the door post." In a half hour the house was still and nothing was to be heard but the occasional rattle of the cows' walnut bows and the barking of a small Indian dog down at the Dean place, where some wolves were trying to get at the shoats.

It may be here observed that the selectmen warned Peg Willoughby out of town the day following and broke up the bough house where she simmered her noxious herbs.

As we have now set forth the common belief in witchcraft and in the supernatural generally in colonial times, by the supposititious conversation and conduct of the old folks at the East quarter husking party, we will observe that the view on this subject as entertained by the laity was perhaps more strongly entertained by the professional class.

Ministers and magistrates were alike deluded. The fact of bedevilment was assumed by the pulpit, and the judges at the bench charged jurors in the laying down of rules for the weighing of evidence in the case of witchcraft with the same confidence as in cases of theft or assault. It is thought probable that the judges of the Province Court sought to employ in the Province laws the rules and practice which had been employed at the Colonial Court in Salem, and the judges who presided over that court were reappointed, William Stoughton, Esq., being chosen chief justice. In the works of Rev. Cotton Mather on subjects relating to the marvelous, doings as strange as those related around Goodman Baker's fireside were set forth. Among other supposed manifestations of witch power he mentions persons afflicted with "sore paynes" and "vomiting" and "frequent swooning." He gives an instance of a child being "lame on one side and then on the other," and of sometimes pretending to see mice. He states that on one occasion the child catching a mouse threw it upon the fire, whereupon it snapped like gunpowder. He said that several standing by saw the flash, but only the child saw the mouse. In speaking of witch marks he intimated they might be caused by the devil touching the person; that these marks were insensible, and upon being pricked would not bleed, and that they were sometimes bluish and sometimes red. Among the ways of testing witches which he referred to were the being heard speaking to their "familiar" or telling what they have done, or telling of their "transportations," or being seen with their spirits or feeding their imps.

But it should be said to the credit of the colonial clergy that the witchcraft delusion which ran its course before the century closed was dissipated as much perhaps by their efforts and influences as by all other agencies combined.

Its cessation may have had its beginning in the attitude of the Mathers, who while they stood ready to coincide with the judiciary in the correctness of witch conviction upon proper evidence, yet considered it a cruelly and a great travesty of justice to make use of some of the evidence which was admissible in the courts of England, or to abide by such principles and precedents as were sanctioned by them.

While they believed as did Sir William Blackstone, who wrote his commentaries about three-quarters of a century later, that demoniacal possession was a possibility and scriptural, yet they believed the devil and not his victims should be held responsible. Rev. Increase Mather declared it to be unlawful to use herbs to keep off the evil spirits, and he disparaged the curing of diseases by means of charms, saying that they who obtained health in that way had it from the devil. He considered white witches who pretended to cure in that way as bad as black ones, and a good witch as bad as a bad one. He said "Balaam was a black witch and Simon Major a white one, but the latter did more hurt by his cures than the former by his curses."

113

He took a decided issue with the English courts of the time, which held that "If a specter practicing diabolical molestations appeared to anyone it was conclusive and legal evidence that the person so represented was a witch," which theory was accepted by Sir Matthew Hale and adopted at the Salem trials. The attitude of the Boston ministers was that the devil himself and not the person accused caused the representations.

In 1692, Rev. Increase Mather wrote a work at the request of the ministers of Boston, which was published in this country and also in England, the object of which was to show the illegality and wrong of using spectral testimony which was used at the Salem trials. The preface to this work was written by Samuel Willard and signed by fourteen ministers, who made the following statement: "That there are devils and witches the scriptures assert and experience confirms; they are the common enemies of mankind set upon mischief. But certainly the more execrable the crime is, the more critical care is to be used in the exposing of the names, liberties and lives of men (especially of a godly conversation) to the imputation of it." Mather said: "I declare and testify that to take away the lives of any one merely because a specter or devil in a bewitched or accused person does accuse them will bring the guilt of innocent blood on the land." He maintained that the oath and testimony of confessed witches and of persons possessed should never be received, and that a trial for witchcraft ought to be conducted by the same law and rules of evidence as a trial for murder, burglary or any other felony.

If the Mathers and the other ministers here referred to were representatives of their profession at this period they were more than abreast of the judiciary and the laity, and far in advance of English law generally.

CHAPTER XXI.

Return to the East quarter — Forest Ride— Game Birds — Goodwife Hart-well's Kitchen — Cooking by the Fireplace — Evening talk of the Farm Folks — Laws Relative to Domestic Animals — Historic Sketch of Hartwell Family— Visit at Home of Constable Thomas Brooks — His Official Duties— Rules Relative to Colonial Dress—Homestead of Goodman William Hunt — Early Military Matters — History of the Hunt Family.

TO return now to our original narration, after the bag was replaced and Farmer Hartwell was reseated there was no further interruption to our journey; it was jolt after jolt all the way; but we rather enjoyed it, for the swaying of the ox cart was somewhat soothing, and our slow pace gave us an opportunity to see the birds. In one instance a wild turkey ran before us with a surprising fleetness; upon expressing our surprise we were informed that this was a means of their safety, for on the wing they were heavy, the largest specimens weighing forty or fifty pounds. In a moist hollow by the roadside we flushed several woodcocks. Upon inquiring if they were flight birds we were told they were; and that there were also plenty of natives; that they nested near every runway and spring hole, and that the corn fields in low places were full of their borings.

As we approached a reach in the road several wood ducks whistled over us, and we learned that their nests were made in the woods adjacent to the meadows and that when their young were full-fledged they carried them to the water in their bills.

Emerging from the forest into a sunny opening, where Farmer Farwell had a small patch of Guinea wheat, there arose from it a flock of purple grackles; and so large was it that we could easily understand why a bounty was placed upon them, for as they alighted on a large oak they almost covered it and the overflow settling on a willow caused it to bend like a reed.

When we reached Goodman Hartwell's home his wife and children were at the door looking for us, having heard the rattle of our cart in the distance, and soon we had entered and were seated at the dinner table. The afternoon was mostly spent in one of the front rooms chatting about matters pertaining to the East quarter, for the prediction of the wild ducks about the weather had proven true and the rain was now beating against the east windows.

At early twilight Goodwife Hartwell set about preparing the supper; and as we heard her clinking the tongs against the andirons while she pulled from underneath them the hard wood coals which during the afternoon she had taken care to have in readiness, the desire seized us to see a meal cooked by a fireplace. The wish was no sooner expressed than Goodman Hartwell led us into the kitchen and seated us close by the wood box, where we could see everything.

The sparks ascended thickly from beneath the long, stout crane, the tea-kettle hummed, and the steam gracefully ascended among the various objects that were pendent above the mantlepiece upon a pole stretched over it; and every now and then as there fell upon the fire a few rain drops, which had been driven by the blast down the chimney, there was a hissing and sputtering as if the coals were conversing with the storm sprites.

Amid all this snugness, Goodwife Hartwell was busily "plying her evening care;" being at the outset of her work particularly engaged with a plump ball of rye dough which she was stirring and patting in a wooden bread trough or tray in an earnest endeavor to mix the ash and butter-milk which she had poured into it to make it rise. When the dough had been thoroughly stirred she scraped it into a compact little heap, being careful to leave nothing on the tray; and after cutting it in halves, deftly slipped one part into a frying pan and the other upon an iron disc the size of a bucket top, which she set on edge and tipped slightly towards the coals. The frying pan after covering she placed on the longest hook of the crane, saying as she did so that she usually cooked shortcake in that manner, but thought we might like to see it done both ways.

While the cakes were baking Goodwife Hartwell brought in a jack and a spit, informing us that this was used in cooking meat, the jack turning the spit so that it would "do evenly."

As we were company there was "boughten" tea that evening, instead of the usual malted beverage, and in place of the usual wooden trenchers we had pewter plates of a pattern that showed that Jazen came of a good family, for she said she brought them with her from England.

Grace was asked before eating, and thanks returned afterwards, forcibly reminding us of the poet Burns' beautiful picture of "The Cotter's Saturday Night."

After supper we sat about the fireplace and talked while the children popped corn and cracked nuts, and the rain ran down the east window pane. The corn they popped in the ashes, occasionally stirring it; the nuts they cracked on the stone hearth.

In the course of the evening Nathaniel Ball came in and soon after Thomas Brooks, for they lived near. Nathaniel Ball wanted some garget for a sick cow, and Thomas Brooks brought back a couple of cart ladders which he had borrowed.

The room was savory with the roasting of a spare-rib which Goodwife Hartwell was getting in readiness for the men folks' dinner next day, as she was to attend a quilting at Farmer Miles'. The smell of the pork suggested some queries respecting the raising of swine, which we had seen frequently running at large by the roadside and in pasture places. We learned that swine were of great importance to the settlers. They were not only prolific, but at certain seasons could subsist on the abundant acorn mast with which the woods abounded. They also fed upon ground nuts and succulent roots and wild cherries and berries. At some seasons they were restrained from running at large; and at town meeting in Concord and towns adjacent, laws were enacted to regulate them, of which the following are specimens: "In 1641, it was ordered that everyone that keeps any hogs more than his own within one fortnight after this day shall rid them out of this town, only that for every hog that shall be taken in to be kept by any one more than his own, for every week shall pay five shillings."

In 1643, it was ordered "That every inhabitant should drive out his hog every morning into the wood, and when they come home at night to see them shut up safe, or else, if they be about the street, to ring and yoke them."

In 1648, it was voted in town meeting "That every swine that should be found of every man out of his own property without a sufficient yoke and ring, after the first of March next the owner thereof shall forfeit for every swine so taken one shilling, and if the swine be yoked and not ringed or ringed and not yoked then six pence for any swine so taken, beside all the damage done by any such swine." It was also "Agreed that all yokes should be under the throat of the swine, and so long as the swine was high, and a rope go up on each side to be fastened above, and that swine should not be accounted sufficiently ringed if they could root."

In 1643, it was ordered by the freemen of the town "that all the cattle within this town shall this summer not be turned abroad without a keeper, and the keeper shall not keep any of the herd in any of the great river meadows from Bridle point downwards towards Concord." The intent of the order was to preserve the river meadows.

In 1655, it was ordered that "All young new weaned calves shall be herded all the summer time."

In the town of Concord there appeared to be a separate territory assigned to the swine, when under restraint during planting time. This territory was in the vicinity of Concord Junction, near Annursnuc hill, and is known in the records as the " hog pen" and "hog pen walk." After the crop was gathered these animals were allowed to run at large, provided there was placed upon them an ear-mark, so called; so that each settler might know his own swine and be held responsible for their mischief. The Indians were not allowed to mark their swine, and if they sold any pork they were to bring the hog's ear with it. In the records mention is repeatedly made of the "hog pen walk"; and in the land divisions this territory was held as a reservation. The hill Annursnuc is one of the highest three in the town of Concord. Its name is supposed to mean the same as Quinnursnuck, which signifies pestle, from the fact that rocks such as the Indians made their mortars and pestles of were found there. (Mr. Davis, Plymouth, Mass.) It is said that porphyry, of which arrow heads were made, was found there also.

After the neighbors had departed Goodman Hartwell related to us some of his family history; and as this and that of his numerous descendants has long been identified with the annals of Concord, we will give a brief outline of it.

According to Densmore, the historian of the Hartwell family, William and Jazen Hartwell came to America probably about 1635 or 1636. It's supposed William was about 23 years of age when he went to Concord, and in 1642 he was made a freeman of the Massachusetts Bay Colony. He was one of the town's original grantees and a most estimable citizen, holding office and serving on important committees. He had a large family and his descendants are widely scattered throughout the country, many of whom are holding responsible positions. He died March 12, 1690, aged 77. His wife died August 5, 1695.

In his will he mentioned among his children, John, Samuel, Sarah, and Mary. The following are the earliest vital statistics relating to the family in this country, and these have been preserved among the colonial archives:

"John, the sonne of William Hartwell, was born the 23-12-1640.

"Samuel, son of William and Jasan Hartwell, borne 26-1-45.

"Martha, daughter of William and Jassin Hartwell, the 29th-2-1649."

It is not known where William Hartwell was buried.

As has been stated, his house was situated on the " Old Bay road" leading from Concord to Lexington and was about a mile more or less from the public square. His original house lot consisted of nine acres and was near the eastern boundary of property lately owned by the originator of the famous Concord grape. His subsequent land possessions were large. At the time when a disturbance arose because of titles, and a committee was chosen to adjust land matters at their discretion, William Hartwell was allowed 247 acres, which were in three separate lots. It is thought that all his children were born in Concord.

Bright and early on the morning following the night spent at William Hartwell's we started for the farm house of Constable Thomas Brooks. Crossing over the field we observed one of the ditches which were used for fencing.

We saw by the size of the stubble within the enclosure that the corn stalks which grew upon it were very large; we also pulled up several turnips and found the quality good, which satisfied us they were raised on comparatively new land, or that which had lately been broken up, disabusing us of the theory that only old Indian fields were planted by the settlers.

We heard above us the scream of an eagle and the honk of some wild geese flying southward; and as we suddenly saw through the cold gray of the thick mist, for the wind had become easterly, a barley stack a little back of Constable Brooks' barn, which through the tog looked larger than ever before, there flew from it several brant which had alighted there the night before in the storm and were foraging on the unthreshed grain.

We soon came to the house which was the second erected on the spot, the owner, like others of the hamlet, having years before exchanged the little log shelter for one more substantial of frame work.

We met Constable Brooks with a small shepherd dog turning the sheep into the pasture lane, leaving the dog for their sole keeper during the day, and to bring them home by night-fall at his master's call.

Our host was right glad to meet us, as he stated, because our conversation on several subjects the night before was interrupted for want of time, and moreover he said his good wife, after seeing us at the meeting house, had many things to say about the Sunday training of children in things religious.

As Constable Brooks had several duties to attend to that day that could not be put off, he invited us to go with him; and he had in the barn an extra horse which he had brought over from Joshua Wheeler's, thinking we would be glad to accompany him about Concord town in the performance of his official duties.

It was nearly mid-forenoon when we rode out of the door yard, Farmer Brooks with his wife seated on a pillion behind him on one horse, and we on the other. Goodwife Brooks was going with us as far as Parson Bulkeley's, where she was to join a party going to the quilting.

Behind us upon our horse were thrown a couple of saddle bags in which were put, among other things, " Fox's Book of Martyrs," which he had borrowed of the parson and was now returning, and a string of plump, pink sausages as a present. By this time the day had become beautiful, the sun which had burned through the fog now shone brightly, and the glint of the moisture from the late rain upon the fallen leaves and mossy tree trunks looked gorgeous, and everything had the clean, still, and suggestive appearance of an October day after a storm.

Our animals were far from being fast but jogged along with the motion of veritable plow horses as they were, and it was past noon when we rode over the north bridge and entered the lane leading to Goodman Hunt's in the north quarter, after having left Goodwife Brooks and the contents of the saddle bags at the parsonage.

Among the duties performed by Constable Brooks that day was the warning of Richard Rambler out of town; he having gotten into Concord without a sponsor in case he or his family should become a public charge; and what made the case more aggravated was that the selectmen of Watertown had warned him away on at least two occasions, and when he at last left there and came to Concord he had taken another person with him who was as much given to idleness as himself, and who withal was profane and used lewd language and was considered a little light-fingered and given to beer. Another service had been to notify two parties who had presumed to dress with undue regard to colonial law, which forbade vain display in personal dress, that they should be more circumspect and leave off some of their flummery and furbelows and take less pains about their Sunday head-dress.

As we rode along we made some inquiry as to the laws regulating dress; and for substance the following were some of them: In 1634, it was enacted in view of "some new and immodest fashions, that no person, either man or woman, shall hereafter make or buy any apparel, either woolen, silk or linen, with any lace on it, silver, gold, silk, or thread, under the penalty of forfeiture of such clothes; also, that no person, either man or woman shall make or buy any slashed clothes other than one slash in each sleeve, and another in the back; also all cutworks, embroidered or needlework caps, bands and rails are forbidden hereafter to be made and worn under the aforesaid penalty; also all gold or silver girdles, hat bands, belts, ruffs, beaver hat, are prohibited to be bought and worn hereafter under the aforesaid penalty." A few years later a law was made against "short sleeves whereby the nakedness of the arm might be discovered in the wearing thereof," "sleeves more than half a yard wide in the widest place thereof," "immodest great breeches, knot of ribbon, broad shoulder bands and rails, silk rases, double ruffs and cuffs."

In 1561, the General Court enacted that if a man was not worth two hundred pounds, he should not wear gold or silver lace or buttons or points at the knees, and women holding a less property than this were forbidden to wear silk or tiffany hood scarfs. The same year the court put upon record as the occasion of the law, "its utter detestation and dislike that men or women of mean condition should take upon themselves the garb of gentlemen."

From our observation of Constable Brooks' day's work, we learned that the office of constable was an important one, and that it was with propriety that after being chosen by the town he was sworn in by officers of the colonial government. At one place he collected fifteen shillings and six pence for the use of the town of Concord from a person who had brought in a stranger presumed to be of a questionable character, this being the usual amount per week required in such cases.

He also stopped at the house of one Loren Little and censured him in behalf of the town for "taking in and harboring" Dothan Doolittle, who, common report said, was of "a vicious nature and had an evil tongue." The last official acts of the day were to stop at the meeting house and fasten to one of the hitching trees a couple of wolf pates, which Samuel Smedley had sent up; and post upon the door the notice of a marriage in place of the one which the rain had soaked off; and to "right up" amort stone by Sorrel lane which had been leaning a little since the last heavy corpse was laid upon it.

As we passed into the North quarter we soon arrived at Goodman Hunt's. His house was a model one for the times, being of convenient proportions and so situated as to catch every sunbeam and having no isolated best room on the north side. As we walked in we found dinner awaiting us, for the household had been apprised of our coming by Goodman Buttrick, who lived a little below and had come up to bring a letter which had been brought up from Watertown and left with him for delivery. After dinner we repaired to a shed where some men were hatchelling flax, about the first which had been raised in Concord for a commercial purpose. As there was in one corner a triangular fireplace, we seated ourselves before it and talked and whittled until the sun shining through the windows showed that it was about time we were starting home.

During the afternoon, part of our conversation was on military matters; and as the subject was an important one in those days, we will relate some facts concerning the military history of Concord in its first century. Almost all able-bodied men except ministers and magistrates were furnished with arms and ammunition and expected to be present and drill on stated occasions. They were also required to go on expeditions and scoutings if necessary, and to stand in readiness for "watch and ward." So invariable was this rule that it was necessary to apply to the General Court for exemption. The officers of a company consisted of captain, lieutenant, ensign, and four sergeants. A regiment had a field officer called a sergeant-major, and over them all was a major-general. The commissioned officers carried swords, or leading staves and pistols: they were elected by the members of the company and approved by the General Court.

The sergeants bore halberds; the common soldiers were armed with matchlock or firelock muskets and had horns and pouches for powder and ball; sometimes a forked stick was carried to steady their aim. Officers were required to be church members, and the military exercises were preceded or followed by prayer. Sometimes a military election was the occasion for doing the civil business of the town.

As early as 1636, Sergeant Willard was appointed to exercise the military company at Concord and was commissioned captain in 1646, at which time Timothy Wheeler was made ensign. Mr. Willard served as captain fifteen years. In 1671, Ensign Wheeler was made captain, Thomas Hinchman lieutenant, and Henry Woodis quartermaster. Two years afterwards Woodis was made cornet and Corporal William Hartwell was appointed quartermaster. After the death of the old Indian fighter, Wheeler, Thomas Hinchman was made captain and John Flint lieutenant. In 1677, Peter Bulkeley was appointed captain. July 2, 1689, James Minot was elected captain, Simon Davis lieutenant, and Humphrey Barrett ensign. About a year after the close of Philip's War the military force of Concord consisted of upwards of 150 men, besides some enlistments in a horse company. Nov. 6, 1689, it was ordered by the representatives "that the foot company of Concord having 250 men be divided into two companies."

The afternoon passed quickly at Goodman Hunt's, and there were so many things to talk about that it was late before he said anything about his family history; a subject which, if not introduced voluntarily, we were quite apt to inquire about, especially when we called upon an original grantee of the first quarter century; only a few facts however were elicited concerning the Concord Hunts, but from other sources we have received the following information: William Hunt was in Concord as early as 1640, and became a freeman in 1641. He died in Marlboro, Oct., 1667, leaving an estate of £496 and children named Nehemiah, Isaac, William, Elizabeth,

Hannah and Samuel. He was born in 1605, and married Elizabeth Best, who died in 1661. While in Marlboro he married Mercie Heard Rice, widow of Edmund Rice, in 1664. The Hunt family has been a prominent one in Concord, and in the adjoining towns of Acton and Sudbury. Those in the former town are descendants of William; and of these was Simon Hunt, Captain of a company in the 3rd Regiment of Massachusetts militia in the Revolutionary war. Those in the latter town are in part descendants of William, and in part of Robert Hunt, who came from Charlestown, or of Isaac Hunt, a blacksmith, who came from Cambridge and early settled in the Lanham district, owning at one time about four hundred acres on Pelham's Island. The old house, built tradition says about 1750, is still standing about a half mile from Heard's (Pelham's) pond.

Nehemiah Hunt, son of William, who has been called "Lord of Punkatassett," lived on the estate bought by his father of Rev. Peter Bulkeley; which estate has been owned and occupied in recent years by his descendant, William H. Hunt.

The following is the only mention of the Hunt family among the vital statistics of the town of Concord down to 1654: "Hannah, the daughter of Wm. Hunt, was borne 12 (12) 1640."

CHAPTER XXII.

Visit at Goodman William But trick's — His History — Situation of his House — Reflections upon a prospective Wedding — Historic Sketch of Thomas Brooks — Curious Laws and Customs relative to marriage — Bachelors, Match Making, Widowers — Wedding Gifts—Attend "Lecture Day" Service — Its Nature and Importance — Religious Character of the Colonists—Care of the Poor—Visit at the home of Goodman Richard Rice.

AS we were about starting on our return to the East quarter, Thomas Bateman drove into the yard, and leaving his horse to feed at will, stepped to the door and stated that there was to be a meeting of the land committee at Goodman William Buttrick's that evening for the adjustment of some matters relative to boundary lines; and that he called to notify Constable Brooks, who was one of the committee, and also to request us to be present.

Here let us pause and briefly notice some facts about this estimable family, which has long been conspicuously connected with the history of Concord.

William Buttrick came from England to America in 1635, on the ship Susan and Ellen, in company with Rev. Peter Bulkeley and Thomas Brooke. He embarked from London, May 9, 1635, and was m Concord at its beginning. His English home was at Kingston-on-the-Thames in Surrey.

When he came to this country he was probably about twenty years old, since in 1684, when he deposed concerning the purchase of the township from the Indians he declared himself sixty-eight. He served many years in the town militia as Sergeant, and when sixty-five years of age petitioned the Court to be exempt from further military duty. He married for his first wife Sarah Bateman, who died in 1664. He died June 30, 1696. His descendants are of illustrious memory. Among them was Major John Buttrick of the Middlesex yeomanry in 1775, whose gravestone in the Hill burying ground sets forth his estimable character and distinguished services.

The homestead of William Buttrick was situated on the west bank of Concord river upon the upland, an eighth or a quarter of a mile from the North bridge, where he could look down upon the spring floods as they sometimes spread themselves far out over the low meadows; and where, to the south-westward, he could see the smoke wreaths curling upwards from the snug homes of the Willards, Busses, Woodses and Hosmers. At the northerly the Barretts had built, and far over the marsh, as the broadening river flowed downward towards the Blood farm and Winthrop grant was a country broken by scant settlements.

It is easy to suppose that on account of their early acquaintance and because they had sailed the seas together, a peculiar neighborliness should exist between the two townsmen, Brooks and Buttrick, and that whenever either was in the other's quarter he should visit him; and that often they should meet together with Parson Bulkeley in each other's homes and talk over what they had seen and known of things abroad. There is also every reason to believe that the Batemans were frequent callers at the Buttrick home for kinship's sake, and that altogether there was about this rural manor house an air of sociability and comfortableness not surpassed in the Musketequid plantation.

The "committee of nine" all came except two, who, as they lived at a considerable distance, were doubtless detained by the storm which towards sunset had again set in with a prospect of continuing till morning.

It was a pleasant and cozy scene as around that evening fireside the group sat, while the sparks snapped briskly, and with an unusual activity chased each other over the old crane.

The east wind blew up from the meadows; the big raindrops pelted against the small diamond-shaped window panes, and sometimes a tiny stream ran under the door, until Goodwife Buttrick threw against it a husk mat.

But little cared we for the storm, housed warmly as we were and our "cattle," and with the assurance of clean, soft couches in case the storm continued so as to render a return that night to the East quarter unwise; moreover, Constable Brooks had said there was no concern on his part about his wife, as she was expecting to stop over night at the Miles's in case the quilt was not finished.

In the morning we did not return to Constable Brooks but remained to go with the Buttrick family on the day following to the wedding.

It was with regret that we bade Constable Brooks goodbye, and as he drove down the hill he called back to us and said that a seat would be reserved for us beside him in the meeting house next Sunday, and that if we would go home with him after service, he and his wife would tell us about the Sabbath catechumenal exercise; a matter we were exceedingly desirous of knowing about, for we thought by what we had heard that it savored very much of a modern Sunday school, and if so this was the first in the country.

After his departure we retired to the little chamber that had been assigned us under the double gable whose end window faced to the south, and there, as preliminary to the marriage, we recalled whatever we knew of colonial customs as they related to courtship and marriage and the conditions consequent upon remaining single. It was a fit time for the consideration of such a subject, for the morning was lovely, and we were reminded of the words of the poet:

"Sweet day, so calm, so clear, so bright,
The bridal of the earth and sky,"

and these words together with the preparations which were going on in the room below for the prospective wedding lent a suggestiveness which was very helpful.

In fact things were in pleasant keeping one with another on that bright autumnal morning, with its crisp white frost and genial sunshine, and we thought if the beauty of a day is an auspicious omen to those who are so near their bridal hour, then the twain may be happy indeed.

We had talked about marriage customs the afternoon previous, as we sat by the triangular-shaped fireplace in Goodman Hunt's shop; and as one of the tithing men came in and conversed with the constable about an especial espionage which they were keeping upon a certain bachelor in the Shawshine district, who was acting frivolously toward a giddy and flirtish maiden who occasionally rode over to Goodman Meriam's grocery store with a pannier filled with eggs and dried apple, and who had ordered the storekeeper to get her a "smartish gown" when he went " below," we learned, upon intently listening, about all there was of common or statute law on the subject. It only remained, therefore, for us to put things together on that bright morning.

Before doing this, however, let us notice a few facts relative to the family record of our late host, Goodman Thomas Brooks; for our tarry with him and his household had been a delightful one, and we had received in our conversations with him much information that was useful.

Thomas Brooks, as we have stated, came to America from England in 1635, in the ship "Susan and Ellen," leaving London in company with Messrs. Buttrick and Bulkeley, May 9th. He was one of the earliest settlers at Concord, and through the long interim between then and now, the name has passed along, with here and there someone to make it exceptionally illustrious.

The common ancestor of the Brooks family in Concord, Shattuck says, was Capt. Thomas Brooks. But as Lincoln, Acton, Bedford and Carlisle were once largely included in this township, some of the inhabitants who have borne the name in these towns may lay claim to the same honor as those living in Concord. Thomas was made a freeman in 1636. He was representative ten years. He died May 21, 1667; and his wife, Grace, died May 12, 1664. They left children as follows: Joshua, Caleb, Gershom, Mary, and probably, Thomas and John. Mary married Capt. Timothy Wheeler of Concord. Caleb sold his estate at Concord in 1670 and moved to Medford and was the ancestor of Governor John Brooks and Hon. Peter C. Brooks. Joshua married Hannah, a daughter of Capt. Hugh Mason of Watertown, an officer of Philip's war fame, and was the ancestor of nearly all by the name of Brooks in Concord and Lincoln, among whom was the late Hon. George M. Brooks, a former Judge of Probate of Middlesex County and representative to Congress. The following are the only records among the town's vital statistics as late as 1654, relative to the Brooks family: "Joseph the sonne of Henry Brooks was borne the 12 (2) 1641."

The next following record is "Grace, daughter or Joshua Brooks & Hannah his wife borne 10 March 1661."

To return now to our narrative. In early times wedded life found much public favor, and was greatly encouraged, while an unmarried life was discouraged, as is indicated by the fact that almost from the beginning the colonists placed upon their town records or upon their statute books resolves and enactments designed to make the married state easy and the unmarried state hard.

Bachelors were under a special surveillance, or "spying and tattling" of the constables and tything-men; and so a man might properly be said to gain his liberty instead of losing it by entering into the marriage state. As an inducement for one to marry sometimes a house lot was offered.

In Eastham, Mass., it was ordered that " Every unmarried man in the township shall kill six blackbirds or three crows while he remains single; as a penalty for not doing so he shall not be married until he obeys this order." In 1670, Thomas Tally, who had lived in Concord four years, was summoned into court to answer for not living with his wife.

His defense was that she was in England, and that he had sent for her, and if she did not come he would go after her. This defense, however, was to no purpose, for the Grand Jury, before which he had been brought, banished him from its jurisdiction. Contracts relating to marriage were sometimes written out and signed by the contracting parties. One, which has been preserved and given in detail by the historian Walcott, is for substance that one was to give lands, and the other pounds, shillings and pence, and Robert Blood was to "stand good" for the fulfillment of this pre-nuptial agreement.

In early times people were very cautious about "match making." Fines or the whipping post awaited the reckless, and it was no safe thing to be imprudent in such a matter. The traveler Joslyn, speaking of an evening's courtship in Boston in 1663, said: "On the south there is a small but pleasant common where the Gallants, a little before sunset, walk with their marmalet Madams till the nine o'clock bell rings, then home to their respective habitations."

In 1672 Jonathan Coventry was indicted " for making a motion of marriage to Catherine Dudley without obtaining formal consent." In 1647, m Stratford, Will Colefoxe was fined 5 pounds for "laboring to inveigle the affection of Write, his daughter." The reason given for such carefulness was "to prevent young folks from entangling themselves by rash and inconsiderate contracts of marriage." If an engagement to marry was made and had been permitted by the father he could not without reason break it off. In Plymouth in 1661, Richard Taylor sued Ruth Whieldom's father; and it is said that another man sued the father for loss of time in courting. A person "jilted " was said to be "shabbed."

Marriage of old widowers was in vogue in the Massachusetts Bay Colony, as we infer from the correspondence and conduct of Judge Sewall, who married Hannah Hull of " Pine Tree Shilling" fame and received her weight in silver for dower. Having lived with his wife forty-three years and having had fourteen children, the Judge made the following entry in his diary after her death: "Wondering in my mind whether to live a married or a single life."

Before his wife had been dead two months it is said he had "gazed admiringly at Widow Winthrope in her sley," and that he gave her as tokens of his admiration works entitled "Smoking Flax Inflamed" and "My Small Vial of Tears.

For two centuries the wedding bans were published three Sundays in the meeting house. Ministers were forbidden to perform the marriage ceremony, but it was done by the magistrate or by some appointed by law for the purpose. The minister, however, sometimes preached a sermon on the occasion of an engagement on such a text as the prospective bride might select. One minister, it is said, preached on a text in Ephesians, showing that the married state was a warfare. In this case probably the minister selected his own text. The coming out" or as it was sometimes called "the walking out" was considered an affair of importance, and Cotton Mather thought it expedient for the "bridal couple to appear as such publicly with some dignity." It was quite customary for a long period for ministers' sons to marry ministers' daughters.

For many years "sack posset" was drank at weddings, but, it is said, "not with noisy revelry." "Bride cake" and " bride gloves" were sent by friends. Jewelry engraved with a skull and cross-bones has been known to be given to a bride who was in mourning for a deceased friend. The garter of the bride was sometimes scrambled for to bring good luck.

As the family had been unusually busy we had the forenoon all to ourselves, and when the call came for dinner we were ready to leave our reflections and join the family below. While we were seated at the table Goodman Buttrick surprised us by the announcement that it was "lecture day," and that the family that afternoon would attend service at the meeting house. We had heard of this mid-week meeting and knew that it was made much of but were amazed at the importance which was actually attached to it, and we only needed an invitation to go with them to their little church home on the hill where we could observe for ourselves. On the way thither a Sunday stillness pervaded everything. No sound of work was heard anywhere, and even the chimneys were smokeless, showing how empty the houses were of inmates. As we fell in just before reaching the North bridge with the Brownes and Billingses they at once commenced talking about the last lecture, and the remarks made upon it showed a most commendable knowledge of the theology of the times and evinced also a high type of intelligence. The discussion was clear, the language was concise and the logic convincing. In short, what we heard and saw on the way was ample evidence that there was with the average colonist an independence of religious thinking which corresponded well with his robust self-reliance in coping with the obstacles to be met with in subduing a new country or the formidable ones which he afterwards met with from abroad. We found that his mind was by no means merely imitative, neither absorbent nor vacant, waiting to be filled with whatever a stronger might give it, but it was analytic and constructive and had an original and individual strength; that where an acquired wisdom was wanting there was a supply of good common sense; that he had as nice a discernment between the reasonable and the unreasonable as he did between the right and the wrong, and that these terms were with him practically interchangeable. We found that the colonist firmly believed that he had a good foundation for the hope that was within him. That foundation he unswervingly believed, by the most concise rules of logic, the truest testimony of history, the fullest endorsement of conscience, the strength of divers providences in the shape of guidance and special deliverance, was God's word. Armed and aided by such Divine authority and by various spiritual quickenings and visitations he went forth to what he considered was his heaven directed mission. On the strength of his convictions he enacted such a code of rules for his civic procedure as he believed only supplemented that word and embodied its pure principles and made it practicable for all secular purposes and such as he deemed necessary for its protection and unobstructed progress.

By the doing of these things he was able to succeed as a colonist where others in this country had failed, and by these things he endeavored to set up in each township a genuine theocracy with a government that would have God for its King, His word for its statute book and His Spirit for its sole Interpreter and Director.

As we drew near the meeting house we saw Parson Bulkeley and Major Simon Willard coming on foot over the Milldam path, and we learned after service that the former had been to administer spiritual consolation to an afflicted family up by the Darby bridge, where a child had died. As the family were poor, Mr. Bulkeley had taken with him Major Willard with the design of making some betterment in their material circumstances by bringing them nearer the central village, where the father could be furnished with work and the family could be looked after.

The consideration of these two worthy magnates of the town for one of the poorer class was to us significant and suggested an inquiry as to the charities of the Concord colony: whereupon we discovered that there was a kindness of heart that suffered not the needy to be neglected and that contributions were taken occasionally in the meeting house for the worthy poor.

As the parish included the entire town, so the poor everywhere within its borders were subject to its material ministrations; but it was only the deserving poor who were looked upon with complaisance, for idleness and wastefulness were utterly frowned upon. It is true the colonist was exceedingly saving because circumstances required it: it was nevertheless a part of his religion to recognize the claims of honest poverty upon his purse as well as upon his heart. His parsimony might lead him to deny himself luxuries, but not to deny his neighbors the necessaries of life.

Goodman Richard Rice with whom we had been conversing informed us that the funeral of the child was to take place on Saturday, and we resolved to attend. He also invited us to go home with him and accompany his family to the wedding next day. As it was our purpose to visit as many households as possible during our short stay in the settlement we accepted the invitation after having obtained the reluctant consent of the Buttricks.

As the minister approached the meeting house door all entered as quietly as if it were Sunday, or the Sabbath, as the settlers called the day, because they deemed that the word Sunday savored of Paganism in that it suggested sun worship; and when once within, the service was conducted with all the seriousness and sanctity of the sacred day itself.

The lecture was as the name implies an instructive discourse. The people were literally lectured with respect to their duty, and the subject had particular reference to their daily spiritual experience. At the close few lingered to talk for it was a work day and they hastened home to complete the unfinished task.

As Goodman Rice had but one horse we went on the "ride and tie" system, although as a matter of fact we ourselves rode the most of the way, our host insisting upon walking by our side.

CHAPTER XXIII.

A Wedding at the House of Goodman "John Miles — Description of Bride s and Bridegroom s Dress — The Marriage Ceremony — Throwing the Garter — Situation of the Miles' Homestead — Historic Sketch of John Miles — Visit at the home of Thomas Flint Esquire, His Official Duties — As Assistant — As Commissioner — Early Colonial Law Books — Primitive Courts and Court Practices — Talk Relative to Servants.

DURING the ride our conversation was about the river and its meadows, both of which subjects were interesting to us, inasmuch as the river meadows were found to be not only a means of reliance for food for the stock, but to some extent a quasi means of value or basis upon which to establish the "minister's rates," the division of upland, and rights in commonage, as of planting fields, public pasturage, and the taking of timber trees from forest reservations.

Long before we had exhausted the subject of our conversation we found ourselves at the Rice homestead, and as we entered the lane that led to it we saw that like others it had passed through the pioneer stage and that the log cabin of the first years had given place to a substantial frame structure, with commodious outbuildings.

We received as usual a hospitable welcome, and after supper gathered about the cheerful hearth and spent the evening in pleasant conversation upon things pertaining to the settlement of the town and its future prospects and the family history of our host, which history in brief outline is as follows:

Richard Rice went to Concord at an early date, and first erected a small house at the center, near which he planted an orchard. He lived on the present Walden street, and his house came within the south quarter, but was considered in the territorial apportionment as in the east quarter. He had John Adams for a neighbor, and the two dwelt in the vicinity of the present almshouse.

In 1684, Richard Rice testified with William Buttrick and others as to the purchase of Concord territory from the Indians, giving his age at that time as 72. The name has long been familiar in Concord, and some bearing it have been conspicuous in the town's annals. The name was also a prominent one among the first settlers of Sudbury and Marlboro, and as these towns are in close proximity, it may be difficult to decide to which ancestor all of the descendants belong. Richard Rice died June 9, 1709, being accounted, the record alleges, more than one hundred years old.

After a night of refreshing rest we arose early, and spent the forenoon in strolling about the neighborhood, seeing new objects and gathering some additional data for future reference.

After dinner we prepared for the wedding, and as the time for a start to the Mileses drew near, plans were made for the conveyance of each member of the household.

Goodman Rice and his wife were to go on horseback with the pillion; another horse was provided for us, and it was left with the hired man to so seat the ox cart that it would accommodate all the rest. We drove out of the yard together, but those on horseback soon outstripped the others, so that soon the rattle of the cart and the "gee-up and hishhaw" of John were no longer heard. A half hour more brought us into that part of the south quarter that has long been known as the "nine acres" and identified with the homesteads of some of the Wheelers and Mileses and is situated at that corner of Concord which borders the Sudbury town line.

The house was illuminated for the occasion by the light of several fire-places and many candles. Some of the latter were in brightly burnished brass candlesticks, a part of which had been borrowed of the neighbors, others in the more common kind, while a half dozen were set in a candle beam. Goodman Miles met us in the yard, his man took our animals, and soon we were within, welcomed by a score or more, among whom were several of our new acquaintances. By early nightfall the guests had all come, and only awaited the arrival of Mr. Thomas Flint, whom the court had "appointed to join persons in marriage," no clergyman being permitted to do it.

And now as we wait, it is a good time to describe the dress. Both the bride and the groom were attired as richly as the law of the land with its limitations to vain display, and their moderate circumstances would allow.

The bride wore a neatly-fitting gown of pale pink "calamanco" (good substantial woolen material), beneath which was a white petticoat bordered with orris (fine lace) the edge of which just showed above a pair of high-heeled shoes, which were fastened at the instep with a bunch of ribbons.

A sacque of blue, with "inkle," (a delicate braid), was characterized by a single slash in each sleeve, being all that the law would permit, and just showed the linen garment beneath, which the law required should be sufficiently long to admit no undue exposure of the bare arms. Her hair was bedecked with a sprig of evergreen, in which was entwined a small cluster of bright berries of wild bitter sweet, making a contrast with her dark hair that was beautiful.

The bridegroom was correspondingly attired. His duffel coat stood out at the skirts in true colonial style, and upon its top rested a snow-white ruff, which was starched with an excessive stiffness and tied at the front with tiny tasseled strings. Beneath the coat was a silk and woolen waistcoat and the small clothes, which were fastened at the knees with bright but not costly buckles to a pair or somewhat gay stockings made up a costume which though not extravagantly expensive was picturesque.

Not long after the time set for the ceremony Mr. Flint drove into the yard, accompanied by a servant. As he entered the house he explained that his delay was occasioned by an afternoon call from one of the "Assistants" from Boston, who was on his way to Sudbury town to aid in settling an ecclesiastical dissension which had arisen there concerning a "stinting of the cow commons," which difficulty the colonial court had been called upon to adjust.

Soon the contracting parties "stood up," and the " Commissioner," with a gravity of countenance commensurate with the solemnity of his sentences, spent a few moments in an attempt to impress all present with a true sense of the greatness of the event and the importance of entering upon the matrimonial state with a due regard to its sanctity and a resolve to live up to its requirements with an unswerving fidelity. He said, drawing closer to the bride, "Love is the sugar to sweeten every condition in the married state," and exhorted each to cultivate it and not let their ardor grow cold.

After this hortatory exercise he offered prayer; and the parson, Peter Bulkeley, " improved the occasion" by saying some things corroborative of what had been said

129

and cautioned all to be circumspect and to cultivate those graces which would fit them for any condition.

After these things the main issue was attended to, and the couple were pronounced man and wife. Immediately after this, servants, some of them belonging to the neighbors, brought in the "sack posset," a beverage that was usually drank on marriage occasions, yet, as we were told, without " noisy revelry."

For edibles there was the usual country course for colonial times, conspicuous among which was the bride's cake. After the wedding meal was partaken of, merrymaking was in order, which, as in modern times on similar occasions, was made up of such things as pertained to a pleasurable bantering of the bridegroom and bride.

Soon the "garter" by some mysterious agency was obtained and thrown out, and the scramble for it by the eager company indicated how much the person who finally possessed it prized the good luck it was supposed to bring.

During the evening while others were engaged in the festivities, we sought an acquaintance with several families whom we had not before met, among whom were the Bloods and Heals from the extreme north quarter, and we accepted an invitation from Goodman Blood to visit him the following week. We were also introduced to Mr. Flint, and were soon engaged in an animated conversation concerning his large estate and his duties as a colonial official. As our interview was suddenly interrupted by the great commotion caused by casting the garter and the subsequent scramble for it, Mr. Flint kindly invited us home with him, that we might continue our talk in the quiet ride through the woods, and on the morrow look about his estate, see his family and become acquainted with that portion of the south quarter in which he dwelt. We accepted most gladly the invitation, and explanations having been made to the Rices and to Timothy Wheeler, we bade the Miles's good-night and departed, carrying with us the pleasantest of recollections.

It was with regret that we left the Miles domicile in the midst of the nuptial merry-making, for we were beginning to feel young again in the midst of so much hilarity and exuberance of spirit; besides, we were feeling quite at home there, for everything we heard about the family had been fully corroborated by what we saw.

The house was the first one built upon the spot, and had been erected by John Miles, a pioneer grantee, who was in Concord in 1640. His first house lot which consisted of three acres was in the center, but later he left it and went to the " nine acres," where, with some of the Wheelers for neighbors, he opened a clearing and set up a home which has long been identified with his name.

The spot selected for his homestead was picturesque. It was in a close of nine acres, which in process of time came to be called the "nine-acre corner," and the term is surely no misnomer, since the plot of land thus termed is literally cornered by two streams, the river and gulf brook.

John Miles married for his first wife Sarah, who died in 1678, leaving one daughter, who married Edmund Wigley, and afterwards Joseph Lee. He married in his old age Susannah Redit. He left John, Samuel and Mary. John married Mary Prescottin 1702, and died October 23,1725, leaving an estate of £1,768 and two sons, John and Jonathan, the latter being a graduate of Harvard College.

Samuel, son of the first John, was a deacon in the Concord Church, and died March 13, 1756, leaving as children Samuel, Joseph, Sarah, Ezekiel, Esther, Martha,

Nathan, Reuben and Charles, the latter of whom was a captain in the Revolutionary war.

It was arranged beforehand that the servant who accompanied Esquire Flint should remain overnight with Mr. Miles' hired man that we might have the use of his horse.

The moon was low when the bars were dropped for our egress from the short lane that led out to the country road.

The air was balmy and the night was still, save as when we neared the river was heard the quacking of a flock of belated ducks, who were taking advantage of the bright moon to move a little farther south before the Indian summer was over. Now and then there was also heard the soft tread of a surprised fox as he suddenly turned for a safe retreat upon hearing us. Once a buck stalked so near that our horses stopped; and as we turned the bend of the pond and were about descending the hill, at a point where the evergreen tips almost came together over the road, there clumsily crossed our pathway a large, lumbering form, looking so unshapely as it loomed up in the shadows that Mr. Flint's horse, which was a little ahead of ours, for we were too timid to ride alongside, suddenly sheered and pranced, while ours almost unseated us.

Mr. Flint exclaimed that we had encountered a bear, but that bruin being without cubs was perfectly harmless, and our only fear need be for our horses, as the uncouth appearance of bears and their shambling gait was to them a matter of suspicion. Soon after this little episode we approached the Flint homestead and knew by its looks that a warm welcome awaited us; for, although the hour was late, there was a light in the front windows and the bright fire gleamed cheerily from the half-open door of the kitchen, where a servant stood looking and listening. Once within, we saw steaming upon the crane a large teakettle, and standing between the andirons, whose great brazen tops reflected the crackling flames, a skillet of broth. A beaker of hot cordial was at once offered us with a bowl of the broth, but we took only the latter, saying it would answer both for food and drink.

After being thus warmed and refreshed, we were shown to our lodging place, which of course was the guest chamber, and being at the house of Mr. Flint, "Commissioner" and a "man of means," it was unusually capacious. Next morning we were astir early, but none too early, for in families that were "well to do" slothfulness was in no wise encouraged, and it was the custom soon after sunrise for the hired men to "go afield." The same punctiliousness regarding the daily religious observances was noticeable here as elsewhere, for Mr. Flint opened the leather covered lids of the well-worn Bible and read in true patriarchal style, while the family reverently listened. Breakfast and devotions over, our host led us into his private room, which in modern times would be called an office. On an antique table were a bunch of unsharpened goose quills, a capacious ink horn, some unruled paper of coarse quality, a stick of sealing wax and a seal stamp. For books, there was a work of comments on the English law, "Coke on Littleton," and an old volume of "Notes on the Pentateuch." There was also a pile of letters folded and fastened with red sealing wax in readiness to be delivered to the first person going to Boston; for mail matter was only transmitted by such trustworthy travelers as might chance to come along.

After making a record of the marriage just consummated, Mr. Flint seated himself by the fireside, and in response to our inquiries, defined his duties as an "Assistant" and a magistrate. We found that the functions of the former were highly honorable, and that aforetime they were of a nature legislative, executive, and judiciary; and there being but a dozen Assistants in the Bay colony, only a few towns could boast of one. So important was the office, at the first, that the Assistants could choose a Governor and Deputy Governor out of their own body, and make laws which later only the General Court could do; also while formerly they had to do with the making of freemen, or in other words, empowering the Colonists to vote, this now could only be done by the Court. But though the office had been stripped of some of its prerogatives, it was one of the most conspicuous in the colony, and the possessor of it was in a position of great influence. In a certain sense the Assistants were still the Councilors of the Commonwealth, assumed the name of Magistrates, and were looked up to with great reverence. They were chosen by the people, and because of traditional associations and still existing authority, they took a first rank in society. As to the work of Mr. Flint as a "Commissioner to end small causes" within the territory to which he was specifically appointed his sphere was more circumscribed. His jurisdiction extended over Sudbury and Concord only, and the causes were limited to such as had an issue of not over twenty shillings. But even with these restrictions there was considerable scope for authority, since he might act as judge, juror, and barrister, and also furnish the law, the authorities for the latter being extremely few and meager, as is shown by the following enactment in 1647: "It is agreed by the Court, to the end we may have the better light for making and proceeding about laws, that there shall be these books following procured for the use of the Court from time to time: 'Two of Sir Edward Cooke upon Littleton; two of the books of entryes; two of Sir Edward Cooke upon Magna Charta; two of the New Terms of the Law; two Dalton's Justice of Peace; two of Sir Edward Cooke's Reports.'" Those books furnished the first foundation of law not only for the General Court, but for all others.

Curious incidents are related as taking place in these early courts. Sometimes there was interference which at present may appear incredible and it is said that those who intermeddled most were clergymen. An instance is recorded in an action of alleged slander brought by a minister against a layman. Another minister dining with the judge stated to him that when the case was tried he would like to make a few remarks. When the plaintiff's counsel had opened the case, he began questioning the plaintiff, and the regular proceedings were suspended until the reverend gentleman was through. At the close of the argument for the defendant, the accommodating justice gave the clergyman another chance, whereupon he begged the magistrate to dismiss the action, which he forthwith did.

In another instance one juror, who was standing out against the eleven others, was especially interviewed by the state's advocate and directed as to what to do. When the obstinate man refused to obey, it is said he was starved into compliance, while his fellows received meat and drink; it being remarked that it was better one man should be destroyed than eleven.

It is said that verdicts were sometimes rendered to the effect that there was "strong ground for suspicion though falling short of proof"; in such case the Court might sentence the defendant for such crime as it appeared probable he had committed, though it had neither been alleged in the complaint nor found by the jury. It is recorded that "a man indicted for forgery which could not be proven was reported by the jury to be a cheat and had to stand upon the court-house steps for half an hour with the forged bond and the word 'Cheat' in large letters pinned upon his breast."—Boston Bench and Bar.

Our conversation was interrupted by a call to dinner, which we were glad to hear, for the odor from the kitchen suggested something delicious for us. In the afternoon we set out to attend the funeral at the house by the Darby bridge. As Mr. Flint was to be busy, he sent his servant to accompany us. We rode on horseback, single file, along the way "that goeth to Mr. Flint's," till if merged in the county road, where there was less need of watchfulness for roots and rocks, and where we could ride abreast of each other.

As we walked our horses through the roadway, we had a chat about servants, a subject we had been seeking an opportunity to converse upon before. The man was intelligent and also communicative, so we received some valuable hints which led us to conclude that in colonial times there was but little difference either in intelligence or pedigree between some who worked for hire and some who did not; moreover, the term servant was sometimes used differently from what it is now, and might designate one who transacted business for another as an agent. Some denominated servants in a ship's passenger list might be coming to America to act for parties in England in land matters, or to substitute for them as settlers, thereby enabling the principal to share in land allotments, or in any profit that might accrue from the enterprise.

It is also supposed that some in the passenger lists who were recorded as servants were only ostensibly such for the purpose of disguising themselves, the intent being to evade the unjust immigration laws. As England was at that time agitated by religious and political dissension, there was unusual surveillance over its outgoing population, and permits were not easily obtained; hence the occasional resort to strategy.

An apprentice was considered a servant, and as such was obligated to his master for from three to seven years. He might have come from one of the best families, the old homestead not being sufficient to support several sons. A child during non-age was really a servant, unless he "bought his time" of his father, which was often done. Others might be servants for a term of years by agreement.

Over all servants the master was supposed to maintain a quasi-control, and the law looked to him as a sponsor for their good conduct and expected such watchfulness and wholesome tutelage as was reasonable. Among early town records we find the appointment of certain persons "for to take pains for to see into the general families in town, to see whether children and servants are employed in work and educated in the ways of God and in the ground of religion according to the order of the General Court." In later times the term servant was made to include African slaves, some of whom were in Concord.

CHAPTER XXIV.

Funeral at the House of a Cottager — Absence of Floral Tributes and Artificial Adornments — Sad and Simple Services— The Burial — The Procession to the Grave—Talk with the "Saxton" in the Burying Ground—Early Colonial Funeral Customs — The Bearers, Mort Cloth, Mourning Gloves, Scarfs and Rings — Grave Stones and Epiphs — Start for the Flint Homestead—Evening Adventure by the Way — The Strange Surprise — A Pleasant Discovery — Entertained by Nantatucket and Tissansquaw.

BY the time we had reached the foregoing conclusions we were on the Darby bridge and the house of the poor cottager appeared in sight. It was unpretentious with a low roof, and the thatching so drooped below the two diminutive windows as to give it an appearance of being even smaller than it was.

There was a porch covered with wild clematis, and on either side of the path leading to it were several clumps of lilies and pinks, while in the open yard were the blighted stalks of several hollyhocks. There was a garden nearby in which were still green the leaves of parsnip, cabbages and carrots, but all else had a sterile and withered look quite in keeping with our errand. We knew before we reached the place that the funeral was to be held there, for we saw people standing about as if waiting for something; and just outside the door stood the grewsome bier, covered with a pall or "buryin' cloth."

As we entered we found the room full of people, for it appeared as if everybody from the South quarter was there, besides some from outside. The coffin lay on a table in the narrow entry way, and was made of coarse pine boards, stained dark, giving it a still more somber appearance.

On the lid was a piece of paper giving the name and age of the deceased, which each one picked up and read as he passed by. Not a flower was in sight — no, not so much as an evergreen spray or myrtle sprig to remind the mourners of a coming resurrection, when fresh with an immortal youth they could again see their dead. Every aspect was of death; and as the cold gray of that autumnal afternoon with its low circling sun brooded over the cottage, it was all in accord with the coffin, the bier and the pall, and the sad company standing about them. Presently it was whispered that the clergyman was coming, and then all settled into that solemn hush which had deference both for the living and the dead, broken only by the deep breathing of the sorrowful and the responsive sigh of such as were in sympathy with them.

No Scripture was read at that house of sorrow; no psalm was sung; no prayers were said; and after a few words of consolation, and all present had viewed the remains, even little children being raised up to look at them, the bearers placed the coffin upon the bier, covered it with the cloth and lifting it upon their shoulders, started for the burying ground. We joined the procession. The cloth was kept in place by extra bearers, who walked along by the side of the others, spelling them when tired.

After moving with slow and measured step a quarter of a mile or more, they halted and set the body on a mortstone, while the first set of bearers gave way to the others.

In a few moments the procession resumed its mournful march, and after several similar halts it reached the grave yard, just as the slant beams of the fast setting sun were trying to stretch themselves beyond the little meeting house.

The burial was performed in silence; the cold earth rattled harshly upon the coffin; and when all was over and the "saxton" had heaped the last turf upon the newly made mound, each turned sorrowfully away as if carrying with him fresh evidence of his own mortality.

We lingered about the spot for a little time, thinking to learn from the old "saxton" something more about old burial rites; for this faithful public servant, although it was late, appeared in no hurry to get away, but leisurely folded up the burying-cloth and wiped his clumsy spade on the clean grass, as if to have it in good order when he should want it again.

The wind had gone down, and the moon was just creeping over the great fields to the easterly, and as there was no dampness on that dry knoll there was no discomfort in remaining, while John, the servant, had a loose shoe fastened at the smithy.

It would not take long to relate what the "saxton" told us, but after he had gone there came up the hill path one of the villagers, who was accounted handy at funerals and in laying out the dead, looking for a glove which someone had lost, and from him we obtained some valuable information relating to burial customs. And now before leaving this subject we will state some facts concerning these. In Colonial times there were few religious services at funerals; and but little was said in public, either to mitigate grief or lead to resignation. The coffin was carried to the grave and buried in silence.

Letchford says of it: "All the neighborhood or a goodly company came together at the tolling of the bell". The minister was commonly present, but only as a silent witness. As was the custom in England, laudatory verses were sometimes fastened to the bier or "herse" as the draped platform upon which the coffin rested was called. The funeral carriage called "hearse" was not then in use.

After the funeral printed verses were often procured, and the slips on which they were printed were decorated with black borders, skull and crossbones, a scythe and hour glass. Occasionally an attempt was made to solemnly pun in verse or play facetiously upon a name in a way that might be almost painful to people of the present time.

As a rule there were two sets of "bearers," one called under bearers, usually young men who carried the bier, and the other old men or relatives, who held the corners of the pall; if the distance was long there was a double number of under bearers. The pall or mort-cloth was usually made of velvet and owned by the town. The bier was often kept in the porch of the meeting house, but in some cases it was left standing over the grave awaiting another funeral.

Sometimes there was no regularly appointed grave digger, but a friend or relative of the deceased might perform this service. In some towns the news of a death was the signal for the cessation of all work. Liquors were universally used, and even if the deceased were a pauper, gallons of rum and a barrel of cider might be called for, but if a person of distinction the expense was correspondingly greater. The custom was to look at the corpse and then pass on to the table and take a drink.

Mourning gloves and scarfs were often given. Sometimes there were printed invitations to "follow the corpse," and great care was taken to have all walk in the proper order with respect to relationship and rank. The mourning gloves were usually furnished by the bereaved family, if in well-to-do circumstances, and a minister after a long pastorate usually had in store a large number. It is said that one Boston minister received in thirty-two years, two thousand, nine hundred and forty; being more than he wanted he exchanged them for other goods.

"Mourning rings," engraved with skull and crossbones, were sometimes given to bereaved friends and not infrequently they were quite costly.

Funerals were forbidden to be held on Sunday. Many of the gravestones came from England and were of hard black slate from North Wales. The Welsh stones usually had on them a death's head or that of a winged cherub. Weeping willows and urns came in vogue later, and these were afterwards superseded by the hour-glass and clock face or dial. Capital letters were used in inscriptions till the time of the Revolution.

The epitaphs were sometimes curious to a remarkable degree, as for example:
Here lies cut down like unripe fruit
The wife of Deacon Amos Shute.

There was often the manifestation of great resignation, showing the strong and simple faith of the bereaved friends.

They looked upon death as a liberator from care and toil, and believed it was the entrance to a blessed immortality; hence a bier or burying ground savored of blissful associations: and this accounts for such expressions as that of Judge Samuel Sewall who, after visiting the family tomb and seeing the coffins therein, said: "It was an awful yet pleasing treat:" and of another, that the two days wherein he buried his wife and son were "the best he ever had in the world."

In the twilight we passed from the place of old graves and descended the narrow pathway that led to the "little strate strete", and as we emerged from the shade into the open ground, where it broadened out toward the milldam and town pound, we beheld over the western horizon some of those purple and pink tints which are in striking contrast to the approaching darkness.

Here we thought is a fit illustration of the settler's experiences as relates to such somber scenes as we have just witnessed. He sees light in every condition, however gloomy it may appear to others. That light is his faith. Through it comes his steadfastness in sorrow, his submissiveness in view of death, and his apparent indifference to consolation afforded by external objects. He needs no flowers at his funerals, hence he has none. He desires no burnished trimmings to his coffin, neither does he care for any costly paraphernalia to his grave carriage. If he had these he would look above and beyond them all for his comfort.

The primary design of the absence of ceremony on these occasions was to steer clear of everything that savored of popery. The rude and grewsome decorations on the tombstone were designed only to remind the careless passerby that he too was mortal and must share the common lot.

The darkness deepened. The sluggish mist of the mill pond was settling about us. An east wind suddenly springing up brought from the place of old graves the murmur of pines and the rustle of tree branches. As it was Saturday night an unwonted stillness prevailed about there.

The mill had stopped, the cattle were housed, the roads were vacant, and nothing was seen or heard in the vicinity except the monotonous roaring of the water at the milldam as it fell over the splashboards, and the occasional lone bellowing of an impatient yearling in the town pound.

For an instant we stood motionless, as if to realize where we were, and then it suddenly occurred to us that John only went to get a shoe fastened, and that the time for him to return was passed.

We looked in the direction of the south bridge, if perchance we could see him, but in vain. We turned towards the Meriam grocery, thinking some errand might have called him there; but it was in vain, for no one appeared, and we were about sitting down on the turnstile that guarded the path to the meeting house, when we heard the measured tread of a horse's hoofs, and it flashed upon us that John had gone home, and was even then jogging along over the planks of Potter's bridge in the comfortable assurance that we had walked along expecting him to overtake us.

It needed but little reflection to understand the seriousness of the situation. We were left, and John would have to return for us on finding we were not at home on his arrival. Were it not for this our way would have been clear, for we had only to repair to Goodman Heywood's, or the Buss Tavern or call at the parsonage to be sure of a welcome. But to have John come all the way back was out of the question. Neither would we alarm the family by a night's absence. So springing over a brush fence and breaking off a dry sapling which, the last spring, had been placed there as a part of a "sufficient fence", which the town ordered, we started.

We had not gone far, however, before we wished ourselves back. The country was strange to us. The path in the dim moonlight was ill defined because of the overhanging branches, and every now and then we stumbled over a rock or a protruding root. As we got farther from the village the way grew more and more dreary.

The lights faded in the distance, and the last one seen through a break in the woods was the faint glimmer of John Adams' firelight as it shone forth through his open doorway when he entered after the evening cattle foddering. No sooner had the last light vanished than difficulties began to thicken. The shrubbery crowded closer into the pathway, so we had sometimes to brush back the drooping birches and hazel bushes laden with the night damp, and every now and then when wood ways parted from the main road, it was necessary to stoop in order to discover if possible the footprints of John's horse.

As the stillness of the forest became more and more apparent in the deepening gloom, and its dreariness became more intense, the denizens of the woods became more demonstrative.

Several times there came to us the low call of a coon, which was quickly answered by another in a minor key, as if amicable relations were not being maintained by them. The surly cry of something which by a subsequent description we concluded was a snarling lynx was once heard, and the sound was so new to us that we thought of the spectral wolf, of whose midnight marauding we had heard at the Baker husking party.

Another startling, though harmless episode, was the flying of a large hoot owl so near us as to fan our faces with his furry wings.

But in spite of these impediments we kept on, intent upon putting as much space as possible between us and the hamlet before John should meet us.

It was not however given us to get far in carrying out our intent, for still other obstacles were to arise, the climax of which was reached when we arrived near the pond.

We had heard legends connected with the Concord ponds and especially this one. How that spirits flitted over it, and even stalked forth upon its lone shores, and that wood nymphs danced about and sometimes allured timid and incautious travelers into the deep woods.

The recalling of these and other stories of a like nature was a poor preparation for passing the pond, which was now but just ahead, and remembering that nothing but a Bible in one's pocket or a silver bullet from a gun barrel would avail anything in case of an assault by the Evil One, we dropped our staff, which we had carried for a defense, and resolved to trust to our heels in case anything should occur out of the usual.

We had reviewed all our legendary lore concerning the pond and knew by the damp murky atmosphere that it was close at hand, when with startling suddenness there came a weird and melancholy sound as if the very woods uttered a wail. We stopped. Our hair bristled and we listened spellbound. A moment and it came again, and nearer than before, and we believed that the next it would be in the road.

We had heard forest sounds of every nature before, as we supposed, from the low night call of the little wood bird to the deep booming of the lank bittern, but here was a noise entirely new and incomparable to anything else.

Our first thought was to turn back and quickly put ourselves as far as possible from the locality if not from the source of so dismal and frightful a sound. We had never practically believed in ghosts, and as for spirits we had never seen one nor met with one who we supposed had.

Our theories were of the age in which we lived. But we were in another age now, and we had been sitting beside ancient firesides and listening to gruesome tales by those in whose houses were old garrets, and in whose cellars were dark archways, and along whose winding woodland paths the shadows chased each other gloomily, sometimes taking strange shapes, and over whose low gables the clouds lowered scowlingly. We had been sitting where the wind whistled down old chimney stacks, and where groups instinctively drew the settle near to the hearth's edge and listened timidly to the mystical wiseacre as he interpreted strange sounds, until no one cared to go upstairs or down stairs or step outside. In fact we had been living amid a different environment, one in which every predilection to a belief in the supernatural had been thoroughly aroused, and we only needed the present evidence of our senses, together with what we supposed had been an exhaustive observation of all of nature's strange sights and noises, to lead us to abandon old conclusions and accept new ones.

In fact we learned by this sudden experience that it is the objects around which superstitions cluster which differ, rather than the nature of the persons who are influenced by them, and that it is by an easy transition through the pathway of circumstances that we come to believe in the goblin of the quaint old burying ground, the elf of the woods or the latest product of modern spiritism.

The nomenclature of an age may disguise its real beliefs, and the character of the homes of the living may determine the character of the spirit tenantry.

In other words, the nature of a genuine New England apparition is such that it would never be seen flitting about among the flowers of a modern cemetery. Its nature is too rugged to live there. Like the white polar bear it requires cold and barrenness, where folks shiver and seldom go.

Given right conditions and it may come to you. It loves the cobwebs beneath low rafters, and the smell of mice among old cradles and empty meal barrels. It would browse among bunches of brown herbs and squeak forth its magical utterances, where the wind plays through angular knot-holes and blows the light out if anyone enters.

These conditions withheld and those of an opposite character substituted, and you have an up-to-date tenantry, and one that is coy and cultured, and is at home in the presence of the velvet carpet and satin paper, stuffed couches and chairs.

But they are all of the same kith and kin, it matters not where we find them, whether on the public platform or in the drawing room, or by "the way that goeth to Mr. Flint's." Let it not then be thought foolish that our hair started, and that we were stirred to our very extremities by that startling, inexplicable wail that came from pondward.

We were in Rome doing as the Romans did, and our first thought and impulse was to flee from the swamp sprites without stopping to question what they were.

Pursuant to this purpose we turned about when we saw in the direction whither we were going a flash of light, or rather the illumination of reflected light, as if cast up by an unseen fire in the brush wood.

Here was a new development, only little less surprising than the first, since we thought it might be a part and parcel of it, for almost simultaneous with the strange sight came a succession of the strange sounds, this time as if they would split the very darkness which they pierced.

We were brought to a standstill; we could neither retreat nor go forward. It was peril before us and peril behind us and peril on both sides.

As we stood wondering with what little there was left of us to wonder, and waiting for another outburst of the terrific wail, we saw under the low hemlock boughs a couple of upright forms, which under other circumstances we should have called human, but which looming up as they did in the shadows and amid its lurid light we thought had the appearance of something inhuman. They looked like Indians, and were dressed like them, a fact which only increased our dread of what they might be, for we were aware that supposed manifestations from the spirit world were made by Indians, hence naturally we thought it might be so now.

Just as we were about settling ourselves into a clump of evergreens, whose friendly branches almost touched the dilapidated top of an ancient windfall, this being the only available hiding place, one of the forms turned toward us, and we saw at a glance, and to our great surprise and delight that it was no other than Nantatucket whom we met at Nashawtuck; and that his companion was Tisansquaw, whom we once saw at the lower fishing falls.

In an instant we were ourselves again, for in these we knew we had friends, and that whether the sounds we had heard were of man or devil they would be explained, and if the situation was serious we would share it together.

As we sprang forward the Indians recognized us, and their greeting was as warm and demonstrative as their rude ways and stolid natures would admit of. It took but a moment to inquire concerning the sound, and to be informed that what we had heard was a pair of migratory loons, or great northern divers, which in the fall and spring occasionally drop into our New England waters, where they remain a few days prior to their journey southward. They had been disturbed among the low water brush on the pond shore by the fire and had sent out their wild screams as if in protest.

No one need wonder at our recent alarm, for the notes of this remarkable bird at any time sound strange, but stranger yet in the night's stillness, with the medium of a dense, swampy atmosphere to intensify them.

We were soon sitting by the camp fire of our two friends, which was just outside the bushes, by the pond's edge, beyond which was the dark, outlying water where the loons were.

We learned that Nantatucket and Tisansquaw had been to Natick, to attend an Indian service held there by Apostle John Eliot, and that being late in getting home, and growing hungry, they had encamped beside the pond and were engaged in broiling a rabbit, which they had thrust through with a wooden spit.

CHAPTER XXV.

Arrival at the Flint Farm — Sunday Morning in a Home of Colonial Concord— Start for Meeting — Gathering of the Worshipers — Neighborly Inquiries — The Church Service — The Sermon — Singing — The Noon Intermission — Catechistical Exercises — Afternoon Service — Colonial Church Customs — Sacred Music — Succession of Sinking Books —"Lining Off"— Triple Time — "Fuging" — Pitch Pipes — Introduction of Musical Instruments — Talk with Goodman James Hosmer — Conversation Relating to the Installation of Rev. Peter Bulkeley — Facts of History Concerning this Subject.

JUST as Nantatucket had drawn the spit from the rabbit and placed it upon a broad flake of clean bark, which Tisansquaw had pealed from a birch tree, we heard the clatter of horses' feet, and knew that John was coming. It was with regret that we closed our interview with our swarthy friends for we could have contented ourselves to remain with them over night, but we knew that the next day was the Sabbath, and that all traveling was forbidden, and that even the short journey to the Flint farm, though undertaken with so good an excuse, might subject us to great prejudice, so we sprang into the empty saddle and were soon away.

We received a warm welcome on our arrival. Supper had been delayed awaiting our return; after which Mr. Flint gathered the household together, including the servants, for no servant was omitted in this exercise, and opening the Bible, read and commented upon it, being assisted by his "Notes on the Pentateuch."

After reading, each of the family was catechized, and all showed such a commendable acquaintance with the Holy Scriptures as might put to blush many a youth and adult also in a Sunday school of today, with all their so-called "Lesson Helps" and "Side Lights." After the religious exercises were over, and the younger members had retired, Mr. Flint and myself conversed upon several topics of public interest, and it was not until the low burning candle reminded us that it was getting late that we retired to our room there to enjoy another night of well-nigh perfect slumber.

The morning sun arose giving promise of a beautiful day. Not even a low-lying cloud was visible to show the possibility of unpleasant weather. But the quiet was without, for the noise down-stairs betokened that the Sabbath was not with them a day of indolent repose. It was but a short time after going below before breakfast was eaten, and the sun had hardly dried the night's moisture from the sparkling earth when we were all on our way churchward, passing over the same way which the night before had brought to us such discomfort. As we ascended the hill path to the meeting house, we found that the parson had not yet arrived, so, intent upon hearing the news from the whole countryside, we leaned up against an unused hitching post to look and listen.

After the usual salutations by each new comer, conversation commenced on the events of the week in their several quarters, as these related to things of a nature sufficiently serious to admit of Sabbath inquiry.

Goodwife Brown wanted to know if the "arbs" she sent Susan Ann, poor child, did her good, and if her pain was gone. Patty Underwood asked after the condition of old Aunt Lois, and whether the crutches which she had left at the mile post by the corner for Goodman Billings to carry to her were the right length. Dame Woods was anxious to know of the Darby boys, and if they had sufficient clothing for winter, for, said she, "Since their mother died they have fared hard."

With these and similar inquiries the time was occupied till someone said, "The minister is coming," when all stepped from the beautiful sunlight into the cool stillness of the sanctuary and remained standing till he had passed into the pulpit.

The service was opened by an invocation immediately followed by the reading of the Scriptures with comments.

Then came the singing of a psalm from "Sternhold and Hopkins' Edition," set to the tune of "St. David." The lining of the psalm was by Deacon Griffin, and the congregation endeavored to make the repetition of it musical and in accord with the tune assigned, but we observed that before the exercise was over there was a compromise between "St. David," "York" and "Old Winsor," and that the tune varied as much as the time. It was, however, evidently satisfactory to the worshippers, and the devout demeanor of every participant assured us that singing in those days was really worship.

It was noticeable that there were only a few copies of the Psalter in the congregation, which showed that lining off was a necessity. The sermon was exegetical, expository, doctrinal, and hortatory, with an application at the close, and occupied an hour. Psalm singing followed, and the service ended with the benediction.

At noon came the catechistical exercise, of which we had heard much but had not yet seen. We do not know whether or not on every Sunday it came at this hour, for we did not inquire, and the intermission the Sabbath previous being taken up with the sacramental service and a baptism, we have nothing to judge from.

We conjecture, however, that the noontime was its regular hour, because it was the only practicable time for it, and the one which in later days has been given to the Sunday school. If from nine or half past to twelve, and from one or half past to nearly four, was taken up with the regular service, almost of necessity, the catechistical would come between.

But whatever the hour, the nature and order of it was the same, and we will describe what we saw of it. There was a short interval after the morning service, in which the middle-aged men could stretch their legs and go to the Buss tavern and eat the lunch which they carried with them, and the younger women could repair to the houses nearby and warm their barley coffee or steep a little "store" tea, and the old people could go to one of the "noon houses" which were nearer at hand and replenish their foot stoves with coals and warm some cider or sack posset, the latter of which they brought with them, while the former was kept in storage to be had on tap.

This brief intermission was followed by a prompt gathering together at the drum beat, and a seating of the people in a way that had special reference to age, the younger and unmarried portion, who were the catechumens, being nearest to the minister. As in the morning, the sexes sat separate, except in the back seats, where the grave heads of households sat and where there was allowed a latitude of promiscuousness which would not be tolerated among the younger element.

There was no prelude, and when Parson Bulkeley arose there evidently ran through the younger portion that feeling of embarrassment which usually prevails on occasions of public examination; while upon the faces of the elders there was plainly depicted that flush of anxious suspense which betokened a deep desire that the children do well.

The questions were all simple and admitted of Scriptural answers. The purpose evidently was to inculcate a knowledge of the doctrines and duties taught in the Bible. A short intermission followed this exercise, when all assembled to listen to the second sermon, which consisted of a gathering up and application of the points brought out in the noon exercise, together with comments upon them.

As the order of the second service was similar to the first, we will not stop to note any change, but proceed to state a few facts of colonial church customs as related in history.

A singing book in common use was Ainsworth's, "Book of Psalms," printed in Amsterdam in 1612, of 348 pages.

It contained annotations and the tune in which each psalm was to be sung. The annotations explained the psalms, as for example, "The Leviathan is the great whale fish or sea dragon used to represent great tyrants."

The books were very few from which came the custom of lining off, called "deaconing." Judge Sewall said with regard to the harmony on a certain occasion, "I set York and the congregation went to St. David." Another writer says: "Not two persons quaver alike but each may drop off, alter, twist or change to suit him." Bye and bye the "Bay Psalm Book" came; then "Tate and Brady's Version."

When note singing was introduced, there came heart burnings, with assertions that it was popish. In process of time lectures were given in singing, from which may have been evolved the singing school; and by allowing those who had learned to sing by rule to sit in the front seats may have been evolved the choir.

After a while "triple time" tunes came into use. This gave offence to those who wanted to drawl out the notes in uniform length, and the time was derisively called "a long leg and a short one." Then came the style of singing called "fuging", introduced by Billings, which system spread like wild-fire.

Pitch pipes made of apple-tree wood were used at the first; afterwards, metallic tuning forks. In 1714, there came from England "a pair of organs," so called. It was given by Thomas Brattle to Brattle Street Church, Boston, but it was refused, and then it was given to King's Chapel, where, after remaining unpacked for several months, it was made use of.

The bass viol was about the first musical instrument used in the New England churches. Violins were opposed because they savored too much of dancing music. A compromise was made in some places by which the fiddle might be played if played the wrong end up, as in this way it could be called a small bass viol.

In Concord the version of "Songs and Hymns" by Sternhold and Hopkins was used prior to 1666. In 1775, it was voted to sing from Tate and Brady's version three months on trial. The June following Watt's version was introduced and used till 1828.

The singers were first "seated" about 1774, when the custom of lining ceased and the church voted that Deacon Wheeler should lead the singing one half the time and the singers in the gallery the other.

In 1779, the church took into consideration the "melancholy decay of singing in public worship and chose 20 persons who should sit together in the body pews below and take the lead in singing, the women to sit separate from the men."

As to the early catechistical service, Letchford's "Plain Dealing" mentions the church in Concord as the first one to adopt the custom of catechizing the children. Mather says, "This was one of the constant exercises of the Sabbath at the Concord church." He states further that "All the unmarried people were required to answer questions, after which expositions and applications were made to the whole congregation."

As the sun was fast settling behind the trees by the mill dam, we were descending the narrow hill path with Goodman James Hosmer, who had entertained us at his "noon house," and had there invited us to go home with him.

On the way to his house we had an opportunity for conversation on several subjects appertaining to the Concord settlement, about which we desired information, prominent among which was the installment and ordination of Rev. Peter Bulkeley. We had known something of these events, but not all.

Neither had we much knowledge of the history of the church; for as its records for the period since its establishment were wanting, one person's conjectures about this as well as about the civil history, were as good as those of another provided each followed the analogy of common procedure.

It was quite opportune that a subject of this nature was suggested, since it would hardly have been in keeping with the strict Sabbath observance of the time to discuss certain other matters.

We ascertained in the course of our conversation that some embarrassment attended the first installation at Concord; and as the subject is interesting we will give some facts as we have found them stated in history.

The church was organized July 5, 1636, and preparatory to the installation of Mr. Bulkeley a day of fasting and prayer was observed April 5, 1637. As usual, Colonial dignitaries from Boston, both civil and ecclesiastic, were invited to the council; for the state as well as the church were interested in clerical settlements and assumed to have a quasi-jurisdiction or influence over ministers although theoretically it might have denied it.

Not all, however, of the invited guests of either class were present, although delegates were there from most of the churches. Winthrop says, "The Governer and Mr. Cotton and Mr. Wheelwright and the two ruling elders of Boston and the rest of the churches which were of any note did none of them come to this meeting."

"The reason was conceived to be, because they counted these as legal preachers and therefore would not give their approbation to their ordination." A reason given for the Colonial absence of some of the notables was that the call came at too short notice, but as a matter of fact, it was sent three days beforehand.

It may not be proper at this late day to decide as to the force any informality about the letters missive may have had, for there may have been both law and fact in the case, of which we know nothing. This much, however, is certain, that controversy then prevailed concerning both doctrine and church polity. And as at that time Mr. Bulkeley was supposed to attach much importance to good works and was therefore considered a legal preacher, it might be natural for some to remain absent.

Besides the question of theological fitness for the clerical office there had arisen a question as to whether a minister ordained in England after the forms of the

144

Episcopacy could by this act be rightly recognized as a properly constituted clergyman.

Both questions were probably settled in the case of Parson Bulkeley, for the council ordained and installed him. And concerning the matter of church polity, one of the delegates proposed a question which led to a passing of the following resolution: "That such ministers as have been clergymen in England and ordained by the bishop were to be respected as having there legally sustained the office of minister by the call of the people, and such ordination was considered valid here; but, for having received this ordination by the bishop, they should consider it a sin and in this country they should not consider themselves ministers till called by the people; but when thus elected, they were to be considered ministers even before ordination."

It may be here stated that ministers who held to a covenant of works or who believed in the doctrine of the law rather than the doctrine of grace were known as "legalists", and those believing in the latter "antinomians."

CHAPTER XXVI.

Visit at the home of Goodman James Hosmer — — Reflections upon the Settler's Fireplace — Invitation to Humphrey Barrett's Log Rolling — Situation of the Hosmer Farm — Outline of Hosmer History — The Old House Site — Scenes at the Log Rolling — Early Forestry — Care of Concord's Poor — Process of Clearing New Lands — Facts Relative to the Barrett Family.

WE had just finished our subject when the home of our host appeared in an opening among the trees, and as we beheld it beyond the purple and yellow of the maples and willows, we thought that nothing we had seen in the settlement surpassed it in picturesqueness.

As we entered the yard we were met by his good wife, who had hastened out to tell her husband that James who was ill in the morning was better, after which she lost no time in saying that supper was ready.

After partaking of the evening meal we all seated ourselves about the cheerful hearth fire and chatted about various neighborhood matters and about some things Colonial. It was indeed a social season and scene. There was domestic and homelike business about everything.

The pale moonlight which streamed in from over the window sill was met at its entrance by such a fervid, animated light from the fire place that it was hardly perceivable and there was nothing whatever wanting to complete the fireside comfort.

So snug were our surroundings and so cheery was everything that we mentioned the fact to Goodman Hosmer and suggested that a settler's hearth was a place of great privilege. "Yes", he replied "it really is for we lay our plans there."

His last utterance made us thoughtful, and we pondered over it that night after the lights went out, as we looked over the still meadows and saw the stars twinkle and were impressed with the silence that pervaded everything; and were also reminded of the half-burnt black logs which were even then smoldering beneath the banked fires of the slumbering house-keepers ready to sparkle the next morning at break of day.

What, thought we, has the fireplace been to the settler? What part has it played in his history, and have we given it its due? These queries came to us in rapid succession and quickly responsive came the unqualified conclusion that the open fire had been a potent element in the development of colonial character. Fire is always a source of interest if not of inspiration when it is not really mischievous, and the poet has done well to sing about it, the philosopher to muse over it, and the pagan to eulogize it.

The fire of driftwood upon the ocean beach, the vivid reminder of wrecks on the dark waters, the tidings of which never come shoreward; the watch-fire of the lonely garrison, beyond whose glimmer none durst venture; the camp-fire in the forest where slow sentinels pace through night's stillness; and the fires in dark evergreens made by Indians — all these have their value and suitably impress one; but not any or all of them are comparable to the fire on the settler's hearthstone, where the flames are reflected up and among braids of corn and grey herbs and out upon pewter platters on the old dresser and into the corners of the great kitchen and over the broad floor boards.

Before the open fire was the settler's council chamber. Beside it was his children's nursery. There they laughed and played and popped corn while the fathers whistled and sang and cracked jokes. The settler's austerity was softened by the fireplace, and the hard lines of his exposed life were toned down. There he forgot his homely toil while the tea kettle sang and the flames crackled and the winds swept over the dry moorlands and vacant meadows.

Without his fireplace he might have been lonely, for stoves and furnaces could not have supplied the want of companionship that these did. The gentle motion of a fire upon the hearthstone is almost akin to the friendly presence of a human form.

Thoreau said of his hut in Walden woods when he gave up his fireplace, that though there was more warmth in a stove there was less company in it. The labor necessary for maintaining the open fire was another advantage. To obtain the requisite amount of fuel the settlers were obliged to spend a large part of the long winter in the woods, swinging the axe and ponderous beetle, for it was only by means of the beetle and wedges that he cleft in twain the gnarled oak and knotted hickory. Further time was spent in hauling it from the rugged hillsides and the frozen swamps. After it was hauled it was to be cut in the dooryard, then seasoned and housed, and by the time all this was accomplished the robins came. The amount of wood required for the open fire was enormous, for the fireplaces were very capacious and consuming, and the rude carpentry of the houses was such as to let in much cold.

If we can judge of the average fuel supply of the settler by the quantity sometimes stipulated for in the settlement of a minister we should conclude that from twenty to thirty cords would be required and sometimes more.

Moreover, the chimneys with their broad flues were health-giving. Through them in the night time, when the fires were low, pure oxygen came down, and there ascended upward every impurity, so that it was almost as if the inmates of the house lived in the open air.

The fireplaces might be from six to eight feet in width, in some instances even more. In this case the black log required the strength of two men to lift it into its place.

Between this and the forelog was heaped brush wood and chips and cleft pine, all to be enveloped in a grand pyramid of flame which went aroaring up the chimney as if mad, while into every corner and cranny of the great unfinished apartment the light danced and cheerily crept, and the warmth melted the frost on the small window panes and drove back the cold from under the door. Before such a scene the settler sat with his family, and the neighbors came and sat with them, and in the flames they thought they saw horsemen and in the ashes heard men walking as in snow.

When at the hour of retiring the flames faded and the spent fuel had become reduced to a bed of coals the householder covered them carefully with hot ashes to be used the next morning to start a new fire. If for any reason during the night the coals went out, some were borrowed, if a neighbor was near, but if not, they resorted to the flint, steel and tinder box, or to the use of a gun.

The settler's fireside has often been pictured in both prose and poetry, but perhaps by none more fitly than by Whittier in his poem called "Snow Bound", where in the following words he sets forth the cheer and snugness of the open fire in a winter's storm: We piled with care our nightly stack Of wood against the chimney back, — The oaken log, green, high, and thick, And on its top the stout back-stick

The knotted forestick laid apart, And tilled between with curious art The ragged brush; then, hovering near, We watched the first red blaze appear, Heard the sharp crackle, caught the gleam On whitewashed wall and sagging beam, Until the old rude furnished room Burst, flower-like into rosy bloom.

As it was near the sun setting when supper was over, Goodman Hosmer did not get through with his chores till early evening, and since we were quite weary with our Saturday night's escapade among the ghosts we talked but little and retired early. Before going to bed, however, we were informed that there was to be a neighborhood log-rolling over at Goodman Humphrey Barrett's the next day and as our host was going with his hired man he would like to have us accompany him. "Besides," said he, "Goodman Barrett sent a special invitation to you Saturday night and would have spoken to you about it at the meeting house had it not been Sunday."

A log-rolling in a new country was attractive. We had heard of such but never expected to be present. It was therefore with bright anticipations that we retired and awaited the morrow.

Before the "shell" sounded for breakfast, for Goodwife Hosmer blew a conch shell in some mysterious yet apparently easy manner at the kitchen door, we sat down at the raised window that overlooked the river course to consider the relative position of the Hosmer homestead to the central village. The outlook was a pleasing one and showed the taste and sagacity of Goodman Hosmer in his selection of the locality for a home.

In a northerly direction at a distance of a half mile more or less was Annusnac, forest crowned and symmetrical, standing like a sentinel beside the plain. To the westerly and southerly was the winding Assabet with its occasional clumps of yellow willows, while upon its channel as seen through a near clearing was just passing the canoe of Nipanum of Nashoba.

A flock of wild ducks were flying from river to river, and along with a couple of cows on the meadow was a small deer, all feeding together as if belonging to one family. It was a scene worth lingering upon, and so loth were we to leave it that we were a few minutes late at the breakfast table, with no better excuse than that we had been enraptured by what we had seen.

As the annals of the Hosmer family have been conspicuously connected with Concord and its members are many and widely scattered, let us leave our story and notice a few outline facts of their history as these have been preserved by record and substantial tradition.

The first progenitors of the Hosmer family in America were Thomas and James, who were brothers. Thomas Hosmer was at Cambridge as early as 1632 and went to Connecticut about 1635. James Hosmer with his wife Ann and two children left England in April 1635 and went to Concord in the following September. No record of the death of his wife is known to be extant, but it is known that his second wife was buried March 11, 1641, and that his third wife, Alice, died March 3, 1645. He had seven children, — Marie and Ann who were born in England; James, Mary, Stephen, Hannah and Mary.

James, the eldest son, married Sarah White who was a sister of the Rev. Joseph Rowlinson, minister of the church in Lancaster, Mass., and who was captured by the Indians in King Philip's war and ransomed at a place near Wachusett mountain in what is now Princeton. James was killed at the Sudbury Fight, April 21, 1675 Stephen,

148

his youngest son, married Abigail Wood in 1667. He had six children, among whom were James and Thomas. Thomas married in 1631, Prudence, a granddaughter of the first Abigail Wood Hosmer; and a son by this marriage was Hon. Joseph Hosmer, a noted patriot who was born December 25, 1735 and died Jan 31, 1821, aged 85.

An early house lot of the first James Hosmer, tradition informs us, was at the Central village on or near the residence of the late Hon. Samuel Hoar on the present Main street, near the Public Library. His next house lot was situated between the Assabet and the south branch of the Musketaquid rivers. It is stated that faint traces of the cellar hole are still visible and deeds of a portion of the original farm are still in possession of one of James Hosmer's descendants.

South west of the paternal estate was the home of James Hosmer, Jr., who was killed by the Indians at Sudbury. His house was near the present bridge of the Fitchburg Railroad a little to the eastward of the depot at Concord Junction. Formerly, a little stream nearby afforded sufficient water power for a small flax mill which the Hosmers owned and operated.

James Hosmer, Sr., added to his original land grant till his domain extended nearly to the "Nine Acres," and included various detached and outlying parcels of land. His grave is unknown; but probably is among many of his contemporaries in the Hill Burying Ground.

The site of the ancient homestead is now grass grown; only an earth dent remaining to identify it; and the surroundings are silent save as sounds come to it from afar or as Nature breaks into the stillness with song of bird or chirp of insect. But the associations to those who are conversant with them are eloquently suggestive and remind one of distant years when the elder James Hosmer drove his cattle to pasture and perhaps plodded on from this early morning-task to raise the gate of his little flax mill, thereby to furnish the prepared material for the fine linen of the town's folk.

It took but a short time after breakfast for the men to yoke up the oxen and start for the log-rolling. We met several other teams on the way, for everybody in the north quarter appeared to be going there, and there were some from as far south as Mr. Flint's. They were a lively company, and the great jargon of "Gee off, Buck!" and "Hish-haw, Star!" reminded us of hurried military orders and the long line of staid oxen, of an army mule train.

At length we reached the place and entered the enclosure, which was a large opening in the forest, where Goodman Barrett the year before had cut his fire wood and was now clearing to sow to rye. He had left on the ground the untrimmed branches as they had been cut from the logs and the cord wood, and these having become thoroughly dry during the warm season were now to be burned, thereby affording fertility to the soil and a clean surface to sow his rye upon. The men went to work lustily for there was much to be done. There were knotty trunks to be piled together; furrows to be ploughed around the field to prevent the fire from spreading; "windfalls" to be pulled apart and a few logs to be removed.

While this work was going on Goodman Barrett came to us with the request that we go home with him when the rolling was over. His genial countenance was a sufficient assurance that his home would be a hospitable one, and we cordially assented, whereupon we sat down upon a log and conversed about the early forests. The facts brought out were in full accord with the records, the substance of which is as follows: the settlers did not waste their timber trees, but passed laws for their protection; they even ordered, sometimes, that the trees by the wayside should not be cut down, but spared as shade for the cattle; people were restricted also from taking only a certain number of trees from the common land. A reason for this restriction may have been the scarcity of some kinds of trees, as the pine and oak, upon which they much relied for building purposes. The settler used no scantling stuff in his house frames; his work was massive and designed to stand and the great beams were hewn out of the "clear" tree trunks.

Probably the annual fires of the Indians set to clear the woods of underbrush had done much mischief to the timber lands and the common use of wood for fuel had greatly diminished the number of timber trees.

The subject of forestry naturally led us to inquire about the climate, and from what we learned we concluded there had been less change in it than many suppose. True we speak of the heavy snows when we were children, but we forget that a child has short limbs and that a comparatively shallow depth would appear great to us then. There are some records that give light on this subject. In one of the towns adjacent to Concord the town ordered that the fences should be put in proper condition early in March, and various things were to be done at a date which might indicate no great change in the temperature of the season.

While busy in conversation about the climate, Goodman Barrett was called away by one of the neighbors, saying as he left us that he might be gone an hour or more. We were not however to be left for so long a time alone, for he soon returned with the two sons of a poor widow, who, he afterwards told us, had applied to him for work, their mother being partially dependent upon what they could earn as farm hands. After setting them to work at the easy task of gathering into heaps the lighter brushwood, Goodman Barrett again seated himself on the log and we resumed our chat. Our conversation was on the subject of town charities, — this being suggested by the circumstance just alluded to.

We soon concluded that the town of Concord took care of its poor and on this point let us leave our story to present the following records. In 1645, William Halsted bequeathed "unto the poore of Concord fyve pound to be layed out in a Cow which I would have So ordered by the Deacons & my executors that it may be a continual help to such as are in need. God giving a blessing thereto."

In 1654, when a second land division was made, it was enacted "that all poore men of the Towne that have not commones to the number of foure shall be allowed so many as amounts to foure with what they all ready shall have till they are able to purchase for themselves and we mean those poore men that at the present are householders."

In the will of Robert Meriam who died in 1682, was the following clause, "I give to the poor of the Town of Concord four pounds in corn." Peter Wright, weaver who died Jan. 15, 1718, devised property to the town which was the origin of a fund for what were called the "Silent Poor." About noon the work ceased and all gathered in a corner of the clearing to eat their lunch, which had been supplemented by a pail of new milk and a firkin of "sack posset" which Goodman Barrett had provided.

It was a merry company in that clearing by the roadside, and when the noon hour was over and the work was resumed it was with many a cheery hallo and lively call. By mid-afternoon the task was completed and the field was ready to be burned over.

The log-rolling had brought together the dismantled tree trunks, and the dry branches which had been thrown upon them made the piles inflammable.

In rapid succession they were set on fire till all were ablaze and a great volume of smoke and cinders and sparks showed how efficient was the element of fire for clearing the fields for planting.

Before sunsetting the fires burned low, and the smoldering, grey ash heaps indicated the kind of fertilizer the settlers used in raising their winter rye and "guinny" wheat.

CHAPTER XXVII.

Invitation to visit the "Blood Farms" — Homestead of a "Borderer" or "Outdweller — Pastoral Visitation with Parson Bulkeley and Deacon Griffin — Religious Exercise at the house of Goodman Thomas Dakin— Use of Ardent Spirit — Possible Mistakes about Ministerial Drinking Habits — Social Standing of the Clergy — Safeguards against abusing Clergymen — Installation Dinners — Relation of Pastor to his Parish — The Dakin Family — Legend of Hidden Treasure.

WE met James Blood from the so called "Blood Farms", who with his men had come all the way from his home by the town's northern border to assist in this land clearing. We had met him the Sunday before at the meeting house and promised to visit him sometime. As he was urgent that we accompany him home after the "log-rolling" we acceded after obtaining the kind but reluctant consent of Goodman Barrett who had expected us to go home with him.

The sun was near setting when we started, and long before we reached our destination the darkness had so deepened that it was difficult to keep the narrow pathway. But little was said during the journey for the men had enough to do to manage the cattle, one yoke of which was but half broken, and all impatient to get to their stalls sprang forward by jerks so that we progressed with much unsteadiness. At length we saw in the distance a light and conjectured, because homesteads were scarce in that locality, that we were nearing our destination; which conjecture was confirmed by the hurrying team and by the announcement of James Blood that we were almost there.

A hired man met us as we approached the dwelling; the rattle of the wheels had brought the "women folks" to the door, and we were soon within, partaking of a settler's substantial supper. Of course there were the usual excuses about the menu, for human nature was then the same as now, and the same pride was manifested by the housekeepers as to their culinary skill; but we made a practical demonstration that the supper was all we could wish; and soon, the meal time ended and the table cleared, we were seated by the ample hearth-side for an evening chat.

We learned very much that evening concerning the life of "borderers", as the Blood settlers were called, because a part of their lands at least were supposed to only border on those of Concord township.

Among the conclusions arrived at from our conversation was that much hardship was experienced on account of their isolated condition and especially their distance from the central village of the township. It was a difficult journey to meeting; there were no near neighbors from whom to borrow if anything was needed; and whatever of accident or incident occurred there might be none to share in the joy or the grief. In short, to be a "borderer" was almost like colonizing a new country alone.

The main drawback to these "outdwellers," as they were sometimes called, was the anomalous attitude that they sustained in not being considered citizens of the town of Concord, while at the same time they were expected to pay "rates".

We did not ascertain whether it was the design of James Blood when he settled in this remote district to eventually make it a distinct municipality or only to occupy a land grant, but we concluded it was the latter.

After a long and interesting conversation we retired, and early next morning arose to look over the farm. It was indeed a new country and we thought of the possibilities of peril which might menace the family should hostilities at any time break out with the Indians or should fire burn their dwelling in the winter season.

After an early breakfast we started for the village with one of the hired men who was going to mill. We went on horseback and behind the saddle was a couple of grain sacks thrown across the animal in a way to make them balance. One of the sacks contained corn and the other rye, and, we were informed, their bread was made of equal parts of each.

An hour's ride brought us to Concord town and as we approached the minister's house he rode out of his yard accompanied by Deacon Griffin. After passing the morning salutation, Parson Bulkeley informed us that he was just starting off for a day of pastoral visitation taking the Deacon as one of the committee which had been appointed at the last town meeting to ascertain and report concerning the moral and spiritual condition of the children and youth. The announcement was coupled with an invitation to go with them, the invitation perhaps being suggested by some queries we had put sometime previous relative to the minister's pastoral work. As all was fish that came to our net we were not slow in accepting and we were soon on our way to Cornet Wood's just beyond the south branch of the river to procure if possible one of his horses, he having, as the parson informed us, a good saddle horse which would not be in use that day since the owner was picking his cranberries.

It was a fortunate circumstance that we were to obtain a horse at Cornet Wood's, for the Parson and Deacon were to begin their calls at Thomas Dakin's, which was further on. It took but a short time to get the horse ready and we were soon off and away through the woods.

We found that the Dakin place was in a lonely locality as much so as any we had visited. Not a house was in sight and woods were on every side; for since he had settled there late, there had been no time to enlarge the clearing. It was a most cordial welcome that we received from the Dakin family; for not only were visitors infrequent there but everything relating to ecclesiastic matters was most acceptable. It was not long after we entered before Parson Bulkeley began his perfunctory work, for Goodman Dakin, seeing us coming up the lane, had called in the boys and the hired man and a couple of wood choppers who were temporarily working for him. All were soon seated and silence reigned as if at the meeting house; and moreover all seemed to enter into the exercise with a relish.

Questions were asked to test the children's knowledge of scripture and the personal experience of the elders was inquired into; and after Deacon Griffin had ascertained what measures were being made use of for the spiritual nurture of the young, all kneeled while Parson Bulkeley implored a blessing upon all present. As we were about to go, Goodman Dakin with an importunity which we were reluctant to ignore entreated us to remain till night, offering to return with us at evening to Cornet Wood's; so earnest was the request that we felt constrained to comply; and especially so since Parson Bulkeley had informed us that he usually held the same exercises at each house, making everything professional on these occasions.

Before the Parson and Deacon took their leave, and after those who had been called in were excused, Goodwife Dakin brought in a glass decanter and a couple of beakers, requesting the visitors to help themselves, which they did, although with a dignity and decorum which showed no inordinate desire for the drink and indicated that they partook as much out of courtesy and deference to custom, as for any craving within themselves.

This attitude of the minister so impressed us that we afterwards inquired concerning it and also about some other things pertaining to the ecclesiastics of the period, and from the answers given and from old records together with the revelation of the sparks at several fireplaces, we came to the conclusion that the colonial clergy and perhaps the clergy of a later date likewise had not always been rightly represented concerning the drink habit, but that isolated cases have been held up as the rule. In fact from all that we have gathered we have concluded that the profession, neither by preaching nor practice, encouraged intemperance, and that it never was true that pastoral visits as a rule were characterized by excessive dram drinking. The pulpit was perhaps as outspoken then as now against drunkenness, if not more so.

It was a subject for discipline, and church discipline in those days meant something. A person who was set aside in his church membership came as near both civil and ecclesiastical ostracism as one could and not be an outcast.

The average character of the colonial preacher forbids the belief in such stories as picture him staggering from house to house on his round of pastoral visits, sipping to excess wherever he stopped and going home half intoxicated.

That they drank is not denied, but they considered that they drank moderately, and strove to teach others that it was a disgrace and a sin to drink to excess. This was likewise the position of a large part of the laity. Moreover distilled liquors were expensive and to waste money upon any luxury was sinful.

From necessity the early colonist was economical almost to penuriousness. He had nothing to throw away. Generally speaking he may have used spirit on the principle of value received. He would drink only so much as he believed would enable him to hoe more corn or cut more wood or get in more hay; but to pay much money for the mere fun of getting fuddled, the more thrifty would not.

Later, when the country became more settled, luxury through wealth began to prevail, and distilled drinks being less expensive, the drinking customs changed. But even then the clergy were, we believe, by their character, their example and their teaching the same stalwart guard to beat back the encroachment of an evil appetite.

And now that we are on the subject of ministerial standing, we would state, that as a class they were greatly respected and revered. Their social position was on a level with that of the magistrate and the wealthy. Books being few they were referred to as to a living encyclopedia and it might be said of the New England minister as of the schoolmaster in Goldsmith's Deserted Village, "And still they gazed and still the wonder grew That one small head could carry all he knew." So great was the respect for ministers and churchly ordinances that strict laws were made to enforce it.

A person who unduly criticized his minister was subject to public censure, if not to trial and the penalty of a fine. In one town, a man was publicly whipped for speaking derisively of the Bible and its ordinances as the clergyman taught them.

A woman was once ordered to stand before the public with a cleft stick upon her tongue, because she showed a lack of respect for the Elder. It is related that one Philip Ratcliffe in 1631, was publicly whipped and banished for speaking against the churches. Absenting one's self from church was a fault punishable in public.

But, notwithstanding all this, ministers were subject to great censure from their people at large, when it was thought the case justified it. One was bitterly rebuked for having saved eight hundred dollars by selling produce from his farm.

Another was reproved for wearing stockings, "footed up with another color." He was also rebuked for jumping over a fence, instead of going though the gate when calling upon a parishioner. One was mildly reproved for wearing too worldly a wig.

The installation of a minister was a great event, sometimes attended by a dinner at the tavern. This consisted of all kinds of New England fare with a liberal supply of liquors. Liquors were sometimes mixed on the meeting house steps, and portable bars were sometimes located near the house of worship. The installation dinner was sometimes extravagant, as one given at the house of Rev. Dr. Sewall in 1761, when it is said that so great was the preparation for it that the price of provisions in Boston raised "a part for several days." It was said of it, "There were six tables that held one with another eighteen persons each. Upon each table a good rich plum pudding, a dish of boiled pork and fowls and a corned leg of pork with sauce proper for it, a leg of bacon, a la mode beef, a leg of mutton with caper sauce, a roast loin of veal, a roast turkey, a venison pastel, besides cake, cheese, tarts and butter."

Various quaint adjectives were made use of in describing the preachers. They were sometimes spoken of as "painful preachers," meaning pains-taking, "fit to teach," "soul ravishing," "soul piercing," "angel rivaling," "septemflous," "holy savored," "soul affecting." The relation of the pastor to his parish was substantially the same as now in churches of the congregational order, except that his authority was considered much greater, and although theoretically a fiction yet he was a bold parishioner who attempted to overthrow it.

They called themselves "a church without a bishop," but practically the pastor sometimes took the place of a bishop and came near being a king.

When a minister was settled after the "old standing order" it was difficult to unsettle him. According to a supreme court decision he could hold the meeting house, church records, church funds, and draw his salary unless dismissed by a council.

The contract entered into between the pastor and people was evolved from the congregational common law, as principles are crystallized by acts of the civil courts.

But notwithstanding the strong position held by the minister, he was sometimes subjected to such sorties by the laity as made the throne tremble; occasionally there were severe controversies, — it might be over creed, church polity, or some simple town affair.

In Concord there was great dissension concerning the preaching of Mr. Bliss about the time of Whitefield's visit. In the Sudbury Church there was a great strife concerning the stinting of the cow commons, and the contention was carried so far, that the Colonial Court sent delegates to meet with it in council, and Rev. Edmund Brown was one of the chief actors; all of which goes to show that peace cannot be maintained by ecclesiastical metes or bounds however firmly set.

After the conversation about ministers we walked around and looked over the locality in which Goodman Dakin had cast his lot. His first settlement was near the central village where he had a house and barn which he sold to John Hayward, when he took up his abode beyond the river. His neighbors were Michael Wood, Obadiah Wheeler, and Edmund Wigley; the two latter living near Broad Meadow.

As the history of this family is an interesting one we will give some of the outline facts. Thomas was the common ancestor in this country and was at Concord before 1650. His first wife died in 1659, his second wife, widow Susan Stratton died in 1698. He died Oct. 21, 1708.

After a generation or two, a branch of the family moved just over the line into Sudbury and established there an estate which long bore the family name. For many years there was in the family a long succession of deacons, one of whom Deacon Samuel Dakin, grandson of Thomas, fell in battle in the last French and Indian war, July 20, 1758, at Half Way Brook near Fort Edward while connected with the expedition of General Amherst.

The site of the home-where Deacon Dakin dwelt was a little over the Sudbury and Concord boundary line, and not far from the old farm long owned by his descendants in the former town. The spot is marked only by an earth dent. The locality of the Dakin homestead on either side of the town boundary line has been a lonely one and there have been traditions about it of concealed booty. The spot is quite near the well known Concord woods which consist of many acres concerning which, legends might naturally arise. The stories represent that a part of the pirate crew of Captain Kidd repaired to a spot about there for secreting their spoils; and it is certain that strangers were seen about there under suspicious circumstances, remaining for some hours without divulging their errand.

The place where they went has been approximately pointed out and traditions have been passed down from generation to generation until doubtless some came to believe them and to search for the treasure supposed to be buried. On one occasion as one of the proprietors was plewing by the help of a neighbor in a pasture in close proximity to the spot, he noticed that the plow struck a large, flat, stone. The team passed on and the day's work was ended.

Early the next morning the Deacon repaired to the spot to examine the aforesaid stone. But what was his surprise on arriving to find his neighbor there before him intent on the same errand. They looked at each other and laughed over the humorous situation, but neither carried back any treasure except a cheery good morning.

Probably the stories related of this locality are similar and have no more truth than those related concerning the visits of the Pirates to other towns. In some instances it has been said that the Evil One stands guard over the booty and that in searching for it silence was to be maintained, for a single word might break the spell and the treasure would vanish, but in process of time better conclusions were entertained and it is now supposed that the Pirates were profligate rather than provident and spent as they went.

We have now, as we believe, sufficiently set forth by fictitious representation, intermingled with fact, what Were some of the customs, experiences and pioneer processes of the first settlers of Concord; and now we propose no longer to give descriptions of supposed visits to their families, neither to draw inferences from analogy nor to resort to conjecture to supply any absence of record or lack of authentic tradition. Our purpose will be hereafter to deal purely with history; and in a plain matter of fact manner, state in the present book some further annals of the township during the first score of years; reserving for a future volume events that occurred during its continuance as a colony and then to the close of its history as a province.

PART II. HISTORY OF THE SETTLEMENT
OF CONCORD, MASS. 1654-1692
CHAPTER XXVIII

Early Record Relating to the Concord Plantation — Permission to Purchase Territory — Land Sale — Indian Deed — Depositions Confirmatory of title to the Township — Original Boundary — Additional Land Grants — Petitions to the General Court.

AMONG the remaining things to be considered that are related to the first two decades of the town's history are further matters appertaining to real estate.

We have already noticed that a tract of land six miles square was purchased of the Indians in 1636, and that the price of it was paid in wampum and merchandise. We stated that a deed was delivered and lost, and that depositions concerning this transaction were taken in after years confirmatory of a bona fide sale.

The land then purchased was lotted out and divided up, additions were made to it, records made of it, and such regulations provided as would secure to all their rights.

It is our purpose in the present chapter to produce the evidence of these things by giving a transcript of some of the original documents and some statements taken from old writers.

The first recorded statement about a proposed plantation at the place which was later to become Concord is the following, in vol. 1 page 57 of the state Archives, bearing date Sept. 2, 1635: "It is ordered, that there shallbe a plantacon att Musketequid, & that there shallbe 6 myles of land square to belong to it, & that the inhabitants thereof shall have three yeares imunities from all publ[ic] charges, except traineings; Further, that when any that plant there shall have occacon of carryeing of goods thither, they shall repaire to two of the nexte magistrates where the teames are, whoe shall have power for a yeare to presse draughts, att reasonable rates, to be payde by the owners of the gootls, to transport their goods thither att seasonable tymes; & the name of the place is changed, & here after to be called Concord."

This order of the Colonial General Court was succeeded the next March by the following: "It was further 'agreed, that the imunitie ot Concord for three years shall begin the first of October nexte, & that none shall have benefitt thereof but those that lyve there, & with respect only to the stocke they have there.'" (Mass. Records, 1. 167).

A permission for the Concord settlers to purchase territory was given by the General Court and the record of it made May 17, 1637, is as follows: "Concord had leave graunted them to purchase the ground w'hin their limits of the Indeans, to wit, Atawans & Squa Sachim." (Mass. Records 1. 196).

A record relating to a land sale at Concord whether of the original grant or of some other transaction, a matter that has perhaps never yet been settled by any published history, is the following dated August t, 1637: "Webb Cowet, Squa Sachem, Tahatawants, Natan quaticke alias Oldmans, Caato, alias Goodmans did expresse their consent to the sale of the weire at Concord over against the towne & all the planting ground wch hath bene formerly planted by the Indians, to the inhabitants of Concord of wch there was a writing, wth their marks subscribed given into the Court expressing the price given." (Mass. Records, 1. 196).

With regard to the Indian deed of the original land grant Shattuck states, History of Concord, page 7.

"I have sought in vain for the Indian deed. It was probably lost very early, since measures were taken in 1684, when the colony charter was declared to be void, and the claims of Robert Mason to large portions of the country were asserted to establish the lawful title, which the inhabitants of Concord had in their soil. The original petition was also lost."

The measures referred to by Shattuck as having been taken to confirm the evidence of a legal ownership, are the following depositions which have been preserved in the records of both Middlesex County and the town of Concord: "The Testimony of Richard Rice aged seventy-two years Sheweth that about the yeare one thousand six hundred Thirty six there was an Agreement made by some undertakers for the Towne since called Concord with some Indians that hail right unto the land then purchased for the Township. The indians names was Squaw Sachem, Tohuttawun Sagamore, Muttunkatucka, and some other indians y' lived then at that place, The Tract of land being six miles square, The center of the place being about the place the meeting house standeth now, The bargaine was made & confirmed between ye English undertakers & the Indians then present, to their good satisfaction on all hands.

"7. 8. 84. Sworne in Court

"Tho Danforth Record'"

[Middlesex Deeds, Lib. 9, fol. 105.] "The Testimony of William Buttrick aged sixty-eight years or thereabouts Sheweth, That about the yeare one thousand six hundred thirty & six, there was an Agreement made by some undertakers for the Towne since called Concord with some Indians that had right unto the land then purchased of them for the Township; the Indians names was Squaw Sachem Tohuttawun Sagamore & Nuttankatucka & some other Indians that lived and was then present at that place & at that time. The Tract of land being six miles square, The center being about ye place the meeting house now standeth on. The bargaine was made & confirmed between the English the Indians then present & concernd, to theyr good satisfaction on all hands "7, 8, 84. Sworne in Court

"Tho Danforth R."

[Middlesex Deeds, Lib. 9, fol. 105.] "The Deposition Jehojakin alias Mantatucket a christian Indian of Natick aged. 70 years or thereabouts, "This Deponent testifyeth & sayth, that about 50 years since he lived within the bounds of that place which is now called Concord at the foot of an hill named Nawshawtick now in the possession of Mr Henery Woodis & that he was prsent at a bargaine made at the house of Mr Peter Bulkly (now Capt Timothy Wheeler'sbetween Mr Simon Willard Mr John Jones, Mr Spencer & severall others in behalfe of the Englishmen who were setling upon the sd Towne of Concord & Squaw Sachem, Tahuttawun & Nimrod Indians which sd Indians (according to yr particular Rights & Interests) then sold a Tract of land conteyning six mile square -the sd house being accounted about the center) to the sd English for a place to settle a Towne in.

And he the sd Deponent saw sd Willard & Spencer pay a parcell of wompompeag, Hatchets, Hows, Knives, Cotton Cloath & Shirts to the sd Indians for the sd Tract of land: And in prticular he the sd Deponent perfectly remembreth that Wompachowet Husband to Squaw-Sachem received a Suit of cotton cloath, an Hatt, a white linnen band, shoes, stockins & a great coat upon account of sd bargaine And in the conclusion thesd Indians declard themselvs sattisfyed & told the Englishmen they were Welcome. There were also present at the sd Bargain Waban, Merch' Thomas his brother in law Nowtoquatuckquaw an Indian, Aantonuish now called Jethro "taken upon oath. 20'h of October 1684 "Before Daniel Gookin Senr. Asisis'

"Tho: Danforth. Dep'. Gov',"
[Middlesex Deeds, Lib. 9, fol. 100.]

As regards the shape or form of the territory contained in the original grant, the historian Walcott says, "The original grant was laid out in the form of a square. Right angles and straight lines were preferred by the early settlers whenever they could be had. No other grants had been made near this place; consequently it was not deemed necessary to notify any adjoining owner of the running of the line, and the simplest possible form was adopted.

"The original grant may be bounded as follows: Beginning at the southwest corner at a stone post which marks the present southwest corner of the town, the line runs north 400 east (approximate needle course) on the Acton line to a stone at the present northwest corner of Concord, near the Dudley place. When Acton was made a town, the statute bounded it on the east by 'Concord old bounds;' from which it appears that Acton includes no part of the original Concord, and that the dividing line between the two towns is a portion of the old Concord line on that side. The Acton boundary extended leads to a heap of lichen-covered boulders surmounted by a stake.

This ancient monument is near the top of a hill in the southwesterly part of Carlisle, and undoubtedly marks the old northwest corner of our town. It was identified and pointed out to the writer on the ground by Major B. F. Heald, of Carlisle, who says that he has often heard his father and other ancient men, long since deceased, speak of this bound as marking the old Concord corner; and everything goes to corroborate this testimony. The place was commonly known by the name of "Berry Corner" and was the original northeast corner of Acton; but, in 1780, a portion of that town near this point was included in what was then constituted as the District of Carlisle, and subsequently formed a part of the town of the same name.

Making a right angle at this corner the line runs southeasterly through the lower part of Carlisle, coinciding in two places with our present boundary, and, crossing the river, runs about a quarter of a mile to the southward of the main street of Bedford and parallel with it, to a point on the upland about forty rods east of the Shawsheen River. Ancient stone walls preserve this line in part.

The bound at the northeast corner must have been removed at some time after Bedford was incorporated; and, as it stood in cultivated land, near a house, the farmer would not be likely to value it so highly as we should, had he allowed it to remain. The corner can be located with sufficient accuracy however, by the intersection of the north line, just described, with the line on the east; and it appears from the Billerica records of 1700 that the corner was then marked by a stake and stones.

159

Returning to the southwest corner, we run southeasterly on the present Sudbury line to the river, and thence in the same course, on the Way land line, to the corner at Lincoln; then striking across the lower corner of Lincoln and keeping in the same straight line, we come to a heap of stones situated near a brook, and in a line with that part of the boundary between Lincoln and Weston which extends southwesterly from the great road at G. F. Harrington's house. Turning and making a right angle at this corner, we proceed towards the northeast, on old stone walls, just touching the eastern edge of Beaver Pond and including a portion of the boundary between Bedford and Lexington, thus meeting our north line and completing the square."

Besides the territory contained in the grant of six miles square, other lands were subsequently petitioned for, an account of which is thus given in Shattuck's History: "Additional grants of land were occasionally made, adjoining Concord, after the first purchase. On the 2nd of May, 1638, Governor Winthrop had 1,200, and Thomas Dudley 1,000 acres granted them below Concord. When they came up to view it, "going down the river about four miles, they made choice of a place for one thousand acres for each of them. They offered each other the first choice, hut because the deputy's was first granted, and himself had store of land already, the governor yielded him the choice.

So, at the place where the deputy's land was to begin, there were two great stones, which they called the Two Brothers, in remembrance that they were brothers by their childrens' marriage, and did so brotherly agree, and for that a little creek near those stones was to part their lands. At the court, in the 4th month after, two hundred acres were added to the governor's part." The governor's lot lay southerly, and the deputy governor's northerly of those rocks, and they were divided by a little brook, which may now be seen a short distance below Carlisle bridge. Governor Winthrop selected (judiciously, I think) a lot in Concord, which "he intended to build upon," near where Captain Humphrey Hunt now lives. The changes, which took place in his property and family, probably prevented him from putting his plan into execution.

In Nov. 1636, 500 acres of land were granted to Increase Nowell, Esq." on the north side of the bounds of Concord beyond the river against the governor's 1200;" and 500 acres to the Rev. Thomas Allen of Charlestown, on the north side of Mr. Nowell's; and, Oct. 7, 1640, to the Rev. Thomas Weld of Roxbury 533 acres, next to Mr. Allen's. Another tract of 400 acres, was also granted to Mr. Atherton Hough. All these lands were sold about 1650 to John and Robert Blood, and comprised what was afterwards known as the Bloods' Farms, which became a part of Concord and which will be hereafter noticed." But notwithstanding tract after tract was bestowed upon the people of Concord they still wanted more territory.

This is indicated by the following petition dated Sept. 7, "Whereas your humble petitioners came into this country about four years agoe, and have since then lived at Concord, where we were forced to buy what now we have, or the most of it, the convenience of the town being before given out: your petitioners having been brought up in husbandry, of children, finding the lands about the town very barren, and the meadows very wet and unuseful, Colonial especially those we now have interest in; and knowing it is your desire the lands might be subdued, have taken pains to search out a place on the north west of our town, where we do desire some reasonable quantitie of land may be granted unto us which we hope may in time be joined to the farms already laid out there to make a village. And so desiring God to guide you in this and all other your weighty occasions, we rest your humble petitioners."

Thomas Wheeler
Timothy Wheeler
Ephraim Wheeler
Thomas Wheeler, Jr.
Roger Draper
Richard Lettin.

Indorsed: "We think some quantitie of land may be granted them provided that within two years they make some good improvement of it."

In addition to the foregoing statement of Shattuck relating to land transactions of Concord he further states as follows on page 38 of his History: "It has already been intimated that additional grants of land were made to Concord about 1652. The following details relate to these and other grants.

"'To the Honored Generall Court assembled at Boston.

The returne of the nommber of acres of land granted as an addition to the Towne of Concord according to the order of the General Court in 1654.

"'Whereas the Court was pleased to grannt to our Towne a village some fouer years since upon condition they should improve it betore others, but neglecting their opportunity, the plantation of Chelmsford have taken a good parte of the same, also Nattatawants [Tahattawan] having a plantation granted him which takes up a good some also, we whoes names are subscribed have taken a survey of the rest remayning, and wee finde about seven thousand acres left out, of which Major Willard hath two thousand acres, except a little part of one end of his farme which lyes in the place or parcell of vacant land being by the last court granted to our Towne on this condition that at this Court we should acquaint the Court of the quantitye of what wee have.

"This is a true copie compared with original on file, as it was exhibited to the Generall Court may 1655 as attest.

Edward Rawson, Secretary.
Tho. Brooks
Timothy Wheeler
Joseph Wheeler
George Wheeler
George Heaward
John Jones."

Other territorial acquisitions followed, but as these belong to a subsequent period mention of them here is omitted.

CHAPTER XXIX

Land Allotments and Divisions — Early Records Relating to Real Estate — Public Reservations — Undivided Territory — Location of Land Tracts — Amount of Acreage — 'The grant of Thirty-one Acres to Rev. Peter Bu Ike ley.

THE settlers did not long allow their landed possessions to remain undisposed of or unused, but soon divided them. The first apportionment was of house lots and a limited quantity of lands outlying. The second was by what were called land divisions.

Of the first method, Walcott, in his History, page 18 states as follows: "As soon as the most pressing needs of the situation were met, allotments of land were made to the members of the company, and house-lots were laid out with some regularity on both sides of the Mill Brook, eastward as far as the Kettle place lately owned by Mr. Staples, and on Walden Street to the Almshouse; in a westerly direction as far as the Damon place; and to the Old Manse and the Edmund Hosmer place on the north. Besides his house-lot, each one received his due proportion of the planting-ground and meadow lying in the near vicinity. This was the first division of lands, the price paid into the common stock being a shilling per acre, or, in some special cases, a sixpence per acre. The land thus divided constituted a small part only of the whole grant, and the remainder was held in common and undivided, subject to such regulations as the inhabitants thought fit to establish, until the second division in 1653, by which, substantially, the whole remaining portion of the original grant was disposed of."

About the second division the same author writes: "By the first division of lands, which has already been alluded to, a small portion only of the township passed into the hands of individual owners and became private property."

A rule relating to the second division of land is the following, which was voted upon at a town meeting held on January 2nd, 1653: "A meting of the Towne of Concord the 21h of the 11 mo. 1652 about second devitiones as foloweth, lmpr it is agreed that 20. acres of land shall be for one Cow Comon (of all the land men hold) and two yearling shall goe for one grown beast, and one horse for one beast, and 4. sheep for one beast.

I' The bounds of the Towne is devided into three parts; as foloweth: only the hogpen walke is not to be devided; Impr All on the north sid of the great Rivre shall be for them, on that sid of the same; and all on the east sid to Mr Bulkelyes,

I' the second part of the devition is on the East sid of the aforesid rivre, beyond Cranefild to Shawshine corner, and to Mr fflints pond to the gutter that comes out thereof, and to the goose pond and along the path that comes to the Towne medow & to the Towne; and the psones to Inioye this part are all the Inhabitants from Mr farweles to the East end of the Towne, also Thomas Brookes is to come in amongst them for two, thirds of his land, and Robert Meriam; Sargent Wheler and Georg Meriam to Joyne with them;

I' the third pt of [the] devition is from the gutter that comes from Mr fflints pond as aforesaid; to the south rivre & betwen the rivres; and those appoynted for that devition, are the Rest of the towne not beforementioned.

It is agreed that if the mair pt of any of the Companyes shall agree for the laying out of the devitiones as before exprest then the minor pt shall be Compeled to agree there to, but in Case the maior pt shall not agree; then any particular pson shall not be hendered of ther wright, but they shall have power to call on indeferant man and the Company to whome he belongs shall choose one other, or if they refeuse so to doe, then the Townsmen shall choose on man, who with the suerveyer shall indeferantly lay out his or there lands so requiring it, this votted.

It is forther agreed that every pson shall have som, quantity of upland adioyning to his medow, where it is in Comon except som more then ordenary ocation may hender it, and in Case any defarence be therein; it is to be ended by indeferent men; and this is to be pt of there second devition; It is agreed that second devitiones shall not hender, heighwayes to menes propriaties that they have in particolers, but they shall be inioyed without charge of purchies to be layed out by indeferent men; It is agreed that all those that have grants of lands given them, shall have three acres for one as others have."

Of the second division, Shattuck says, "The town met several times to consider in what new manner this division should be made. On the 2nd of Jan.

1654, it was voted to divide the town into three parts or quarters, and to have the lands first divided into the quarters; but this was not entirely satisfactory to the inhabitants. "Much uneasiness," say the Records, "took place before the system was matured." On the 8th of March, 1654, "at a publique training", nine men were chosen, "three out of each quarter, empowered by the town to hear and end former debate, according to their best light, and discretion, and conscience: only eight of the nine must agree to what is determined, or else nothing be of force; and none voted to the contrarie, but Georg Wheeler, Henry Woodis, Joshua Edmands, William Buttrick, and Thomas Stow." The labors of this committee resulted in the following agreement:

"We whoes names are under written conclude that 20 acres of meadow shall be reserved for a minister in the Hogepen-walke about Annursnake, and 20 acres of plowland out of the south quarter, and 20 acres of woodland in the east quarter. We agree also that 20 acres of woodland shall be reserved for the public good of the towne lying neer the old hogepen, at each side of the townes bounds line. — That some particular persons shall have some inlargement, who are short in lands, paying 12 d. per acre, as others have don, and 6d. per acre, if the towne consent thereto :— tht persons are as follow: Georg Wheeler 20 acres; Obadiah Wheeler 20 acres; Michel Wood 12 acres; Thomas Daken 10 acres; Thomas Batman 15 acres; Bapties Smedly 14 acres. These to have second divition as others have had. That all pooremen in the towne that have not commons to the number of four, shall be allowed so many as amounts to foure with what they have already, till they be able to purchase for themselves, or untill the townsmen shall see cause to take it from them, and bestow it on others that want: and we mean those poore men, that at the present are householders. And upon these conditions and those that follow, the Hogepen-walke is resigned up to the north quarter."

By the several divisions and allotments a large part of the towns territory was early disposed of. Some however remained for years undivided, and of this latter were several large strips which belonged to each of the Quarters, the Great Fields; and a tract in the vicinity of the Bateman Pond containing about four hundred acres and formerly known as the "Twenty Score", a name derived from the area of the reservation.

Years after land matters had largely been adjusted, here and there was found remaining a lone parcel that might be considered the property of the public, several of these being determined by actual survey reported upon as late as 1845, to contain about two hundred and twenty-six acres.

One of these parcels was a small island in the crotch of the River below Mr. Woodis's Rock where the Rivers meet; another, a plot of a little less than an acre, reaching upstream from where the Minute Man statue is situated.

Besides the grants and allowances in which the inhabitants in general shared, there were allotments to individuals concerning which Walcott states: "James Blood, father and son, received as part of their second division five hundred acres in one parcel, extending southward from the town line. Henry Woodis and Thomas Stow jointly owned a tract of six hundred and sixty-six acres, situated south of Fairhaven and east of the river, which was sold in 1660 to Thomas Gobble and Daniel Dane for £72, and was afterwards occupied by them.

Large tracts were held for a long time afterwards by the Quarters, or by joint proprietors, in common and undivided; as for instance, the "Great Fields" adjoining the Great Meadow; and the "Twenty Score," which extended to the southward from Bateman's Fond and contained, as the name would imply, four hundred acres, and many other parcels besides, in various parts of the town."

There was also, as stated in an earlier chapter, a tract of thirty-one acres of land situated at the center of the town, granted to Rev. Peter Bulkeley in consideration of his erecting a mill "to grind the town's corn."

It would be interesting to know where all the lands thus allotted and divided were situated. To determine this, however, in every instance would be a difficult matter, for time, in many cases has left little or no trace of their boundary lines: but there has been preserved in the public records sufficient to determine their general location.

At a town meeting supposed to have been held at the suggestion of the selectmen and Rev. Edward Bulkeley, Thomas Brooks and Joseph Wheeler, Jan. 26, 1663, measures were taken taken for the purchase of a new town book.

The book was purchased and it was decided that "what is in the old book that is useful shall be transcribed into the new with all lands which men now hold" "that every man that hath not his proportion of lands laid out to him, that is due him shall gitt it laid out by artis." This was to be done by 1655 and each one was to give the town clerk a description of his land approved at a meeting of the inhabitants of the quarter in which he lived and certified by the quarter clerk.

Referring to data afforded by the foregoing measure, Shattuck, in his History which was written in 1835, states: "From these records I have compiled the following table which gives the greater part though not all the names of the proprietors of the town at that time. The places of their residence, when known, are indicated by the names under which they now pass."

The following is the list with a change of arrangement.

The estates with the names of their owners in each quarter, we have grouped together and the names of the owners at the time of Shattuck's writing are in parentheses.

NORTH QUARTER.

Widow Heald, 6 lots, 161 acres (Joshua Buttrick,) John Heald, 4 lots, 86 acres (North of Joshua Buttrick). William Buttrick, 12 lots, 215 acres (Jonas Buttrick). John Flint, 9 lots, 534 Acres (John Flint). James Blood Sr. and James Blood Jr., 12 lots, 660 acres (Rev. Dr. Ripley). John Smedly, 17 lot, 668 acres (South of J. Jones). Thomas Bateman, 7 lots, 246 acres (Near R. French.) Baptise Smedly, 10 lots, 186 acres (Ephraim Brown). Humphry Barrett, 11 lots, 316 acres (Abel B. Heywood.) Richard Temple, 5 lots, 291 acres (Barretts Mills). John Blood, 1 lot, 61 acres (Near Thomas Blood). John Jones, 9 lots, 311 acres (James Jones'). Samuel Hunt, 13 lots, 277 acres. Boaz Brown, 6 lots, 86 acres (The Dakin House). Thomas Brown 14 lots, 186 acres (Reuben French.)

SOUTH QUARTER

Joseph Dean, 1 lot, 22 acres (Wm. Heyden). Luke Potter, 22 lots, 249 acres. John Heywood, 13 lots, 385 acres. George Haywood, 10 lots, 505 acres. Daniel Dean and Thomas Gobble, 1 lot, 600 acres (Jones Tavern). Henry Woodhouse, 1 lot, 360 acres. Joseph Barrett and Joshua Wheeler, t i lots, 77 acres (John Vose). Nathaniel Billings Jr. 7 lots, 54 acres (Amos Baker.) John Billings, 6 lots John Wheeler, 1 lot, 67 acres. George Wheeler, 24 lots, 434 acres (near James Adams). Edward Bulkeley, 11 lots, 183 acres (near Meeting House.) Samuel Stratten, 6 lots, 254 acres. (Alms-House). Edmund Wigley 4 lots, 31 acres. John Miles, 23 lots, 459 acres (Josiah Davis). William Buss, 19 lots, 319 acres (Elijah Woods). Thomas Dakin, 4 lots, 87 acres. James Hosmer, 4 lots, 164 acres. Samuel Wheeler, 2 lots, 21 acres. James Smedley, 9 lots, 287 acres. John Scotchford, 10 lots, 120 acres (near Cyrus Stow) Michael Wood, 13 lots, 230 acres. (Samuel Dennis).

EAST QUARTER.

Thomas Wheeler, Sr. 16 lot, 373 acres. (Jonathan Wheeler). Francis Fletcher, 17 lots, 437 acres. Richard Rice, 3 lots, 189 acres. George Meriam, 16 lots, 239 acres (near Alms-house). Moses Wheat, 22 lots, 339 acres, (Bedford Road). Robert Meriam, 16 lots, 595 acres, (Eb. Hubbard). Ephraim Flint, 750 acres (Lincoln). Grace Bulkeley, 1 lot, 750 acres. Thomas Pellet and Joseph Dean, 7 lots, 244 acres. Joseph Wheeler, 29 lots, 357 acres. Joshua Brooks, 11 lots, 195 acres (Isaac Brooks). Caleb Brooks, 12 lots, 150 acres. Eliphalet Fox, 14 lots, 106 acres (Bedford Road). John Meriam, 8 lots, 262 acres, (Virginia Road). William Hartwell, 20 lots, 241 acres, (Bedford Road). John Hartwell, 3 lots, 17 acres, (Bedford Road). Nathaniel Ball, 11 lots, 137 acres, (Bedford Road). William Taylor, 14 lots, 117 acres, (Bedford Road). James Farwell, 18 lots, 280 acres. Joseph Wheeler, 29 lots, 357 acres. William Baker, 5 lots, 43 acres.

Besides the foregoing list Mr. Walcott has also located some of the allotments, a part of which we gave in the chapter on early streets, and the remainder are the following together with the names of the occupants at the time of Mr. Walcott's writing, given in parentheses.

On the west side of the highway of Monument street in the direction of the North Bridge was the early home of Humphrey Barrett, his lot containing twelve acres. (D. G. Langs.) On the same street John Jones had eight acres. (Sarah J. Prescott.) John Smedley owned ten acres to the easterly. (John S. Keyes). And James Blood and son had twelve acres at what was afterward the Old Manse estate. (Dr. Ripley).

The tract of land early granted to Rev. Peter Bulkeley which contained thirty-one acres, was situated at Concord Center and on its southerly side extended in a straight line from a point where now stands the publishing house of Albert Lane, which is the site of the Bulkeley Mill, beyond which Mill the west end of the Milldam began, and going to the corner of the Lexington highway and Bedford street, to nearly the spot where the Catholic Church stands.

On the south side of this line was a public reservation or a portion of the town's common land.

In connection with the grant of this land it was agreed that Mr. Bulkeley for the purpose of repairing his milldam should be permitted to take sand or clay from the parcel reserved for the town's use.

To the northerly the thirty-one acre grant extended in the direction of what are now Lowell and Monument streets, the latter, or a portion of it at least being then perhaps but a mere path to the home of Mr. Bulkeley and the river meadow beyond.

The strip extended westerly to the Millbrook, and easterly to the hill.

Soon after the death of Rev. Peter Bulkeley which occurred March 9, 1659, his widow conveyed the entire tract to Capt. Timothy and George Wheeler; and in 1687, the former by bequest left to the town a large portion of the land tor schools and a training field.

By this gift the town's common land at the center was made to comprise, with the exception of the mill privilege, and perhaps here and there a small strip, all the territory intermediate between the brook and the top of the hill east and west; north to the present Colonial House; and to the south as far as the premises now owned by the First Parish.

Thus by the accession of the newly acquired territory by the Wheeler bequest, the town obtained an uninterrupted space for public purposes, and the place already occupied by the meeting house, the burying ground, the pound, the whipping post and the stocks was made a part of a large tract which was afterwards to contain the schoolhouse and training field and still later the present public square upon or about which have been erected the Middlesex Hotel, the Catholic Parsonage, the Masonic Hall, and the Soldier's Monument. The collateral events connected with this combination of public property are of much interest.

The town, after the acquisition of its new territory had ample encouragement to improve it. Soon the "Little Strate Strete" of which mention has been made so often was no longer to have the land between it and the milldam disfigured by the gaping gravel or clay pit, but by some adjustment or exchange of rights, the work of removing earth from the place near the meeting house for mill repairs ceased, and gravel was taken from the hillside at a point between the town house and the Catholic church until the hill was dug through, and by the continuation of the way so opened the present Bedford street was made. Nor was this all the alteration of the central village in the vicinity of its prospective public square. Gradually the old foot-path over the milldam by the south west corner became a necessary way to the tavern, the store, and the road westerly beyond the mill brook. From a foot-path it became a cartway, and from this it developed into a county road; so that perhaps soon after the middle of the 18th century the town folks from the East Quarter were no longer obliged to drive their vehicles around by way of Potter's bridge at the head of the millpond an eighth or a quarter of a mile south, but could pass over a convenient causeway at the dam, while those from the opposite Quarter could drive direct to the meeting house without any detention at the milldam, at which place it is said, the west side people formerly dismounted from their wagons on Sunday that they might walk to the house of worship while the team drove around over Potter's bridge.

CHAPTER XXX

Successive Ownership of Land Grants — Historic Sketch of the Major Simon Willard Farm at Nashawtuc — Change of Occupants of Old Estates.

NEXT in point of interest to a knowledge of the location of the allotments is a knowledge of their successive ownership; but to obtain this in every case would not be easy if indeed it were possible. Some of them probably changed ownership in a very few years and some were doubtless soon divided up between several owners.

During the town's second decade many new settlers arrived, and as fresh ships entered the ports of Massachusetts Bay and the passengers found the older townships largely occupied, they pushed back into the interior. As Concord had meadows and was the first settlement beyond tide water, so it would naturally receive its due share of the new comers and would sell them portions of their estates.

It is true there are instances where farms descended from sire to son with all the apparent precision of the English law of primogeniture, and if the children bounded off it was not to go far, but to settle about the paternal estate by the occupation of a part of it or of lands contiguous to it; for this reason some of the first estates were for generations identified with their first owners but these were doubtless exceptions, and in many instances a Jones place may soon have become a Smith place and the Smith place become identified by some other name. Illustrative of this process, we have in a manuscript work entitled "Homes and People of Concord," written by Mr. Edward Jarvis, and now in Concord Public Library, the following compilation of facts namely: There were in Concord by 1654, eight families, who in the first quarter of the last century were "the most numerous families of farmers in the town," who yet by the last quarter had largely parted with their estates.

The names of these families were Buttrick, Barrett, Brown, Hunt, Hosmer, Dakin, Flint and Wood.

Of five farms owned by the Buttricks; four went out of the family while there were five voters by the name in town.

Of eight farms owned by the Barretts only two were left in their name, with ten voters in town.

Two generations ago four farms belonged to the Browns; in 1881, they held the same number in their possession while the voters had increased to eleven.

Of three farms owned by the Hunts only one was known by this name in 1881, notwithstanding there were seven voters of the name.

The Hosmers owned six farms early in the first quarter of the nineteenth century while only three remained in the family name in the last quarter, with eleven voters of the name in town.

The Flints occupied and owned three farms in the first quarter of the nineteenth century while in 1881, all were sold and four voters remained.

As against these instances of change, Mr. Jarvis gives several where estates have been conspicuously retained in the family; among these is the Derby estate. This family have held their farm from the first, the property descending in a single line until as late as least as 1881, at which time eight of the name are on the voting list. The Wheelers who have been among the most numerous families in Concord have also kept their estates.

Thus farms have changed owners and persons their occupation in the last quarter century and so presumably in the century preceding. A farm which has had many owners but whose title may be traced through them all is the Major Simon Willard or Lee farm at Nashawtuc.

As the successive owners have been celebrated and the History of Concord would not be complete without a description of this farm we will give it; taking our data from Dr. Grindall Reynolds.

The first English owner was Major Simon Willard before spoken of as one of the progenitors and principal promoters of the plantation of Concord. His house was situated at about the spot where now stands the Abbott House, and the lands connected with it probably included those upon the hill and immediately about it.

The successor of Major Willard was Thomas Marshall, formerly a soldier in the army of Oliver Cromwell, and living, before he went to Concord, in Lynn from which place he was sent to the General Court.

Mr. Marshall was something of a military man having attained to the rank of Captain in the service of Cromwell and having had command of some soldiers in America during one of the Indian wars. He bought the Willard farm Nov. 19, 1659, for two hundred and ten pounds. Shortly after the purchase he received a license to sell "strong water" to travelers and others.

After a sojourn of sixteen months on the farm at Nashawtuc, Capt. Marshall sold the place to Henry Woodis or Woodhouse for the sum of two hundred and forty pounds. At this time the farm was said to contain three hundred and fifty acres.

Five years later the house was destroyed by fire and the only son of the owner, an infant, perished in the flames. The building which was burned at this time, it has been supposed, was not the one erected by Major Willard, but the one erected by Mr. Woodis.

Before his ownership of the Nashawtuc farm or prior to 1661, Mr. Woodis was a land owner and a man of considerable prominence. He was an officer in King Philip's war and for several years represented the town at the general court.

In 1699, the farm, excepting one fifth, was sold to Joseph Lee, son in law of Henry Woodis. The property was kept in the Lee family for the space of one hundred and thirteen years. During this period the town of Concord passed through many and eventful changes, some of which were conspicuously connected with the Lee farm.

Joseph, the first Lee who lived on the farm was from Ipswich and married Mary Woodis in 1678, going to Concord from that town, the records state, in 1696.

In 1719, the first Joseph Lee, gave his son Joseph one hundred and fifty acres, and his other children the remainder, except the one fifth before referred to which was given to the fourth daughter who married Elmer Dakin.

The second Joseph Lee was a physician. He bought of each of his brothers and sisters their portion; and in 1730 increased the acreage of the old farm by the purchase of two additional plots.

The next owner was Joseph Lee, the third of the name and he also was a physician, but practiced his profession, as is supposed, quite inconstantly. He was considered wealthy; and it is conjectured that he dealt somewhat in real estate. He took part in several important church quarrels and was one of a number who left the First Parish church and formed what has been termed the Black Horse Church, because its meetings were held in the hall of the tavern that once stood near the present Public Library.

He was a tory, and that probably of the rankest kind, for he was not only in sympathy with England, but, it is stated, conveyed the secrets of the Patriots to the officials at Cambridge, even after the Revolution had set in. For this misdemeanor he was confined to his Nashawtuc farm fourteen months. He died at the age of eighty.

While Joseph Lee was confined at his farm in the Revolutionary war, Harvard College found an abiding place at Concord for a short time and about a dozen of the students made their home at his house.

The last owner of the entire farm of the name of Lee is supposed to be Silas who obtained it from his brother John who had previously owned it jointly with his brother Joseph.

In 1814, the widow of Silas sold her right of dower to William Gray for $1,000, and the place passed out of the possession of the family of Lee. William Gray, well known in his day as "Billy Gray," was a noted Boston merchant, born in Lynn in 1750.

About the time of the conveyance of the Willard or Lee farm to William Gray, the war broke out between the United States and Great Britain, and it is stated that it was the gold of Mr. Gray that fitted out the Constitution which captured the Guerriere in that noted fight which showed the supremacy of American Seamen over the British. It has been stated also that it was with timber from Nashawtuc that the Constitution was built. A large growth of wood covered the hill at that time, and one who itis asserted worked for Mr. Gray lumbering, said that one winter fourteen or fifteen teams were employed hauling to the river logs of pine and oak, some of which were from three to four feet in diameter. These logs were floated down and taken to Boston to be used partly at least in ship building.

In 1821, the farm was sold by Mr. Gray for $3,000 less than it cost him and passed into the possession of Samuel Phillips Prescott Fay, a native of Concord and son of Jonathan Fay.

Samuel Fav was Judge of the Probate Court from 1821 to 1856. But his possession of the property was said to be only nominal, he only holding it for Joseph Barrett the husband of his sister.

Joseph Barrett the twelfth owner of the Nashawtuc farm was a man perhaps no less noted for his personal characteristics than his predecessors. He was familiarly known in Concord as Squire Joe Barrett, and conspicuous both for his social and physical qualities. He had a powerful physique, being, it is said, over six feet tall and weighing over two hundred and fifty pounds. He carried on the farm himself for some years and then placed it in charge of his son Richard only working on it when he wished. Like other owners of this remarkable farm, Mr. Barrett was extensively connected with public life, being for some years and until his death in 1848, Treasurer and Receiver General of the Commonwealth.

From 1844 to 1852 the property belonged to Captain Richard Barrett, son of General Richard, and was sold by him in the latter year to Samuel G. Wheeler, Mr. Barrett serving as Treasurer of the Middlesex Fire Insurance Company. Mr. Wheeler was an energetic business man of New York. He made many improvements in the farm house, built a barn and planted a row of elms on the road to Acton.

After an ownership of four years he sold the place to David Elwell, a sea captain. The new owner like his immediate predecessor was a person of thrift and one who had been prominent in his calling, being the first American ship master to sail through the straits of Magellan. He was about sixty-eight years old when he took the farm and he gathered at his Concord home a collection of curious articles which he had collected in his voyages to various parts of the world.

The building with its contents was burned in the winter of 1856-7, and upon the chimney, which for a time was left standing, it is said, was inscribed a half-effaced date which indicated that the house was erected in 1646 or '56.

From Elwell the farm passed successively into the possession of Joseph L., and Charles H. Hurd, grandsons of Dr. Isaac Hurd. In 1891, the property was sold by the heirs to Mr. William Wheeler. The lands once composing this famous farm are now more or less made use of for residential purposes and various elegant buildings with finely kept lawns are now situated upon it, and afford a fine lookout over the river.

The Concord Reservoir is situated upon the highest point and nothing but the eminence itself with its aboriginal name now remains to remind one of Tahattawan and his wigwam as it once nestled near the rivers by Egg Rock, or of the farm building, formerly erected by the sturdy Simon Willard, or of the tall timber trees that long ago stood there until "cut down by the orders of 'Billy Gray' the merchant, and carted to the seaboard, there perhaps, as before intimated, to become a part of Old Ironsides "whose thunders shook the mighty deep."

In closing this sketch of the farms at Nashawtuc perhaps nothing could be more appropriate than the following from a paper of Dr. Reynolds read before the Antiquarian Society and since published in a book containing his works.

The paper is entitled

"The Story of a Concord Farm."

"Rightly viewed this farm has been in itself a little world.

All trades, all professions, all human interests, seem sooner or later to have come to it. The Indian, the fur trader, the planter of new towns, the Cromwellian soldier and innkeeper, merchants, doctors, lawyers, mechanics, farmers, a judge, a minister, a sailor, a railroad manager, — all these have possessed the land, and for the most part have departed and left little trace of themselves behind. I count that nine different stocks or families have in two hundred and fifty years owned the farm, and that only two of them are represented in the town today, unless it be by remote side branches. But on the soil there are nothing but surface changes. The beautifully rounded little hill, the green meadow, the winding rivers, — these are just what they were two hundred years ago.

Instinctively, as I close, I recall Emerson's words, which seem simply concentrated history:

"Each of these landlords walked amidst his farm,
Saying, "Tis mine, my children's and my name's;
How sweet the west wind sounds in my own trees!
How grateful climb those shadows on my hill!
I fancy these pure waters and the flags
Know me, as does my dog; we sympathize;

171

And, I affirm, my actions smack of the soil."
 "Where are these men? Asleep beneath their grounds;
And strangers, found as they, their furrows plough
"The lawyer's deed
Ran sure
In tail,
To them and to their heirs
Who shall succeed,
Without fail,
Forevermore.
"Here is the land,
Shaggy with wood,
With the old valley,
Mound and flood.
But the heritors?
Fled like the flood's foam,—
The lawyer and the laws,
And the kingdom,
Clean swept herefrom.
"They called me theirs,
Who so controlled me;
Yet everyone wished to stay, and is gone.
How am I theirs,
If they cannot hold me,
But I hold them?

CHAPTER XXXI.

Old Houses — The Elisha Jones House — The Block House— Hunt House — Abel Hosmer House — Wheeler House — Joseph Hosmer House — Woods House — But trick House — Barrett House — Old Manse — Wright Tavern — The Colonial — The Meriam, Tut tie, Fox, Brown, Heywood, Beal, Bull and Alcott Houses— Ancient House Sites — Site of the Rev. Peter Bulkeley Parsonage — Site of the Major Simon Willard House — Deserted Districts and their suggestiveness.

IT would be a matter of much interest to know of the houses or even their sites where the original owners of allotted lands first lived. It is exceedingly improbable however that any of the first houses of the persons whose names are on the list of earliest granters is now standing, and only one is known to exist which belonged to one of the settlers who next succeeded them.

The following is a list of some of the older houses of which we have any knowledge and a sketch of the history of a portion of them: The Block house, Elisha Jones house, Hunt house, Barrett house, the Wright Tavern, the Old Manse, the Colonial, Wheeler house, Abel Hosmer house, Joseph Hosmer house, Woods house, Buttrick house, Meriam house, Tuttle house, Fox house, Reuben Brown house, George Heywood house, the Beal house, Alcott house and the house once inhabited by Ephraim Bull the originator of the Concord grape.

THE ELISHA JONES HOUSE.

The Elisha Jones house now occupied by the Hon. John S. Keyes is situated on Monument street a short distance from the lane leading to the Battle-ground and just beyond the Old Manse on the opposite side of the way. Its first owner was John Smedley an original grantee, of Huguenot descent who arrived at the Concord plantation probably before 1640.

It is not certain that the house stood where it now stands since there are early records which indicate that it may have been on either the east or west side of the highway as it then existed. The road however may have been changed in subsequent years, so that to follow it might mislead as to the original house spot.

As first constructed the house contained but two rooms, one above the other and faced the four points of the compass. The frame was of ash, the boarding of pitch pine, the latter having edges that overlapped to protect from the weather. The lower portion of the chimney was made of stone and clay mortar and its dimensions were twelve feet by eight. John, the son of John, the first proprietor who married May 5, 1669, was the second owner of the house, and he added two rooms on the south side and between them an entry and stairway, and perhaps the east leanto. From John the second, the house passed to Ebenezer Hartwell who married Sarah Smedley, daughter of John, Junior.

In 1724, the third owner sold the place to Samuel Jones, his next neighbor, for 210 pounds. It was afterwards occupied by his son Thomas Jones, who in 1727 married Mary Mills.

The last-named couple were blest by a numerous family, all born in this house the youngest of whom, Elisha, received the old home by the last will and testament of his father. Elisha Jones was a blacksmith, and in 1770, married Elizabeth Farrar. Through his ownership of the house comes its Revolutionary history and fame.

173

Hon. John S. Keyes, the present occupant and owner, in his sketch of the old homestead in a paper prepared and published by the Concord Antiquarian Society, writing of Elisha Jones states as follows: "He became the prominent man of the family, was Lieutenant according to some authority, and Captain according to others. In the troubles preceding the Revolution Elisha was active on the right side; he received of the military stores sent to Concord in 1775, fifty-five bbls. of beef and 170 x3 lbs. of salt-fish, to be stored in his cellar and shed.

His family of two small children were greatly disturbed by the events of the morning of the 19th of April. The early alarm roused them, and the Militia and minute men who fell back at the approach of the British troops halted on the hill behind their house and waited there some time before crossing the bridge. The confusion and excitement increased as the five companies of the red coats marched up the road, and left two companies near his house, while two more went on to Col. Barrett's and one remained to guard the bridge.

The soldiers of the two companies then halted near this door yard, soon surrounded the well in front, drinking the cool water that was so delicious after their long march that hot day. It seems to have satisfied them as there are no report of any depredations. Mr. Jones had prudently taken his wife and babies down cellar, where they cowered in fear and trembling in the dark corners, while he stood guard over the barrels of beef. Soon the chatter and noise of the Britishers ceased, and all was still. Then the silence was broken by the volleys of musketry at the bridge. He could stand it no longer but rushing up from the cellar followed by his wife and crying children, they saw the regulars retreating in confusion back to the village, bearing their wounded, some with ghastly faces, supported by their comrades, others with bloody limbs hastily bandaged to stanch the flow. It was a shocking sight to the oldest child, a girl of four years, which she remembered to her old age, and often described. To her father it lent new excitement and patriotic rage; he pointed his gun out of the bedroom window on the north-west corner of the house, determined to have one raking fire at the foe. His wife clung to his arm begging him not to risk their burning the house if he fired from it and succeeded in preventing his purpose and getting his gun away. Then he went to the door of the shed and stood there looking at the retreating soldiers in scorn and triumph. One of the rear guard who may have seen his attempt to shoot, or "misliked his look," drew up as they passed the house, and fired a "British musket ball" at Elisha. It was a well-pointed shot considering that the red coats fired from the hip, and not from the shoulder with a sight along the gun barrel, as the Yankees did. The ball struck at the height of Jones' head about three feet to the right, and passing through the boarding, glanced from an oak joist, and out through the back side into the ground behind. The hole in the front board still remains, to be seen of "pilgrims and strangers," some of whom content themselves with putting their fingers in it, while others have been known to try to cut out and carry off the hole. Whether, after this narrow escape, Mr. Jones joined in the pursuit to Charlestown, or remained at home to care for his frightened family, tradition does not tell."

The old house is in the midst of an interesting locality. Not far away towards the west is the Old Manse with its gray, gambrel roof and antique pose, extending back riverward from the historic highway as if modestly shrinking from the multitudes that visit it.

Towards the east and on a large unoccupied lawn in full and open view from the Jones doorway is ground supposed to have been inhabited by the Indians as indicated by the stone arrow heads found there.

To the northerly through the pines is the "Battle Ground" including the monument, the bridge, and the "Minute Man" Statue. To the east and south are still the rough pastures over which the Provincials passed to intercept the British in their retreat back to Boston; and before the doorway is the same old road along which the Regulars ran after the firing in the first conflict.

Truly if time has dealt favorably with any spot about Concord where a century ago men wrought mightily it is here.

The river moves onward with an unchanged course; the willows as of old grow beside it; the floods rise and occasionally sweep over the meadow lands as of yore; and when by the winds of gray November the trees are stripped of their foliage, their is disclosed over the brown reaches of marsh land an interesting expanse of historic country.

From Elisha Jones the property passed to Nathan Barrett, from whom it was purchased by a daughter of the last owner of the Prescott place which was nearby, Mrs. John S. Keyes.

The improvements made by the present owner Judge Keyes we will give in his own words: "With much labor and expense it was carefully repaired and renovated; a new outside and inside finish put on the building; the old chimneys taken down and replaced by new; the rooms finished in native woods; the small windows enlarged; and Lutheran, long and bay windows, porch and piazza added, and the interior so changed that its former owners would hardly recognize it. The outside retains the lean-to roof on the North, and the general shape of the old house. The barn was moved across the road from where it had long been an eyesore to the Manse and placed nearly on the site of the blacksmith shop, and the view over the meadows and battleground improved."

THE BLOCK HOUSE.

The Block house, or what remains of it is situated on Main Street, the first building west of the Bank. It is owned now by Miss Louisa Kennedy and occupied by F. Holland. As it stands on land adjacent to the second burying ground its location may indicate that it was on land of the town since it may be inferred that the burying ground was on such land if not given by two sisters as tradition has it. The Block house was supposed to have been built as a garrison in King Philip's war and to have been made largely of solid pine logs. Judge John S. Keyes says, in 1839, when there was an enlargement made on the west side for a window, he witnessed the workmen sawing through solid pine logs.

It might be difficult to trace the entire succession of owners of this ancient structure. It is presumable that after being used as long as needful for a public purpose, it was sold to private parties for a dwelling place.

The first private owner of whom we have any knowledge was Rev. Daniel Bliss, a royalist who lived there before the Revolutionary war and is supposed to have made the first alterations in it. From Bliss it passed into the possession of Dr. Isaac Hurd, who at one time owned nearly or quite all the land between this building and the river at the south bridge. From about 1850 to 1880, it was occupied by Dr. Henry A. Barrett.

Associated with this old house is much that is suggestive of a stormy period in olden times. It is true that Concord, unlike some of the interior towns of Middlesex County, in King Philip's war was spared an attack by the Indians; nevertheless it was subject to the liability of sudden assault, and hence on more than one occasion the inhabitants of the lone outlying hamlets may have been summoned to this little central stronghold by the firing of significant signal guns, warning them that suspicious forms had been seen lurking by the wood side, or that the tracks of strange feet had been discovered along the meadow paths, or that mysterious smoke rising from lonesome localities where no settler was known to live, might betoken the presence of savages who very soon would be at their doors; and as down through the years we come in thought we can perhaps faintly conceive of events that transpired about this building, when about a century later in 1775 the British Regulars marched past and may be, visited it in their search for public stores.

In former years, an ancient jail stood near and was reached perhaps by a path along its very garden fence if it had one, and the poor debtor whose board in the little grim prison house may have been paid by some obstinate creditor might have been reminded of home comforts and sighed for restoration to them, by sight of this house.

In its present appearance it shows but little sign of antiquity and as it stands smiling by the roadside near the place of old graves, there is nothing to remind the traveler that in that city of the dead may be the dust of many who have passed in and out of this old building.

THE HUNT HOUSE.

The Hunt house is situated at Punkatassett. It bears the mark of great age and is supposed to have been built about 1725. The original clapboards were of an old-fashioned length. The place is now the property of Mr. William Hunt, a great-grandson of the original owner.

THE ABEL HOSMER HOUSE.

The Abel Hosmer House is situated on Elm street near Concord Junction and is owned or occupied by George M. Baker. It is on a part of the original James Hosmer estate whose lone homestead by the interval of the Assabet river to the westerly was at its beginning one of the town's outpost houses. It is supposed to have been built about 1750, by one of the Hosmer family.

The Wheeler House, This house with its leanto-roof to the rearward, and its little well-kept front porch pleasantly facing towards the wayside is very old, having been built probably from 160 to 200 years ago. It well deserves the name it is known by since it has always been identified with the Wheeler family which is one of the most numerous in Concord. It stands on the Sudbury road on the most direct way from the Public Library to the R. R. Station, and is now the property of Miss Helen Blanchard, a lineal descendant of the first owner.

THE JOSEPH HOSMER HOUSE.

This is situated a little beyond the South bridge and was probably erected in 1751. It was the home of Joseph Hosmer at the time of the Concord Fight. The house was searched at that time by the English soldiers for military stores while its proprietor was acting as Adjutant of the assembling provincials by request of Col. James Barrett. It is now owned by Prescott Keyes, Esq.

THE WOODS HOUSE.

This is now used as a school for boys and is known as the Concord School. The present master of the school and manager of the estate is Thomas H. Eckfeldt, A.M. The house was built soon after 1760 and was also searched April 19, 1775 for military stores supposed to be secreted there.

THE BUTTRICK. HOUSE.

This old and historic homestead is near the North bridge and now owned by Joseph Derby. It was built, it is asserted, by Jonathan Buttrick in 1712, and April 19, 1775 was owned and occupied by Major John Buttrick, who took a conspicuous part in the Concord fight. Before this old building to the eastward is the "Battle Lawn" lately so called, where the militia and minute men were formed, preparatory to their march to the bridge; and near it the detachment of Regulars under Capt. Parsons passed on their way to and from the home of Col. James Barrett.

THE BARRETT HOUSE.

The Barrett House is perhaps better known to the public than any other in Concord, because of its former owner and occupant Col. James Barrett of Concord Fight fame. An extended account of this house was given in a former chapter. It is in the vicinity of Annusnuck hill and was probably built about 1725—50. The L is supposed to have been added years after the erection of the main building.

In the dooryard of this house the British made a bonfire of the Provincial gun-carriages, while Capt. Parsons's command were searching the house for other Provincial property.

THE OLD MANSE.

The Old Manse stands a little back from the road on Monument street, a short distance from the public square.

The plot of ground upon which it stands was originally the property of James Blood father and son who had fourteen acres allowed them in this vicinity. Various have been the owners and various and distinguished have been the occupants of this old mansion. Few if any homes in our land have associated with them more features of historic and classic interest. It was for a long time the home of Rev. Ezra Ripley, a prominent pastor of the Concord First Parish. As for many years it was occupied by successive ministers many of the New England Clergy have been entertained there, and the walk from the memorable highway that passes it, to the little vine clad front has many times been trod by the feet of distinguished visitors, and the "prophet's chamber" has doubtless witnessed the presence of guests, whose names if we knew them all would make a long and honored list.

To the rear is the river flowing onward as tranquil and bright as is the memory of the lives that were lived within those peaceful precincts.

THE WRIGHT TAVERN.

The Wright Tavern which apart from its age is among the historic objects in Concord was built about 1747. It stands near the spot where there was an earth pit from which the owners of the Bulkeley Grist Mill obtained material with which to repair the mill-dam, a right which was stipulated for when the mill privilege was granted.

The plot of ground which was a part of the small portion at the central village owned by the town was sold by a committee appointed for the purpose at a town meeting in May 1744, to Ephraim Jones in consideration of his paying the sum of thirty pounds and also an agreement that the "broken ground" in said town between the training field and the meeting house "be improved in such way and manner as to prevent the Training field from wasting away the town's land."

The record of a conveyance of this property was dated June 22, 1785 and describes a small piece of land with bounds "Beginning at a stake at the Northeasterly corner and leaving the highway full fore rods wide." Not long after the purchase of the aforesaid property Mr. Jones began to build, and a tavern was established there as early at least as the middle of the 18th century.

Nov. 25, 1751, Landlord Jones sold the premises to Thomas Munroe who came to Concord from Lexington. Munroe kept the place open to the public as an Inn until he died in 1766. After his death the place was sold at a mortgagee's sale to Daniel Taylor, the deed passing from Deacon Thomas Barrett who held the mortgage.

In 1775 Amos Wright was carrying on the business of inn keeper at this house, either as agent or proprietor. While thus engaged the Concord Fight occurred, and from that time forth the old tavern stand has been associated with his name.

In the colonial period when this old hostelry was open to the public it was prominently identified with town business. Its first proprietor Jones having been a leading town officer as well as militia captain, more or less of the officials met there for the transaction of town business.

Sometime during the year 1775, the property passed into the hands of Samuel Swan of Charlestown, who kept tavern there till 1785. From that time till a comparatively recent date the house ceased to be used as a place of public entertainment.

The next owner was Reuben Brown a saddler who once lived in the Antiquarian House. Since the house was closed as a tavern a variety of callings have been represented there, among which is that of the livery man, the baker, the book binder, the store keeper, the tinsmith, and the shoe dealer.

At present the property belongs to the "First Parish Society," it having been donated to it by the late Reuben Rice and Judge E. Rockwell Hoar who were joint owners.

The house some years since again became an Inn, and at present is kept by Mr. John J. Busch.

As it stands on the corner of Main and Lexington streets, west of the Burying ground hill and just northerly of the First Parish Meeting house, it is one of the conspicuous objects near the Public Square.

The historic features of this old hostelry are such as to render it much sought for by sightseers; and it is said that as many as fifteen thousand guests registered there the last year.

For a long time the old fireplaces, of which there is one in nearly every room, were closed up, but of late they have been re-opened, and the present proprietor has attempted to give the old house somewhat of its former antique appearance. Visitors are welcomed for an inspection of the premises, and whatever of cheer modern appliances can afford may be expected. As reference has been made in another part of this volume to the relation of the Wright Tavern to the Concord Fight, it is unnecessary to repeat it here.

The old picture by Doolittle and Earle, painted in 1775 represents the British soldiers as halting before the door while their commander, Lieutenant-colonel Smith and his Major, Pitcairn, are in the burying ground on the hill, looking over the village where the soldiers are in search of military stores. Before the Wright Tavern and along the way toward the public Square, the Royal troops are drawn up with martial precision, in close ranks, apparently awaiting the return of their officers for orders.

Of all the works of man set forth in this picture, which though crude in perspective, may nevertheless be comparatively accurate in detail, there is probably not one that has undergone less of change than the Wright Tavern. It stood there then as now it stands, defiant of storms and untouched by the embellishment of modern art, while its main companions of that old and memorable day are the moss-stained tomb stones nearly opposite, the ancient roadway, the meadows and the brook.

THE COLONIAL.

The Colonial House, or what we call the Colonial, is composed of three houses which were formerly distinct and separate from each other, viz: the White house, a public store house, and the Thoreau House. Each of these portions is supposed to antedate the War of the Revolution.

The White house takes its name from a former occupant by the name of White. The middle portion was used as a deposit for Provincial military supplies, and the Thoreau house was once owned by aunts of Henry Thoreau. An interesting fact connected with the Colonial House is that the portion of it which was once a public store house was probably visited by John How, a British spy, as he styled himself, whose diary was printed at Concord, N. H. in 1827.

How left Boston by order of Gen. Gage given April 5, 1775, to examine the roads, bridges and fording places, and ascertain which was the best route for an army to take to Worcester to destroy military stores deposited there. He returned by way of Concord where, he states, he was introduced to Major Buttrick and several other gentlemen and was invited to dine at the tavern. He states: "I was now invited to take dinner at the tavern with a number of gentlemen. The conversation at dinner was respecting the Regulars at Boston which they expected out." After relating further conversation he continued as follows: "By this time we had got through dinner. After dinner we walked up to the storehouse to examine some guns. I told them I could make any they wished. Here I found a quantity of flour, arms, and ammunition. After examining the gates and doors attached to yard and storehouse, I returned to the tavern, where, after taking some brandy and water I took leave of them."

The Colonial House is situated at Concord center fronting the Public Square, and the proprietor is William E. Rand. It is resorted to by tourists at all seasons; and in summer especially, because of its abundant foliage and pleasant southerly outlook upon the town's common land, the soldier's monument and the old burying ground.

Of the other houses in this list we have too limited a knowledge to make more than a passing mention. The Heyward, Alcott, Brown, Bull, Beal and Meriam houses are all situated on Lexington street and probably antedate 1750. On the Bull estate the Concord Grape was originated.

Besides the history of old houses in Concord there are several sites that merit especial notice. One of these is on Lowell street and marked by a tablet designating it as the place where the house of the town's first minister stood. Great care was taken by the committee on erecting tablets in Concord, that there should be no mistake as to the identity of the spot marked.

Tradition has always asserted it, and according to a statement of one of the oldest inhabitants there was visible at this place an ancient earth dent; but the evidence does not rest wholly with these things. Several years ago when workmen were engaged in this immediate locality making excavations for a public purpose they came upon the remnant of an old cellar wall just where one might be expected to be found provided the conclusions of the committee were correct. There has also been collected about the premises, building material of an antique pattern in the shape of brick or tile. The brick or tile, for it is stated that neither term will hardly describe them, were made of lime obtained from clam shells, and were evidently manufactured many years ago.

The Major Simon Willard house site is near the Concord School for Boys just beyond the South Bridge and is also marked by a tablet. The identity of this spot is unmistakable; and there is no question but that there the daring and energetic major made his early home which was probably the farthest westward of any in the Bay colony; and when the wigwam of his Indian neighbor that stood near Egg rock, and the homes of his fellow townsmen on the "Little Strate Strete" were about equidistant from him.

Probably the house when erected ended the road towards the wilderness and was literally "out west" and when the floods swelled the Musketequid or thin ice covered it, he and his household were completely isolated from the settlement.

It may be the location of this pioneer homestead on the west bank of the Musketequid that occasioned the erection of the first "town bridge" near there, of which Walcott writes: "The first bridge over the South River is said to have been placed a short distance below the bend in the stream against Mr. Hurd's land, a location afterwards abandoned for the present one, in order to obtain a more direct course for the road to Lancaster."

The first neighbor to live at the westward beyond Mr. Willard was perhaps James Hosmer.

Of the road that may have been extended westward for his accommodation, the writer just referred to says: "The earliest way from the South Bridge to the Derby place ran in a curved line, between Nashawtuck Hill and the house of Charles H. Hurd, to the old Colburn house lot, and then turning more to the westward, reached the Hosmer's, and crossed the river by a ford-way near the railroad bridge. When, however, a bridge was thrown over the river, where it is now crossed, at this point, the commonly travelled way to and from the town was by the John Hosmer place."

Thus step by step the various ways as they radiated into the deep woods from the little hamlet that gathered and grew at Concord's geographical center might be traced by the sites of old homesteads, were it not that time with its "ever effacing finger" has almost obliterated them.

As it is difficult to ascertain where many of the early house sites are, for the same reason it is hard to determine what of a town's outlying portion may at different periods have been the most populous.

There are in more or less of the New England townships districts now abandoned to a wild vegetable growth, which may once have resounded with the activities of busy life.

Illustrative of this is what Thoreau says of Walden pond. He informs us that in that vicinity were dwellings which in his day were nearly obliterated. Among those who lived there as he gives them were Cato Ingraham, Zilpha, Brister, Freeman, Stratton, Breed, Gondibert, Nutting, Le Grosse and Hugh Quoil. Of the homes in which they lived he says: "Now only a dent in the earth marks the site of these dwellings, with buried cellar stones, and strawberries, raspberries, thimble-berries, hazel-bushes, and sumachs growing in the sunny sward there; some pitch-pine or gnarled oak occupies what was the chimney nook, and a sweet-scented black-birch, perhaps, waves where the door-stone was.

"Still grows the vivacious lilac a generation after the door and lintel and the sill are gone, unfolding its sweet-scented flowers each spring, to be plucked by the musing traveler; planted and tended once by children's hands, in front-yard plots, — now standing by wall-sides in retired pastures, and giving place to new-rising forests; — the last of that stirp, sole survivor of that family. Little did the dusky children think that the puny slip with its two eyes only, which they stuck in the ground in the shadow of the house and daily watered, would root itself so, and outlive them, and house itself in the rear that shaded it, and grown man's garden and orchard, and tell their story faintly to the lone wanderer a half century after they had grown up and died, — blossoming as fair, and smelling as sweet, as in that first spring."

CHAPTER XXXII.

Development of the Settlement — Indications of Progress — Various Hindrances — Discouraging Report — Unsatisfactory Condition of the River Meadows — Measures taken for a Betterment of the Meadows—Unproductive Uplands — Emigration to Connecticut — The Towns Recuperative Energy — Condition in 1654.

ABOUT the time of an adjustment of matters relating to the town's territory, rules and regulations were made and adopted regarding its municipal management. As the town was divided into several districts termed quarters, the work of constructing and maintaining highways and bridges was also provided for and apportioned.

These things together with the usual town meeting enactments in matters pertaining to public convenience are indications that the town steadily kept pace with its sister settlements. But any prosperity whether of township or individuals in those strenuous times was only obtained by dint of great and persevering effort. We judge from a paper presented to the General Court within ten years after the settlement began that there were grave doubts as to the ability to survive the hindrances that beset them on every hand. In a petition, presented May 14, 1645 the signers stated: "Many homes in the Towne stand voyde ot Inhabitants and more are likely to be: and we are confidenta that if conscience had not restrained, fearing the disolution of the Towne by their removal, very many had departed to one place or otherwhere Providence should have hopefully promised a livelihood."

After this plain statement of fact which set forth the state of temporal affairs in Concord and at the same time almost in a single sentence showed the devout and worthy character of the signers there is a pathetic explanation of their attitude in words as follows: "This our condition we thought it oure duty to informe you of, fearing least if more go from us we shall neither remayne as a congregation nor a towne, and then such as are most unwilling to depart, whiles there remayne any hopes of ordinance amongst us, will be enforced to leave the place, which if it should come to pass, wee desire this may testify on the behalf of such, it was not a mynd unsatisfyed with what was convenient, which occasioned them to depart, but meerly to attaine a subsistence for themselves and such as depend on them, and to enjoy ordinances."

One great cause of discouragement was the condition of the river meadows in times of high water. Sept. 8, 1636 an order was passed by the Court which is supposed to be a response to a petition for river betterments.

"Whereas the inhabitants of Concord are purposed to abate the falls in the ryver upon wch their towne standeth, whearby they conceive such townes as shalbeee hereafter planted above them vpon the said ryver shall receive benefit by reason of their charge & labor, it is therefore ordered, that such townes and ffarms as shalbee planted above them shall contribute to the inhabitants of Concord portionable both to their charge & adventure, and according to the benefit that the said townes or ffarms shall receive by the dreaning of their medows." (Mass. Records Vol. 1 page 178).

As evidence that the agitation of this subject was continued at times during subsequent years we have the following record bearing date Nov. 13, 1644, which relates to commissioners appointed at that time "to the better surveying, improving and draining of the meadows and saving and preserving of the hay there gathered either by draining the same or otherwise and to proportion the charges laid about it as equally and justly (only upon them that own lands) as they in their wisdom shall see meete."

Johnson says that in 1654, "The falles causeth their meadows to be much covered with water, the while these people together with their neighbor towne (Sudbury) here several times essayed to cut through but cannot; yet it may be turned another way with an hundred pound charge." The way proposed was a channel across the country to Watertown or Cambridge.

It may be difficult at this distant day to conceive of the inconvenience and deprivation occasioned by the river floods, for conditions are different. Then, the farmers depended largely upon the hay produced on these marsh lands not only for their dairy products but also for fertilizer for their upland. This latter was a very important matter.

The settlers could raise their corn at the first by placing in the hill a single alewife yet later when the ground had become partially exhausted by successive crops, something more substantial was needed as a plant stimulant so that considering the circumstances there is little wonder that the people complained and called for meadow betterments.

Neither may we doubt as to the results of these disadvantages. Johnson says the people "were forced to cut their bread very thin for a season" and Walcott, writing of the first year, states: "It cannot be wondered at that some sickened and died by reason of the unaccustomed hardships and severity of the winter weather, while others lost all faith in the success of the enterprise, sold their estates for a little, and departed. The cattle died, wolves preyed upon the herds; homesickness and fear of an Indian attack increased the burden of their lives, so that it became well-nigh greater than they could bear."

Besides the loss occasioned by the wetness of the meadows, some of the uplands were considered poor, for we find the following records concerning them: "Finding the lands about the town very barren." "Neither have we found any special hand of God gone out against us only the povertie and meannesse of the place." Again we find in a petition presented about 1655, "and our land much of it being pine land which affords very little feeding for cattle." It is hardly to be supposed that the soil was very unlike much of the uncleared land of Concord at the present.

The Indians had not exhausted much of the land, for it was not in accord with Indian nature to work much, and we believe their corn fields were comparatively few and small; and perhaps the lands earliest cleared were the pine lands because it would be an easier task to effect the clearing and the planting of them and these lands might have had lighter soil than the hardwood lands.

But in addition to these adverse circumstances in the natural world, the people of Concord early encountered obstacles in the little social and religious world in which they lived. As has been already stated, some friction existed early between the minister and the elder. Whether it was of an ecclesiastical or of a financial nature, we do not judge. It may have been both, as is indicated by the following statement of Winthrop in his history: "Some of the elders went to Concord, being sent for by the church there to advise with them about the maintenance of the elders &c. They found them wavering about removal not finding their plantations answerable to their expectation, and the maintenance of two elders too heavy a burden for them. The Elders advice was that they should continue and wait upon God, and be helpful to their elders in labor and what they could, and all to be ordered by the deacons, (whose office had not formerly been improved this way amongst them,) and that the elders should be content with what means the church was able at present to afford them, and if either of them should be called to some other place, then to advise with other churches about removal."

By the combination of these untoward circumstances during the first decade, was the going forth of a large company of the inhabitants to Connecticut. The movement was doubtless led by Elder Jones; and those who went with him were some of the staunch men of the settlement.

Among them are supposed to have been Dagget, Evarts, Mitchell, Odell, Barron, Tomkins, Jenney, Middlebrook, Bennet, Coslinor Costin, Ephraim and Thomas Wheeler.

John Evarts of the foregoing list is said to be the ancestor of Secretary of State William Evarts of President Grant's cabinet.

As to the scene when the company set forth tradition is silent, but it doubtless was a sad one. Mutual services associated with days of danger and deprivation in which there was a sharing together of a common lot would naturally create friendship and endearment.

The route taken by the emigrants it is not unlikely was the "Old Connecticut Path" which they could enter at a point about four miles southerly in the part of Sudbury now Wayland. Once on this trail of the Nipnet Indians, the party would probably have a fairly beaten track for a long distance towards the place they sought which was the territory of the present town of Fairfield, Long Island.

As about one eighth of the entire population of the Concord township were included in this company, it doubtless was a great blow to the settlement. Yet so great was the recuperative energy of the plantation that within ten years after the exodus, the inhabitants had extended their homesteads to the territorial limits of the town and asked for additional land grants. The lands already possessed were being developed and the resources of the town increasing generally. In 1653 a subscription of five pounds a year for seven years was ordered for the benefit of Harvard College, and Johnson informs us as follows relative to the condition of the town a year later: "The number of families at present are about 50, their head of great cattell are 300, the church of Christ here consists of about 50 souls."

CHAPTER XXXIII.

Death of Mr. Thomas Flint and the Rev. Peter Bulkeley — Departure from Concord of Major Simon Willard— Walcott's description of the Nature and Value of Major Willard's Public Services — Biographical Sketches of Thomas Flint Esquire and the Rev. Peter Bulkeley.

HARDLY had the little colony at Concord fairly recovered itself and entered upon a period of renewed prosperity after the dissention and discontent of the first two decades, when it lost three of its most prominent citizens each of whom had more than a local reputation, Thomas Flint, Rev. Peter Bulkeley and Major Simon Willard. Of these three Concord worthies the historian Walcott writes: "On October 8, 1655, the town lost one of its foremost men by the death of Thomas Flint. Two years later, Major Willard received, as a reward for his distinguished services to the country, a grant of five hundred acres of land, which he selected and laid out in the southerly part of Groton. Rev. Peter Bulkeley died March 9, 1659; and in November following, Major Willard sold his estate in Concord to Captain Thomas Marshall, of Lynn, and removed to Lancaster, whither he had previously been urged to go, and where he filled a high position. Subsequently he removed to Groton, where his son Samuel was settled as minister; and after the destruction of the town by the Indians, he took up his abode at Charlestown, where he died April 24, 1676, at the age of seventy-one years."

The departure of these men was doubtless severely felt and greatly deplored not only on account of the loss of material and moral support but because of the severance of kindred ties and associated experiences. Mr. Bulkeley had been under God, their chief spiritual guide.

Mr. Willard had surveyed their lands and represented them in places of legislation and served them as civic counselor at a time when the town needed strong men to lean upon; and Mr. Flint had doubtless long enough "ended small causes" and joined young men and maidens in marriage to endear himself to the whole community, and make his name a household word. Mr. Bulkeley and Mr. Flint were taken away by death. Major Willard moved to other places to be as bold a pioneer there as he had been in Concord town.

As a biographical sketch of Mr. Willard has been given in a former chapter we will here only quote the following relative to him from the history of Walcott: "Knowledge of men, skill in surveying lands, experience gained by trading with the natives, were qualities that fitted him in a peculiar manner to take the lead in locating the land granted by the colonial government, and fortifying the title by peaceful negotiations with the Indian occupants.

As deputy and assistant he was well known in the colony, and by the aid of his influence with those in power, the controversy with Watertown about the eastern boundary was brought to a favorable termination.

"As captain of the train-band, Willard directed the military spirit of his neighbors when military distinction was second only to that of the church. He surveyed the lands allotted to the settlers, made their deeds, was arbitrator in their controversies, kept their records, and, last office of all, settled their estates after they were dead. A person like this, — useful in any community, at any stage of its history, — was indispensable to the plantation at Musketaquid."

The lack of space prevents a very extended statement as to the place that was occupied by Mr. Thomas Flint in both the township of Concord and the Colony of Massachusetts Bay, but it may be said of him as of Mr. Willard and the Rev. Peter Bulkeley that a complete history of either could not be written without giving him prominent notice.

Thomas Flint, Esq., came from Matlock in Derbyshire, England, to the township of Concord in 1638. We are informed that his native place was beautifully situated and had a rare attractiveness; but, presumably, like many another English worthy of the non-conformist class, he preferred the great outer world in which to act as his conscience dictated, to an ecclesiastical restraint in his native land.

Walcott informs us that both Mr. Flint and Rev. Peter Bulkeley had sufficient property to bring them within the degree of subsidy men, and therefore it is supposed that embarkation from England was achieved by obtaining a special license or through the connivance of the authorities.

Mr. Flint brought to America, as a genealogy of the family states, £4000, and hence would be considered wealthy, since all the other settlers, with the exception of Messrs. Willard and Bulkeley, were, as has been said, "mere plain people with small means."

In 1639, he was made "Commissioner to hear and end small causes," having with his colleagues Simon Willard and Richard Griffin, judicial authority corresponding in modern times to a trial justice, or judge of a district court.

He was representative of the town four years and was an "Assistant" eleven years. When Assistant in 1649, he joined Governor Endicott in protesting against the wearing of long hair, taking the stand doubtless as did Mr. Bulkeley, by his example "that it was a thing unmanly."

Mr. Flint assisted in drawing up a code of simple rules and regulations for the Indians, restraining and constraining them in a wholesome manner.

He possessed one of the largest land tracts of any individual in Concord, and the fact that a way was early laid out to his farm indicates that his estate was an important one.

His real estate was mostly in what is now the town of Lincoln and extended from "Flint's Pond to Beaver Pond and the town bounds." The area contained about seven hundred and fifty acres and included the land now comprising Lincoln Center.

For many years the "Flint Farm" was occupied by descendants of the family or by their lessees. His character, we infer was a very worthy one. Johnson calls him "a most sincere servant of Christ, who had a fair revenue in England, but having improved it for Christ by casting it into the common treasury, he waits on the Lord for doubling his talent if it shall seem good unto him so to do, and in the meantime spending his person for the good of his people in the office of magistrate." In verse, he says of him as follows:

"At Christ's command thou leavest thy land and native habitation,
His folks to aid in desert-straid for Gospel exultation.
Flint, hardy thou, wilt not allow the undermining fox
With Subtile skill, Christ's vines to spoil: thy sword shall give them knocks;
Yet thou, base dust and all thou hast is Christ's, and by him thou
Art made to be, such as we see: hold fast forevermore."

The will of Mr. Thomas Flint is the first one recorded in Middlesex Probate Records. His brother Rev. Henry Flint of Braintree, and his uncle William Woods were his executors. His sons were John and Ephraim, who lived in Concord and perhaps Edward and Thomas, and William of Salem. John married Mary, daughter of Urian Oakes, President of Harvard College in 1667. In 1680-1, he was one of a committee to seat the meeting house. He is mentioned in the Indian deed of 1684 as one of those who paid for the township, and who were spoken of in the deed as "agents of the town of Concord." In 1660, he was town clerk. His children were Abigail, John, Mary, Hannah, and Jane. John Jr. married Mary Prescott and died Oct. 23, 1725, leaving an estate of £1708, and for children, John, Jonathan, a graduate of Harvard College, Mary, Elizabeth, James and Benjamin.

As in the case of Mr. Thomas Flint space forbids a complete account of the character and services of Rev. Peter Bulkeley, but enough has been stated on the foregoing pages to convince the reader that the beginning of Concord history is identified with him, and that perhaps it might be said that its success and his personal impress are inseparable. Although his later life was spent in a wilderness, by his gentle birth he was fitted for the most cultured environment and by his scholarly attainments he might have adorned any position.

Rev. Peter Bulkeley descended in the tenth generation from Robert Bulkeley, Esq., an English Baron, who, in the reign of King John, was Lord of Bulkeley in the County palatine of Chester.

As we get our starting point in that stormy period of English history, 1200-1300, when liberty was wrenched from a wicked monarch and crystalized in Magna Charta under circumstances that called forth much valor, we need not be surprised that such illustrious stock showed itself long afterwards in one whose life has elicited unusual praise and reverence.

He was born at Odell, Bedfordshire, Jan. 31, 1582, O.S and when about eighteen years old became a member of St. John's College, Cambridge, from which he received the degree of Bachelor of Divinity, which title his brother Edward also possessed.

His first pastorate was in his native town, where he succeeded his father and where he preached about a score of years as a non-conformist minister. His career in this field was terminated by Archbishop Laud, who because of his nonconformity to the established church deposed him, which act led Dr. Bulkeley soon afterwards to embark for America.

In 1635, after his arrival in this country, he went to Cambridge and was made a freeman May 6, of the same year.

He was possessed of considerable property for colonial days, the amount being estimated at several thousand pounds, but his intense enthusiasm and broad liberality in the colonization of Concord, together with other outgoings of his noble nature greatly reduced his possessions, so that at his death, which occurred March 9, 1659, his estate, as mentioned, amounted to only 1302 pounds, of which 123 pounds was in books.

So benevolent was Mr. Bulkeley that his gifts extended not only to the public but to his servants, of whom it is said he had many, and to whom he gave farms.

The scholarly traits of Mr. Bulkeley have long been known both by tradition and by the traces of them in his published works, prominent among which was one entitled "The Gospel Covenant," which was issued in 1646.

He was considered a powerful preacher, and the representations of those living near to his time are that he was evangelical and that the chief aim of his ministry was to impress upon men their religious needs and to lead them to the Gospel as the only source of supply.

As a pastor, we conclude he was full of zeal for the spiritual wellbeing of his flock, as it is said that seldom did a person leave his presence without having heard some word that impressed him with the importance of religion.

As a man he was large-hearted, public spirited, and attracted people through his personal affability. He was considered the father of his parish, exemplary in conduct, wise in counsel, tender and appreciative to the law-abiding and severe in his judgment of evildoers. His dress was plain and he wore his hair short. We infer that his constitution was robust since he endured much and lived to the age of seventy-seven.

The names of his children by his first marriage are as follows: Edward, Mary, Thomas, Nathaniel, John, Mary, George, Daniel, Jabez, Joseph, William and Richard.

The following are the names of children by his second marriage: Gershom, Eleazer, Dorothy and Peter.

Edward became a minister and succeeded his father in the pastorate at Concord.

Peter, born Aug. 12, 1643, went to Fairfield Conn, to which place his two brothers, Thomas who married a daughter of Elder John Jones, and Daniel went in 1644.

In a will of Gershom made May 12, 1712, is the following item; "To my brother's children, Gershom, Peter, Grace, Margaret and Dorothee, I give each of them ten shillings."

In a will of Peter Bulkeley of Fairfield Conn, dated March 25, 1691, the testator speaks of himself as being in the 49th year of his age; and mentions a son Peter and daughters Grace and Margaret.

The name Bulkeley has been variously spelled. The first Peter wrote it "Bulkeley;" his son Edward wrote it "Bulkely" or "Bulkeley;" and the Hot Peter son of Edward followed the form used by his grandfather. The common pronunciation of the name is as if spelled Buckley.

Rev. Peter Bulkeley in the second division of land received a tract of seven hundred and fifty acres in what is now Lincoln, a part of which is the present Codman place.

It is not known where the distinguished pioneer pastor of Concord was buried. The Rev. Dr. Ripley in his "Half Century" sermon says "There is reason to believe that the three first ministers viz, Peter Bulkeley, Edward Bulkeley and Joseph Estabrook were laid in the same tomb."

His will is among the Probate records of Middlesex County, and in this will are the following clauses, which serve to reveal much of his character "In case any of my children before named in this, my will, to whom I have bequeathed the legacies named shall prove disobedient to their mother or otherwise vicious or wicked (which God in his mercy prevent) then, I will that the legacy shall be virtually in the power of my said widow, their mother, to deal with them therein as she herself in Christian wisdom shall think meet, either to give their legacy or to keep it herself."

He alludes to his "wasted estate," which he says "is now very little in comparison of what it was when I came first to these places, having made great sacrifices in the beginning of these plantations and having little to leave to the children God hath given me and to my precious wife, whose unfeigned piety and singular grace of God shining in her doth deserve more than I can do for her." He gave a portion of his library to Harvard College.

In connection with the foregoing account of the town's first minister it may be appropriate to publish copies of the following papers. The first of these Shattuck informs us is endorsed as the "Concord Church Covenant" and although without signature or date it has internal evidence of authenticity and of being the first covenant.

We present it as it is given by Shattuck, the orthography only being changed: "Considering the instability and inconstancy of our hearts in cleaving to the Lord in that which is good, we do bind ourselves one with another this day before the Lord, that we will endeavor by the grace of God assisting us, henceforward to walk as becometh the people of God, according to the gospel of our Lord Jesus Christ. And more particularly do we promise and covenant before the Lord, that, whereas he hath of his great goodness brought us from under the yoke and burdening of men's traditions to the precious liberty of his ordinances which we now do enjoy, we will, according to our places and callings, stand for the maintenance of this liberty to our utmost endeavor, and not return to any human ordinances from which we are escaped. And we further covenant to subject ourselves to every ordinance of Christ, which he shall please to make known to us to be his will. Also we do take him to be our only Priest to instruct us, our only High Priest to make peace with the Father for us: so we will set him up as our King and Sovereign to command us, to rule in us and reign over us by the help of his word and Spirit. And that we may the better be kept in an holy subjection to him and his will, we will both watch over each other in the Lord, admonishing one another, both to prevent the evils into which we might fall, and to recover ourselves out of those that we have been overtaken with, not suffering any raging pollution or spiritual uncleanness amongst us, but labor to cast it forth by the power which Christ hath given to his church. And further, considering that we are members one of another, and have civil respect and are liable to be oppressed and devoured one of another; and considering also the increase of this evil, daily getting strength through the abounding of self-love so mightily prevailing in us; we do therefore here solemnly promise before the Lord, that we will carefully avoid of oppression, griping, and hard dealing, and walk in peace, love, mercy, and equity towards each other, doing to others as we would they should do to us. And in testimony of our willing assent to this covenant we have hereunto subscribed our names."

The second paper is a letter written by the Rev. Peter Bulkeley to Mr. Cotton of Boston. "To the Reverend his honored friend Mr. Cotton, Teacher of the Church at Boston, give these.

"Reverend in the Lord, "Some other things I am full of, but will not write with paper and ink; only in a word I bless God for what I hear, how the Lord doth fill your ministry with abundance of grace, life, and power, to the exceeding joy of those that are true-hearted towards the Lord. But withall I stand amazed and wonder att God's forbearance, considering what I hear in another kind; which I doe also believe to be true in some parts; true I mean, as done and spoken by some, though untrue, in respect of any cause given on your part. Truly, Sir, it is to me a wonder, that the earth swallows not up such wretches, or that fire comes not downe from heaven to consume them. The L. hath a number of holy and humble ones here amongst us (in the country generally), for whose sakes he doth spare, and will spare long; but were it not for such a remnant, we should see the L. would make quick work amongst us. Shall I tell you what 1 think to be the ground of all this insolency which discovers itself in the speach of men? Truly I cannot ascribe it so much to any outward thing, as to the putting of too much liberty and power into the hands of the multitude, which they are too weak to manage, many growing conceited, proud, arrogant, self-sufficient, as wanting nothing. And I am persuaded, that except there be means used to change the course of things in this point, our churches will grow more and more corrupt day by day; and tumult will arise hardly to be stilled. Remember the former days which you had in old Boston, where though (through the Lord's blessing upon your labours) there was an increase daily added to your church, yet the number of professors is far more here, than it was there. But answer me, which place was better governed? Where matters were swayed there by your wisdom and counsel, matters went on with stength and power for good. But here, where the heady or headless multitude have gotten the power into their hands, there is insolency and confusion. And I know not how it can be avoided in this way, unless we should make the doors of the church narrower. This we have warrant for from the word; which course, if it should be taken, would bring its conveniency also in another kind. But of these things no more. Only I pray the L. to heal the evils of the places and times we live in, and remove that woful contempt of his gospel which doth abound. O what mischief doth one proud, lofty spirit that is in reputation for understanding, amongst a number of others that are weak; and some of both such there are in every place. But our comfort is, God's end and work shall go forward. Some shall be converted, some hardened. The God of mercy carry on his work in our hearts and hands to the gloryfying of his rich grace in Christ Jesus. I pray remember my harty love to good Mrs. Cotton, thanking her for her kind remembrance of my little ones. I pray God give us both to see his grace increasing in those that he hath continued towards us. Farewell, dearly beloved and honoured in the Lord, comfort yourself in him, who is most ready to be found in time of need. In him I rest. Yours ever, Pet: Bulkeley.

"April 4, 1650.

To close this brief sketch without the expression of a thought concerning so conspicuous a character, or without a personal tribute, might be to pass it unworthily. We would say, therefore, that perhaps, all in all, no life has been more consequential in the history of any colonial town. It is a tradition that Concord was saved in the war with King Philip by his exemplary conduct and benign influence over the Indians, in that when they were assembled on a neighboring hilltop on April, 1675-6, and undecided whether to attack Sudbury or Concord, they concluded to avoid the latter for "Big Pray" had lived there.

Upon the altar of the municipality he placed his prayers, his personality and his property. Going to it rich, he passed from it comparatively poor, and if through the dark and discouraging places in the early annals of this ancient township there has never ceased to be seen a bright spot, we may account for its presence by his influence, who while living always blest and when dead lived in the lives of others.

CHAPTER XXXIV.

Settlement of Rev. Edward Bulkeley — Rev. Joseph Estabrook called as Colleague Pastor — Measures taken for their Maintenance—Biographical Sketches of Rev. Edward Bulkeley—Peter Bulkeley Esquire—Acquisition of New Territory—Stow, Littleton, Carlisle and Acton—Iron Industry.

AFTER the death of Rev. Peter Bulkeley the church extended a call to his son Edward at a salary of eighty pounds a year. In 1667, the Rev. Joseph Estabrook was employed as his colleague at the same salary. It thus occurred that the town within the space of a score and a half of years after its settlement was the second time called upon to support two religious teachers at the same time. But the people did not flinch from fulfilling their obligation to their ministers.

Feb. 3, 1680 it was voted "that every house holder that hath a teame greate or lesser shall accordingly carry yearly one loade of wood to the ministe and every other house holder or rateable person to cut wood one day and for the ministers: and that the wood is to be equaly devided to too ministers as the selectmen for the time being shall appoynr."

Even in old age when his usefulness as a pastor had for the most part ceased the Rev. Edward Bulkeley was provided for by his people as indicated by the following vote passed March 5, 1694, "Whereas their Reverd Pastor Mr. Edward Bulkeley is under such Infermatyes of Body by Reason of great age that he is not capeable of Attending the worke of the ministry as in times past, being Also sensible of the obligation that they are under to Afford to him a comfortable maintenance dureing the Terme of his natural life, that thereby they may Testefy their Gratitude for his former service in the Gospell that they the sayd People of sayd Concord do hereby oblige ye sayd Towne to pay to ye s'd Mr. Bulkeley or to his certain order yearly each year dureing his natural life the sum of thirty pounds of mony the one halfe at or before the first of May sixteen hundred ninety five, which sum as above shall bee yearly and each year upon the sayd Termes, and which sum of Thirty pounds truly payd as above, shall be in lieu of the former sallary of eighty pounds which the sayd people were obliged to have payd yearly to him the sayd Mr. Bulkeley for his ministerial service."

The Rev. Edward Bulkeley was born at Odell, England June 17, 1614. He was admitted as a member of the First Church in Boston in 1634. He acquired his professional education under the direction of his father; and was ordained at Marshfield in 1642 or 3. He died at Chelmsford Jan. 2, 1696 and was buried at Concord. It is stated by William Prescott Greenlaw, Librarian of the New England Historic Genealogical Society, that the name of Rev. Edward Bulkeley's wife was Lucyan; that she was living in 1668, and that her name is repeated in the Emerson branch of her descendants. They had four children: Peter, Elizabeth, John, Jane and Mary.

Peter was born Jan. 3, 1641, at Concord. He graduated at Harvard College in 1660 and died in 1688.

Elizabeth married for her first husband, Rev. Joseph Emerson Dec. 7, 1665; her second husband was John Moody of Reading. John, the third child died young at Marshfield and was buried Feb. 26, 1658. Jane married Ephraim Flint. Mary was born about 1655 and married about the year 1678 Rev. Thomas Clark of Chelmsford.

Peter became the Hon. Peter Bulkeley who early began a political career in which he became quite distinguished. He was admitted as a freeman May 11, 1760, and on May 7, 1673 ne was elected deputy to the Colonial Court where he served three succeeding terms, and the last year he was chosen Speaker.

For eight years he was Assistant; and Sept. 6, 1676, he with William Stoughton was sent to England to negotiate with the King relative to certain matters of dispute in the Bay Colony. In military and also in judicial affairs he held high positions, being made a Major and by the appointment of Governor Andros an Associate Justice with Chief Justice Dudley. He married Rebecca, daughter of Lieut. Joseph and Sarah Wheeler on April 16, 1667. Their children were Edward, Joseph, John and Rebecca. The latter married Jonathan Prescott Jr.

Peter Bulkeley died May 24, 1688, at Concord after a long illness at less than fifty years of age. His life had been full of activity but was somewhat unfortunate towards its close. Before his death his estate was in an insolvent condition. His honors had faded; he was separated from his early associates in public life, and he repaired to his native town worn and broken in health.

At the time of his decease he lived "next ye Millpond,"

Walcott states, perhaps where Dr. Barrett now lives.

Elizabeth the third child who married for her first husband Rev. Joseph Emerson in 1680, and for her second, John Moody of Reading, had children as follows: Peter, Edward and Joseph.

Peter married a Miss Brown, Edward married Mary Moody and Joseph married Rebecca Waldo.

A descendant of Joseph and Rebecca was Ralph Waldo Emerson.

The following is the lineal order of successors to the great essayist.

4 Rev. Joseph Emerson—Eliz. Bulkeley.

12 Edward Emerson — Rebecca Waldo.

28 Joseph Emerson— Mary Moody.

123 William Emerson — Phebe Bliss.

307 Rev. William Emerson Ruth Haskins.

601. Ralph Waldo Emerson

A portrait of Peter Bulkeley Esq. supposed to have been painted by Sir Godfrey Kneller at the time when Mr. Bulkeley was in England as agent for the Massachusetts Colony in 1676-79 is now or was in the possession of Mrs. George D. Sargent of Boston. This picture has been reproduced and furnished by William Prescott Greenlaw a descendant of Hon. Peter Bulkeley for the Genealogical Advertiser Vol. 1 1898.

In the early part of the third decade of the town's history it again petitioned for more land and a tract was granted which afterwards became the town of Acton and a part of Littleton and Carlisle.

A movement was also made by several citizens of Concord in conjunction with some others to colonize a tract to the west and southwest a result of which was the granting of territory which became the town of Stow.

As a concise and consecutive account of these transactions has been given by Shattuck in his time-honored history we quote it as perhaps the most suitable description that can be given by us.

"On the 23rd, May 1655 "Five thousand acres of Land were granted to the Inhabitants of Concord for feeding, according to their petition, provided it hinder not any former grants." This was all the tract of land described in the above return, excepting the farms belonging to Major Willard. When his farms were granted I have not been able to find out. One of them lay in the southeast part of the tract, and the other at the northeast. This distinguished individual had several subsequent grants. On the 6th of May, 1657, he had "for services to the colony, 500 acres of land in any place where he could find it according to law;" and 21st of May, 1658, he had 500 acres more "on the south side of a river that runneth from Nashua to Merrimack, between Lancaster and Groton, and is in satisfaction of a debt of £44" due from John, sagamore of Pawtucket. His execution was to be given up. This farm was laid out in May, 1659, by Thomas Noyes.

The Praying Indians claimed some right to the land granted to Concord "for an enlargement to the towne; " in consideration of which, "the town of Concord doth give to them the planters of Nashoba, fifteen pounds at six a penny, which giveth them full satisfaction. In witness whereof they doe set to their hands this 20 of the 10 mo. 1660." This agreement was signed by "Nassquaw, marchant Thomas (Thomas Waban), Wabatut, great James Natototos—a blind man, Ponpant, and Gomgos," by their marks; and John Thomas and John Tahattawan, by their names; and witnessed by Joseph Wheeler, John Shepard, and John Jones "At a generall court held at Boston the 11th of October, 1665. In answer to the peticion of Concord for an enlargement of their bounds, this court doe grant them a tract of land conteyned in a plott returned to this court under the hand of Ensign Noyes, by estimation the whole being about five thousand acres, whereof the town reserveth two thousand acres to be layd out to either Indians or English, as this court shall see meete hereafter to dispose and grant, and the remaynder, being about three thousand acres, this court grant to Concord so as the same doe not abridge any former grant made by this court; and doe order Leift. Beers and Leift. Thomas Noyes to lay out the same and to make returne thereof to the next Court of Election. A true copie. Attest, Edw. Rawson. Seer."

The following is a copy of the return made 25 May, 1667 and approved by the proper authorities. "We, Richard Beers of Watertown and Thomas Noyes of Sudbury, being appointed to lay out and measure to the inhabitants of Concord a tract or tracts of land next adjoining to their first grant; in order to which, we the above said, did lay out and measure unto the inhabitants of Concord their second grant, being five thousand acres of land granted in the year 1655, as also their grant of three thousand acres granted in the year 1665, next adjoining to their first grant, beginning at the southwest angle of their old bounds (near Maj. Hayward's), extending their said southerly line upon a northwest point, four degrees northerly (according to the Meridian compass) two miles and 280 rods: there making a right angle on a bare hill, and from thence a line upon a northeast point 4 degrees easterly two miles one half and fifty rods, there meeting Nashoba plantation line, running the line of the said plantation to their angle one mile one quarter and 60 rods, nearest hand upon an easterly point, there making a right angle, running a line, being the line of the Indian plantation, two miles one quarter and 60 rods, there being bounded by Chelmsford line and Bilrica line as is more plainly described by a plott; in which plott is contained nine thousand and eight hundred acres of land, one thousand eight hundred acres being formerly granted to Major Willard, the other eight thousand being granted to the inhabitants of Concord, and laid out the 5th May, 1666. Given under our hands.

Richard Beers,   surveyors.
Thomas Noyes,

"The town agreed 20th Jan. 1668, that these additional grants of land 'shall lay for a free comon to the present householders of Concord, and such as shall hereafter be approved and allowed to be inhabitants; except such parts of it as shall be thought mete to make farms for the use and benefit of the towne.' A full title was then acquired from the Indians, though it was thought proper in 1684, for reasons already mentioned, to obtain the following confirmatory deeds.

"'To all people to whom these presents may come, greeting; Know ye that we, Mary Neepanaum, John Speen and Sarah Speen, Dorothy Winnetow, Peter Muckquamuck, of Natick, and James Speen, and Elizabeth Speen, his wife of Waymeset, Indians, for and in consideration of a valuable sum of money payd to us in hand by Capt. Timothy Wheeler, Henry Woodis, James Blood, and John Flint, the receipt whereof we do by these presents acknowledge, and therewith to be fully satisfied and contented, have sold and by these presents do sell, alien, enfeofe, and confirm unto the said Capt. Timothy Wheeler, &c. of Concord in the county of Middlesex in ye Massachusetts Colony, in New England, for the use and behoof of themselves and the rest of the proprietors of the s'd town of Concord a certain tract or parcell of land conteyning by estimation a thousand acres, be the same more or less, and is situate, lying, and being within the last grant of land by the Generall Court to ye s'd town of Concord, and is bounded south-east by Sudbury and the land of Stow alias Pompasititcutt, and norwest by the s'd Stow, running by them upon that line about a mile and a quarter, near to the hill called by the Indians Naauuhpavil; and from thence by a streight line to the North River at the old bounds of ye s'd town of Concord, unto them the said Timothy Wheeler, &c. &c. to them their heirs and successors for ever. And we the said Mary Neepanaum, &c. do hereby covenant and promise to and with the foresaid Timothy Wheeler, &c. &c.

that we are the true proprietors of, and have good right and full power to grant, bargain, and sell, the above granted and bargained premises unto the said Timothy, &c. &c. and that the said Timothy, &c. &c. shall and may at all times and from time to time for ever hereafter have, hold, occupy, possess, and enjoy the above granted premises in full, be the same more or less, without any let, denial, or contradiction of us the said Mary Neepanaum, &c. or any of us or any of our heirs, or any other person or persons whatever, lawfully claiming or having any right, title or interest therein, or to or in any parcel thereof. In acknowledgement of this our act and deed, we hereto put our hands and seals this fifth day of May in the year of our Lord one thousand six hundred eighty and four.' "All the above-named Indians signed this deed—James Speen by writing his name, and the others by their marks, in presence of Moses Parker, Noah Brooks, Samuel Wheeler jr., Benjamin Bohow and Sarah Bohow (the two last of whom were Indians), and acknowledged 'before Pet: Bulkeley, Assistant.'

The foregoing deed applied to the south part of the tract. The same individuals, in behalf of Concord, bought of 'John Thomas, and Naaunoushqua, his wife;

194

Tasunsquaw, the relict of Waban, deceased, and eldest daughter to Tahattawan, Sagamore, deceased; Thomas Waban her son; Solomon Thomas; John Nasqua; James Casumpal, sen., and Sarah, his wife; and Sarah, the relict widow of Peter Conaway, Indians,' for £21; by estimation, 8000 acres, lying in "the last grants of land by the General Court to the town of Concord, and is bounded southeast by the old bounds of the said town of Concord, easterly partly by Bilrerca, partly by a farm formerly layed out by Major Willard for himself, and partly by Chelmsford, till it meet with Nashoba line, and then westerly by the said Nashoba to the southeast corner of the said Nashoba, then northerly by the said Nashoba till it meets with Stow, and so bounded norwest by the said Stow, till it comes near to a hill by the Indians called Naaccuhpavil, and then running upon a straight line to the North River, at the old bounds of the said town of Concord.' This deed was executed and acknowledged in the same form as the preceeding, on the 13th of Aug. 1684; and witnessed by Ebenezer Engoldsbey, Joseph Wooley, Joseph Shambery, and Andrew Pittemey. These several grants were afterwards known as the 'Town's New Grant' — the 'Enlargement of the Town by the General Court,' — and generally 'Concord Village'; till after about seventy-five years they were in great part separated from Concord and incorporated as the town of Acton.

"Lieutenant Joseph Wheeler, by trading with the Nashoba Indians, became their creditor, and petitioned the General Court, in 1662, for a grant of 200 acres of land at the southerly part of their plantations as payment for his debt; but it was refused. In 1669, he, with several inhabitants of Concord, petitioned for a tract of land at Pompasiticutt: and the Court appointed him, with John Haynes of Sudbury, William Kerley of Marlborough, James Parker of Groton, and John Moore of Lancaster, a committee to view it and report at their next session. This report was made May II, 1670; and it was found 'to contain 10,000 acres of country land, whereof 500 is meadow. The greater part of it is very mean land, but we judge there will be planting ground enough to accomodate 10 families. Also there is about 4000 acres more of land that is taken up in farmes, whereof about 500 acres is meadow. There is also the Indian plantation of Nashobah, that doth border on one side of this tract of land, that is exceedingly well meadowed, and they do make but little or no use of it.' George Hayward, Joseph Wheeler, Thomas Wheeler, John Hayward, William Buttrick, Sydrach Hapgood, Stephen Hall, Edmund Wigley of Concord, and Joseph Newton and Richard Holdridge, petitioned for this tract of land; and it was granted to them 'to make a village, provided the place be setteled with not less than ten famyles within three years, and that a pious, an able, and orthodox minister be maintained there.' Daniel Gookin, Thomas Danforth, and Joseph Cook, were appointed 'to order the settlement of the village in all respects;' and the various proceedings in relation to it resulted in the incorporation of the town of Stow, May 16, 1683; which has since been found able to accomodate more than twenty families!"

Not only did the people of Concord during its first century set themselves to subduing the soil and seek assiduously to extend their domains even to the extent of obtaining territory from which might be made new townships but they sought to bring forth treasures from the earth other than those of a vegetable nature. Soon after the arrival of settlers it was ascertained that iron ore existed in the south-west part of the town in such quantities as might pay to establish iron works. Promoters of the enterprise presented themselves, prominent among whom was Oliver Purchis who had been in the iron business at Lynn.

March 5, 1658, a company was organized "To erect one or more Iron Works in Concord."

May 30, 1660, the Colonial Court gave the Company permission "To dig iron ore without molestation in any land now in the Court's possession." It also granted one thousand acres for the Company's purposes.

The industry continued with more or less success until the close of the century, when it closed as it is supposed, through lack of ore.

As the result of these operations a dam was built over the Assabet river at what is now Westvale, and near its upper portion iron works were established.

Among the names of Concord people who were stockholders are Rev. Edward Bulkeley, Robert Meriam, Timothy Wheeler, Jr. William Buss, John Niles or Miles, Joseph Hayward and Mary Griffin.

After various transfers the property passed to an owner who by 1715 had erected upon it a Grist Mill and a Fulling Mill, and in process of time a mill was built for the manufacturing of woolens. The lands in this vicinity have long been known as the Ironworks farm. The scene of some of the operations is still known as Mine hill.

It is stated that when one Leihtenegger "did attend the work of a mine at a place called fair haven" he "did build a bridge to facilitate his passage to and from said work."

At the farm formerly owned by George H. Wright at "Nine Acre Corner" indications of this industry have long been visible.

CHAPTER XXXV.

King Philip's War—Activity Preparatory to its Coming — The Part taken in the Conflict by Concord — Its Cause — The Havoc — Condition of the Country at the Outbreak of Hostilities— The State of Society — The Towns Means of Defense — Its Militia—Its Garrison Houses — The Foot Company— The Troop of Horse — Means Provided for the Relief of Refugees — Miscellaneous Military Matters.

WE have thus far considered some of the chief civic events, incidents and episodes that occurred at Concord during its first half century. We will now notice some military events of the period.

Hitherto the progress of the town was marked by a reign of peace. No shout of hostile Indian had been heard in the home of any inhabitant. No public proclamations had been issued for the levying of war-accoutered soldiers; and there had been no mortal combat. The struggle had been with the rough conditions of a new country; with rocks and brambles of unsubdued hillsides and the gnarled and mossy tree trunks of the timberlands. But at the beginning of the last quarter of the seventeenth century the scene changed. A season of strife was at hand. Along the horizon a cloud was gathering which as it arose and burst over the feeble settlement was to cause a consternation of which we in the present can but faintly conceive.

The Colony was on the eve of King Philip's war; a war which for atrocity, destructiveness, and for various dismal features was exceptional. For months before the tempest broke out, its coming was announced by a variety of unmistakable forerunners. Messengers from the forest brought intelligence that the Indians in distant places were sharpening their hatchets and tightening their bow strings; that a conspiracy was being brewed, and that soon they might expect savage invaders to prowl about the farm houses and haunt every highway and bypath and bridge.

Because of these forerunners the settler was put on his guard and in preparation for the issue he became correspondingly active. He set himself to meet prowess with prowess, and to pit strength against strength. He took down from over the mantlepiece his old musket, scraped its flint, inspected its lock, and scoured the rust from its priming pan. Bullets were cast by him on the old kitchen hearth, the contents of his powder horn were replenished from the public stock, — and everything possible was done to protect his home.

While these things were going on there was much consternation, and doubtless households were disturbed to an unusual degree. The children probably wondered why their mother looked worried and furtively glanced toward the woods. They did not understand why the cows were kept in the barnyard during the day and why outbuildings were closed early at night. To them it was all a mystery that the neighbors talked together in small companies and that after the trundle bed had been pulled out at evening there were whispered voices at the fireside. But the insignificance of all this at length showed itself and soon all were made aware that experiences were threatened such as were without parallel in their pioneer history and that the peaceful relations that had hitherto existed between the Indians and whites were to give place to a period of strife the result of which none but Heaven could foresee.

The town of Concord was so situated and circumstanced and a kind Providence so favored that it suffered no general attack as did some other places. It was however

197

subject to dire contingencies and was called upon to bear in common with the whole colony grievous taxation and to contribute its quota of soldiers to be in readiness to take the field at short notice. Moreover, it was ordered to furnish garrison houses and to provide relief measures to such as fleeing from distant frontier farm houses or neighboring towns sought refuge there.

The town also near its western frontier in the part then known as Nashoba was the scene of a dismal tragedy which was doubtless long a subject of fireside conversation for the inhabitants of that region. But although no portion of the town became a battle ground during the period of King Philip's war some of its citizens became conspicuous by their services on the battle fields of other towns and in several instances these were of a character quite distinguished. Before entering in detail upon the narration of these or other matters pertaining to Concord in Philip's war, let us notice the cause and nature of the conflict and some things concerning the condition of the country and the state of society at its commencement.

The cause of the war was a feeling of jealousy or unrest on the part of some of the aborigines engendered by a belief that the English were trying to crowd them from the soil.

This feeling culminated in an Indian alliance of several tribes for the purpose of exterminating the English and appropriating or destroying their property.

The principal progenitor of this alliance and director of its operations was Philip, a chieftain of the Wampanoags who dwelt at a place called Pokanoket or Mount Hope or Montaup near Bristol R. I.

Philip was called King by Governor Prince but his aboriginal name was Metacomet. His father was Massasoit a friend of the Plymouth pilgrims. The means King Philip employed were very sagacious, and savage though he was his energy and exploits have elicited the admiration and wonder of many writers and been the subject of ballad and song.

He is supposed to have personally visited the tribes with which he sought to form an alliance and to have fanned into a flame whatever sparks of hatred already existed, and by his example and enthusiasm to have stirred his followers to deeds which with a less daring leader, would never have been committed. By his savage torch homesteads were reduced to ashes in an hour; whole households were destroyed by his tomahawk and scalping knife; and farms once smiling in plentitude and peace were left abandoned and desolate.

Of the results of the war Trumbull in his history of Connecticut says, "About six hundred of the inhabitants of New England, the greatest part of whom were the flower and strength of the country, either fell in battle or were murdered by the enemy. Twelve or thirteen towns in Massachusetts, Plymouth Colony and Rhode Island were utterly destroyed and others greatly damaged." Another writer has stated that were all the events of the Revolution comprised in a single twelve month, they would not exceed the horrors of King Philip's war.

The condition of the country at the breaking out of the war was such as to augment the terrors even of civilized warfare. Much of the territory was still uncleared. There were vast areas of impassable swamps and thick timberland. The roads were many of them through deep forests; the bridges were frail and infrequent and those over the smaller streams may have been mere log crossings that might be swept away by a sudden flood or easily destroyed by the foe. More or less of the outlying farms were situated in exposed places without means of repelling assaults, and where the drear shadows that crept out from the woods were suited to increase the disquietude of the defenseless family. Moreover the settler was subjected to seasons of suspense; it was difficult to obtain news; the foe might be near or remote, he could not determine which. It might be venturesome to go beyond his own dooryard, and all the information he could get from the outer world may have been brought by some scout or circumstance or sign.

Another factor in the case was the nature of the enemy. The Indian when on the warpath was implacable, cunning and capable of any cruelty by which he could cripple his foe. His knowledge of the country enabled him to move about with remarkable celerity. He was acquainted with the location of every village and hamlet and no lone farmhouse had escaped his notice.

All these things King Philip took advantage of, and a characteristic of the conflict was the suddenness with which he struck, the rapidity with which settlements widely separated from each other felt the blows. So swift were his movements and so unexpectedly did he attack towns that the inhabitants almost considered him possessed of supernatural powers.

The state of society when the war broke out, may be best indicated by saying that it was just prior to the witchcraft delusion and about the time which has been designated as New England's dark age. The early fathers of the colony were dying off and with them the learning which they had brought from the old country, for there were few schools through which to transmit it to their children. It was in this period perhaps more than in any other when people signed their names with a mark. As ignorance usually begets superstition, so there was a tendency at this time to accept the marvelous, and to believe that Philip's war was preceded by omens. Mather informs us that strange sights were seen. The perfect form of an Indian bow was supposed to appear in the air at New Plymouth.

This was regarded as a "prodigious apparition." The inhabitants of Hadley, Northampton, and other towns in that vicinity thought they "heard the report of a great piece of ordinance with a great shaking of the earth and a considerable echo." Some believed that on a still morning there was a noise of discharged musketry; that bullets flew past them; that a noise of drums was heard; and that there was a sound as of the galloping of horses.

Thus the condition of the country and the state of society were such that the community and individuals were kept constantly on the alert and became suspicious of all inexplicable phenomena. To them there was a significance either natural or supernatural in every unusual sound or sight. The report of a gun fired far off in the forest, the bellowing of cattle in the pastures, flocks of birds flying affrighted from the shrubbery, a wounded deer, a missing shoat, the loud barking of a dog in a distant clearing, the mysterious imprint on the soft earth of strange footsteps, and fresh camp coals in the woods, either of these might betoken the approach of Indians and send families to the friendly garrisons.

For the reasons now considered Philip's war has been associated with exceptional hardships, and its annals, long after its occurrence were related to curious and half reluctant listeners about the home hearthside, the rude campfire, and wherever companies were gathered together under circumstances that tended to recall them. The farm boy became familiar with its leading actors and events through frequent rehearsals; and the few objects that came down through the years as grim reminders of the dismal experiences were looked upon by him as something which, if it could speak might utter strange things. Around the rusty firearms that stood in the old shed corner were gathered memories which were fraught with thrilling adventure. The snow-shoes stowed in the cold garret, the bullet molds in the little closet over the wood box, the cocked hat and faded waistcoat which clothed the dummy that relieved the weary night watch, were each suggestive in their turn. The grim walls of the old garrison, worn and weather-stained by time and storm were long associated with things that had been said of them; whether of the midnight assault and repulse, or of the timely rescue of beleaguered inmates, or of the ruse of the savage who sought to approach it behind the slow-moving bush. The stone hatchet that was unearthed in the plow land, though silent and unshapely, was eloquent nevertheless by its suggestiveness. The low grave by the meadow side, the stone heap under the trees, the faint outline of a cellar hole about which were coals yet uncrumbled,— all of these were pointed out to succeeding generations as memorials of King Philip's war.

The military history of Concord in this war comprises a description of the means employed for its own defense, the measures for a maintenance of such soldiers as the Colonial authorities might send into the town as a convenient place from which to operate by marchings and scoutings, the payment of its share of such extra taxation as was superinduced by the war, and the special service that the town by its own soldiers rendered to other places.

We will now consider each of these in the order here given.

First its means of defense. — This consisted in the town militia and garrison houses. At the outbreak of the war the organized militia of Concord consisted of one-foot company and a troop of horse. The foot company was organized in 1636, with Simon Willard, then a sergeant, as acting Captain or drill master. About a quarter of a century later the appointment by the Court was as follows: Timothy Wheeler, Captain; Jos. Wheeler, Lieut.; William Buss, Ensign; Richard Rice, Thomas Bateman and Thomas Wheeler, Sen. Sergeants; William Buttrick, Samuel Stratten and John Scotchford, Corporals.

The horse company had its organization Oct. 13, 1669 and included beside members belonging to the town also some from places adjacent. It first captain was Thomas Wheeler; its first Lieutenant Thomas Henchman; and its Quartermaster was Henry Woodhouse (or Woodis.) Shattuck says that the Horse Company was "the second and western horse company in the county and from it the present Concord Light Infantry descended." It is probable that a portion of the members of the aforesaid companies saw service in the Old Narraganset War in 1654, as its former captain, Simon Willard was at that time the commander of an expedition which set forth by order of the United Colonies against Chief Ninigret. In this expedition which was composed of 250 infantry men and 40 cavalrymen there were several soldiers from Concord.

Concerning the garrison houses of Concord Shattuck states as follows: "We have no other means than tradition to ascertain the number or situation of the garrison-houses in Concord.

The house now occupied by Dr. Hurd was originally one; another stood near John Flint's; another near Meriam's corner; two others within the present limits of

Bedford; another near John Hosmer's; and another near Silas Holden's. An Indian fort was built near Nashobah Hill in Littleton, then in Concord. These were not all. The number and situation varied, at different times, for the subsequent twenty years." That these were all the defensed places of the town we are not to infer, since ordinary farm houses were sometimes fortified and used as places of rendezvous.

In relation to the militia and other means of aggressive warfare Shattuck says, "In October, 1675, the government ordered that the militia of Suffolk and Middlesex be put in a posture of war; and be ready to march at a minute's warning to prevent danger;' and at the same time authority was given to Capt. Timothy Wheeler 'to impress an able gunsmith to repair to Concord to be resident there for the fixing up of arms from time to time during the war for this and the towns adjacent.' 'Committees of militia,' somewhat resembling the committees of safety in the revolution of 1775, were appointed in the several towns. The Hon. Peter Bulkeley was chairman of that committee in Concord. He and Joseph Dudley were appointed in November to 'attend the forces that are now to go forth against the enemy, and to be ministers unto them.'" The work of the militia and garrison houses of Concord we conclude proved a benefit to the people outside the town as well as to those living within it. They served as a protection for the people living on the Blood farms on the North, and after the burning and sacking of Lancaster and Groton the inhabitants of those places found these garrison houses a safe shelter. Shattuck says, "March 14th the Council ordered 'that the companies of militia of Concord and Sudbury, doe forthwith impress so many carts as may bee sufficient to bring off the goods and provisions belonging to the people left at Lancaster, unto Concord or any other towne, they desire to come unto; and for guarding the said carts it is ordered that Sargant Lamson, commander of the garrison soldiers at Lancaster, do send two files of soldiers, to guard the said carts up and down.' Besides the inhabitants of Lancaster, several of Groton and other frontier towns resided in Concord till after the peace."

As the war progressed and the destruction of town after town threatened a common calamity, Concord became a general rendezvous for colonial soldiers that from time to time were sent out to meet sudden emergencies. Of these soldiers Shattuck states, "The detachments of soldiers for the relief of the frontier towns were frequent and heavy in May. Early in that month 80 from the troops of Essex, Suffolk, and Middlesex, were ordered to repair to Concord for the country service. On the 20th, 270 garrison soldiers from the same counties, were ordered to be stationed at the following 'frontier towns for the better security of them from the incursions of the enemy.' Concord 20, Sudbury 30, Chelmsford 20, Billerica 20, Andover 20, Haverhill 20, Bradford 10, Exeter 20, Medfield 30, Dedham 20, Milton 10, Braintree 15, Weymouth 15, Hingham 20. These soldiers were to be maintained at the cost of the several towns, and to be under the direction of the committees of militia.

"Major Daniel Gookin succeeded Major Willard after his death in April, in command of the military forces in Middlesex; Thomas Clark was commander in Suffolk, and Daniel Dennison in Essex; all of whom were in Concord, May 30th."

"Capt. Joseph Sill commanded one of the companies which were at Concord several months and was frequently sent out on scouts." An early and important military service during King Philip's war in which Concord was represented is the famous Hutchinson Expedition to Brookfield, Massachusetts.

The object of this Expedition was to pacify the Nipnet Indians living in the vicinity of the Connecticut river, and to gain their favor, and perhaps to secure their sympathy in behalf of the colony.

The person selected by the Council at Boston for this important mission was Captain Edward Hutchinson, who was to take with him Capt. Thomas Wheeler of Concord and a part of his troop of horse, together with Ephraim Curtis, a noted scout of Sudbury, well skilled in Indian diplomacy, to repair at once to the rendezvous of these Indians and assure them of the kind intentions of the Colonial authorities toward them and that no harm would come to them if they would submit to the government.

On July 28, Capts. Hutchinson and Wheeler with about twenty or twenty-five of the latter's troop of horse marched from Cambridge to Sudbury and by August 1 found themselves at Brookfield or Quaboag as the Indians called it.

Upon their arrival they were informed that the Indians were at a place about ten miles to the westward. Whereupon Capt. Hutchinson dispatched Capt. Wheeler and Ephraim Curtis to inform them of their coming and the nature of their errand. The messengers found a body of about one hundred and fifty Indians to whom they delivered their message and after some perilous parleying and surly treatment by the savages, an agreement was reached by which Capt. Hutchinson and his company were to meet the sachems the next day on a plain about three miles from Brookfield. They went according to agreement, but the Indians were not there, but were, they were told, at a place seven miles distant. The English captains thought it unwise to proceed further, knowing as they did the treacherous traits of the enemy with which they dealt. Several citizens of Brookfield however who had accompanied them advised an advance, feeling assured from their acquaintance with several of the sachems that no harm would come of it.

The Captains acted upon their suggestion and pursued their way till they found themselves on the border of a swamp and in a pathway so narrow as to necessitate their marching in single file. As the mission of the English was a peaceful one and the Indians had been so informed and their good behavior had been vouched for by the three citizens of Brookfield, perhaps the usual precautions of the Indian fighter were not observed, for after marching quite a distance to a place where there was a hillside on one hand and a swamp on the other, the Indians with a startling suddenness poured upon the little company a most murderous discharge of musketry. Eight men were killed and five were wounded, among the latter of whom was Capt. Hutchinson. For a moment all was in confusion; the savages, having the advantage of concealment and a picked battle ground, offered no visible force for the English to oppose so the main body fell back. Capt. Wheeler finding himself unhurt and seeing that none of his men had fallen, wheeled, as he states, upon the enemy and rushed toward them without calling upon his men to follow, but almost immediately he received a severe wound and his horse was struck. Thus disabled and almost alone, the bold captain was left in the midst of the enemy with some of them but a few rods away. When he turned upon the Indians, his men were some distance from him and in an opposite direction, they having been forced back at the first fire. As, however, a kind Providence would have it, Capt. Wheeler's son Thomas, finding that his father was not among the surviving company, and fearing that he was dead or in danger, rushed back single handed, and although wounded himself yet upon finding his father and seeing his sore straits, dismounted, and placing him upon his own horse, started him to the rear following on foot as rapidly as possible, receiving as he did so a second wound. As the Indians did not take immediate advantage of the terrible plight into which the English had been thrown nor follow hard upon their precipitous flight, the survivors of Hutchinson's force soon found themselves emerging from the forest and making their way unmolested towards Brookfield.

They kept in the open country not daring to leave it lest they again be beset, and tracing their way as best they could, for they were all strangers to the place, at length found themselves back to Quaboag.

The tidings of what had occurred spread through the town like wildfire and from every farm house the occupants fled to the strongest building in the village which was quickly fortified and put in preparation for a stout defense.

Soon after all had entered the house it was surrounded by the savages who by wild ravings and terrible gesticulations sought to intimidate the inmates, and by every art and device known to them sought to batter in or to burn down the building. But the first assault was to no purpose and the Colonists showed by their vigorous defense that the assailants were to pay dear for their victory if they obtained it. After the first onset the Indians settled down for steady work and then and there began that memorable siege of the Brookfield garrison that was for a generation rehearsed at the farmhouse fireside and which has passed into history as one of the most notable events of the period.

CHAPTER XXXVI

Authentic Account of the Hutchinson Expedition to Brookfield by Captain Thomas Wheeler — The Ambuscade—The Attack—The Escape—The Siege of the Garrison House — Ephraim Curtis the Sudbury Scout — The Rescue by Major Simon Willard as a detailed account of the Brookfield expedition has been written out by Capt. Thomas Wheeler we believe that it is better to print portions of it in full, than to write it in our own words.

"When we came near the said swampe the way was so very bad that we could march only in a single file, there being a very rocky hill on the right hand and a thick swampe on the left. In which there were many of those cruel, bloodthirsty heathen, who there waylaid us, waiting an opporto cut us off: there being also much brush on the side of the said hill, where they lay in ambush to surprise us.

"When we had marched there about sixty or seventy rods, the said perfidious Indians sent out their shot upon us as a showre of haile, they being (as was supposed) about two hundred men or more. We seeing ourselves so beset, and not having room to fight, endeavored to fly for the safety of our lives. In which flight we were in no small danger to be all cut off", there being a very miry swamp before us, into which we could not enter with our horses to go forward, and there being no safety in retreating the way we came, because many of our company who lay behind the bushes and had left us pass by them quietly; when others had shot they came out and stopt our way back so that we were forced as we could to get up the steep and rocky hill; but the greater our danger was the greater was God's mercy in the preservation of so many of us from sudden destruction. Myself being gone up part of the hill without any hurt and perceiving some of my men to be fallen by the enemies' shot, I wheeled about upon the Indians, not calling on my men who were left to accompany me, which they in all probability would have done, had they known of my return upon the enemy. They firing violently out of the swamp and from behind the bushes on the hillside wounded me sorely and shot my horse under mi, so that he faltering and falling I was forced to leave him, divers of "the Indians being then but a few rods distant from me.

My son, Thomas Wheeler, flying with the rest of the company, missed me amongst them, and fearing that I was either shot or endangered, returned toward the swampe again, though he had then received a dangerous wound in the reins, where he saw me in the danger aforesaid. Whereupon he endeavored to rescue me, showing himself therein" a loving and dutiful son, he adventuring himself into great peril of his life to help me in that distress, there being many of the enemies about me. My son set me on his own horse and so escaped, awhile on foot himself, until he caught an horse whose rider was slain, on which he mounted, and so through God's great mercy we both escaped. But in this attempt for my deliverance -he received another dangerous arm wound, by their shot, in his left. There were then slain, to our great grief, eight men, viz: Zachariah Philips of Boston, Timothy Farlow of Billerica, Edward Coleborn of Chelmsford, Samuel Smedley of Concord, Sydrach Hopgood of Sudbury, Sergeant Eyres, Sergeant Pritchard, Corporal Coy, the inhabitants of Brookfield, aforesaid. It being the good pleasure of God that they should all these fall by their hands, of whose good intentions they were so confident and whom they so little mistrusted. There were also then five persons wounded , viz: Captain

Hutchinson, myself, and my son Thomas, as aforesaid, Corporal French of Billerica, who having killed an Indian was (as he was taking up his gun) shot and part of one of his thumbs taken off, and also dangerously wounded through the body, near the shoulder. The fifth was John Waldo, of Chelmsford, who was not so dangerously wounded as the rest. They also then killed five of our horses and wounded some more which soon died after they came to Brookfield. Upon this sudden and unexpected blow given us (wherein we desire to look higher than man the instrument) we returned to the town as fast as the badness of the way and the weakness of our wounded men would permit, we being then ten miles from it. All the while we were going, we durst not stay to staunch the bleeding of our wounded men for fear the' enemy should have surprised us again, which they attempted to do, and had in all probability done, but that we perceiving which way they went wheeled off to the other hand and so by God's good providence towards us they missed us, and we all came readily upon the town, though none of us knew the way to it, those of the place being slain as aforesaid, and we avoiding any thick woods and riding in open places to prevent danger by them. Being got to the town we speedily betook ourselves to one of the largest and strongest houses therein, where we fortified ourselves in the best manner we could in such straits of time, and there resolved to keep garrison, though we were but few and meanly fitted to make resistance against such furious enemies. The news of the Indian's treacherous dealing with us, and the loss of so many of our company thereby, did so amaze the inhabitants of the town that they being informed by us, presently left their houses, divers of them carrying very little away with them, they being afraid of the Indians suddenly coming upon them, and so came to the house we were entered into, very meanly provided of clothing or furnished with provisions.

"I perceiving myself to be disenabled for the discharge the duties of my place by reason of the wound I had received, and apprehending that the enemy would soon come to spoyle our town and assault us in the house, I appointed Simon Davis, of Concord, James Richardson and John Fiske, of Chelmsford, to manage affairs for our safety with those few men whom God hath left us, and were fit for any service, and the inhabitants of the said town; who did well and commendably perform the duties of the trust committed to them with much courage and resolution, through the assistance of our gracious God who did not leave us in our low and distressed State but did mercifully appear for us in our greatest need, as in the sequel will clearly be manifested.

"Within two hours after our coming to the said house or less, the said Capt. Hutchinson and myself posted away Ephraim Curtis, of Sudbury, and Henry Young, of Concord, to go to the Honoured Council at Boston, to give them an account of the Lord's dealing with us in our present condition. When they came to the further end of the town they saw the enemy rifling of houses which the inhabitants had forsaken. The post fired upon them and immediately returned to us again, they discerning no safety in going forward, and being desirous to inform us of the enemy's actings that we might more prepare for a sudden assault by them, which indeed presently followed, for as soon as the said post was come back to us, the barbarous heathen pressed upon us in the house with great violence, sending in their shot amongst us like haile through the walls and shouting as if they would have swallowed us up alive, but our God wrought wonderfully for us so that there was but one man wounded within the house, viz — the said Henry Young who looking out of the garret-window that evening was mortally wounded by a shot, of which wound he died within two days after. There was the same day another man slain, but not in the house, a son of Serjeant Pritchard's, adventuring out of the house wherein we were to his Father's house not far from it, to fetch more goods out of it, was caught by those cruel enemies as they were coming towards us, who cut off his head, kicking it about like a football, and then putting it upon a pole they set it up before the door of his Father's house in our sight.

"The night following the said blow they did roar against us like so many wild bulls, sending in their shot amongst us till towards the moon rising which was about three of the clock, at which time they attempted to fire our house by hay and other combustible matter which they brought to one corner of the house and set it on fire. Whereupon some of our company were necessitated to expose themselves to very great danger to put it out. Simon Davis, one of the three appointed by myself as Captain to supply my place by reason of my wounds as aforesaid, he being of a lively spirit encouraged the soldiers within to fire upon the Indians; and also those that adventured out to put out the fire (which began to rage and kindle upon the house side) with these and the like words, that God is with us, and fights for us and will deliver us out of the hands of these heathen, which expressions of his the Indians hearing they shouted and scoffed, saying, now see how your God delivers you or will deliver you, sending in many shots whilst our men were putting out the fire. But the Lord of Hosts wrought very graciously for us in preserving our bodies both within and without the house from their shots and our house from being consumed by fire, we had but two men wounded in that attempt of theirs, but we apprehended that we killed divers of our enemies.

"I being desirous to hasten intelligence to the Honoured Council, of our present great distress, we being so remote from any succour (it being between sixty and seventy miles from us to Boston, where the Council useth to sit), and fearing our ammunition would not last long to withstand them if they continued to assault us, I spake to Ephraim Curtis to adventure forth again on that service, and to attempt it on foot, as the way wherein there was most hope of getting away undiscovered; he readily assented and accordingly went out but there were so many Indians everywhere thereabouts, that he could not pass without apparent hazard of life, so he came back again; but towards morning, the said Ephraim adventured forth a third time and was fain to creep on his hands and knees for some space of ground, that he might not be discerned by the enemy, who waited to prevent our sending, if they could have hindered it. But through God's mercy, he escaped their hands and got safely to Marlborough, though very much spent and ready to faint by want of sleep before he went from us, and his sore travel night and day in that hot season till he got thither, from whence he went to Boston; yet before the said Ephraim got to Marlborough, there was intelligence brought thither of the burning of some houses and killing some cattle at Quaboag by some who were going to Connecticut, but they, seeing what was done at the end of the town, and hearing several guns shot off further within the town, they durst proceed no further, but immediately returned to Marlborough, though they knew not what had befallen Capt.

Hutchinson and myself and company, nor of our being there, but that timely intelligence they gave before Ephraim Curtis his coming to Marlborough occasioned the Honoured Major Willard's turning his march towards Quaboag for their relief, who were in no small danger every hour of being destroyed, the said Major being, when he had that intelligence, upon his march another way as he was ordered by the Honoured Council as is afterwards more fully expressed.

"The next day being August 3rd, they continued shooting and shouting and proceeded in their former wickedness blaspheming the name of the Lord and reproaching us his afflicted servants, scoffing at our prayers as they were sending in their shot from all quarters of the house, and many of them going to the town's meeting-house (which was within twenty rods of the house in which we were), who mocked, saying, come and pray and sing psalms, and in contempt made an hideous noise somewhat resembling singing. But we to our power did endeavor our own defense, sending our shot amongst them, the Lord giving us courage to resist them and preserving us from the destruction they sought to bring upon us. On the evening following we saw our enemies carrying several of their dead or wounded men on their backs, who proceeded that night to send in their shot as they had done the night before, and also shouted as if the day had been certainly theirs, and they should without fail have prevailed against us which they might have the more hopes of in regard that we discerned the coming of new companies to them to assist and strengthen them, and the unlikelihood of any coming to our help.

"They also used several stratagems to fire us, namely, by wild fire in cotton and linen rags with brimstone in them, which rags they tied to the piles of their arrows sharp for the purpose and shot them to the roof of our house after they had set them on fire, which would have much endangered the burning thereof, had we not used means by cutting holes through the roof and otherwise to beat the said arrows down, and God being pleased to prosper our endeavors therein. They carried more combustible matter as flax and hay to the sides of the house and set it on fire and then flocked apace towards the door of the house either to prevent our going forth to quench the fire as we had done before or to kill our men on their attempt to go forth or else to break into the house by the door, whereupon we were forced to break down the wall of the house against the fire to put it out. They also shot a ball of wild-fire into the garret of the house which fell amongst a great heap of flax or tow therein, which one of our soldiers, through God's good Providence soon espyed, and having water ready presently quenched it, and so we were preserved by the keeper of Israel both our bodies from their shot which they sent thick against us and the house from being consumed to ashes, although we were but weak to defend ourselves, we being not above twenty and six men with those of that small town who were able for any service, and our enemies as I judged them about (if not above) three hundred. I speak of the least, for many there present did guess them to be four or five hundred. It is the more to be observed that so little hurt should be done by the enemies shot it commonly piercing the walls of the house and flying amongst the people, and there being in the house fifty women and children besides the men before mentioned.

But abroad in the yard one Thomas Wilson, of that town, being sent to fetch water for our help in further need (that which we had being spent in putting out the fire) was shot by the enemy in the upper jaw and in the neck, the anguish of which wound was at the first that he cried out with a great noise by reason whereof the Indians hearing him rejoyced and triumphed at it, but his wound was healed in a short time praised be God.

"On Wednesday, August 4th, the Indians fortifyed themselves and the barns belonging to our house, which they fortified, both at the great doors and at both ends, with posts, boards, rails and hay, to save themselves from our shot. They also devised other stratagems to fire our house on the night following, namely, they took a cart and filled it with flax, hay and candlewood and other combustible matter, and set up planks fastened to the cart to save themselves from the danger of our shot. Another invention they had to make the more sure work in burning the house: they got many poles of a considerable length and bigness, and spliced them together at the ends one of another, and made a carriage of them about fourteen rods long, setting the poles in two rows with peils laid cross them over at the front end, and dividing said poles about three feet asunder, and in the said front end of this, their carriage, they set a barrel, having made a hole through both heads, and put an axle-tree through them, to which they fastened the said poles, and under every joynt of the poles where they were spliced, they set up a pair of truckle wheels to bear up the carriages, and they loaded the front or fore end thereof with matter fit for firing, as hay and flax and chips, &c.

"Two of these instruments they prepared that they might convey fire to the house with the more safety to themselves, they standing at a distance from our shot whilst they wheeled them to the house. Great store of arrows they had also prepared to shoot fire upon the house that night, which we found after they were gone, they having left them there. But the Lord, who is a present help in times of trouble, and is pleased to make his people's extremity his opportunity, did graciously prevent them of effecting what they hoped they would have done by the aforesaid devices, partly by sending a shower of rain in season, whereby the matter prepared, being wett, would not so easily take fire as it otherwise would have done, and partly by aide coming to our help. For our danger would have been very great that night had not the only wise God (blessed forever!) been pleased to send to us about an hour within night the worshipful Major Willard, with Captain Parker, of Groton, and forty-six men more, with five Indians, to relieve us in the low estate into which we were brought.

"We continued there both well and wounded towards a fortnight, and August the thirteenth Capt. Hutchinson and myself, with the most of those that had escaped without hurt, and also some of the wounded came from thence, my son Thomas and some other wounded men came not from thence, being not then able to endure travel so fair as we were from the next town till about a fortnight after.

We came to Marlborough on August the fourteenth, where Capt. Hutchinson, being not recovered of his wound before his coming from Brookfield, and overtyred with his long journey by reason of his weakness, quickly after grew worse and more dangerously ill, and on the nineteenth day of the said month dyed, and was there the day after buried, the Lord being pleased to deny him a return to his own habitation and his near relation at Boston, though he was come the greatest part of his journey thitherward.

The inhabitants of the town also not long after men, women and children removed safely with what they had left to several places, either where they had lived before their planting or settling down there, or where they had relations to receive and entertain them.

"I tarried at Marlborough with Capt. Hutchinson until his death and came home to Concord August the 21 (though not thoroughly recovered of my wound), and so did others who went with me. But since I am reasonably well, though I have not the use of my hand and arm as before. My son Thomas, though in great hazard of life for some time after his return to Concord yet is now very well cured and his strength well restored. Oh, that we could praise the Lord for his great goodness towards us.

Praised be his name, that though he took away some of us, yet was pleased to spare so many of us and adde to our days; he help us whose souls he hath delivered from death, and eyes from tears, and feet from falling to walk before him in the land of the living till our great change come, and to sanctifie his name in all his ways about us, that both our afflictions and our mercies may quicken us to live more to his glory all our dayes."

CHAPTER XXXVII

Devout Nature of the "Narrative" by Captain Thomas Wheeler — Religious Character of the Colonial Soldiers — Instances of Alleged Divine Interpretation — Original "Title of the Wheeler Document — Pacific Object of the Hutchinson Expedition — Preparatory Work by the Sudbury Scout — Salutary Effect of the Disaster — Biographical Sketches of Captain Thomas Wheeler, Simon Davis, and Ephraim Curtis — Names of Soldiers Credited for Services about Brookfield

In this wonderful narrative which has been repeatedly referred to as the epic of Colonial times, Capt. Wheeler has not only given to posterity a noble example of heroic conduct and unflinching fidelity to duty when the wellbeing of his fellow men was at issue, but he has also exhibited a wonderful reliance upon a protecting Providence to render help in time of need, and the passages in this paper which set forth his trust are no less remarkable than those that indicate a courage and composure that was undaunted by any circumstance of battle. And what he says of himself will apply equally to Simon Davis, and presumably to those who were with them.

Everything in this document savors of sincerity which was begotten of an experience that was most serious; and written as it was after the noise and smoke of battle had subsided, it shows that its pious author was not forgetful of the Power that preserved him and his command in their dire straits, but who the rather made haste to render Him a reverential recognition when a place of safety had been reached.

In short the history of this event as written out by one of its principal actors shows that Capts. Wheeler and Davis and their men believed in a prayer answering Providence and that it is the province of Christianity to sustain the human soul in the dark hour of earthly abandonment.

With much propriety the Hon. John S. Keyes in referring to Capt. Wheeler's wonderful paper has stated in his sketch of Concord History concerning the matter as follows, "The combination of bravery and piety, of trust in the Lord and keeping their powder dry, that characterizes this expedition is a marked example of the spirit of the times.

The men who could do and suffer and believe as this troop did, were true founders of 'A Church without a Bishop, A State without a King.'" In the character of Capt. Thomas Wheeler as we conceive of it by the facts he has given, there is set forth that combination of soldierly qualities and religious fervor which we believe characterized many of the Colonial military commanders.

Capts. Wadsworth and Brocklebank who fell at the Sudbury fight a few months later were men who took an interest in matters both political and religious; the latter being a deacon of the church.

Capt. Samuel Dakin a descendant of Thomas of Concord, who commanded a company in one of the Canadian campaigns and was slain at Half Way Brook near Fort Edward, writes just before his departure from home in a paper which is still extant dated September 29, 1756. "'And now going on an Expedition against the enemy at Crown point, I have given myself up wholly to God, to be at his disposal in life or death, and O that God would accept of me again for Jesus Christ's sake."

In a letter to his wife he says, "I have never yet heard one thwarting word in my company, but they seem all to have a brotherly love one for another, and have never heard one profane word among them, and their forwardness in attending services is delightful to me, so that I have many mercies."

In a letter of June 10, 1758, he states concerning the men of his command "they are very ready to attend prayers and the singing of Psalms which we have practiced on our journey."

Such was the religious faith of the soldiers who fought in the Colonial and Intercolonial wars, and so great was their confidence in the God of battles to befriend them.

And who shall say that their confidence was misplaced or their faith misapplied? Who can deny that Ephraim Curtis was divinely directed as he crawled over the greensward in his third attempt to evade the watchful savages, and go for relief; or who will dare to assert that the timely arrival of Major Willard and his companions at Marlboro just in time for the rescue of his former Concord neighbors at the Brookfield garrison was not ordered of Heaven?

And who furthermore can say that the sudden shower that quenched the burning combustibles which were rolled up against the house was not sent in answer to their supplications? These instances are only in exact accord with many others, notable among which is the unexpected aid from Goff, the regicide judge at Hadley, when the town's immediate destruction was threatened by the Indians and the efforts of the inhabitants had been exhausted; and of the upsetting of the cart loaded with burning material at Sudbury which, tradition says, the savages were rolling down the hill back of the Haynes garrison house in order to destroy it.

Surely, if it is foolishly venturesome to deny these facts or to disclaim a belief in the deductions which the fathers drew from them, then it is wisdom for their descendants to profit by them and to make Him who has been

"Our help in ages past,
Our hope in years to come."

After the return of Capt. Thomas Wheeler and the Concord survivors of his company, the town observed October 21, 1675 as "A day of praise and thanksgiving to God for their remarkable deliverance and their safe return", and a sermon was preached by Rev. Edward Bulkeley. The welcome to the survivors of the Brookfield battle and siege was doubtless a most ardent one. For weeks the town had been kept in a state of sorrow and suspense not knowing what the fate of their fellow townsmen might be; for in those early times surgical skill was in a comparatively undeveloped state, and the lacerations made by the large musket balls then in use would be difficult to heal.

The sermon of Mr. Bulkeley and the narrative of Capt. Wheeler were published not long after they were written. The complete title of the original Wheeler document is the following.

"A True Narrative Of the Lord's Providence in various dispensations towards Edward Hutchinson of Boston and myself, and those that went into the Nipmuck Country, and also to Quaboag, alias Brookfield. The said Captain Hutchinson having a Commission, from the Honoured Council of the Colony to Treat with several Sachems in those parts, in order to the pulick peace and my self being also ordered by the said Council to accompany him with part of my Troop for Security from any

211

danger that might be from the Indians: and to Assist them in the Transaction of matters committed to him."

Probably the "Narrative" was written soon after the author's return to Concord, and not unlikely while waiting for a recovery from his wounds and other hardships.

This paper written by one so trustworthy when the facts described were fresh in memory, and with an impression of the stirring events set forth in it still vivid, renders the document a most valuable one. It has been much quoted and was referred to by contemporary writers. The historian Hubbard used it freely, and Major Daniel Gookin in his "History of the Praying Indians" also referred to it.

The mission which Capt. Wheeler was sent on was of great importance and much depended upon its successful accomplishment. It was preeminently a peaceable one.

Before he started out, the council had twice sent Ephraim Curtis, the Sudbury scout into the Nipmuck Country to see if he could placate the Sachems by assuring them of the pacific attitude of the Colonists towards them. This measure was considered necessary on account of the warning received through Waban, the ruler of the Christian Indians at Natick, Curtis did his full duty.

Taking with him several friendly Indians he proceeded on his way to Brookfield, and from thence westward according to his account to the Colonial Council, till he discovered an Indian trail which he followed many miles to "the low river by Springfield old road," where he discovered some of the Nipmuck Sachems. Several villages were visited and satisfactory assurances were received from the inhabitants of fidelity to the English. As a result of a visit to the Quaboag tribe whose sachem was Mattaump, a document was delivered of which the following is a copy, the original being among the State Archives.

"The Ruler of Quabage being examined by us where his men were: he said they were at home. Then we asked him whether there were none of them gone to help King Philip to fight against the English of Plymouth: he said No; and neither would he help him: for he has been false to him already, and, therefore I will not help him: but I will still continue our subjection unto the English of the Massachusetts Colony: neither will I suffer any of my men to go and help him; and in Confirmation of the same I do set my hand, 25: 4: 75; Conkcascogan, alias Conkganasca."

But notwithstanding their fair promises, the Nipmuck and Quaboag Indians shortly after the visit of Curtis, showed a disposition to join Philip, for the cunning chieftain of Pokanoket, whom the English believed would remain peaceable at Pocasset, whither he had fled upon their pursuit of him after the disastrous work at Swanzey on July 4, had been among the tribes, and probably by his persuasive eloquence and promise of prospective spoils had stirred them to the verge of strife. By the middle of July and in less than a month after Curtis left them at their ancient town of Neminimisset, a place in the northwesterly part of the present New Braintree, several of their sachems had again assembled and this time with a warlike purpose neglectful of their declaration to Ephraim Curtis. But the Colonial Council in spite of indications to the contrary, not despairing of peaceful relations with these tribes of the interior or at least of securing from them neutrality, again sent for the Sudbury scout.

On July 16 an order was issued to the constables of Sudbury directing them "to impress two or three valuable horses as Ephraim Curtis shall require." These were to be delivered to Curtis who was to take with him two or three "able and confiding Indians which Capt. Gookin would provide to go with him on the country's service."

To this second summons to go to the Nipmuck country as a friendly messenger of the English, Curtis promptly responded. Taking with him two or three Christian Indians of Natick he started. Upon arriving at Marlboro he learned that a house built by him at Quinsigamond now Worcester, where he had done some frontier work had been pillaged by the savages, and that Matoonas the Nipmuck chieftain whose tribe he had so recently visited in the interests of peace, with a considerable company of his own warriors and a portion of King Philip's men were on the warpath to the southward doing much mischief. The bold scout was nothing daunted by this disheartening intelligence but went forward and met the Indians near Brookfield. The savages were ugly; their demonstrations showed evil designs; and it was evident that Curtis had a dangerous task before him.

After considerable parley and adroit maneuvering, during which both Curtis and his allies were subjected to great danger, a description of which Curtis set forth in his report to the Council which report is among the State Archives Vol. 67 p 215, he found opportunity to deliver his message. But it was of little avail. The second mission of Curtis to secure the friendliness of the tribes of the interior was utterly fruitless; for notwithstanding his shrewd diplomacy and formal assumption while in the presence of the savages of their having no disposition to actually harm him, he was too accustomed to their wily ways not to know that he and his company were in a position of extreme peril, and that all the friendly overtures of the Colonial Council had been flippantly and defiantly refused so with his little party he retreated as best he could and making his way back to Boston promptly rendered a report that was unmistakable in its meaning. The Colonial Council saw that a crisis was coming and that it was of no use to send messages by an embassy which was so small that the Indians would treat it with contempt, but that an expedition should be sent consisting of such a force and leadership as would command respect. The Hutchinson expedition was accordingly fitted out.

Capt. Hutchinson had lived in the Nipmuck Country and had a farm there upon which he had employed several of the Nipmuck sagamores. He was popular with the natives and had been sent on several occasions to negotiate with them concerning matters of importance. He was the oldest son of William and Ann and came to America with his uncle in 1633, his parents arriving a year later. Capt. Wheeler was equally well fitted for the position he was tJ occupy for he also was well acquainted with the Indians, having had an opportunity to learn their wiles and weaknesses while trading with them some years before along the Merrimac river.

The exact place of the Brookfield ambuscade has been the subject of much conjecture and controversy. Some years ago an ancient map was discovered by Dr. Green of the Mass. Historical Society entitled "A new plan of several towns in the County of Worcester." It bears the date March 30, 1785, and was the work of Gen. Rufus Putnam, at that time of Rutland, but formerly of New Braintree.

Upon this map is located in the northwesterly part of New Braintree the Indian town Meminimisset or Wenimisset and in the swamp to the east is found the inscription "Hutchinson & Troop Ambushed between Swamp & Hill." Dr. L. R. Paige of Cambridge in the "New England and Genealogical Register" dated October, 1884, before the discovery of this map, brought forward strong and convincing arguments to prove that the scene of the battle was near this spot. Rev. J. H. Temple author of the "History of Brookfield" adduces arguments also strong and convincing that the scene of the battle was the ravine near the New Braintree and Brookfield line some two and a half miles from Wickabaug pond. Both gentlemen are considered authorities in matters of historical research; and both probably argued from the same general facts.

Rev. G. M. Bodge author of "Soldiers in King Philip's War" states that after reading the arguments on both sides he is unable to state which spot is the correct one.

One thing, however, is certain, that in 1785, the date of the map referred to, the former place was known as the scene of the conflict. It is not supposed that Philip was personally present in the attack on Brookfield, as he left the swamp at Pocasset to which he had been driven by the English July 31, and arrived at "Quaboag, Old Fort" on Thursday Aug. 5.

The work is supposed to have been done entirely by the Nipmucks, the chief among whom were the Quaboags, Wabbaquasets and Nashaways. It is said that when the victorious Nipmucks told Philip of their work at Brookfield he gave three of their Sagamores viz: Apequinask, Quannasit and Mattaump, about a peck of unstrung wampum apiece.

Capt. Wheeler and his command left Brookfield Aug. 10 and arrived at Marlboro Aug. 14 Capt. Hutchinson went with the return party but died the day after the arrival and was buried at Marlboro.

A few weeks after the return of Capt. Thomas Wheeler we hear of him again as doing military duty; and the indications are that this time it was in the scouting service which was kept up between towns in companies or squads. Before closing our narrative of events about Brookfield it is due that at least a short sketch should be given of some of the leading characters. Capt. Thomas Wheeler it is supposed was of the family of Wheelers who were at Concord as early as 1640—1 and which Shattuck says according to tradition, came from Wales. That the tradition is incorrect is strongly probable since the name of Wheeler was a common one among English families who early emigrated to America.

It is believed that the families of Wheeler who went to Concord dwelt, before coming to this country, at a place a few miles from Odell, Bedfordshire, England, at which latter place Rev. Peter Bulkeley formerly lived In this locality, it is stated, that in the 17th century more people bore the name of Wheeler than any other This fact renders it quite presumable that the Concord families of Wheeler emigrated from that vicinity.

Another significant circumstance is that a few miles from the old home of Peter Bulkeley was a small parish known as Cranfield and in that parish was formerly a locality or precinct that went by the name of Virginia. As both these terms are familiar in Concord history designating places the earliest in which some of the Wheelers have lived, it may not be too much to suppose that the terms were brought to this country by the Wheelers or Bulkeleys. The Virginia road according to Mr. Albert E. Wood was the earliest or one of the earliest in the plantation.

Capt. Thomas Wheeler it is supposed, was a brother of Capt. Timothy and Lieut. Joseph Wheeler of Concord. He married Ruth, a daughter of William Wood and died Dec. 10, 1676. He had five sons.

Thomas Wheeler Jr. who was with his father in the Brookfield fight died unmarried Feb. 16, 1676—7. In the record of his death he is referred to as "Thomas ye son of Widow Ruth Wheeler" That his estate was administered upon is evidence that he was past nonage and not a mere lad of thirteen as has been asserted. Nothing of a documentary nature that we know of indicates that the Capt. Thomas Wheeler the old Indian fighter was a citizen of Concord previous to 1662. In 1669 the town leased to him a tract of land that has been referred to in a previous chapter. Before his residence in Concord he was engaged in trading with the Indians along the Merrimac river.

Timothy Wheeler mentions in his will which was probated Sept. 7, 1687, "Joseph, Ephraim and Deliverance, my brother Thomas his sons." Children of Capt. Thomas and his wife Ruth were Alice, died March 17, 1641; Nathaniel, Jan. 9, 1676—7; Thomas died Jan. 17 1676—7; Ephraim died Feb. 9, 1689.

Joseph and Deliverance, mentioned in Timothy's will, were, it is supposed, the sole survivors of their parents.

Joseph in 1677, administered upon the estate of his brothers Thomas and Nathaniel. The estate of Thomas consisted of "a horse, pistols, cutlash, and gun; "and was prized at £6—12s.

Capt. Thomas Wheeler was admitted a freeman in 1642. He became Sergeant of a foot company of Concord in 1662; and was appointed Captain of a horse company at its organization in 1669. The horse company was made up of troopers from several towns.

Jan. 12, 1669, a lease of land for twenty-one years containing two hundred acres of upland and sixty acres of meadow lying west of Nashoba brook was made to Capt. Thomas Wheeler. The terms were that he should pay a yearly rent of five pounds after the expiration of seven years and build a house and farm. The house was to be forty feet long, eighteen feet wide, and twelve feet stud, "covrd with shingles, with a payer of Chimnes." The barn was to be forty feet long, twenty four feet wide, and twelve feet stud. At the expiration of the lease the buildings were to be left for the use of the town, with thirty acres of fenced tillage land.

It was further stipulated in the lease that he was to receive and pasture the dry cattle of the town's people, the cattle not to be more than one hundred in number, nor less than eighty. The cattle were to be marked by their owners and delivered at Capt. Wheeler's barn. The price fixed was two shillings a head, payable one third in wheat, one third in rye or peas and one third in Indian corn. The owners were to "keep the said herd twelve Sabboth dayes yearely at the appointment & according to the proportion by the said Thomas or his heires allotted."

Simon Davis was a son of Dolor Davis who was a petitioner for the town of Groton in 1656 and had lands granted him in Concord in 1659. He was a carpenter and died at Dunstable 1673. He married Margery, a sister of Major Simon Willard; and their children were Ruth, who married Steven Hall and Simon and Samuel, both of which sons were settled in Concord. Simon Davis married Mary, a daughter of James Blood in 1660; and died June 14, 1713 aged 77. Simon Davis and Mary had a numerous family; and their descendants are widely scattered, some of whom have been distinguished.

To close our account of the Brookfield affair without some further notice of Ephraim Curtis would leave it incomplete although he was not a Concord citizen.

Ephraim Curtis was the son of Henry Curtis an original grantee of the town of Sudbury which was settled in 1638. He was doubtless well acquainted with his fellow soldiers of Concord, his father's house having been situated, it is supposed near the border of the two towns. Although only about thirty years old at the breaking out of the war, yet his knowledge of woodcraft and Indian ways were exceptional.

It is said that he understood their language. The fact that the Colonial Council twice sought his services to bear a message to the Nipmucks, unaccompanied but by two or three friendly Indians showed remarkable confidence in him.

Before his appearance as an emissary for the government to negotiate with the Indians, he penetrated the western wilderness as a pioneer and built a house at a place near Quinsigamond pond now in Worcester.

Mr. Falls in his "Reminiscences of Worcester" says "For a time he claimed the whole town of Worcester but had to be content with two hundred acres near the upper part of Plantation Street and another plantation near Grafton Gore."

Although noted for his venturesome nature we infer he had a heart gentle as a child, for it is said that in his later life he was accustomed to tell how after working all day, he would sit down and look towards Sudbury and shed tears in spite of himself.

It would be vain to attempt adequately to set forth the boldness of Curtis in his thrice repeated endeavor to pass the enemies' lines before Brookfield. It may be doubtful if in the chronicles of the early wars of America acts more heroic have been recorded. It was a desperate strait that led Capt. Wheeler to send him forth; and it was a forlorn hope of a fearful character that Curtis entered upon and no one better than he knew its possible consequences.

The garrison door opened and he went out, it closed, and he was left alone with his enemies. His main protection, apart from Providence, was the damp, dust laden atmosphere made heavy by the smoke of gunpowder, the friendly darkness, and the drowsy condition of the savages wearied by the work of the day previous. A slight incautious movement might betray him, the breaking of a stick, the rustle of the wood grass or the unlucky displacement of a small stone. But none of these things deterred him.

Dropping on his hands and knees and creeping silently on the greensward he eluded the vigilance of the watching guard and when through the cordon of savages and fairly within the outskirts of the welcome woodland he arose and ran, and hours later "much spent and ready to faint" he reached Marlboro to find to his joy that Major Willard was already on his way to Brookfield to rescue his beleaguered comrades. Ephraim Curtis died at Sudbury at the age of 92; and was probably buried in the town's old burying ground.

CHAPTER XXXVIII.

Removal of the Christian Indians from Nashoha to Concord—Indian Mission Work — The Establishment of Christian or Praying Indians in Villages or Towns — The Character and Conduct of the Christian Indians — Their Fidelity and Service to the English — Rules for their Restraint — Humane Act of John Hoar— Circumstances Explanatory of Harsh Treatment of the Christian Indians by the Colonial Communities— Historic Sketch of Indian Mission Work at Nashoba by Herbert Joseph Harwood of Littleton — Disposition of the Nashoha Territory.

THE next event of importance to the town in the course of the war was the removal of the Praying Indians from their plantation at Nashoba now a part of Littleton and placing them at Concord under the care of John Hoar Esq.

As before stated, years previous to the breaking out of King Philip's war a portion of the Indians dwelling in this part of the country were gathered together in the following towns and villages, viz: Wamesit (Lowell), Nashoba, (Littleton), Okkokomimesit (Marlboro), Hassamnanesit (Grafton), Makunkokoag (Hopkinton), Natick, and Punkapog (Canton).

Besides these places of ingathering, which were called the "Old Praying Villages,' there were several others among the Nipmucks called the "New Praying Towns;" and the Indians thus congregated and those affiliated with them were known as "Christian" or "Praying Indians" They were under the surveillance of Daniel Gookin as their civic sponsor and Rev. John Eliot was their teacher in spiritual things.

While thus sequestered they attained a goodly degree of thrift, laid aside their Pagan practices and lived peaceably with their white neighbors. When Philip's war broke out these Indians proved themselves not only friendly to the English, but very serviceable as scouts and guides.

So great was the confidence the English placed in them that they formed them into military companies, and it was suggested at one time that the Friendly Indian stations be used as frontier forts, forming not only a line of defense against hostile tribes in the interior, but places of rendezvous for Colonial soldiers who might cooperate with them.

In several instances, by the personal solicitude of the "Praying Indians" and by special service rendered by them, signal advantages accrued to the settlers and severe catastrophes were averted. Before the breaking out of the war, Waban informed the English of the hostile intent of King Philip, and told them that as soon as the trees were leaved out the Indians would begin their attack.

In the expedition of Hutchinson and Wheeler the Christian Indians acted as guides and interpreters; they also warned the Colonial soldiers of the wiles and strategies of the enemy. The two sons of Petuhanit, Joseph and Sampson, strongly advised against an advance when the hostile Nepmucks were urging them on towards the swamp; and had their advice been followed, the sad surprise might have been averted. When the retreat came they carefully avoided an ambush by keeping the broken expedition in the open field, directing them along a course unknown to the English but which brought them in safety to the garrison.

When, after the fight at Narraganset it became important to know the movements or the Indians toward the Connecticut river, Major Gookin sent as spies, the two Christian Indians Kattenanit and Quanapohit. These went among the

Indians at Brookfield and after ascertaining their plan reported it to the Council, which plan was to assault all the frontier towns beginning at Lancaster. The Council acting on their report sent messengers to Concord, Lancaster and Marlboro. Captain Wadsworth at once with forty men from Marlboro, marched to Lancaster and the town was saved from entire destruction; and had the advice of Quanapohit been heeded it is believed that the Rowlinson garrison would have been saved.

It is asserted by Mr. Bodge, " There can be little doubt that if in the pursuit of Philip in the Nipmuck country the counsel of the native Indians had been heeded by Captain Henchman, Philip and most of his company would have been destroyed." But, notwithstanding these evidences of fidelity to the English, as threatening events thickened and the very existence of the colony was menaced, there crept over the community a feeling of distrust towards these Indians and there was a growing suspicion that some of them were in sympathy with King Philip and had even assisted him.

This feeling which was not shared in so much by the ministers and magistrates, was so strong among the laity that at length an order was issued to disband the Christian Indian military companies, that all Christian Indians should repair to one or another of five Indian villages designated, that they should never go more than a mile from their centers unaccompanied by an Englishman, and if anyone was discovered breaking these rules he might be arrested or shot.

Notwithstanding, however, the stringency of the regulations the masses were not satisfied but went so far in their impatience to be rid of the presence of any Indian, that at length the Court, wearied perhaps by the people's complaints, ordered the removal of all the Indians to Deer Island in Boston harbor.

The work began by the attempted removal of the Wamesits; the direct occasion of which was the alleged setting fire to a haystack, which act a hostile Indian who was afterwards executed at Boston confessed to have done.

The Punkapogs were next to be disturbed; and soon after, a clamor was raised against the Naticks, who were unjustly accused of burning an old and disused building in Dedham.

The Naticks were conducted from their homes by Captain Prentice who was their friend. They were met by the Apostle John Eliot and Major Gookin and other friends at the "Falls of the Charles river " and carried to Deer Island in boats.

The Hassanamesit Praying station was attacked by the hostile Indians and having been disarmed by the English, about two hundred of them were captured.

The same month the remnant of the Nashoba Indians, which consisted of not more than a dozen able-bodied men and their families, were ordered to Concord, and General Gookin, Rev. John Eliot and Major Simon Willard were a committee of the Court to carry out the order and see that they were properly cared for.

At Concord they were placed in charge of John Hoar, their unfailing friend, the only man in town it is said who was willing to receive them. Standing up stoutly against a strong public sentiment, for the tragic affair at Brookfield and other Indian atrocities which it was suspected some of the Praying Indians had sympathy with were still recent, Mr. Hoar acted as a protector, erecting for them a building where they could be secure from all indignities whether from within or without the town, and providing employment by which they could earn a livelihood.

This act of John Hoar stands out in strong contrast with the treatment they received at other hands. After the Natick Indians were driven away, the English entered and plundered their deserted homes while the banished inmates were landed upon a bleak island with insufficient clothing and compelled to subsist almost entirely on fish and clams.

When the Marlborough Indians were removed, the soldiers stripped them of everything, even taking from them the pewter communion cup that was given their minister by Mr. Eliot. These and other startling incidents of cruelty all unavenged and apparently acquiesced in by the community in general, were the overt expression of a feeling of hostility to some of the Indian converts of the saintly Eliot.

It is true that something may be said explanatory of such severe conduct, if not in mild palliation of it. Society was terribly stirred by recent and startling events. Public calamities were accumulating. Each day might bring the report of a new disaster. Every wood path or the long and circuitous frontier was unsafe to the unarmed traveler. The dark war cloud was casting its shadow from the Connecticut river to the sea board. A quota of citizen soldiers from every town where they could be spared, were by Colonial impress assisting by guarding garrison houses or ranging the forests it: scouting squads to beat up the enemy and upon their discovery to fall back and warn the endangered inhabitants. Under such circumstances it is not altogether remarkable that it became unpopular to befriend the Praying Indians; and even that such good and true men as Gookin and Eliot who had the best means of knowing the nature of the Christian Indians and the actual facts concerning their conduct became the targets of public scorn because of their advocacy of the cause of these helpless creatures.

The spot where the workhouse provided by Mr. Hoar probably stood was not far from the town's central garrison house.

Gookin says of its situation that it was "about the midst of the town and very nigh the town's watchhouse." As showing the interest of Mr. Hoar by this friendly act, we quote the following from Gookin's "History of the Praying Indians."

"About this time there befell another great trouble and exercise to the Christian Indians of Nashobah, who sojourned in Concord by order. The matter was this; the Council had, by several orders, empowered a committee, who, with the consent of the selectmen of Concord, settled those Indians at that town, under the government and tuition of Mr. John Hoare; the number of those Indians were about fifty-eight of all sorts, whereof there were not above twelve able men, the rest women and children. These Indians lived very soberly, and quietly, and industriously, and were all unarmed; neither could any of them be charged with any unfaithfulness to the English interests.

"In pursuance of this settlement, Mr. Hoare had begun to build a large and convenient work-house for the Indians near his own dwelling, which stood about the midst of the town, and very nigh the town watch-house.

"This house was made, not only to secure those Indians under lock and key by night, but to employ them and to set them to work by day, whereby they earned their own bread, and in an ordinary way (with God's blessing) would have lived well in a short time."

That any suspicion of treachery on the part of the Nashobah Indians was ill founded is evident from the fact that they who knew the most about them had an

219

unstinted belief in their sincerity. Their conduct from the beginning had inspired confidence. Tahattawan, the Sachem of Nashoba who once dwelt at Nashawtuc, as tradition has it, became one of the first converts to Christianity by the preaching of Eliot at Nonantum. The tribe or clan which he represented went to Nashoba from the region of the Musketequid, by the advice of Mr. Eliot that they adopt the government that Jethro proposed to Moses in the wilderness, whereby they were to choose rulers of hundreds and of fifties and of tens. In this way they came to live in towns separate from the English, and upon this principle, Natick and Nashoba and the other Indian villages or "Praying towns " were originated.

As the sequel to the removal of the Nashobah Indians to the place provided for them by Mr. Hoar is of a later date, the subject will be left here to be resumed in its chronological order.

Before dismissing the subject however it may be appropriate, since these Indians are properly associated with the history of Concord in other relations than those which are religious, to print the following sketch of them which by permission is quoted from a paper prepared by Herbert Joseph Harwood, Historian of the town of Littleton and published in a pamphlet of the Littleton Historical Society entitled Proceedings No. 1.

"John Eliot in his 'Brief Narrative' written in 1670 says, 'Nashope is our next Praying Town, a place of much Affliction; it is the chief place of Residence, where Tahattawans lived, a Sachem of the Blood, a faithful and zealous Christian, a strict yet gentle Ruler; he was a Ruler of 50 in our Civil Order; and when God took him, a chief man in our Israel was taken away from us. His only son was a while vain, but proved good, expert in the Scripture, was Elected to Rule in his Father's place, but soon died, insomuch that this place is now destitute of a Ruler.' "This was the earliest Nashoba sachem of whom we have any knowledge, he is spoken of in different publications and records by the various names, Tahattawarre, Tahattawan, Tahatawants, Attawan, Attawance, Ahattawance and Nattahattawants, under which last name he is recorded in Suffolk deeds, Vol. 1 No. 34 as the grantor in a sale made in 1642, of a large tract of land on both sides of Concord River to Symon Willardin behalf of Governor Winthrop, Mr. Dudley, Mr. Nowell, and Mr. Allen.

"The tract was in extent 3760 acres and the consideration 'six fadom of waompampege, one waistcoat and one breeches.' In the deed Nattahatawants is referred to as 'sachem of that land' and is referred to by some writers as sachem of Musketaquid (Concord), in view of which it is important to note that Eliot states that 'Nashope' [Nashobah] was his, 'chief place of Residence.' "Barber gives Tahattawan jointly with Squaw Sachem as the vendors of Concord to the white settlers in 1635.

"Tahattawan's only son who succeeded him as sachem of Nashobah was John Tahattawan, also referred to as Tahatooner by Samuel G. Drake.

"Old Tahattawan had two daughters (at least), the elder of whom, Tassansquaw, married the celebrated Waban, and another Naanasquaw or Rebeckah married Naanishcow or John Thomas.

"Tahattawan's son referred to by Eliot, John Tahattawan, was one of the signers to 'an agrement mad betwene the Ingene of mashoba and the Town of concord' dated '20 of 10 mo. 1660' and if the record on Concord books is an exact copy, both he and John Thomas signed their own names, while seven other Indians made marks, but the fact that John Thomas in 1714 signed a deed by mark, and also that the word 'and' occurs between these two signatures on the record would tend to show that perhaps there is an inaccuracy in the record and all may have made marks.

"This 'agreement' of 1660 conveyed land which was afterwards known as Concord's second grant.

John Tahattawan died before 1670, and left a widow Sarah, daughter of Sagamore John of the Wamesits, and children, a daughter Sarah, otherwise called Kehonosquaw, and a young son who was killed at the age of 12 years, Nov. 15, 1675 at Wamesit, near Lowell, when a party of armed men of Chelmsford went to the Indian camp and wantonly fired upon them in retaliation for the burning of a barn of which the Indians were suspected. Five women and children were wounded, among whom was the boy's mother Sarah, who was then a widow for the second time, having had as her second husband Oonamog, ruler of the praying Indians of Marlborough. In my 'Historical Sketch' I made the error of confusing Sarah the widow of John Tahattawan with his daughter Sarah or Kehonosquaw.

"After the death of John Tahattawan, Pennakennit or Pennahahnnit was the chief of the Nashobah Indians, and was also 'marshal general' of all the praying Indians and attended court at Natick. He was also called Capt. Josiah and was no doubt the last who could be called Sachem of the Nashobahs, as he is spoken of by Gookin as chief in 1674, and in the year following the settlement was broken up by King Philip's war.

"Waban, as before stated, married Tassansquaw, the eldest daughter of old Tahattawan, and is supposed to have originally been of this vicinity, though it is not by any means certain; his name is also spelled Waaubon or Waubon, and according to Samuel Gardner Drake, signified 'wind.' He is said to have been about the same age as Rev. John Eliot and consequently was born about 1604.

"Winthrop says that Eliot in beginning his labors among the Indians in 1646, preached ' one week at the wigwam of one Wabon, a new sachem near Watertown mill, and the other or next week in the wigwam of Cutshamekin near Dorchester mill.' "Being Eliot's first convert to Christianity and a man of much strength of character, Waban was of great assistance in gaining the good will and attention of other Indians and was recognized as a powerful man both by the white people and by the Indians, both Christians and those hostile in King Philip's war.

"An instance of this is shown in the letters from Sam Sachem and other Indians begging for peace, printed by Samuel Gardner Drake. The first one dated July 6, 1676 is superscribed 'To all Englishmen and Indians, all of you hear Mr. Waban, Mr. Eliott,' and the addresses of three of these letters include Waban's name.

"Waban was of Natick in 1674 and the chief man there when Gookin wrote in that year, adding 'He is a person of great prudence and piety: I do not know any Indian that excels him.' "He was alive as late as March 19, 1684, at which date he signed by mark the first of sixteen Natick Indians who sent a letter to Mr. Gookin inviting him to lecture and is said to have died at Natick the summer following.

"Waban's son, Thomas Waban of Natick, signed in 1714, a deed to the heirs of Col. Peter Bulkeley and Maj. Thomas Henchman of half of Nashobah plantation. I own the original document, showing Thomas Waban's signature in a good hand. Two other Indians who signed by mark were John Thomas and John Thomas, jr., also of Natick.

221

"The town records of Natick were written at one time by Thomas Waban in the Indian language, and it is said he was also a justice of the peace and once issued a warrant as follows: 'You you big constable; quick you catchum Jeremiah Ofrscow; strong you holdum; safe you bringum afore me, Thomas Waban, Justice peace.' "A story is told by Samuel Gardner Drake of Waban, which may perhaps more properly be told of his son, as follows: A young justice asked Waban what he would do when Indians got drunk and quarreled; he replied 'Tie um all up, and whip um plaintiff, and whip um fendant, and whip um witness.' "Thomas Waban's Indian name was Weegramomenit, as we learn from the deed to Hon. Peter Bulkeley of Concord and Maj. Thomas Henchman of Chelmsford dated June 15, 1686 conveying half of Nashobah plantation.

At that time the Indians could not legally sell but were afterward given permission by the General Court to do so, which accounts for the second deed of the same land in 1714, previously referred to.

"John Thomas or Naanishcow who married one of old Tahattawan's daughters is referred to by Gookin as follows: "Their teacher [i. e. at Nashobah] is named John Thomas, a sober and pious man. His farther was murthered by the Maquas in a secret manner, as he was fishing for eels at his wear, some years since, during the war. He was a pious and useful person, and that place sustained a great loss in him." By 'teacher' he meant minister. John Thomas had sons, Solomon or Naahkenomenit and John Thomas, jr.

"Several of these relationships I established by the signatures to the deed of June 15, 1686, to Bulkeley and Henchman, and there also signed that deed,' Nuckomraewosk, relict of Crooked Robin,' 'Natahoonet' and 'Wunnuhhew alias Sarah, wife to Neepanum alias Tom Dublet' from which I infer they may have been also descendants of old Tahattawan.

"Other Nashobah Indians were Nasquan, Merchant Thomas or Marchant Thorns, Wabatut, Great James Natocotus a blind man, Pompant, Gomps and 'Mr. John Sagamore ' who was the father of Sarah the wife of Tom Dublet.

"The petition of Rev. John Eliot for the incorporation of the several Indian towns is of date May 3, 1654 and the portion of his petition that relates to the Nashoba plantation is the following: "First, therefore the inhabitants of Nashoba living 7 or 8 miles west of Concord, desire to have liberty to make a town in y' place, with due accommodations thereunto. And though Concord have some conditional grants of lands y' way, yet I understand that we shall have a loving and Christian agreement betwixt them and the Indians."

The response to the petition is as follows, and of date May, 14, 1654 "In ansr to the peticon of Mr. Jno. Elliott, on behalf of several Indians, the Court graunts his request, viz.: liberty for the inhabitants of Nashop [Nashobah] and to the inhabitants of Ogkoontiquonkames [Marlborough] and also to the inhabitants of Hasnemesuchoth [Grafton] to erect severall Injan tounes, in the places propounded wi'h convejent acomodacon to each, provided they prjudice not any former graunts; nor shall they dispose of it wi'h out leave first had and obtajned from this Court."

In his history of Concord Mr. Shattuck has the following reference to the Nashoba territory.

"Nashobah, lying near Nagog Pond, partly in Littleton and-partly in Acton as now bounded, accordingly became an Indian town; and here a part of the Praying

Indians in Concord, with others in the vicinity, gathered and adopted civil and religious order, and had a Ruler and other municipal officers, though no church was formed. Such as were entitled to Christian ordinances probably went to Natick to celebrate the communion after a church was organized there in 1660."

Mr. Harwood states that he has found no authority for supposing that the town of Concord ever had any title to the territory of Nashoba, but he locates the original grant outside of any English town boundary lines.

He states in his History: "If the reader will look at a map of Littleton and note the following points, he will have the four corners of the ancient Indian plantation Nashobah: the northwest corner of Littleton on the side of Brown Hill, near the road to Ayer, was one corner; a point near the center of Boxboro', found by prolonging the present west and south lines of Littleton, till they meet, was another corner; the westerly end of Nagog pond was a third corner, and a point on the Westford line, between the Dodge place and Forge Pond, was the fourth corner. It was uniformly spoken of as four miles square, but was not exactly that, being, as we have seen, only three miles on one side, and having corners which varied slightly from right angles."

Repeatedly in ancient documents relating to lands lying in the vicinity of the Nashoba grant are references to this tract of territory in a way that leads one to infer, as we believe, that it was a distinctive area of wilderness land, entirely independent of any that had hitherto been granted.

Petitioners from other places in being allowed their requests are cautioned not to intrude upon this Indian reservation nor in any way to interfere with it in the establishing of boundary lines; and this precaution was observed in response to petitions from the people of Concord and made even after the granting of land for the "feeding grounds" from which " Concord Village ", afterwards Acton, was formed.

The lands of the Nashoba Indians in process of a few years after Philip's war were transferred piecemeal, or in parcels to the English owners or occupants. Lieutenant Joseph Wheeler of Concord by trading with the Nashoba Indians, while they were living on their plantation, became their creditor and besought of the Colonial Court in 1662, a tract of two hundred acres in the south portion of Nashoba byway of satisfaction of his claim, but was refused.

Among the first purchasers of land of the Nashoba Indians, if not the very first, were Peleg Lawrence and Robert Robbins of Groton. The tract purchased by these persons was, according to a plan on file at the State House bearing date Jan. 2, 1686-7, was located in the north east corner of the Nashoba reservation, with an area of a half mile in width by two in length. The next purchaser of a portion of the plantation from the aboriginal owners and the first for which a deed was passed was made June 15, 1869, by Hon. Peter Bulkeley of Concord and Major Thomas Henchman of Chelmsford. These vendees bought the eastern half of the territory, for the sum of seventy pounds. The deed of this tract was placed upon record and the following is a description: "And it contains one moyety or half e part of said Nashoba plantations, & the easterly side of't; It is bounded by Chelmsford plantation (about three miles & three quarters) on the easterly side; by Concord village Land Southward, about two miles & three-quarters; Northward it is bounded by Land sold by the aforesaid Indians to Robert Robbins and Peleg Lawrence, both of Groton Town, which land is part of the aforesaid Nashobah plantation, & this is exactly two miles in Length &

runs Hast three degrees Northerly, or West three degrees southerly, & the South end runs parrallell with this Line; On the Westerly side it is bounded by the remainder of said Nashoba plantation: & that West Line runs (from two little maples marked with H for the Northwest corner) it runs South seven degrees & thirty minutes east, four miles & one quarter; the most Southerly corner is bounded by a little red oak marked H, the north east corner is a stake standing about four or five pole southward of a very great Rock that Lyeth in the line between said Nashobah & Chelmsford plantation."

After the foregoing conveyances there was left in possession of the Indians, says the historian of Littleton, " only that portion of the plantation which Danforth in his plan designated as 'Nashobah the Indians part' being the westerly portion, four miles long on the west line, two miles theoretically on the north line, but actually only one, and 412 poles on the south line." Deeds from the Indians relating to the transfers are on record at the Cambridge Registry of Deeds, one with date May 9, 1694, from Thomas Waban of Natick to Walter Powers of Concord and the others with date May 10, 1701 from Solomon and John Thomas, Jr., both of Natick, to Josiah Whitcomb of Lancaster. A deed confirmatory of the title to the tract bought by Bulkeley and Henchman was given in 1714 by Thomas Waban, John Thomas and John Thomas Jr., to Major Henchman and the heirs of Hon. Peter Bulkeley. The original deed which is ancient in appearance and bears the signature of Waban and the marks of the other grantees is in the possession of Herbert Harwood.

For years it was a grave question with the General Court as to what should be done with the territory once occupied by these Indians. Some of the inhabitants of Concord wished to settle upon it and make it an English town. Some of the neighboring towns, as Groton and Stow, desired to annex the whole or a part of the territory and thus absorb it in their own township. Their desires found expression in the form of petition and of an actual attempted annexation of the land. Meanwhile as the matter was left open, straggling settlers came upon the land, and some by right of purchase and some without right made their home there. But the colonization element at length prevailed; and in response to a petition of date 1711 when twenty-three who represented themselves "Inhabitants of Concord, Chelmsford, Lancaster and Stow," etc., asked the General Court for permission to settle a township at Nashoba, a committee was appointed to view the land and make a report of it. The result was that in 1713, it was decided that Nashoba should be a town of English people, and on November 1714, an act incorporating it was passed by the Court, and from this and adjacent territory the town of Littleton was created.

Only a few of the Nashoba Indians ever returned to their ancient corn fields and hunting grounds at Nashoba after their exile to Deer Island. The last occupant of her race was Sarah Dublet the wife of " Tom Dublet" whose Indian name as she signed it in the deed to Bulkeley and Henchman was Wunuhhew, sometimes called "Sarah Indian." Traces of the Nashoba Indians have occasionally been discovered about their ancient haunts. Especially have they been found in the vicinity of Nagog Pond where there are indications of ovens and sites of huts, and where it is said there was once an Indian fort.

At the breaking out of Philip's war, several families of white people were living in that part of Littleton known as Nashoba but which was really in Concord Village.

Prominent among these families was Walter Powers whose estate had been called the " Powers Farm " and " Nashoba Farm." Upon this farm there once stood a garrison house which was long called the " Reed House." The ruins of this building are now, or were recently, visible at the foot of Nashoba hill. There was also visible until within a few years vestiges of an ancient burying place which probably contain the dust of the Shepards, the Powers, and others of the earliest pioneers, who soon after the abandonment of the Nashoba plantation, and the fires of Philips war had fairly faded out found their way thitherward.

The old graveyard was years ago ploughed over but some of the grave stones which found their way into a wall give unmistakable evidence that thereabouts they were once used as grave markers. It may be proper to observe before leaving this subject that as a portion of Littleton, which was not of the Indian plantation, may have been associated and known by the name of Nashoba, care may be necessary in making a distinction "between the two tracts of territory. That which has been designated as Nashoba but which was not within the Indian plantation, is a part of what has been called Concord Village, and has been known as " Power's Farm " and " Nashoba Farm."

CHAPTER XXXIX.

The Narragansett Campaign — Its Object and Nature—Names of Concord Soldiers — Company in which they Served — The Officers — Return of Order of Concord Committee of Militia — Object of the Expedition— The Swamp Fort— The Wintry March from Dedham Plain — The Fight — Description by Rev. G. M. Bodge—Causalities to the Concord Soldiers — Burial of the Dead — The Return March — Comments on Criticism of Conduct of the Campaign — Account of Petitions for Land Grants — Concord Names in List of Land Claimants— The "Long" or "Hungry" March — Authentic Account of the Swamp Fight by Capt. James Oliver

THE next prominent movement in which Concord soldiers were engaged was the famous Narragansett Campaign.

In December 1675, after the retirement of King Philip and his followers from the Nipmuck country and his defeat about Springfield, the United Colonies of Massachusetts, Plymouth and Connecticut, perhaps for the double purpose of preventing the Narragansett Indians from rendering him aid and also to punish them for alleged acts of perfidy, fitted out an Expedition.

The project was hastily planned and placed under the command of General Josiah Winslow of Plymouth. The army consisted of one thousand men; five hundred and twenty coming from Massachusetts. The Massachusetts men consisted of six companies of foot and one of horse under command of Samuel Appleton of Ipswich. The commanders of these companies were as follows: 1st Jeremiah Swain, Lieut.; 2nd Samuel Mosely, Capt.; 3rd James Hosmer Oliver, Capt.; 4th Isaac Johnson, Capt.; 5th Nathaniel Davenport, Capt.; 6th Joseph Gardner, Capt.; Cavalry Company., Thomas Prentice, Capt. The Concord men were in Capt. Davenport's company, and the following are from a list of men impressed for it from the several towns. Mass. Archives, Vol. 68, page 100 and pages 67-100. The date is from November 25 to December 3, 1675.

The list is made up of men from Cambridge, Woburn, Sudbury, Cambridge Village, Reading, Medford and Concord.

The names of Concord men are as follows: Joseph Busse, Abraham Temple, Samuel Howe, John Wood, Joseph Wheeler, Thomas Brown, John Wheeler, Timothy Rice, George Hayward, Steven Farre, John Taylor.

The line officers of Company 5 were Nathaniel Davenport, Capt.; Edward Tyng, Lieut.; John Drury, Ensign.

Captain Davenport was born in Salem. He was a man of enterprise and ability and had gained some distinction by governmental appointment. His experience with men and his daring nature fitted him for a military leader. He was said to be popular with his men; and that upon taking command he made a speech to them and also gave them liberty to choose their own sergeants " which pleased them very well." Lieut. Ting or Tyng, who commanded the company after Davenport fell, was son of Capt. Edward Tyng and was born March 25, 1649. He was subsequently made Lieutenant Colonel by Gov. Andros, and after the reduction of Nova Scotia, Andros appointed him Governor of Annapolis, but on his way there, the vessel that conveyed him was captured by the French and he was taken to France where he died.

The following is the return of the order of the Concord Committee of Militia which directed them to impress men for the country's service, a part of which service was in the Narragansett campaign. (State Archives, Vol. 68, page 65).

"To the honord Court sitting in Boston 3d 10th 75.

By virtue of a warrant from Majr. Simon Willard directed to the Comittee of the Militia in Concord requiring them to impresse eleven able souldiers well fitted &c: for the service of the Country in the present expedition: The said Comittee have impressed (& accord: to order of honord Council doe returne the names of) these persons; viz: Joseph Brusse, Abraham Temple, Samuel How, John Wood, Joseph Wheeler, Thomas Browne, John Wheeler, Timothy Rice, George Hayward, Stephen Farre & John Taylour, who were at present (most of them & the rest seasonably will bee) fitted for arms: But several of them doe want & desire to be supplyed with some cloathing (coates especially) & where they may bee accommodated with them they would understand. 3d 10th 75.

Yor worships humble servant.

Tim: Wheeler Capt.

of Concord.

Postscript.

Wee having severall Troopers also impressed in this Towne, & there being a Company of Indians ordered amongst us, wch wee are to take care of: Tis humbly desired, that favor may bee shown us, in the release of some (if it may bee) of the persons above mentioned.

Tim: Wheeler."

The more immediate object of the expedition and that which has rendered it famous was the reduction of the Indian stronghold in what is now Kingston, R. I. This fort, for such it has been called, though of Indian construction, was very strong, having been built, it is supposed, under the direction of an Englishman by the name of Teffe or Tift.

It was situated upon an upland or island in the midst of a large cedar swamp of five or six acres in area. About the place was a circle of palisades or timbers set upright, outside of which, Hubbard states, was a hedge of almost a rod in thickness. The "Old Indian Chronicle" asserts that it was in the middle was a clay wall and that felled trees were about it. At the corners and exposed portions were block houses or flankers for cross firing upon any who might seek entrance between them. Within the enclosure were several hundred wigwams, and there the Narragansetts had ensconced themselves and accumulated their winter stores. At one corner of the fort where the defenses were incomplete, there being neither hedge nor palisades, the entrance was guarded by a fallen tree about five feet from the ground.

It is probable the Indians relied very much upon the nature of the ground for defense; this being such that except when it was frozen an approach to the fort would be very difficult and dangerous, and perhaps this was one reason why the attack was made in the winter.

The Massachusetts forces mustered on Dedham plain Thursday, December 9, 1675. On the same day they marched twenty-seven miles to Woodcock's garrison in the present town of Attleboro. On December (O they arrived at Seekonk, and on the 12th crossed over Patuxent river, and going by way of Providence reached Smith's garrison at Wickford, R. I. at night. Several days were then spent in scouting and skirmishing and on December 18, a march was made to Pettisqnamscott where the Connecticut force consisting of 320 men under the command of Major Treat joined them.

This army it is alleged was the finest that had ever been organized in America. The starting was a sad one. At Pettisqnamscott they found that Bull's garrison house which was a stone building and at the time considered a very strong one had been destroyed by the Indians, and the entire expedition was compelled to bivouac in the open air with a driving snow storm raging about them.

When the morning broke it was still snowing; but chilled though the men were by the night's exposure they moved forward to the Indian Fort which was but a few miles ahead.

The Massachusetts men were in the advance; the Plymouth men next, and the Connecticut contingent at the rear.

The snow grew deeper as the march progressed and it was with difficulty that the men plodded forward with their heavy packs and military accouterments. By about noon the army had reached the border of the large swamp in which the stronghold was situated. As they came in sight of it a body of Indians were discerned which the companies of Capts. Davenport and Mosely, which were in the advance, pursued and fired upon.

The Indians after returning the fire fled into the swamp, the English following without waiting for orders or for the other companies to come up.

Upon arriving, however, near the only possible entrance to the Fort, which was by a long fallen tree " over a place of water" and across which the pursued Indians had just passed, Davenport and Morsely halted their companies, hesitating, doubtless to follow over a path so perilous and not knowing but that the Indians who had just passed over it had been sent to decoy them to a place deadly of entrance.

But the halt was a short one; for they quickly discovered the incomplete portion before spoken of and the two companies dashing forward, then and there was commenced that terrific conflict which for three hours was waged with a most appalling fierceness.

We quote the following description of the battle by Mr.Bodge.

"The companies of Capts. Davenport and Johnson came first to this place, and those officers at once charged through the gap and over the log at the head of their companies; but Johnson fell dead at the log, and Davenport a little within the fort; and their men were met with so fierce a fire that they were forced to retire again and fall upon their faces to avoid the fury of the musketry till it should somewhat abate. Mosely and Gardiner, pressing to their assistance, met a similar reception, losing heavily, till they too fell back with the others, until Major Appleton coming up with his own and Capt. Oliver's men, massed his entire force as a storming column, and it is said that the shout of the commanders that the Indians were running, so inspired the soldiers that they made an impetuous assault, carried the entrance amain, and beat the enemy from one of his flankers at the left, which afforded them a temporary shelter from the Indians still holding the blockhouse opposite the entrance.

In the meantime, the General, holding the Plymouth forces in reserve, pushed forward the Connecticut troops, who not being aware of the extent of the danger from the blockhouse, suffered fearfully at the first entrance, but charged forward gallantly, though some of their brave officers and many of their comrades lay dead behind them, and unknown numbers and dangers before. The forces now joining, beat the enemy step by step, and with the fierce fighting, out of their block-houses and various fortifications. Many of the Indians, driven from their works, fled outside, some doubtless to the wigwams inside, of which there were said to be upward of five hundred, many of them large and rendered bullet-proof by large quantities of grain in tubs and bags, placed along the sides. In these many of their old people and their women and children had gathered for safety, and behind and within these as defenses the Indians still kept up a skulking fight, picking off our men. After three hours hard fighting, with many of the officers and men wounded and dead, a treacherous enemy of unknown numbers and resources lurking in the surrounding forests, and the night coming on, word comes to fire the wigwams, and the battle becomes a fearful holocaust, great numbers of those who had taken refuge therein being burned.

When now the fortress and all its contents were burning, and destruction assured, our soldiers hastily gathered their wounded and as many as possible of their dead and formed their column for the long and weary march back to Wickford."

As the result of the battle about 80 were slain on the side of the English and 150 wounded. The Indians lost about 300 killed, although prisoners reported their dead to be as many as 700, and if their wounded were in the usual proportion to the number of the slain then the causalities of those dreadful hours might run into the thousands.

The casualties to the Concord men were: George Hayward killed, and Abraham Temple and Thomas Browne wounded.

That the position of the company in which the Concord soldiers served was one of extreme peril is indicated by the terrible manner in which Capt. Davenport, their commander was riddled by bullets, the circumstances of whose death is thus narrated in the "Old Indians Chronicle": "Before our men came up to take possession of the Fort the Indians had shot three bullets through Capt. Davenport whereupon he bled extremely, and immediately called for his Lieut. Mr. Edward Ting, and committed the charge of the Company to him, and desired him to take care of his Gun, and deliver it according to Order and immediately died in his place."

Ninigret, chief of the Niantick Indians informed Gen. Winslow that his men buried twenty four bodies of the English at the Fort and asked for a charge of powder for each. Forty of the English soldiers were buried at Wickford, and the spot was long marked by a tree called the " Grave apple tree." But comparatively little is recorded of the march back to Wickford.

The night was bleak, the wild storm of snow which was raging at the start continued. The dread of ambuscade, the scant knowledge of the country, by which some lost their way, not to meet the main body till the next morning, the sad loss of comrades who might have been townsmen or neighbors, all contributed to make the night dreary and the journey a terrible one.

It was, however, considered unwise to bivouac, so the column moved on bearing with them 210 of their wounded and dead, and this after marching from morning till midday and from that time engaging in fearful combat until the sun sank behind the dark storm cloud, leaving them to find their way in darkness over a strange country.

The fort of the Narragansetts was utterly destroyed. The wigwams being of frail inflammable material and fanned by the rough wind of that tempestuous December night, an resting upon no foundation but the bare earth, all vestige of this defensed city of the aborigines and even the identity of the spot might have been lost except for tradition and a few scattered relics; but these have been faithful to their trust, and the spot where the Swamp Fight occurred is pointed out to a certainty. Many bullets have been found in the vicinity and charred corn and cooking utensils and arrow heads. As criticism of the English has sometimes occurred on the ground that the closing scene of an event already sufficiently calamitous was unnecessary we quote from the last-mentioned author.

"I wish here to record my protest against the unjust, often weak, and always inconsiderate, criticism bestowed upon our leaders, in this campaign, and especially in this battle, for their lack of foresight in abandoning the shelter and provisions of the fort, their sacrifice of the lives of our wounded men through their removal and the dangers and fatigues of the long march, and their inhumanity in burning the helpless and innocent in their huts and wigwams.

It is well to remember at the start that many of the wisest, ablest and bravest men of the three colonies were the leaders in this affair. A noble commander, wise and brave: reverend ministers, by no means backward with their opinions; the most prominent and skillful surgeons the country afforded; veteran majors and captains of Massachusetts and Connecticut, with their veteran soldiers fresh from severe experiences in the western campaign, inured to danger and experienced in Indian wiles and deceits: against all these we have recorded only the remonstrance of Mr. Church, who up to that time, at least, had experience in Indian warfare only as a scout, and the only record we have of any protest by him was made many years after the affair. And again, from the standpoint of their conditions as nearly as we can now judge, it seems that their hasty retreat was wise. They were some sixteen miles from their base of supplies (it is doubtful if they had noted the Indian supplies until the burning began). There was no way of reaching their provisions and ammunition at Wickford except by detaching a portion of their force now reduced greatly by death, wounds and exposure. The number of Indians who had escaped and were still in the woods close at hand were unknown, but supposed to be several thousand, with report of a thousand in reserve about a mile distant. These were now scattered and demoralized, but in a few hours might rally and fall upon the fort, put our troops, in their weakened condition, upon the defensive, and make their retreat from the swamp extremely difficult if not utterly impossible, encumbered as they would be by the wounded, whose swollen and stiffened wounds in a few hours would render removal doubly painful and dangerous. Added to this was the chance of an attack upon the garrison at Wickford, and the dread of a midnight ambuscade, which every hour's delay made more likely and would render more dangerous."

When the men of the Massachusetts force were ready to march for the reduction of the Narragansett Fort, a proclamation was made in the name of the Governor to the soldiers that, " If they played the man, took the Fort, and drove the enemy out of the Narragansett country, which is their great seat, they should have a gratuity of land besides their wages."

Years after, a petition was presented to the General Court by the people living in several towns of Essex County dated June 4, 1685, asking for a tract of land pursuant to the foregoing promise.

The Court responded to the petition favorably and allowed the grant of a tract of land eight miles square in the Nipmuck country "provided it be laid out so as not to interfere with any former grants, and that an Orthodox minister on their settlement of thirty families be settled within four years next coming." (Mass. Col. Records Vol. 5 page 487).

For forty years nothing more was done in the matter. The place specified for the grant was remote, and the conditions imposed hard to be complied with. In process of time, however, when the Massachusetts and Plymouth colonies had become one, and went by the name of the Province of Massachusetts Bay, a petition was again presented by Samuel Chandler and Jacob Wright of Concord in behalf of themselves and a number of other persons, recalling the act of the General Court in 1685, and asking that a grant of land might be made to the petitioners.

The result was that a committee was appointed consisting of Mr. Samuel Chandler of Concord and two others who were fully empowered to lay out an area of land eight miles square, in some unappropriated land of the Colony for the purpose set forth in the petition.

A list also was to be prepared by the committee, of those who by reason of service in the Narragansett war or their legal representatives were entitled to a share in the lands thus laid out.

As it turned out that the number of claimants as reported by the committee was so great that the land grant would be insufficient for them all, the committee was instructed to lay out " two tracts of land for Townships of the contents of six miles square," the same conditions being imposed as in the first order.

After some delay and some controversy as to the sufficiency of the lands granted there being disagreement between the Council and House of Representatives with regard to it, the latter body January 19,1731, sent up to the Council a pleading message in advocacy of the claims of the Narragansett soldiers and their representatives. The following is a copy of a part of this paper: "And one great Reason is that there was a Proclamation made to the Army in the name of the Government (as living Evidences very fully testify) when they were mustered on Dedham Plain where they began their March, that if they played the man, took the Fort & Drove the Enemy out of the Narraganset Country, which was their great Seat, that they should have a gratuity in Land besides their Wages; and it is well known, & our Sitting to hear this petition is an Evidence that this was done; and as the Conditions have been performed, certainly the promise in all Equity & Justice ought to be fulfilled; and if we Consider the Difficulties these brave men went through in Storming the Fort in the Depth of Winter, & the pinching wants they afterwards underwent in pursuing the Indians that escaped through a hideous Wilderness famously known throughout New England to this day by the Name of the hungry March; and if we further Consider that until this brave though small army thus played the Man, the whole Country was filled with Distress & fear & We trembled in this Capital Boston itself & that to the Goodness of God to this army We owe our Fathers & our own Safety & Estates, We cannot but think that those Instruments of Our Deliverance & Safety ought to be not only justly but also gratefully & generously rewarded & even with much more than they prayed for, If we measure what they receive from us, by what we enjoy and have received from them.

We need not mention to the Honorable Board the Wisdom Justice and Generosity of Our Mother Country & of the ancient Romans, on such Occasions, Triumph, Orations, Hereditary Honors & privileges all the Riches, Lands & Spoils of War and conquered Countrys have not been thought too great for those to whom they have not owed more if so much as We do those our Deliverers: & We ought further to observe what greatly adds to their merit that they were not Vagabonds & Beggars & Outcasts, of which Armies are sometimes considerably made up, who run the Hazards of War to Avoid the Danger of Starving: so far from this that these were some of the best of Our men, the Fathers & Sons of some of the greatest & best of Our families and could have no other View but to Serve the Country & whom God was pleased accordingly in every remarkable manner to Honour & Succeed."

A result of this message and a renewal of the soldiers' petition was the appointment of a committee for an adjustment of claims; and pursuant to the work of the committee townships were confirmed, among which was Narragansett township No. 6, now Templeton, Mass.

This township was confirmed to one hundred and twenty claimants or their representatives then living in the towns of Concord, Groton, Marlborough, Chelmsford, Billerica, Lancaster, Lexington, Stow, Framingham, Littleton, Sherborn, Stoneham, Southborough and Woburn.

Samuel Chandler of Concord was one of the Committee to have the matter in charge.

The following are the familiar Concord names found in a list given in the old "Proprietors' Record" Book in Templeton, headed "June 24, 1735. Those that drawed their lots in the Narragansett Township No. 6.

"No. of lot	Claimant	Grantees and references.
49	Samuel Chandler for	Joseph Buss
52	Samuel Chandler for	Assignee to John Taley
19	Benjamin Temple	in the right of his father Abraham
9 96	Simon Davis	
39	Johnathan Buttrick	for heirs of Samuel Buttrick
8	Ephraim Brown	for his father Thomas Brown
14	Samuel Miles	
26	John Wood	
80	Joseph Buckley	for his father Peter Buckley
18	George Farrar I	heir to Samuel How
118	Daniel Adams	for his father-in-law Daniel Dean
111	Daniel Billings	for his father Nathaniel Billings
643	Joseph Wheat	for Moses Wheat
117	Abraham Taylor	
7	Samuel Hartwell	for his father Samuel
120	David Wheeler	assignee to Samuel Greeland
79	Thomas Ball	
69	Ebenezer Wheeler	for his father John
23	Nathan Brooks for	"Snow"
42	Eleazer Bateman	
25	John Wheeler for	his brother Joseph
32	Joseph Wood	
43	John Adams	
21	Ephraim Temple	
102	John Barrett	

The following is an additional list which purports to be the names of Concord Claimants.

Claimants Grantees Samuel Chandler assignee to John Griggs Samuel Chandler Jr assignee to John Kent Jonathan Whiting alive Jane Cane for her father John Cane William Clark heir to John Taylor James Russel for his father Benjamin The Concord soldiers were probably absent from home about two months, during which time they were subjected to great hardship occasioned by long marches, hunger and cold.

After the withdrawal of the expedition to Wickford it rested till after the last of January. The snow storm that was raging at the time of the battle lasted several days and was followed by a sudden thaw which swelled the streams and softened the ways making marching difficult.

After the first of February however, the forces broke camp and then and there began the forward movement which for generations was designated as the "Long March" or "Hungry March." The objective point was the Nipmuck Country. The course to it was long and circuitous.

The provisions gave out and the little army was forced to kill some of its horses to sustain life. The foe harassed their flank and rear, and after a long and fruitless attempt to bring him to an open engagement they arrived worn and weary at the region of the Connecticut river, and General Appleton seeing that the Expedition could accomplish no further purpose, came from Marlborough to Boston, reaching there about the first of February.

As Concord was creditably represented both as to the town's soldiers who took part in the Swamp fight and the position which they occupied, it may be appropriate to publish the following account of the engagement as it is given in a letter from Capt. James Oliver who commanded the third company. The letter is taken from Hutchinson's History of Massachusetts, Vol. 1 page 272 third edition.

In this work the authorship of the letter which is without a signature is attributed to Major Bradford, but it has been asserted by Mr. Drake author of "Book of the Indians" who had seen the original, to have been signed by Capt. Oliver.

"Narraganset 26th 11th month 1675.

After a tedious march in a bitter cold night that followed Dec. 12 we hoped our pilot would have led us to Pomham by break of day, but so it came to pass we were misled and so missed a good opportunity. Dec. 13th, we came to Mr. Smith's, and that day took 35 prisoners. Dec. 14th, our General went out with horse and foot, I with my company was left to keep garrison. I sent out 30 of my men to scout abroad, who killed two Indians and brought in 4 prisoners, one of which was beheaded. Our Army came home at night, killed 7 and brought in 9 more, young and old. Dec. 15th, came in John, a rogue, with pretense of peace, and was dismissed with this errand, that we might speak with Sachems. That evening, he not being gone a quarter of an hour, his company that lay behind a hill killed two Salem men within a mile of our quarters and wounded a third that he is dead. And at a house three miles off where I had 10 men, they killed 2 of them. Instantly, Capt. Mosely, myself and Capt. Gardner were sent to fetch in Major Appleton's company that was kept 3 miles and an half off, and coming they lay behind a stone wall and fired upon us in sight of the garrison. We killed the captain that killed one of the Salem men, and had his cap on. That night they burned Jerry Bull's house and killed 17. Dec. 16th came that news. Dec. 17th came news that the Connecticut forces were at Petasquamscot and had killed 4 Indians and took 6 prisoners. That day we sold Capt. Davenport 47 Indians, young and old for 80/. in money. Dec. 17th we marched to Petasquamscot with all our forces, only a garrison left; that night was very stormy; we lay, one thousand strong, in the open field that long night. In the morning, Dec. 19th, Lord's day, at five o'clock we marched. Between 12 and 1 we came up with the enemy and had a sore fight three hours. We lost, that are now dead, about 68, and had 150 wounded, many of which are recovered. That long snowy cold night we had about 18 miles to our quarters, with about 210 dead and wounded. We left 8 dead in the fort. We had but 12 dead when we came from the swamp, besides the three we left. Many died by the way, and soon as they were brought in, so that Dec. 20th we buried in a grave 34, next day 4, next day 2, and none since here. Eight died at Rhode Island, one at Petasquamscot, 2 lost in the woods and killed Dec. 20, as we heard since; some say two more died. By the best intelligence we killed 300 fighting men; prisoners we took, say 350, and above 300 women and children. We burnt above 500 houses, left but 9, burnt all their corn, that was in baskets, great store. One signal mercy that night, not to be forgotten, viz: that when we drew off, with so many dead and wounded, they did not pursue us, which the young men would have done, but the sachems would not consent; they had but 10 pounds of powder left. Our General, with about 40, lost our way and wandered till 7 o'clock in the morning before we came to our quarters. We thought we were within 2 miles of the enemy again, but God kept us; to him be the glory. We have killed now and then 1 since and burnt 200 wigwams more; we killed 9 last Tuesday'.

We fetch in their corn daily and that undoes them. This is, as nearly as I can, a true relation. I read the narrative to my officers in my tent, who all assent to the truth of it.

Monhegins and Pequods proved very false, fired into the air, and sent word before they came they would so, but got much plunder, guns and kettles. A great part of what is already written was attested by Joshua Teffe, who married an Indian woman a Wampanoag. He shot 20 times at us in the swamp, was taken at Providence Jan'y 14, brought to us the 16th, and executed the i8'h. A sad wretch, he, never heard a sermon but once these 14 years. His father going to recall him lost his head and lies unburied."

CHAPTER XL.

The Advance of the English to the Nipmuck Country — Movements of Canonchet — Indian Depredations in the Spring of 1675-76 — Their Descent upon Concord Pillage — Isaac and Jacob Shepard Slain — Mary Shepard made Captive — Place of the Tragedy — Description of the Event — "The Escape of Mary Shepard—The Removal of the Nashoba Indians from Concord — Sketch of Capt. Samuel Mosely — His Antecedents — Character of His Soldiers.

ON Feb. 12, 1675, occurred the "Nashoba incident" or the massacre at "Concord Village" as the Concord "new grant" was sometimes called.

After the desertion of their fort and perhaps while the wigwams with their charred corn heaps were still smoldering, Canonchet and the remnant of his warriors who with some of the families had escaped while the burning was yet going on returned to their ruined homes to gather it may be what little remained of their rude implements for cooking, or any unburnt provision which for the time being they might subsist upon. They buried their dead, cared for the wounded, and after sending their women and children who survived the fight and flames to a place of safety, sullenly and with a savage determination started on the track of their destroyers as they marched forth from Wickford. At every step they harried them till they reached the Connecticut valley where Canonchet formed an alliance with the Nipmucks at their old headquarters at Meminisset near Brookfield.

At this time it is supposed that Canonchet rather than King Philip was the real leader of the great horde of confederated but unorganized Indians, which it is believed at this stage of the war had planned to drive the English from the Nipmuck country. But Canonchet soon went on an errand to the southward where things went adversely to him and he was captured and shot. A little later, Philip went westward, perhaps seeking new alliances in New York, even visiting, it may be, the Maquas or Mohawks.

In the meantime, during the closing months of the year 1675, for the year at that time by the reckoning called "Old Style" ended in March, the Indians were more or less broken up into small marauding parties or squads, which scattered over the country disturbed the inhabitants and every now and then pounced upon the defenseless homesteads. On February 1st, one of these squads made a descent upon the home of Thomas Eames situated upon the southerly side of Mt. Waite near the present South Framingham and burned the buildings after killing or taking captive his family of ten persons while Mr. Eames was absent at Boston to obtain a stock of ammunition with which to defend them.

Feb. 10, Lancaster was burned, the Rowlinson garrison captured, and the wife of Rev. Joseph Rowlinson the minister was carried away captive. On the 12th, the Indians made a raid on Concord village, now a part of Littleton, and killed two men and captured a girl.

The place of the tragedy was on the south side of Quagana Hill, and the persons slain and captured were children of Ralte and Thanklord Shepard who went from Malden near a place since called Bell Rock to Concord village, where he bought of Lieut. Joseph Wheeler of Concord 610 acres lying in the form of a triangle between the Indian plantation of Nashoba and that part of Chelmsford which is now

Westford; Nagog pond forming the base of the triangle, the apex being two miles one-quarter and sixty rods north from the southwest end of Nagog pond.

The names of the persons slain and captured were Isaac, Jacob, and Mary. Isaac was born June 20, 1639, and married Mary Smedley, 1667. Jacob was born in 1653, and Mary the youngest of the family was born in 1660 or 1662.

When the Indians swooped down upon the Shepard homestead the ground was covered with snow to such a depth that snow shoes were used. The event happened on Saturday, and Isaac and Jacob were threshing in the barn.

Being aware of the perilous times, they had set their sister on the summit of a hill to watch for Indians; but the savages eluded her vigilance and before she was aware of their presence she was captured and her brothers were slain.

Tradition does not inform us just where the girl was taken to; some think it was in the neighborhood of Lancaster, others that it was as far off as Brookfield, but wherever it was she soon escaped and returned home.

Hubbard in his narrative of the Indian wars says of Mary Shepard that "she strangely escaped away upon a horse that the Indians had taken from Lancaster a little while before."

Tradition asserts that she escaped during the night following the day of her capture and arrived home the next morning.

Rev. Edmund Foster a former minister of Littleton in a "Century Sermon" preached in the year 1815, stated concerning the event that tradition says the girl was carried by the savages to Nashawa, now called Lancaster, or to some place in the neighborhood of it.

Samuel Gardner Drake in his notes on the "Old Indian Chronicle" says that the leader of the band who slew the Shepard brothers is supposed to have been Netus, the same who attacked the Eames family, and who was sometimes called the Nipmuck Captain. Netus was slain the 22nd of March following, by a company of men from Sudbury, who with some soldiers from Marlboro found him asleep with a company of Indians around their campfire. Foster says that in the dead of night as related by tradition, Mary Shepard took a saddle from under the head of her Indian keeper when sunk in sleep increased by the fumes of ardent spirit, put the saddle on a horse, mounted him, swam him across Nashawa river, and so escaped the hands of her captors and arrived safe to her relatives and friends.

Mrs. Rowlinson says that the only time she ever saw any Indian intoxicated during her captivity was just before her release when John Hoar had given her master some liquor as part of her ransom and he got drunk on it.

The Removal of the Nashoba Indians from Concord to Deer Island.

Soon after the massacre at Quagana hill a movement was made to remove the Nashobas from the care of their friend John Hoar to Deer Island, Boston Harbor.

As we have in an early chapter of this work referred briefly to this event giving some account of it, we will here only supplement it with such additional statements as were not there brought out, and properly belong to the period upon which we are writing.

During the stay of these Indians at Concord under the charge of John Hoar they were given employment and are represented as being contented; but there were intermeddlers in their affairs; and a part of the Concord people allowed their dislike of all Indians to take such acute form as to send for the savage adventurer, Capt. Samuel Mosely to take them away.

And here it is important to pause in our narration sufficiently long to set forth some facts connected with the life and character of Samuel Mosely, whose name and fame in King Philip's war were both savory and unsavory.

Samuel Mosely was the son of Henry Maudsley who came from England to Massachusetts in 1685 in the ship Hopewell. The family was of Lancashire, England, and the name was there spelled Maudesley. Henry lived at Braintree where Samuel was born June 14, 1641. Samuel spelled his name Mosley; he married Ann Addington. In 1688 he was one of a commission sent to treat with the Narragansett Indians, and in connection with this service is called "Captain."

In a work entitled "The Present State of New England," it is said of him "This Captain Mosley has been a Privateer at Jamaica, an excellent soldier and an undaunted spirit; one whose memory will be honored in New England, for his many eminent services he hath done the Public."

That Samuel Mosely had been somewhat of an adventurer upon the high seas is probably true. One writer says of him that "he had visited Jamaica in the way of trade, and the adventurous spirit had been excited and schooled perhaps by Sir Henry Morgan and his associate buccaneers; the result of which was the bringing home to Boston the prizes from some unmentioned enemy."

A part of the experience of Capt. Mosely as a quasi-mariner was obtained by acting on a permit from the Court to take reprisals from the Dutch, who in several instances had captured vessels belonging to the English.

In 1674 and 5, he was given the command of an expedition for this purpose which was fitted out by some merchants in Boston whose commerce had been molested and succeeded in taking three vessels — the "Edward and Thomas" whose captain was Peter Roderigo, the "Penobscot Shallopp" Cornelius Anderson, Captain, and the "Shallopp called Philipp."

The crews who manned these vessels were brought into Boston April 2' 1675 and imprisoned to wait their trial for piracy the following May.

Much excitement existed during the trial of these men and some sympathy was expressed for the Dutch prisoners who set up a defense by pretending to produce a commission given by William, Prince of Orange, and the allegation of an infringement of the law of nations on the part of the American ships by trading with the French while the Dutch were at war with them. The result of the trial was that five out of nine who were indicted for piracy were convicted and sentenced to be put to death. It occurred, however, that on account of the existence of the Indian war an execution of the sentence was deferred, and Roderigo upon his own petition was pardoned; and Anderson, having been acquitted, both entered the Colonial service as soldiers.

When the war broke out by the slaying of Sassamon or Sausamon and the attack upon Swansea which quickly followed, three companies were raised to meet the emergency, one of infantry from Essex county; one from Suffolk; and a company of horse from the various towns of Middlesex. The Suffolk company was commanded by Samuel Mosely and is supposed to have been made up in part of some of these adventurers.

That Mosely and some of this element gravitated together as comrades in arms, "doing duty" near Brookfield shortly after the Wheeler disaster is indicated by the following statement preserved among the state archives Vol. 68 page 7.

"Boston, October ye 13, 1675.

To the honored Governor & Councell of the Massathusets Colony in New England.

These are to signyfie that Cornellius ——— [sic] Consort the Dutchman was uppon the Contryes Servis Att quabage and by the Councle of Warre there was sent out Capt. of the for Iorne And Afterward marched to Grotton & Chemsfort According to my best Advice continued in the Countryes Servis six weekes Cornellius being Reddy to depart the Country & myself being here att boston the Major Willard being Absent I granted this ticket.

Thomas Wheeler, Capt.

Cornelius Anderson was sometimes called Cornelius Consort.

So popular was Capt. Mosely that although he was outside the line of official succession by the stiff rule of colonial promotion, so that he could not hold a commission in the regular way, he raised an independent company of 110 volunteers in three hours.

As late as May 5, 1676, Samuel Mosely received a commission while connected with the command of Major Savage and the wages of his soldiers were raised by popular subscription.

Mosely and his men in addition to their wages were to have all the profits accruing from the plunder or sale of Indian captives; and in case these did not prove sufficient the Court was to make up the balance.

"On August 34, 1676 at a great sale of Indian captives he is charged with 1 boy and girle 6 jf; & 13 squawes & pappooses 20£."

Savage says that Mosely died Jan. 1680. He died intestate. His administratrix was his widow Ann Mosely and among his assets as inventoried mention is made of an old musket and sword in the "Garret."

That all the men that served under Capt. Mosely were adventurers or were recklessly inconsiderate of the claims of humanity is not to be presumed. For even if at the outset his men were unlike the average of those who served in other companies, yet regiments and companies were subject to change. As the ranks were thinned by the enemy and the hardships of marches and exposure to extreme weather, they were doubtless replenished with whatever material came to hand. Hence we may perhaps account for the presence of occasional names associated with some of the old towns of Middlesex county. The discovery of the name of Richard Adams of Sudbury who was wounded in the Swamp Fight while serving in Capt. Mosely's company may have led the writer to make the statement in his History of Sudbury that the quota sent from that town for the Narragansett Expedition served in Mosely's company; whereas the fact is that the men from Sudbury were in the company of Capt. Davenport and served with the soldiers from Concord. The name of Richard Adams is found in a list of Mosely's men who mustered at Dedham Dec. 9, 1675 for the Narragansett campaign. Mass. Archives Vol. 167 page 293. In that list are names that are unfamiliar, some of them perhaps being French or Dutch anglicized in spelling.

In estimating the character of Capt. Mosely we are not to infer simply from the fact that he is accredited with certain Indian captives which were sold to him that he was exceptionally severe in his dealing with the savages, it being asserted in Capt. Oliver's letter that on a certain day "we sold Capt. Davenport 47 Indians, young and old for 80£ in money." It was the common practice to dispose of Indian prisoners in this way. Even the wife and child of King Philip were sold into West Indian slavery. Mosely's character is to be judged by his own isolated conduct, not by practices that he engaged in in common with others.

Neither are we to suppose that he was altogether uncouth in manner, nor wholly lacking in that culture which characterized some of the early colonists. He was, we infer from his influence upon and association with the leaders of the times, their peer in matters of petty diplomacy, and even, it may be, partook of the customary reverence for and recognition of things sacred.

CHAPTER XLI.

Movements of the Indians after the Narragansett Campaign — Expedition into the Nipmuck Country — Dismissal of Soldiers from the Garrison Houses — The Disastrous Results — Advance of the Indians to the Eastward—The Alarm — The Starting of Relief Companies — Soldiers from Boston Watertown and Concord — Capt. Samuel Wadsworth's Command—His Arrival at Marlborough— The Return to Sudbury — The Ambuscade—The Wadsworth Fight at Green Hill — The Forest Fire— The Rout — Escape to the Mill at Hop Brook — Burial of the Slain — The Woodland Grave — Siege of the Haynes House — Attempted Rescue by the Concord Men — Ambuscade of the Concord Soldiers — The Route Taken to Sudbury.

AS before observed, after the Narragansett Swamp Fight and the ending of the "Hungry March," repeated depredations were committed upon the frontier towns from the Connecticut river easterly as far as Concord Village. But these predatory bands were easily concentrated at the call of King Philip who by the departure of Canonchet to Connecticut about this time had become the sole director of the Nipmuck Indians and what few fugitive Narragansett confederates remained with them. Shortly after the middle of February it was reported that there were two large fortified Indian encampments in the central part of Massachusetts, one near the Wachuset hill, the other at Meminesset. To meet the existing conditions, the Colonies of Massachusetts and Connecticut proposed organizing another army consisting of six hundred men. The Massachusetts contingent was placed under command or Major Thomas Savage, and marched to Meminisset about March 16 They found that the foe had disappeared. For some cause the Indians who were gathered about Wachuset, were not attacked and the Council probably considering it inexpedient for the force to remain longer in search of the enemy ordered Major Savage to withdraw his troops and return to Boston. For a time the principal opposing forces were the troops stationed at the central garrison houses and those engaged in the ranging service between them. At some of these central posts the forces were quite efficient and commanded by able captains, as for example, the one at Marlboro, which from about February 5th till into the following April was in charge of Capt. Samuel Brocklebank, who was stationed there after his return from the Narragansett expedition, whither he went with a reinforcing column after the troops left Wickford.

But the forces at these posts were soon after weakened by an order of the authorities dismissing some of the men; the council thinking perhaps that the foe was subdued.

But the opinion was sadly erroneous, and to some of the soldiers and settlers it was a fatal one. Shortly after the order had been complied with the Indians again became active, and along the frontier there were signs of a renewal of hostilities. The forest rang with their shouts of triumph.

The old garrison doors closed; and everywhere the towns were put in a posture of defense. Nor was the preparation premature. Soon reports came of burnings and plunderings; and messengers went speeding through the forest to the Council for relief. On Feb. 21st a part of Medfield was burned. On March 13th Groton was destroyed. On the 26th the Indians fell upon Marlboro burning a part of its dwellings, and on the 28th, Rehoboth was assailed. That Philip was present with this large body that was moving eastward, while it may not be absolutely proven, is altogether probable. According to Mrs. Rowlandson, who was a captive among them, he was in the vicinity of Wachuset about that time with a large force of Indians. It is hardly probable that the wily chieftain, so near a large body of his warriors, would not be present directing their movements on their way easterly.

When the tidings reached the Council at Boston great consternation was created. Never before had King Philip with so large a force been as near the metropolis of the Bay Colony. Messengers were sent out with the news in every direction, the militia was put in motion and everything possible was done to check the enemy's advance. But there was little need of any extra messengers, the towns of Middlesex were already astir. The signal given from hamlet to hamlet had aroused the watchful inhabitants and whatever forces could be spared were sent at once to the line of danger. A force was dispatched from Boston consisting of from fifty to one hundred soldiers. Another was started from Watertown led by Capt. Hugh Mason. Others who hurried to the front were a "ply of horse" from the troop of Capt. Prentice under Corp. Phipps, and Capt. Hunting with forty friendly Indians, also a body of twelve men from Concord.

The company from Concord was made up in part at least and perhaps wholly of the town's citizens, some of whom may have been eligible to impress but not in the service, kept at home it may be for garrison work.

History does not inform us of this matter, neither does tradition. The record says, "Twelve resolute young men;" and there is every reason to infer that upon the first indication of the near approach of the foe to their sister town of Sudbury they presented themselves voluntarily, and without being bidden hastened to the rescue.

It would be interesting to follow in detail so far as there is data for it, the fate or fortune of each of these detachments as they hurried to the scene of action and became a part of it. But as only a portion of them are nearly related to the history of Concord we are called upon to confine our narrative chiefly to those.

The detachment sent from Boston was commanded by Capt. Samuel Wadsworth, an experienced officer who had served in the Nipmuck country under Major Savage, going to the relief of beleaguered Lancaster, a short time previous.

Hastening with all speed up through Sudbury to Marlboro, where it was reported at his starting that the enemy had concentrated, he arrived about midnight of April 20, and reported to Capt. Brocklebank, who had been left in charge of the garrison house there, all other houses having been burned.

It took but a short time for Wadsworth to learn that after sacking and destroying the town the Indians had gone in the direction of Sudbury. Without stopping for needed rest, having exchanged some of his tired soldiers and younger men for a part of the garrison guard and accompanied by Capt. Samuel Brocklebank who desired to go to Boston to speak to the Council, Wadsworth at once retraced his steps back to Sudbury, where he arrived probably by early afternoon the day following.

Upon his entering the town there appeared about one hundred Indians, which Wadsworth may have supposed was Philip's main force, or at least a detachment from it, and one which he could pursue with safety and easily capture; but it was a mistake, and the mistake was fatal.

The Indians had resorted to their old ruse of using decoys; and the same tragic experience that befell Capt. Wheeler at Brookfield and Capt. Lathrop at Bloody

241

Brook, and Capt. Beers near Northfield and notably in one of the later wars Gen. Braddock, was in store for Capts. Wadsworth and Brocklebank, old Indian fighters notwithstanding both officers were.

Upon seeing the savages the English pursued, but suddenly and without warning were surprised by a number estimated at from one thousand to fifteen hundred who fired upon them from a place of concealment at or near the foot of Green hill about a quarter of a mile from the present South Sudbury village. The trap had been cunningly set and as cunningly sprung. The Indians had allowed the English to pass up through the town during the night, and during their march to and from Marlboro had placed in waiting so many of their men as were needed for the ambuscade When Wadsworth returned, as they believed he would upon receiving intelligence of their absence from Marlboro, they were in readiness to meet him with their murderous volleys.

After the first firing by the Indians, which was not so deadly as might be supposed from their vantage ground, Wadsworth closed up his little company for a valiant defense, and from that time, which was probably not far from midafternoon, the fight continued till after nightfall. On the one hand it was a combat for life, on the other for a mastery over the main force of the English which stood between themselves and the spoliation of the town of Sudbury.

No sooner had Wadsworth recovered from the surprise than he attempted to gain the hill top, and so successfully that by night he had reached it, and with a chance that the foe would be held in abeyance till reinforcements reached him.

From tree to tree, from rock to rock, from over fallen logs the fire of Wadsworth's men was doubtless well directed; while the enemy although strong and active were kept well in the distance not daring to fight at close quarters.

The indications as set forth in Philip's war are that the savage was too cowardly for open combat. He depended upon surprises and trickery or upon overwhelming numbers.

A mistake of the Council and Colonial committees may have been in believing that they could capture the Indians by large expeditions by which they were chased from point to point in a vain attempt to draw them into open battle. The Indian's mode of living and familiarity with the country enabled him to elude all such efforts, and except for the destruction of an Indian fort and village large bodies of troops in carefully planned campaigns were a partial failure, and only furnished opportunity for Indian ambushment.

Wadsworth had gained the hilltop and was within night's friendly shelter both of which he had probably longed for, but the wily enemy impatient of the stubborn defense and aware that just over the hill to the easterly was the Watertown company endeavoring to break through to his relief and that with the morning other reinforcements would arrive, as a last resort set fire to the forest. The crisis had come. The flames fanned by the April breeze set out upon their disastrous errand without mercy. Soon they reached the top of the hill where the brave little company stood fearless to face anything human but powerless to do battle with this new agent. The last moment of their remaining together had arrived. They broke, they ran, down through the brushwood and the thickening smoke and through the gauntlet of savages. The Indian's opportunity had come. Before the conflagration was started they had doubtless so stationed themselves as to form a complete circle around the fire enclosed space; so that when there was a struggle to escape from the flames not an Englishman would have a fair chance of escape. Only too successfully was the programme carried out; for of the forty or fifty men more or less, who had fought through the long hours of that April afternoon from the foot to the summit of Green hill less than a score escaped and found shelter in the neighboring mill by the brook. All the others had fallen or been taken captive, and when the morning sun arose and the terrible night shadows had lifted, the charred and mangled corpses of that band of brave men lay scattered over that piece of burnt woodland to be gathered in kind embrace by a company of whites and friendly Indians and laid in one large lone grave in the wilderness.

The burial scene as described in Gookin's History of the Praying Indians is as follows: "Upon the 12th of April early in the morning over forty Indians having stripped themselves and painted their faces like to the enemy, they passed over the bridge to the west side of the river without any Englishmen in the company, to make discovery of the enemy (which was generally conceded quarter thereabout), but this did not at all discourage our Christian Indians from marching and discovering, and if they had met with them to beat up their quarters. But God had so ordered that the enemy were all withdrawn and were retreated in the night. Our Indian soldiers having made a thorough discovery and to their great relief (for some of them wept when they saw so many English lie dead on the place among the slain), some they knew, viz, those two worthy and pious Captains, Capt. Brocklebank of Rowley and Capt. Wadsworth of Milton, who with about thirty-two private soldiers were slain the day before. ... As soon as they had made a full discovery, [they] returned to their Captains and the rest of the English and gave them an account of their motions. Then it was concluded to march over to the place and bury the dead, and they did so. Shortly after, our Indians marching in two files upon the wings to secure those that went to bury the dead, God so ordered it that they met with no interruption in that work."

A rude stone heap was placed over the grave, it may be for the double purpose of protecting and of marking it.

In 1730, President Wadsworth of Harvard College, son of the Captain, caused a slate stone to be erected beside the spot. From this time there was another long season of neglect. The spring time came with its decoration of violets and wood grass, the autumn with its falling leaves, and the winter with its kindly mantling snows, each in its turn tenderly placing its appropriate token upon the lonely grave. At length after the lapse of nearly two centuries the appearance of the place was changed by the establishment of a more imposing memorial.

Having narrated the leading events of the battle of Green hill we are in a position to consider the movements of the men from Concord.

On the night that Capt. Wadsworth left Marlboro and while yet on the march back to Sudbury the Indians were busy in preparation for assaulting the garrison houses of the town. These houses contained at that time in all probability all the inhabitants on the west side of the river; the people on the east side, or what is now Wayland having fled for protection to the fortified meeting house, and fortified parsonage of Rev. Edmund Brown, the former situated at a spot still pointed out in the town's first burying ground, and the latter at the junction of Mill brook and Sudbury river.

243

The principle garrison attacked was that known as the Walter Haynes house. This house stood upon the west side of the Sudbury river, the same stream which in Concord is called the Concord river, near the meadows about midway between the present Sudbury center and Wayland center.

The attack upon this house began, according to the "Old Petition" about six o'clock in the morning and was kept up till after mid-day, at times the fight occurring in the very door yard. To this garrison house the Concord men directed their course. They probably arrived in the vicinity in the early forenoon. The fight at Green hill had not then begun, and part of the Indians had passed over the main causeway and "town bridge," which are a part of the "old road" from Wayland to Sudbury center and were doing mischievous work on the east side. A sufficient force was probably left at the Haynes house to keep up a hard fight with the inmates and to prevent it from being reinforced.

As the Concord men drew near the garrison house, they saw a small company of Indians near it, and doubtless supposing that these were all and that they could easily overcome them and gain entrance to the building, they rushed forward forgetful in their impetuosity of the risk of an ambuscade.

No sooner were they within the power of the designing savages than the latter arose in great force and placing themselves between the English and the garrison house fell upon them with great ferocity and so disastrous was the onslaught hat but one escaped. The "Old Indian Chronicle" says: "They were waylaid and eleven of them cut off." Hubbard says: "These men at the first hearing of the alarm, who unawares were surprised near a garrison house, in hope of getting some advantage upon a small party of the enemy that presented themselves in a meadow. A great number of the Indians, who laid unseen in the bushes, suddenly arose up and intercepting the passage to the garrison house killed and took them all."

That resistance was made we may infer both from tradition and from a fragment of record relating to the estate of James Hosmer who was among the slain. The former says "There was a bold resistance;" the latter, which is a Probate matter, speaks of Hosmer as "being slayne in an engagement with the Indians at Sudbury on the 21st of the 2nd month in the year 1676." The names of the fallen that have been preserved are James Hosmer, David Corny, William Heywood, Samuel Potter, Joseph Buttrick, John Barnes, Josiah Wheeler and Jacob Farrar. Tradition is for the most part silent as to the circumstances or any incident connected with the start, the march, or the exact details of the disaster.

We may presume that the start was an exciting one.

Perhaps the quick ear of James Hosmer was the first to catch the faint sound of distant firing as at nightfall on the day previous he went out to fodder the stock on his father's farm near the Assabet: or it may be that the tidings were brought by a scout from over the Sudbury boundary line, who scouring the forest had seen the impress of many moccasins, the sure sign of the presence of a war party. Certain it is that there were warnings of an Indian invasion in the neighborhood of Concord, for only a few days before, the people of Sudbury had informed the Council at Boston by a letter of Rev. Edmund Brown their minister that the woods were "pestered with Indians" and that several of the town's citizens had been shot at; and asking that men who had been impressed to serve abroad might be sent home.

It was only the day before the little company from Concord started that Thomas Plympton was slain at Boone's plain in the town of Stow, as he was trying to aid Mr. Boone and son to reach a place of safety.

Neither is there any tradition as to the direction that these Concord men took. The main road to the Sudbury east precinct is through what is now the town of Lincoln.

If the soldiers took this road, it would lead them to cross the river at the "old town bridge" and to approach the garrison house from the southerly passing along the causeway from the bridge until they reached the west side of the meadows at a point near the beginning of the old Lancaster road opened about 1663. From this point we have only conjecture to go by in determining the further movements and the exact whereabouts of these men; but assuming that we are correct in the supposition that they went on the east side of the river which would take them over the "town bridge" and the causeway, a route which we believe was the only practicable one in time of high water, we think it fairly safe from the known facts and the lay of the land to make the following supposition; that the majority of the Indians who were assailing the Haynes house on becoming aware of the approach of men to reinforce it concealed themselves in the neighboring shrubbery near the meadow, leaving only a sufficient number in sight to lead the reinforcing party to believe they could easily overcome them or gain entrance to the house in spite of them. The eager English in their usual forgetfulness of Indian trickery and in their impatience to render relief might naturally rush across the arm of meadow which extended from the causeway just mentioned to the upland adjacent to the Haynes house.

When fairly upon the arm of meadow which was covered with water at that time doubtless, the concealed Indians had only to rise up and intercept them. By closing in upon their rear all retreat would be cut off, and the main recourse to be had was to fight where they were, as the broad expanse of flooded meadow to the easterly would make escape in that direction quite difficult, while at the westerly end of the arm of meadow as it terminates in the upland all escape could easily be prevented by a small force.

The foregoing theory not only accords with Hubbard's description of the event but it explains why the men fell on the meadow land.

That this conjecture is correct may be indicated by the following facts relating to the locality. From the point where the causeway proper ended near the Lancaster road as before described, there has been a rude path and a strip of low causeway that extended over the arm of the meadow which in front of the Haynes house reached to the upland at the westerly. This path has served the double purpose of hauling hay and of a way to the house; and it probably extended beyond the house northerly and was perhaps a part of the way which the town voted should extend the whole length of the river meadow to the town bounds. The strip of causeway over the meadow arm is today known as the Water Row road and in time of high water has frequently been flooded in modern times.

The bodies of five of the slain soldiers remained where they fell till the next morning and then were recovered by a searching party who went for them in boats and brought them over the flood to the town bridge, as stated in the petition of Warren and Pierce who helped bury them. The occasion of delay in securing the bodies was the perilous condition of things on the west side of the river. It presumably was not till early afternoon, or the time that Wadsworth reached Green hill, that the savages withdrew from about the garrison houses to concentrate for an attack upon his command. By way of the old "Lancaster road" which passed very near or directly over a part of the Green hill battle ground, it was only about a mile distant. The sound of firing while the action was going on at Green hill could doubtless have been heard during the hours of the late afternoon and into the night quite distinctly; so that the inhabitants to the eastward had cause for believing that the entire territory of the west precinct was dangerous to venture upon.

Moreover every soldier was on duty for defense of the garrisons or was endeavoring to reinforce Wadsworth. On the east side the inhabitants doubtless durst not venture forth on the sad mission of gathering up the slain; for although they had in the morning driven about two hundred Indians over the town bridge and causeway by a running fight, yet they knew not how soon a defeat of Capt. Wadsworth might come and the disengaged savages flushed with victory rush back with overwhelming numbers to overcome them. Those were hours in which to care for the living not for the dead. It was a day of distress and calamity; dark with its disasters, and dreadful in its uncertainties, and it may be a wonder how human hearts could endure the strain.

What became of all the dead we know not: we may conjecture, however, that after the strife had subsided they were sought after and found; and if so were tenderly borne back to Concord or carried to the same lone spot upon the river bank and laid beside the bodies of their late comrades.

The exact locality of the spot where these men were buried may be easily conjectured; as it was high water there would be but one practicable place near the bridge and that would be on the eastern bank of the river just north of the bridge and the road. The place is still a quiet one. No intrusion of farm building or summer cottage has as yet broken the quietude in the immediate vicinity. The place has remained to this day unmarked by any memorial of man's erection but there are land marks which have been there through the centuries. The bridge, which it is said was the first framed one in Middlesex county, has had several successors. The river, although a new channel was long years ago cut by man as a shorter course for its waters, still bends its friendly arm to the banks near which they were laid, as if reluctant to leave it.

As to the story of the sole survivor history and tradition are alike silent. We know not his name nor how he escaped. We may, however suppose that at the first firing the five whose bodies were earliest recovered fell at about the same place being perhaps foremost and where the water was shallow. The seven whose bodies were not at first found may have retreated further back where the water was deeper and scattered about; while the one who survived may have straggled forward to the upland unobserved by the savages and escaped into the woods or crossed over the flood.

Perhaps in no other instance in King Philip's war did a town suffer the loss of so many men on any one occasion in their endeavor to succor others. There were slain in the town of Sudbury on that fateful day not far from fifty armed Englishmen that there is a record of; and of these about one fourth part were from Concord.

As to the substantial value of the sacrifice of the Concord soldiers we may not be able at this distant day to determine. Doubtless anything that drew off the force of savages in their onslaught on the Haynes house was an advantage, as it gave the inmates a respite. It is also presumable that by a detention of a portion of Philip's warriors, he incurred greater loss at the hands of Wadsworth. But whatever the service rendered by the sacrifice it was a most worthy one. The loss was severe in Concord homes and there was mourning in families from which some member, perhaps the head of the household, had gone out never to return. Although no general Indian invasion occurred there during the war yet her loss on that sad spring day was greater than that of some towns that were attacked.

As some of the leading facts and features both of the Wadsworth fight and the burial of the bodies of the slain Concord soldiers are set forth in a petition of Daniel Warren and Joseph Pierce to the Colonial Court, we quote it, Mass. Arch. vol. 68 p. 224: "To Inform the Honoured Counsel of the Service don at Sudbury by severall of the Inhabatance of Watertown as our honoured Captain Mason hath Allready informed a part of thereof in the petion: but we who wear thear can moer largely inform this honoured Councel: that as it is said in the petion that we drove two hundred Indians over the River: wee followed the enimie over the river and joyned with som others and went to see if wee could relieve Captain Wadsworth upon the hill and thear we had a fight with the Indians but they beinge soe many of them and we stayed soe long thar we wear allmost incompassed by them which cased us to retreat to Captain Goodanous Garrison; and their we stayed it being ner night till it was dark and then we went to Mr. Noices Mill to see if we could find any that were escaped to that place all though they wear noe persons dwelling there; but thear we found : 13 : or: 14: of Captain Wadsworths men who wear escaped some of them wounded and brought them to Sudbury towne; On the next day in the morning soe soon as it was light we went to looke for — Concord men who wear slain in the River middow and thear we went in the colld water up to the knees where we found five and we brought them in Conus to the Bridge fut and buried them thear; and then we joined ourselves to Captain Hunton with as many others as we could procuer and went over the River to look for Captain Wadsworth and Captain Brattlebank and the soldiers that wear slain; and we gathered them up and Buried them; and then it was agreed that we should goe up to Nobscot to bring the Carts from thence into Sudbury-Towne and soe returned Horn againe; to what is above written we whos nams are subscribed can testifi: dated the :6: of march

:78; Daniel Warrin .

78: Josep Peirce

There was for several years a controversy relating to the date of Philip's attack upon Sudbury; some considering it April 18th, others April 21st. The probate record referring to James Hosmer gives it the 21st as do some others. The date on the old grave stone gives it April 18; this date having been taken it is supposed from Hubbard's history.

The true date, however, was definitely settled by the discovery a few years ago of an old petition which was signed by a large number of the inhabitants of Sudbury and presented shortly after the war to the Colonial Court.

This document which is among the State Archives Vol. 30 page 205 is interesting and valuable. We quote the following passage from it as it sets forth the condition of things in Sudbury when the Concord men went to its rescue. The date assigned for the fight is ye 21st April 1676.

To ye Honble Governour Dept Governr Magistrates and Deputies of ye Gen" Court assembled at Boston ye 11th October 1676.

The humble Petition of ye poore distressed Inhabitants of Sudbury Humbly Sheweth. That whereas yor impoverished Petition" of Sudbury have received intelligence of a large contribution sent out of Ireland by some pious & well affected p'sons for ye releife of their brethern in New England distressed by ye hostile intrusion of ye Indian Enemy, and that upon this divers distressed townes have presenied a list of theire losses sustained by fireing and plundering of their Estates. Let it not seeme presumption in yor poore petitioners to present a list of what damages we sustained by ye Enemyes attempts hopeing that or lott will be to be considered among our brethren of the tribe of Joseph being encouraged by an act of our Honble Genl Court that those who have sustained considerable damage should make address to this prescnt Session. And is there not a reason for our releife? Not only by reason of Our great losses but alsoe for Our Service p'formed in repelling y' Enemy! Let ye Most High have ye high praise due unto him; but let not ye unworthy Instruments be forgotten. Was there with us any towne so beset since ye warre began, with twelve or fourteen hundred fighting men various Sagamores from all Parts with their men of Armes & they resolved by our ruin to revenge ye releife which Our Sudbury volunteers afforded to distressed Marlborough in slaying many of ye Enemy and repelling ye rest. The strength of our towne upon y' Enemy's Approaching it consisted of Eighty fighting men. True many houses were fortified & Garrison'd & tymously after ye Enemy's invasion, and fireing some Volunteers from Watertowne, & Concord & deserving Capt: Wadsworth with his force came to Our re leife, which speedy & noble service is not to be forgotten.

The Enemy well knowing our Grounds, passes, avenues, and Scituations had neare surrounded Our towne in y' Morning early (wee not knowing of it) till discovered by fireing several disserted houses: the Enemy with greate force & fury assaulted Deacon Haines House well fortified yet badly scituated, as advantageous to ye Enemys approach & dangerous to ye Repellant, yet (by ye help of God) ye garrison not onely defended ye place from betwene five or six of ye clock in ye Morning till about One in ye Afternoon but forced ye Enemy with Considerable slaughter to draw-off.

Many Observables worthy of Record hapned in this assault, Vizt That noe man or woman seemed to be possessed with feare; Our Garrison men kept not within their garrisons, but issued forth to fight ye Enemy in theire sculking approaches: Wee had but two of our townesmen slaine, & y' by indiscretion, none wounded; the Enemy was by few beaten out of houses which they had entered and were plundering; And by a few hands were forced to a running flight which way they would; The spoyle taken by them on ye East side of ye river was in greate p'e recovered."

Almost immediately after the fight at Sudbury, the Indians betook themselves to the westward. Their work had been done but there are reasons for believing that they did not consider it successfully done. Mrs. Rowlandson who was with them writes in her book of "Removes" that "They came home without that rejoicing or triumphing over their victory which they were wont to show at other times, but rather like dogs [as they say] which have lost their ears, when they went, they acted as if the devil had told them that they should gain the victory, and now they acted as if the Devil had told them they should have a fall. Whether it were so or no, I cannot tell, but so it quickly proved, for they quickly began to fall, and so held on that Summer till they came to utter ruin. Hubbard says:

"It was observed by some (at that time their prisoners, since released), that they seemed very pensive after they had come to their quarters, showing no such signs of rejoicing as they were usually wont to do in like cases. Whether from the loss of some of their own company in that day's enterprise (said to be an hundred and twenty, or whether it were the devil in whom they trusted, that deceived them, and to whom they paid their addresses the day before by sundry conjurations of their powwows, or whether it were by any dread that the Almighty sent upon their execrable Blasphemies which 'tis said they used in the torturing of some of their poor captives (bidding Jesus come and deliver them out of their hands from death if he could) we leave as uncertain, though some have so reported. Yet sure it is, that after this day they never prospered in any attempt they made against the English but were continually scattered and broken till they were in a manner all consumed."

The Old Petition states, "Secondly, ye service pformed at Sudbury by ye help of ye Almighty whereby ye Enemy lost some say 100, some 105, some 120, and by that service much damage prevented from hapning to other places whereby y' Country in Generall was advantaged, reason requires some favorable considerations to y' servants of Sudbury. For if it be considered what it hath cost our Country in sending out some forces some of which p ties have not returned with ye certaine newes of such a number slaine as with us."

A variety of facts, circumstances and statements indicate that the 21st day of April 1676 was a day of destiny to King Philip, and that the long hours of stubborn resistance by the combined forces that confronted him were disastrous in the extreme.

His losses can never be known. Probably somewhere in the wilderness many graves were made or else many carcasses remained unburied a prey to the beasts and birds.

It is true that had the battle at Sudbury never occurred victory to the English would have finally come, since it is the rule in history that a superior race supplants the weaker. But at this juncture, time was of much account.

Every day and hour that the strife continued lives were being consumed by an almost intolerable bitterness; homesteads were growing fewer and fewer; households were becoming thinned and hearts sickening with hopes deferred. But whether Philip received the decisive blow at Sudbury or not, certain it is that about that time his fortune began to change. A new army was raised to operate against him; dissensions crept into the ranks of his followers; and after some desultory fighting, the great chieftain turned his footsteps towards his old home at Mount Hope, and in the following summer he was shot by a renegade from his own race. Capt. Hull in his contemporary diary wrote "Aug. 12, Sagamore Philip that began the war was slain."

With the death of Philip the war closed except at the eastward, whither some of the vanquished savages had betaken themselves. With the closing of the war there soon followed an utter downfall of the red race, that once dominated New England.

The overthrow was final; and so complete was the destruction of Indian supremacy that it was stated in a proclamation of Thanksgiving in December of that year "Of those several tribes and parties that have hitherto risen up against us, which were not a few, there now scarce remains a name or family of them in their former habitations, but are either slain, captivated, or fled into remote parts of this wilderness, or lie hid, despairing of their first intentions against us."

The instances where any of the Indians kept their wigwams as permanent homes or became squatters or wild freeholders of the waste woodlands were exceptional. They made up a mere vagrant element, beseeching but little more of their conquerors than a night's shelter, a bit of bread, or some coarse work.

For a while they lingered in the settlements in isolated or fragmentary families as if loth to lose all their identity. But it was to little purpose, and only as a fire which flickers before it goes out; for although men of great heart have sought to fan the fading embers of the race into a flame there yet remains for it of earth but dust and darkness. The race will doubtless have no resurrection except such as will come to all mortals, but the process of total extinction has been slow and painful. Even as late as into the 18th century the latch string of the farm house was occasionally pulled at nightfall by some wayfaring aborigine who came seeking temporary shelter or a place of resting upon the fireside mat. Now and then also there straggled into the village or hamlet, an object of interest to the children, a company of two or three forlorn and neglected creatures who more fortunate than their fellows had survived the hate of one generation and not starved upon the hospitality of another, begging for the small price of a willow basket or a birch broom. But the end of this came, and the years have passed into decades, and decades into scores since the last pure-bred Massachusetts aborigine, a rude lone tenant at sufferance, was seen in the land which he once owned.

As a race the Indians have passed away, without a history except as the white man has written it, or made it a part of his own, and without one work of coarse art wherewith by strange hieroglyphics to inform the world what he once was.

It may never be definitely known just how many men were engaged in the struggle at Sudbury. The following summary perhaps fairly sets forth the English force. In the command of Capt. Wadsworth 50 men. In that of Capt. Cowell 18, soldiers from Concord 12, Sudbury soldiers 80.

Beside these there was a company of Christian Indians in charge of Capt. Hunting and a "ply of horse" from Capt. Prentice's troop under the command of Corporal Phipps.

The following is a summary of the soldiers known to have been killed before the Indians left Sudbury. Of Wadsworth command

two Captains, one Lieutenant and twenty-six private soldiers, 29

Concord soldiers, 11

Captain Cowell's command, 4

Sudbury men, 1 ...

Total: 45

That these are all the fatalities is hardly probable since the records of the events are so scant, the time of fighting was so long and the number of combatants were so many.

It would be almost remarkable if none of the Watertown men were slain and only one of the soldiers of Sudbury.

The Sudbury records give but very little information relative to the Indian invasion. There is an order giving direction as to logs that were used in the fortifications about the meeting house, but this is about all. The inhabitants of the various towns that were the hardest beset by the savages were too much engaged in the struggle for sheer existence to keep a written account of current events, momentous although they were, and the town clerks were only expected to make a record of things that strictly appertained to the public Stationary was expensive; all were not able to write; and the importance of saving data for historic purposes was a matter perhaps little thought of. Family traditions would for a time naturally keep fresh the memory of husbands, fathers, brothers and sons, and it is not improbable that more than one grave in the woods had its lonely pathway which was occasionally trodden by the inhabitants of neighboring farm houses; but after a time new families gave place to the old and these paths were no longer trodden. It may be supposed that after the havoc of battle bodies of scattered combatants were here and there found and buried where they fell. A few years ago a person while digging on the estate of Mr. Francis F. Walker, not far from the Green hill battle ground, found what might have been such a grave. There was a slight discoloration of the earth about the rusty barrel of a firearm and that was all. According to the authority of the Indians, if any reliance is to be placed on their rude reports, more Englishmen were slain at Sudbury than there is any record of. The following letter of Capt. Jacobs of the Marlborough garrison to the Council gives the estimate of the English loss as set forth by the Indians on the morning after their invasion of Sudbury: "This morning about sun two hours high ye enemy alarmed us by firing and shouting towards ye government garrison house at Sudbury." He goes on to state that "soon after they gave a shout and came in great numbers on Indian Hill, and one, as their accustomed manner is after a fight, began to signify to us how many were slain; they whooped seventy-four times, which we hope was only such thing, yet we have reason to fear the worst, considering the numbers, which we apprehend to be five hundred at the most, others think a thousand."

CHAPTER XLII

The Attack Upon Lancaster — Capture of Mrs. Mary Rowlandson— Efforts for Her Release — Heroic Services of Thomas Doublet or Nepanet — Humane Work of John Hoary Esq. — The Process of Ransom — Extracts from the Book of Removes — Rowlandson Rock.

AS stated in a previous chapter the Indians attacked the town of Lancaster on the 10th of February. This however was not the only time, the first being on Sunday Aug. 30, 1675. The attack was led by a chief named Monoco, or one-eyed John, and the point of attack was the house of a Scotch settler named Mordecai Macloud.

At that time seven persons were killed. Other mischievous work was done in the place and its vicinity and taken all together perhaps no other settlement suffered more during Philip's war by the burning of its buildings, the slaughter of its inhabitants and the captivity of the living.

The town is situated in Worcester county along the Nashua river; and the first settlement by the English was begun there in 1643. Lancaster like Groton which also was successively assailed is historically associated with Concord, inasmuch as the three towns had Major Simon Willard as a chief promoter of their early interests.

The Indians who dwelt in the vicinity of Lancaster were the Nashaways, whose tribal relations were with the Nipmucks. After the sad happenings on August 30, the people of Lancaster gathered together in several garrisons and measures were taken to defend them by details of soldiers. But notwithstanding the presence of the soldiers, towards the last of January 1675-6, word was brought by several Christian Indians that the place was in jeopardy.

One of the Indians, Quanapohit, whom the Council had employed to act as a spy in the woods about Wachuset and on towards Brookfield predicted the very day of the proposed attack. Another of them named Kattenanit brought a similar report.

After escaping from the hostile Indians at Meminisset whither he had gone to obtain important facts, he travelled upon snow-shoes about eighty miles to Boston to report to Major Gookin that about four hundred Indians were on their way to attack Lancaster, arriving with his message in a wearied and half famished condition. The authorities at once dispatched messengers to Marlboro, Concord and Lancaster to fortify in great haste; but the order came too late. The blow had fallen. Before Capt. Wadsworth could reach the town, the savages had encompassed it and burned the bridge on the regular road, and it was only by the fidelity of the friendly Indian guides that Wadsworth and his company being led along another route escaped an ambush. By Wadsworth's safe detour a part of the town was saved, but it was only a part. The garrison house of Rev. Joseph Rowlandson was burned and of thirty-seven or forty persons within it only one escaped death or captivity; among the captives was Mr. Rowlandson's wife.

The capture of Mrs. Rowlandson was one of the saddest events of Philip's war and called out unusual sympathy. It was terrible enough to be slain by the tomahawk and to have the body subsequently subjected to the scalping knife, but it was doubly terrible for womankind in helpless captivity to be subjected to a wilderness exposure in time of war with whatever of want or long marches or rough weather might betide her captors and also to be kept in suspense as to what the end might be; but such was captivity among the Indians. They held their prisoners for a ransom. The English sold their Indian prisoners into slavery; the Indians sold their English captives to the white men. To lighten the burdens of the captives and make their lives more tolerable would not hasten the day of their redemption.

Mrs. Rowlandson was held in captivity from Feb. 10 to May 2. During this time she was compelled to travel from place to place with her Indian captors and so be an unwilling witness to many daring and revolting exploits. She was a close observer and after her release wrote and published a detailed account of her captivity, noting the daily movements of her captors and giving a graphic description of their ways of living, their customs, and their treatment of prisoners. The book is known as "Mrs. Rowlandson's Removes;" a title suggestive of the frequent changes to which she was subjected. The author describes the grand pow-wow held by the Indians just previous to their assault on Sudbury, and some of the incidents connected with the event in general so that the book is a great acquisition to the literature relating to King Philip's war.

Soon after the capture of Mrs. Rowlandson great efforts were made to ascertain the amount demanded for her safe delivery to the English, to raise the sum and to secure the services of someone who would be able wisely and successfully to negotiate with the savages. The following description of the release of Mary Rowlandson is by Rev. George M. Bodge in his work on "Soldiers in Philip's War": "Rev. Mr. Rowlandson sought the aid of the Council in his efforts to redeem the captives, many of whom were his own kindred. At first it was impossible to find any one of the friendly Indians willing to venture as messengers among the hostiles, mainly because they had been so cruelly and shamefully abused by the English and were now confined at Deer Island, where they could not be accused or placed under suspicion. At last, however, one Tom Dublet, or Nepanet, consented to go, and was fitted and instructed by Major Gookin, and upon April 3rd started from Cambridge, and returned with the answer of the Sachems on April 12th. The correspondence between the Council and the Sachems is still preserved, in part, though the original letters are lost. The messenger brought back word from Sam Sachem, Kutquen and Quanohit, Samuel Uskatuhgun and other owners of the captives taken at Lancaster that all were well except the youngest child of Mr. Rowlandson, who was dead. At last, after many negotiations by the faithful Nepanet, Mr. John Hoar, of Concord, who, more than any man in the colony, had the confidence of the Indians, accompanied by Nepanet, and another friendly Indian, "Peter Conway," and bearing the ransom, twenty pounds in money and goods, raised by several gentlemen for the redemption of Mrs. Rowlandson, met the Sachems near Wachusett Hill, and on May 2nd received and conducted that lady to Lancaster, and the next day to Boston. The other captives were redeemed at various times and places afterwards.

The place where Mr. Hoar met the Sachems is well identified, being marked by a large rock called "Redemption Rock, " a noble landmark near the ancient Indian trail, between Lancaster and Mount Wachusett, and in the present town of Princton, on the easterly side of a beautiful valley, across which, in the distance, towers Mount Wachusett.

The locality is known as "Everettville," from the name of an ancient family who have lived here for generations. In 1880, Hon. Geo. F. Hoar, of Worcester, a lineal descendant of the chief actor in this transaction, for the English, purchased the land containing this site and set it apart for memorial purposes, and caused the following inscription to be placed upon the face of the rock:

"Upon this rock May 2nd 1676
was made the agreement for the ransom
of Mrs. Mary Rowlandson of Lancaster
Between the Indians and John Hoar of Concord
King Philip was with the Indians but
refused his consent."

As several of the principal actors in the release of Mrs. Rowlandson were connected with the town of Concord, and the graphic description which she gives sets forth some of the methods and something of the character of the combatants with whom the colonists had to deal, we have considered it expedient to publish some portions of the book already referred to, entitled "The Narrative of the Captivity and Restoration of Mrs. Mary Rowlandson": "On the tenth of February, 1675, came the Indians with great number upon Lancaster. The first coming was about Sun-rising; hearing the noise of some guns, we looked out; Several Houses were burning, and the Smoke ascending to Heaven. There were five persons taken in one house, the Father and the Mother and a sucking Child; they were knocked on the head; the other two they took and carried away alive. Their were two others who, being out of their garrison upon some occasion, were set upon; one was knocked on the head, the other escaped: Another there was who running along was shot and wounded, and fell down; he begged of them his life, promising them money (as they told me), but they would not hearkan to him but knockt him in head, and stript him naked, and split open his bowels. Another, seeing many of the Indians about his Barn, ventured and went out, but was quickly shot down. There were three others belonging to the same garrison who were killed, the Indians, getting upon the roof of the Barn, had advantage to shoot down upon them and their Fortifications. Thus these murtherous wretches went on burning and destroying before them.

"At length they came and beset our own house, and quickly it was the dolefullest day that ever mine eyes saw.

The House stood upon the edge of a hill; some of the Indians got behind the hill, others into the Barn, and others behind anything that could shelter them; from all which places they shot against the House, that so the Bullets seemed to fly like hail; and quickly wounded one man among us, then another, then a third. About two hours (according to my observations in that amazing time) they had been about the House, before they prevailed to fire it (which they did with Flax and Hemp, which they brought out of the Barn, and there being no defense about the House, only two Flankers at two opposite corners and one of them not finished, they fired it once and ventured out and quenched it, but they quickly fired it again, and that took.

Now as this dreadful hour came that I have often heard of (in time of War, was as it was the case of others), but now mine eyes see it. Some in our house were fighting for their lives, others wallowing in theirs, the House on fire over our heads, and the bloody Heathen ready to knock us on the head if we stirred out: Now might we hear Mothers and children crying out for themselves, and one another, 'Lord, what shall we do?' Then I took my Children (and one of my sister's), hers to go forth and leave the house: but as soon as we came to the dore and appeared the Indians shot so thick that the Bulletts rattled against the house, as if one had taken an handfull of stones and threw them, so that we were fain to give back. We had six stout dogs belonging to our Garrison, but none of them would stir, though another time, if any Indian had come to the door, they were ready to fly upon him and tear him down.

The Lord hereby would make us the more to acknowledge his hand, and to see that our help is alwayes in him. But out we must go, the fire increasing and coming along behind us, roaring, and the Indians gaping before us with their Guns, Spears and Hatchets, to devour us. No sooner were we out of the House but my Brother-in-Law (being wounded before in defending the home), in or near the throat fell down dead, whereat the Indian scampered shouted and hallowed, and were presently upon him, stripping off his cloaths, the bullets flying thick; one went through my side, and the same, (as would seem,) through my bowels and hand of my dear child in my arms. One of my elder Sister's Children, named William, had then his Leg broken, which the Indians preceiving, they knocked him on head. Thus were we butchered by those merciless Heathen, standing amaized, with the blood running to our heels. My eldest Sister being yet in the House and seeing those wofull sights, the Infidels haling Mothers one way, and Children another, and some wallowing in their blood: and her elder son telling her that her Son William was dead, and myself was wounded, she said, And, 'Lord let me dy with them' which was no sooner said, but she was struck with a Bullet, and fell down dead over the threshold. I hope she is reaping the fruit of her good labors, being faithfull to the service of God in her place.

In her younger days she lay under much trouble upon spiritual accounts, till it pleased God to make that precious Scripture take hold of her heart, 2 Cor. 12. 9. 'And he said unto me my Grace is sufficient for thee.' More than twenty years after I have heard her tell how sweet and comfortable that place was to her, But to return: The Indians hud hold of us, pulling me one way, and the Children another, and said, 'Come along with us :' I told them they would kill me: they answered, 'If I were willing to go with them, they would not hurt me.' "O the dolefull sight that now was to behold at this House! 'Come, behold the works of the Lord, what desolation he has made in the earth.' Of thirty- seven persons who were in this one House, none escaped either present death, or a bitter captivity, save only one, who might say as he; Job 1. 15 'And I only am escaped alone to tell the news.' There were twelve killed, some shot, some stab'd with their Spears, some knocked down with their Hatchets.

****** "That I may the better declare what happened to me during that grievous Captivity, I shall particularly speak of the severall Removes we had up and down the Wilderness."

The First Remove.
"Now away we must go with thos e Barbarous Creatures, with our bodies wounded and bleeding, and our hearts no less than our bodies. About a mile we went that night, up upon a hill within sight of the Town where we intended to lodge, there was hard by a vacant house, (deserted by the English before, for fear of the Indians.) I asked them whether I might not lodge in the house that night to which they answered, what will you love English men still? this was the dolefullest night that ever my eyes saw. O the roaring and dancing and singing, and yelling of those black creatures in the night, which made the place a lively resemblance of hell. And as

miserable was the wast that was made of Horses, Cattle, Sheep, Swine, Calves, Lambs, Roasting Pigs, and Fowl [which they had plundered in the town] some roasting, some lying, some burning, and some boyling to feed our merciless Enemies; who were joyful enough though we were disconsolate. To add to the dolefulness of the former day and the dismalness of the present night, my thoughts ran up on my losses and sad bereaved condition. All was gone, my Husband gone (at least separated from me he being in the Bay; and to add to my grief, the Indians told me they would kill him as he came homeward) my Children gone, my Relations and Friends gone, our House and home and all our comforts within door, and without, all was gone, (except my life) and I knew not but the next moment that might go too. * *

The Second Remove.

"But now, the next morning, I must turn my back upon the Town, and travel with them into the vast and desolate Wilderness, I knew not whither.' It is not my tongue, or pen can express the sorrows of my heart, and bitterness of my spirit, that I had at this departure: but God was with me, in a wonderfull manner, carrying me along, and bearing up my spirit, that it did not quite fail. One of the indians carried my poor wounded Babe upon a horse, it went moaning all along I shall dy, I shall dy. I went on fast after it, with sorrow that cannot be expresst. At length I took it off the horse, and carried it in my arms till my strength failed, and I fell down with it; then they set me upon a horse with my wounded Child in my lap, and there being no furniture upon the horse back; as we-were going down a steep hill, we both fell over the horses head, at which they like inhumane creatures laught, and rejoyced to see it, though I thought we should have ended our days, so overcome with so many difficulties. But the Lord renewed my strength still, and carried me along, that I might see more of his Power; yea, so much that I could never have thought of, had I not experienced it.

"After this it quickly began to snow, and when night came on they stopt; and now down I must sit in the snow, by a little fire, and a few boughs behind me, and my sick Child in my lap; and calling much for water being now (through the wound) fallen into a violent Fever. My own wound also growing so stiff that I could scarce sit down or rise up; yet so it must be that I must sit all this cold winter night upon the cold snowy ground, with my sick Child in my arms, looking that every hour would be the last of my life; and having no Christian friend near me either to help or to comfort me. Oh, I may see the wonderfull power of God, that my spirit did not utterly sink under my affliction: still the Lord upheld me with his gracious and mercifull Spirit, and we were both alive to see the light of the next morning. * * *"

Twentieth Remove.

"On a Sabbath day, the sun being about an hour high in the afternoon; came Mr. John Hoar (the Council permitting him and his own foreward spirit inclining him) together with the two forementioned Indians, Tom and Peter with their third Letter from the Council. When they came near I was abroad: though I saw them not, they presently called me in, and bade me sit down and not stir. Then they catched up their Guns, and away they ran, as if an Enemy had been at hand; and the Guns went off apace.

I manifested some great trouble, and they asked me what was the matter? I told them, I thought they had killed the Englishman (for they had in the meantime informed me that an English-man was come) they said, No; They shot over his Horse and under, and before his Horse; and they pushed him this way, and that way, at their pleasure: showing what they could do: Then they let them come to their Wigwams I begged them to let me see the Englishman, but they would not. But there was I fain to sit their pleasure. When they had talked their fill with him they suffered me to go to him. We asked each other of our welfare, and how my Husband did, and all my friends? He told me they were all well and would be glad to see me.

I now asked them whether I should go home with Mr. Hoar? They answered, No, one and another of them; and it being night, we lay down with that answer; in the morning, Mr. Hoar invited the Saggamores to Dinner; but when we went to get it ready, we found that they had stolen the greatest part of the Provision Mr. Hoar had brought, out of his Bags, in the night. And we may see the wonderful power of God, in that one passage, in that when there was such a great number of the Indians together and so greedy of a little good food: and no English there but Mr. Hoar and myself: that there they did not Knock us in the head, and take what we had: there being not only some provision, but also a Trading-cloth, a part of the twenty pounds agreed upon. But instead of doing us any mischief, they seemed to be ashamed of the fact, and said, it was some 'Matchit Indian that did it.' Oh, that we could believe that there is nothing too hard for God! God shewed his Power over the Heathen in this, as he did over the hungry Lyons when Daniel was cast into the den.

Mr. Hoar called them berime to Dinner, but they ate very little, they being so busie in dressing themselves and getting ready for their Dance. * * * On Tuesday morning they called their General Court (as they called it) to consult and determine whether I should go home or no; and they all as one man did seemingly consent to it, that I should go home, except Philip, who would not come among them. * * * "But to return again to my going home, where we may see a remarkable change of Providence. At first they were all against it, except my Husband would come for me; but afterwards they assented to it, and seemed much to rejoice in it; some asked me to send them some Bread, others some Tobacco; others shaking me by the hand, offering me a Hood and Scarf to ride in; not one moving hand or tongue against it. Thus hath the Lord answered my poor desire, and the many earnest requests of others put up unto God for me. In my travels an Indian came to me, and told me, if I were willing, he and his squaw would run away, and go home along with me: I told him No: I was not willing to run away, but desired to wait God's time, that I might go home quietly, and without fear. And now God hath granted me my desire. O the wonderfull power of God that I have seen, and the experience that I have had: I have been in the midst of those roaring Lyons and Savage Bears, that feared neither God, nor Man, nor the Devil, by night and day, alone and in company: sleeping all sorts together, and yet not one of them ever offered me the least abuse of unchastity to me, in word or action. Though some are ready to say, I speak it for my own credit: But I speak it in the presence of God, and to his Glory. Gods Power is as great now, and as sufficient to save as when he preserved Daniel in the Lions Den; or the three Children in the firey Furnace. I may well say as his Psal. 107, 12 'Ogive thanks unto the Lord for he is good, his mercy endureth forever. Let the Redeemed of the Lord say so whom he hath redeemed from the hand of the Enemy,' especialy that I should

257

come away in the midst of so many hundreds of Enemies, quietly and peacably, and not a dog moving his tongue. So I took my leave of them, and in coming along my heart melted into tears, more than all the while I was with them, and I was almost swallowed up with the thoughts that ever I should go home again. About the Sun going down, Mr. Hoar and, myself and the two Indians came to Lancaster and a solemn sight it was to me. There I had lived many comfortable years amongst my Relations and Neighbors, and now not one Christian to be seen, nor one house left standing. We went on to a Farm house that was yet standing, where we lay all night; and a comfortable lodging we had though nothing but straw to ly on. The Lord preserved us in safety that night, raised us up again in the morning, and carried us along, that before noon we came to Concord. Now was I full of joy, and yet not without sorrow: joy to see such a lovely sight, so many Christians together, and some of them my Neighbors. There I met with my Brother, and my Brother in Law, who asked me if I knew where his Wife was? Poor heart! he had helped to bury her and knew it not; she being shot down by the house was partly burnt: so that those who were at Boston at the desolation of the town, and came back afterward, and buried the dead, did not know her. Yet I was not without Sorrow, to think how many were looking and longing, and my own Children amongst the rest, to enjoy that deliverance that I had now received and I did not know whether ever I should see them again.

Being recruited with food and raiment we went to Boston that day, where I met with my dear Husband but the thoughts of our dear Children, one Being dead, and the other we could not tell where, abated our comfort each to the other. I was not before so much hem'd in with the merciless and cruel Heathen, but now as much with pitiful, tender-hearted, and compassionate Christians. In that poor, and distressed, and beggarly condition I was received in, I was kindly entertained in severall Houses; so much I received from several, (some of whom I knew, and others I knew not) that I am not capable to declare it. But the Lord knows them all by name: The Lord reward them sevenfold into their bosoms of his spirituals, for their temporals. The twenty pounds the price of my redemption was raised by some Boston Gentlemen and Mr. Usher whose bounty and religious charity, I would not forget to make mention of. Then Thomas Shepard of Charlestown received us into his House, where we continued eleven weeks; and a Father and Mother they were to us. And many more tender-hearted friends we met with in that place.

We were now in the midst of love, yet not without much and frequent heaviness of heart for our poor Children, and other relations, who were still in affliction. The week following, after my coming in, the Governor and Council sent forth to the Indians again; and that not without success, for they brought in my Sister, and Goodwife Kristle; Their not knowing where our Children were, was a sore tryal to us still, and yet we were not without secret hopes that we should see them again. That which was dead lay heavier upon my spirit, than those which were alive and amongst the Heathen; thinking how it suffered from its wounds, and I was in no way able to relieve it; and how it was buried by the Heathen in the Wilderness from among all Christians. We were hurried up and down in our thoughts, sometimes we should hear a report that they were gone this way, and sometimes that; and that they were come in, in this place or that: We kept inquiring and listening to hear concerning them but no certain news as yet. About this time the Council had ordered a day of public Thanks-giving: though I thought I had still cause of mourning, and being unsettled in our minds, we thought we would ride toward the Eastward to see if we could hear anything concerning our Children. And as we were riding along [God is the wise disposer of all things] between Ipswich and Rowly we met Mr. William Hubbard, who told us that our Son Joseph was come in to Major Waldrens, and another with him, which was my Sisters Son. I asked him how he knew it? He said, the Major himself told him so. So along we went till we came to Newbury; and their Minister being absent, they desired my Husband to Preach the Thanks giving for them; but he was not willing to stay there that night, but would go over to Salisbury, to hear further, and come again in the morning; which he did, and Preached there that day. At night when he had done, one came and told him that his Daughter was come in at Providence; Here was mercy on both hands: Now hath God fulfiled that precious Scripture, which was such a comfort to me in my distressed condition. When my heart was ready to sink into the Earth [my Children being gone I could not tell whither] and my knees trembled under me, And I was walking through the valley of the Shadow of Death: Then the Lord brought, and has now fulfiled that reviving word unto me: Thus saith the Lord, Refrain thy voice, from weeping, and thine eyes from tears for thy work shall be rewarded saith the Lord, and they shall come again from the Land of the enemy."

CHAPTER XLIII

List of Names of Concord Soldiers in King Philip's War — Miscellaneous Services of the Town — Incidental Hardships — The Loss of Men — Biographical Sketches of the Killed and Wounded.

THE following are lists containing the names of some of the soldiers who served in King Philip's War. A list of the names of soldiers accredited for services performed under Capt. Joseph Sill in 1675-76: William Barrett Lt. John Melvin James Wheeler Thomas Adams Richard Taylor Joseph Bateman Moses Wheate Hopewell Davis Richard Woods John Bateman William Ball In 1675 Capt. Sill was engaged in service from Sudbury westward toward Wachusett Hill; and subsequently by order of Major Simon Willard he was employed in guarding supplies and in guard duty about the various garrison houses.

Among the names of persons who served as soldiers in defense of the garrisons are the following Concord names: Feb. 29. 1675-6.

"Under Capt. Wheeler at Groton garrison":

Samuel Fletcher Senr.	Samuel Fletcher Junr.
Eleazer Brown	Stephen Gobble
Moses Wheate	Richard Pasmore
(perhaps Hosmer)	
Nov. 9,— 1675.	
John Wood	Josiah Wheeler Hugh Taylor

Another list under Capt. Wheeler at Groton in garrison service:

Samuel Fletcher Jr.	Stephen Gobble
Eleazer Ball	Daniel Adams
Moses Wheate	Richard Pasmore
John Potter	Simon Willard
Benjamin Graves	

The following are "later credits for Military Service" of Concord men from the Ledger of John Hull: Nov. 24, 1676 William Jones Jan. 24, 1676 Humphrey Barrett William Hartwell.

The following names are of men accredited as being under Major Simon Willard from Aug. 7th to Jan. 25,1675, whose sur-names were familiar in Concord: Paul Fletcher, John Barrett, John Heale, James Smedly, Josiah Wheeler, Daniel Adams, John Bateman.

In the list from which these are taken is the name of Simon Willard, a son of Major Simon Willard, and Philip Read "Doctor," Dr. Philip Read, we conclude, is the same person who styled himself "Physition" and who having married a daughter of Richard Rice made a home in Concord and practiced medicine there and also in Sudbury, Watertown and Cambridge. We have no means of knowing whether he went to the war acting in any other capacity than as a private soldier although he is designated "Doctor." Neither do we assert that Dr. Read went to the war from Concord, since about the year 1670 he was complained of for making a comparison of Rev. Edward Bulkeley as a preacher with Parson Estabrook saying, that the former was not worthy to carry the latter's books after him.

Dr. Read paid £10 for the offense and for a time left the town
Assignment of Wages.
Concord — Town Cr. By Sundry accts:

John Wheeler, Joseph Wheeler, Abraham Temple, Thomas Wheeler, Junr., David Gobely, Benjamin Graves, James Sawyer, Nathaniel Billings, William Kean, John Haslock, Joseph Chamberlain, Stephen Gobble, Benjamin Chamberlain, John Lakin, Richard Blood.

We do not claim that in every instance in the following lists where a name has been a familiar one in Concord that therefore the person having it is to be accredited as a soldier serving from that town. But we claim that more or less of them belonged to Concord citizens and that in some of the lists nearly all if not everyone did so.

We have no means of knowing whether the names of all the soldiers of Concord who served in King Philip's war were placed on record, neither may we know how many were impressed and how many were volunteers. Furthermore, we may not know how many served as substitutes for soldiers in other towns; nor how many men in other places may have been accredited to Concord.

The method of obtaining a "quota" of troops was for the Colonial Council or commanding officer in charge to issue a warrant directed to a constable, or a committee of militia in each municipality which was returnable to the said Council or General officer.

Besides the service performed in response to calls of the colony to aid other towns and engage in expeditions, much militia work was done at home. The town was near the danger line and repeatedly threatened with invasion, and it was essential to be at all times prepared for an attack.

There were also in the town at various times refugees from other places whose persons and property called for protection. Sometimes carts were required with armed convoys to carry people and their belongings to a place of safety.

To fill all these requisitions and at the same time man their garrison houses and keep up such patrolling of the township as would prevent surprises was an arduous task. To accomplish this not only took every able-bodied soldier but even the youth were sometimes summoned into the service, as

is shown by the following paper, Mass. Archives, Vol. 69, page 134:

"To the Hono :ble Govr: and Councell now sitting in Boston
June 28 : 1677

The Request of the Millitia of the towne of Concord "Humbly sheweth that the millitia of the said towne receiveing a warrant from the worp" Majr Gookin to impress foure men for the service of the Country: and being informed that those that were to be prest were intended onely to scout about Chelmsford; and the said Militia not being able to obtaine those persons that were intended and desired they sent foure youths promiseing to releive them within one week after they went but as soone as they came to Chelmsford they were conducted to black point where they now remaine.

"Our humble request to yor Hon" therefore is; that you will please to consider how unfitt these youths are for the Countryes service: namely Samuell Stratton, John Wheat, John Ball: Thomas Wolley :: and that they may be dismissed from the said service: and be returned home with the first that doe returne, so shall we ever pray for yr Hon" &c.

261

Timothy Wheeler

Capt in the name of ye Millitia."

As a result of the necessity of their keeping soldiers at home excuses were made, as shown by the postscript to the report of the Committee of Militia concerning the men called from Concord to the Narragansett expedition; the request being that some already in service be released.

But the military service was not the only strain upon the community. The soldiers were to be furnished with food and clothing. Their stock of ammunition was to be kept up, and such other commodities as were convenient for carrying on war were to be contributed as occasion called for.

For months the town of Concord was a general military head-quarters, having a gunsmith, and a magazine.

A no small element of hardship to the town of Concord daring Philip's war was its liability to a sudden attack of the Indians. The place would naturally be a coveted one, tor the reason that it had a magazine, and a gunsmith and was a resort of war refugees and was a rendezvous for troops from abroad. As indicating the general solicitude is the following copy of a record relating to the escape of several squaws who were under guard.

"Concord this 13th: June 1676.

Honort Gouerno' Leuer'

"Inasmuch as heare has been a sad accident befallen us through the ocation of nedglegent persons; which had trust Imposed to them: to keep sentery over three old squas & one papoose, these watchmen fell all asleep, and in the meanetime y' squas made theire escape; from them; which may produce a great deale of damage to us y' are resident in Concord; because we are afrraid they are acquainted with ye Condition of or towne, & what quantyty of men we have gon out; & which way they are gone; which may prove very obstructive to or army in their design; we had a Capt; appoynted over the magaseine; which I thought to be sumtient to give a Charge to 12 men; to keep senternalls over three old squas; I hope yor honor will be pleased to take it into Consideration & send us some more strength to suport us from or enemies; for we are in dayly fear; y' they will make an asault on or towne; So hopeing yor honor cannot Impute any Blame to him; who wish to yo' honor ye best y' may be; by yor hono" most Humble Servant John Haywood; Consta"."

Mass. Archives, v. 133, p. 193.

By this report we infer that the condition of affairs was so precarious that it was considered essential to place a strong guard over a few Indian women lest escaping they report the weak condition of the town s defenses. When it was reported to the Council that the squaws had made their escape the situation was considered sufficiently serious to warrant the Council in forwarding immediately a re-enforcement of twenty men.

The actual loss of inhabitants to Concord by the war may never be known. It is considered certain that sixteen were slain outright, but as in all wars more or less deaths were doubtless occasioned indirectly by exposure, sickness and wounds. Neither may it ever be ascertained what were the names of all the slain or where all of them lived.

The following are brief biographical data relating to persons from Concord who were killed or suffered from wounds while engaged in Philip's war.

Samuel Smedley who was slain while with Capt. Wheeler at Brookfield was a son of Baptist Smedley and a brother of Mary whose husband Isaac Shepard was killed at Concord village. He was one of the eight who fell at the first firing in the ambuscade at the swamp. Doubtless his body was buried with his comrades in an obscure grave.

Of the Concord Smedleys or Smeadleys, John and Baptist or Baptiste came to the town prior to 1636. They were of Huguenot descent, and it has been suggested may have come from Matlock, in Derbyshire, England where some of the Smedleys have since lived. Baptiste had his house lot, according to Walcott, near Franklin Dakin's.

John lived at or near the present residence of Hon. John S. Keyes in the vicinity of the Battle Ground. Baptiste Smedley died Aug. 16, 1675. John died the same year.

Samuel Smedley son of Baptiste married Hannah Wheeler in 1667; Hannah a daughter was born July 28 1669; Mary was born 1671; and Samuel Feb. 28, 1673.

The following is the record of his birth. "Samuell Sonne of Babtist and Kathrine Smedley, the 7, 4 mo, 1648." The inventory is on file at the Probate Records by the administrator of Samuel Smedley; and one of the articles specified is the following — "2 horses lost in the Country's sarvice. 06,0,0"

"2 horses was kild with him at the flight at quapoge."

As to Henry Young who was shot at the Brookfield garrison house while looking from the window, we have found nothing but what Capt. Wheeler says of him in his narrative. That he was a brave man is evident from the fact that he was selected to be a companion to Ephraim Curtis in his attempt to elude the vigilant savages and bear beyond their lines a summons for relief. The whereabouts of his grave is doubtless as unknown as that of Smedley. The old burying ground at Brookfield may have received his remains but of the earliest burial place of that town its historians have given but little definite information.

Isaac and Jacob Shepard who were slain at Quagana hill in Concord village were the third and sixth sons of Ralph and Thanklord Shepard. Isaac was born June 20th 1639, and Jacob was born June 1657. The oldest son of the family of Ralph and Thanklord was Abraham who married Jan. 2nd 1673; and a younger son was perhaps Daniel; Mary who was made captive was the youngest child and was born about 1660—1662.

Isaac Shepard married Mary Smedly a daughter of Baptiste Smedly of Concord. A Probate Record informs us that "administration on the estate of Isaac Shepard late of Concord" was allowed to Mary Shepard his "relict widow"

jointly with Abram Shepard her brother. The inventory of the estate sets forth the following property "A farme at Nashobe, one house one barn 12 ac of broken up land 10 of meadow with the rest of the ffarme." The entire estate was valued at £250. From this farm at Nashoba through a long wilderness path Isaac went to visit Mary Smedley the maiden of Huguenot ancestry and thither he took her to dwell among his own kindred.

We know of no record relating to Jacob Shepard except of his birth. Both Isaac and Jacob it is supposed lived on a portion of land formerly owned by Lieut. Joseph Wheeler. Their father Ralph came to America in the ship Abigail from Stepney Parish London in 1635. After residing in several towns he went to Malden where he became deacon.

From Malden he made his way through the woods to the territory near Nashoba called Concord village.

The barn in which the men were threshing was situated it is believed on the south side of a lane to what is now or was lately the Cyrus Pickard place near the road. Mary the sister was on the hill near by, and tradition has pointed out the exact spot, a boulder on the south side of the hill near the top. In the Concord Records is this entry "Thomas Streight and Mary Shepard married by Justice Peter Bulkeley May 28, 1683."

In the case of the Concord soldiers killed at Sudbury there is a great discrepancy between the date of their deaths on the town records and elsewhere.

The record there made is that James Hosmer, Samuel Potter, David Corny and John Barnes died on March 31, 1676. The error is thought to have been occasioned by some imperfect entry or transcription. The following are brief biographical sketches of five of the seven whose identity and connection with the fight at Sudbury has been established as matter of record: James Hosmer as has been stated in a former chapter lived near his father by the Assabet river, at the present Concord Junction. He married Sarah, a daughter of John White, an early and well-to-do proprietor of lands at Lancaster. The following is a Probate record relative to the estate of James Hosmer, Jr.: "An Inventory of the estate of James Hosmer junior, of Concord, in Middlesex, deceased, being slaine in the ingagement with the Indeans at Sudsburie, on the 21 of the second month in the yeare 1676.

Prizers James Hosmer Senr.

Henry Woodis

John Scotchford

Thomas Wheeler

Rev. George W. Hosmer D. D. who was a lineal descendant of James Hosmer and formerly President of Antioch College, and lately pastor of Channing Church Newton, stated in a letter concerning his ancestor who was several generations from him as follows: "My grandfather when resistance was in vain, plunged into the river to swim across and a bullet passed through his head."

James Hosmer Jr. was a brother-in-law of Rev. Joseph Rowlandson of Lancaster. The following is from the old records "James Hosmer and Sara White married Oct. 14, 1658."

Samuel Potter was a son of Luke Potter who early settled at Concord and who was a deacon in the church there as late as 1697. Samuel Potter Senior married for his second wife Mary Edmonds in 1644.

The following are from the Concord early records,—

"Samuell the sonne of hike and Mary Potter the 1, of the 2 mo. 1648."

"Samuel Potter and Sarah Right married 8 Jan . 1673"

"Samuell Potter husband to Sarah his wife: died 31 march 1676."

The house lot of Luke Potter the father was on Potter's Lane since Heyward street.

Joseph Buttrick was a son of William Buttrick who came to Concord in 1635. Joseph married for his first wife Sarah Bateman who died in 1664, and for his second, Jane Goodnow of Sudbury. Joseph Buttrick was a child of the first wife. The following are from Concord old records: "Mary, daughter of Will Buttricke & Sara his wife borne, 17, June: 64"

"Sara, wife of Will Buttricke died 17, July 64."

"William Buttrick & Jeane goodnow married 21 feb. 1667."

Of Daniel Corny, Shattuck says that he was at Concord in 1664. We conjecture that the first name of Corny is David rather than Daniel. There are the following references to David Corny among the early records:

"John son of David & Elizabeth Corny born 18, Oct. 1665."

"David son of David Corny & Elizabeth his wife borne 14, Nom' 1666.

"Ester daughter of David Corny born 14, 12, 75.

"Elizabeth wife of David Corny died 4 March 70, 71."

John Barnes, Shattuck states was at Concord in 1661, and married Elizabeth Hunt in 1664.

Josiah Wheeler was a son of Obadiah Wheeler one of the town's early settlers and one of the first three Wheelers who arrived at Concord, the other three of the six who settled there arriving in 1639. Obadiah Wheeler Sr. died Oct. 27, 1671. aged 63, and his wife Susannah died 1650. Obadiah Wheeler the 4th son married Elizabeth White in 1672, and was father to Obadiah, Josiah, Samuel, Joseph, and others. Obadiah Wheeler lived in the vicinity of Brook meadow.

The following is part of a Probate record relating to the estate of Josiah Wheeler: "An Inventory of the estate of Josiah Wheeler, of Concord in the County of Middlesex, deceased being slain by the engagement with the Indians at Sudsburie on the twenty-first of the second month in ye yeare 1676."

We have discovered nothing concerning David Curry beyond a statement that the Middlesex Probate Records afford evidence that he was a victim to the Indian ambushment at Sudbury on April 21st. Neither have we been able to gather much information relative to Jacob Farrar. A John and Jacob Farrar were proprietors in the town of Lancaster as early as 1653. According to Shattuck John died Nov. 3, 1669 and Jacob either a son of John or Jacob married Hannah, daughter of John Houghton Esq. 1668 and was killed by the Indians August 22, 1675. His sons Jacob, George, Joseph and John, the same author informs us sold their property in 1697 to an uncle of the name of Houghton and removed to Concord.

Among the names of the men who went from Concord to join the Narragansett Expedition in 1675, is the name of Stephen Farre, which name we conjecture may have been pronounced Farrar.

The following is the biographical data of the Concord soldiers who met with causalities in the Narragansett Expedition.

George Hay ward who was killed at the Swamp Fight may have been a son of George Hayward who early built a corn mill at the southwest part of the town and died March 1671. We have no record of his birth but conclude from the fact that we have seen the name of the mill proprietor written in history George Hayward senior, that George the soldier was his son.

Abraham Temple who was one of the wounded at the Swamp Fight was a son of Richard Temple who had a mill on Spencer Brook. An old record states of him, — "Abraham Temple and Deborah hadlocke married 4 desem 1673."

"Richard son of Abraham Temple & Debra his wife borne 6, Oct. 1674."

Thomas Brown the other wounded soldier at the Swamp Fight, lived in the North quarter beyond the Concord river on what has since been the Edwin S. Barrett place and in the neighborhood of Boaz Brown whose home was on the place since occupied by Eli Dakin.

CHAPTER XLIV

Historical Sketches of Major Simon Willard, Lieut. Edward Oakes, Lieut. Simon Davis, Capt. Thomas Brattle.

BEFORE closing the subject of Concord in King Philip's war it is proper to give some further account of Maj. Simon Willard who, as before stated, was one of her most conspicuous citizens, and of several other officers who served at that time and are associated with the town.

The more prominent military service of Simon Willard as related to the public at large began when, in 1653, he was appointed Sergeant-Major of the forces of Middlesex county. In October, 1654, he was made commander-in-chief of a levy of a little more than three hundred footmen and horsemen who were sent out by the United Colonies in an expedition against Ninigret, the Sachem of the Niantics, returning to Boston with his troops by October 24.

The result of the expedition was the obtaining of a satisfactory agreement with Ninigret and also with the Pequod Indians.

Among the earlier services of Mr. Willard in Philip's war was the organizing of the Colonial troops, and one of his first acts in the field was his part in the relief of the Brookfield Garrison. At that time he was, with Capt. Parker, about starting with his company of forty-six men to look after some Indians to the westward of Lancaster and Groton, having five friendly Indians with him as scouts. Soon after this he was in command of a considerable force, consisting, among others, of the companies of Captain's Lathrop, Beers and Mosely, sent to range the country about Brookfield.

According to a paper presented to the Court after the decease of Major Willard, asking payment for his services, there is evidence that from Sept. 20, 1675, to April 18, 1676, "the major was employed about the country business Settling of Garrisons in towns and settling of Indians at Concord and Chelmsford, and other business."

For several months Major Willard was occupied in the various towns assisting in their defense, and soon after the return of the Narragansett expedition at the arrival of Canonchet in the Nipmunck country the Council ordered him to raise a large force of mounted men to do duty in the vicinity of Groton, Lancaster and Marlboro.

The miscellaneous nature of the military services of Major Willard may be set forth by the following copy of a report sent by him to the Colonial Court, giving an account of his movements from March 21 to 29, 1675-6, Mass. Archives, Vol. 68, p. 186: "A short narrative of what I have attended unto by the Councill of late, since I went to relieve Groatton. The 21:1: 75-76, I went to Concord, and divided the troope committed unto me from Essex & Norfolke into three pts one to garde the carte, pressed from Sudbury, one pt for y' carte pressed from concord, both to Lancaster, one pt for y' carte that went from Charlestowne & Wattertowne that went volintiers or wear hiered when I had sent them to their severall places I came downe being the 22:1: 75-6: & went to concord the 25 : 1 : 75, when I come there & inquired how it was with Lancaster the answer was they weare in distresse, I p'sently sent 40 horse thither to fetch away corne, and I went that night to Chellmsfoord to se how it was with them, they complayned, Billerikye Bridge, stood in great need of being fortified, I ordered that to be don, allso they told me, that the Indians made two great rafte of

266

board & rayles, that they had gott, that laye at the other syd of the river. I ordered 20 souldiers to go over & take them, & towe them downe the River, or p'serve them as they se cause, the 27 or this instant I went from Chellmsord to concord agayne when I came there, the troopers that I sent to Lancaster last had brought away all the people there, but had left about 80 bushells of wheat & Indian corne, yesterday I sent: 40 : horses or more to fetch it away, & came down from concord, this day I expect they will be at concord, Some of the troope I relesed when this last worke was don, the other I left order to scout abroad until they heare from me agayne, I thought it not meet to relese men, when we stand in need of men, my desire is to know what I shall do herein concord & chelmsford look every day to be fired, and wold have more men but know not how to keepe them, nor paye them, your humble servant. Simon Willard 29 : 1 : 76."

As a surveyor Mr. Willard was also celebrated. About 1652 he was sent as a commissioner to establish the northern boundary of Massachusetts at the head of the Merrimac river; and it is said that the letters S. W., which some years since were found upon the Bound Rock near Lake Winnepesaukee, were probably the initials of his name.

For prominent service in the settlement of Lancaster Mr. Willard was presented with a large land tract, and it is supposed that he removed to that town in 1659. Subsequent to his removal he acquired a strip of territory in Groton, now situated in the town of Ayer. This land has been known as the Nonacoicus grant, it being adjacent to a brook of this name.

Upon this tract of territory Mr. Willard erected a house which, according to a map made by Thomas Danforth, surveyor, was situated not far from the present county road leading from Ayer to Shirley Village. The exact spot where this house stood has not been positively ascertained; it is believed, however, that it was upon a knoll about twenty-five rods, more or less, from the county road on the southerly side. This conjecture is favored by the nature of the locality. The spot is near the junction of Nonacoicus brook and the Nashua river, where the intervale or meadow extends quite a distance southerly before reaching the upland, thereby affording good land for cultition. Nearby is a considerable rivulet, making convenient the watering of stock and the supplying of the house.

The proximity of the Nonacoicus brook and Nashua river afforded opportunity for fishing and the bottom lands about them for game; moreover, the Nashua river, running, as it did, through Groton and Lancaster, formed a convenient water wav between the two towns: and for this reason Mr. Willard would naturally place his homestead near it. In early times streams passing through a wilderness country were made use of both for transportation and personal passage. The Indians in the upper country were accustomed to make use of them for one or both of these purposes and in the time of the intercolonial wars these waterways were sometimes watched by companies of provincial rangers who lay in wait to intercept any enemy who might use the water courses for reaching the settlements.

The spot just indicated was well situated for defense, it being so elevated as to command a near view of the surrounding country. About this locality formerly there was quite a hamlet; the marks of cellar holes being still visible. Upon the knoll until within about a half century ago a house was standing which when demolished was very old. This may have been the immediate successor of the Willard house, or at least the second. As Mr. Willard went to Groton from Lancaster in 1671, the house was probably erected the same year. We may suppose that it stood quite alone, the estate being a large one and the house according to the plan of Danforth being in the central portion. Another circumstance making presumable its isolated condition, is that it was not called a garrison house which we believe it would have been if there had been homesteads about it.

But although removed from near neighbors and about five miles from any cluster of dwellings at central Groton, the Willard house in Philips war was much frequented by military men for military purposes. As it was on the main line of frontier territory along the region of the Nashua river and the general course of scouting parties as these made their way through the wood from Dunstable to Groton and Lancaster on past Washacum and Wachusett to Quinsigamond, it became a place of rendezvous; and its comfort and geniality were often shared in by the worn soldiers and their tired horses. Bunches of stacked muskets in the door yard may not have been unusual objects, while in the nearer forest to the northerly by the river side and upon the stony ridge at the eastward and along the wilderness road toward Shabbokin, where the road which is now a common highway was then a trail toward Lancaster, may have been many times seen the vigilant sentry. The house was attacked by the Indians and burned March 13, 1676. The family were absent at the time, warning having been given of the approach of the Indians.

March 2nd the town of Groton was put on its guard by the presence of a band of savages who pillaged several houses and stole some cattle. This act of hostility had sent the inhabitants of the scattered homesteads to the several garrison houses of the town and saved many people who would otherwise have perished. When on March 13 the final attack came Major Willard who with his men was scouting among the exposed towns and arranging for their defense went immediately with a squadron of cavalry to the town's relief; but he arrived too late. The town was destroyed. Forty dwelling houses had been laid in ashes, and also the meeting house.

The first house destroyed was that of Major Willard at Nonacoicus and it is not altogether unlikely that he passed the smoking ruins of his own homestead on his way to the rescue of the central village.

There are two scenes in the history of Simon Willard that are especially interesting—one, when the noble old officer over seventy years of age rode hurriedly over the rough wood roads followed hotly by his troop in eager impatience to arrive at Brookefield in season to rescue his former townsmen of Concord or their sons and Capt. Wheeler an associate officer; and the other, his ride to Groton where his own home was situated and his own son was the minister.

After the destruction of Groton, the inhabitants and the porn on of goods that had been saved, as soon as it could be done with safety, were conveyed through the woods to the lower towns; a considerable portion of them being left at Concord.

It is pleasant to contemplate that in selecting temporary unbiding places for his Groton townsmen he showed a preference for his old Concord home, and it may be that the welcome accorded to the Groton exiles was the more hearty because they had been associated in their homes with Simon Willard. The house of Major Willard at Groton was never rebuilt. Soon after, he went to Charlestown where he died April 24, 1676.

When the "piping rimes of peace" returned and the sunlit forest with its kindly sheltering shades again afforded safety and the birds sang there sweetly undisturbed by the harsh war sounds, someone perhaps repaired to the deserted and desolated spot still lovely in its forest environment, and scraping away the cold grey ashes and finding a foundation which the fires of war had not crumbled, built upon it. For years, the structure then erected endured. The storms swept over it and scoured its shingles or tore its thatching. It finally fell; the place again was left vacant, and today the traveler as he passes along the country road may see in the near distance in a pleasant pasture a few bunches of low shrubbery which alone remain to remind one of the former residence of Simon Willard.

But to the interested reader of the town's early history there is about these silent objects and surroundings a special significance. The rough rocks and loosely lying stones may have been resting places for the exulting savage, as he sat on that dismal March morning after applying the torch and watched the flames as they consumed the dwelling place of one whom he intensely hated and feared.

The little rivulet that still creeps down through the grassy runlet and crosses the highway in its passage, affording now the simple service of a wayside watering place, was once it may be rippled by the bucket of Madam Willard or her servants. Where the interval broadens out from the river and brook until by its gentle winding it reaches almost within view from the door, the younger children of the family in the season when the "sound of falling nuts is heard" may have repaired with their coarse baskets to gather walnuts and chestnuts, or to pick cranberries.

Another man who did good service in Philip's war and who spent a portion of his life in Concord was Lieut. Edward Oakes. He came from England in 1640 and lived for many years in Cambridge where he was a selectman twenty-six years. His wife's name was Jane; and the names of four of his children were Urian, Edward, Mary and Thomas, the two former having been born in England. He was a Deputy to the Gen. Court from Concord in 1683,4, and 6.

Lieut. Oakes did service during King Philip's war in the troop of Capt. Prentice, who commanded one of the five troop of horse in the colony. To belong to a cavalry company was a privileged position. The members had extra pay and were generally from the more thrifty and well to do families, each one owning his own horse. Lieut. Oakes was in the summer campaign at Mount Hope. The fact that he was Lieutenant in Capt. Prentice's Command is evidence of a creditable record. He died at Concord Oct. 13, 1689, aged about 85.

Simon Davis was a son of Dolor Davis who was a petitioner for Groton in 1656. His father married Margery a sister of Major Simon Willard. Simon and his brother Samuel made their homes in Concord and had families the descendants of which are widely scattered and greatly respected.

Simon Davis subsequently became a Lieutenant and then a captain, and in King Williams war with forty troopers and thirty foot soldiers was appointed to defend the frontier from Dunstable to Marlborough. Beside serving faithfully as a soldier, captain Davis successively occupied several civic offices, being a representative about 1689. He married Mary a daughter of James Blood in 1660 and Died June 14., 1713 aged 77. It is said that three Governors John Davis, George Robinson and John D. Long have descended from this family.

Another Officer who was connected with the town of Concord was Capt. Thomas Brattle at one time a merchant in Boston and a member of the Artillery Company in 1674. He purchased of the Indians large tracts of territory along the Kennebec and Merrimac rivers and owned the iron works at Concord. From 1678 to 1681 he was a deputy from Lancaster. He was one of the founders of the Old South Church in Boston and married Elizabeth, a daughter of Capt. William Tyng. Thomas Brattle was appointed Cornet of the Suffolk troop on May 30 1670, became Lieutenant Oct. 13, 1675, and captain May 9, 1676.

Thomas Brattle while Cornet on Sept. 8, 1675 conducted a detachment of soldiers for distribution in the towns of Dunstable, Groton and Lancaster, and arranged with the people for their doing garrison duty among them. He was engaged in the organization and supply of several expeditions and was with the Narragansett army after the Swamp fight. He died April 5, 1683 leaving it is stated the largest estate in New England at that time. His sons Thomas and William graduated at Harvard College and both were celebrated and popular.

Before closing the subject of the connection of Concord with Philip's war we would observe that some of the military methods employed during the period correspond quite nearly to some of the practices of the period just preceding the war of the Revolution. For instance the function of the "committee of militia" was similar to the later committee of safety and the latter may have had its origin in or been a continuation of the former. In the time of Philip's war in a town adjacent to Concord, according to its historian, the inhabitants who were capable of bearing arms were divided into two military organizations, one, which was made up of two thirds of the inhabitants, acting as the regular militia, and the remaining third standing in readiness to act at a moment's warning, suggesting both by the number of men in each organization and by the service expected of those in the latter that here may have been the origin of the "Minute men." The company that stood in readiness to act at a moment's notice was known as "The Alarm." If this was the practice in neighboring places, without evidence to the contrary we may suppose it was so in Concord, and perhaps the twelve men who went to the rescue of Sudbury, were Minute men.

The signal service consisting in the firing of several muskets successively may have given rise to the same signal service of a subsequent century.

The making use of the town of Concord as a rendezvous of soldiers, a place for war refugees, for a gunsmith, a "Magazine," and a deposit of military stores may have caused it to be used for a military purpose in both the intercolonial wars and in the conflict of 1775.

Thus closed the tragic and grimly picturesque period of King Philip's war; a period in which the valor of the United Colonies of Massachusetts, Plymouth and Connecticut had been many times demonstrated, and in which the endurance and resources of the respective towns had been severely taxed. Both races left that in their records which they had great reason to regret, and which judged by the standards of later years is far from being commendable.

The English in their fighting qualities even when they were displayed under circumstances which were wild and ill-adapted to the usual conditions of waging war, had shown themselves the masters, although by an inconsiderate rashness or overconfidence they had suffered their greatest losses. Their work had been open and their methods if not unmixed with cruelty had been tactful and orderly.

The Indians had shown themselves coarse adepts in trickery and without successful comprehensiveness of plan. Their chief resource was the ambuscade, and they seldom attacked where the forces were equal. We know of but one notable instance of open siege by them, or of carrying a fortified place by storming it. The incidental references to their traits as brought out in the various war records, and in the literature of the times set forth we believe far less of a native nobility to the life and character of the savage than the poet has associated with him. He was gross in his general habits. The forest cleanliness that belongs to bird or beast was not observed by him, and the precariousness of his manner of living points to him as being lazily improvident. Some of his faultiness in these respects is brought out by Mrs. Rowlandson in a manner so marked as to make the very reading of the descriptions almost repulsive. In short the general testimony of the entire contest is that Indian observation of Europeans for a portion of two generations had not removed him from his ancient barbarity nor led him to abstain from vile practices which he observed before he had ever seen a white man. It is the old story oft repeated in ethnological history that nature alone is ill suited to reform a sin stained soul.

But on the other hand Philip's war remarkably affirmed the province of grace and the gospel to do a work in the human heart that even war with all of hell that there may be in it cannot erase or eradicate.

The Praying Indian although persecuted by his own and his adopted race stood firm between the two fires and amid all the tribulations by which he was tested he could be depended upon in the hour of a "forlorn hope" as none other of his race could be.

Job Kattenanit of Natick dragging himself to the door of Major Daniel Gookin's house in Cambridge a short time before midnight on Feb. 9th after a journey of eighty miles from the Indian village at Meminimisset bringing intelligence in confirmation of a report made by Quanapaug a Christian convert of the Nashaway Indians whom Gov. Leverett had employed as a scout, that the Indians would in twenty days fall upon the English settlements and first attack Lancaster, and Tom Doublet speeding through the long, lonely forest with a message from the Governor in behalf of distressed Mrs. Rowlandson are emphatic tributes to God's saving power among the heathen and to the untiring efforts of His servant the Apostle Eliot who declared it.

These faithful Christians famished and almost overcome by their long fatigue bore witness to their loyalty to the newly found faith by all the eloquence of noble endurance. True there may have been among the Christian Indians religious renegades and cases of mistaken conversion, instances of which Mrs. Rowlandson has cited in her "Removes;" but so it has been with some of the alleged conversions among civilized Christians, and the spurious only proves the value of the genuine.

As to some of the war measures of either side there is but small opportunity to be apologetic. Each dealt with its captives with a cruel commercialism that can under no circumstances be condoned much less commended.

That both contestants believed themselves right we may not question but how this could be is not so easily explained. The same inexplicable way of thinking and of viewing things may have had its influence here as in years later when the pious colonist with a composure of conscience that is remarkable convicted witch suspects.

That the fathers were great in their heroic faith is beyond controversy for this only could have kept them through their hours of trial. That they meant well in what they did few can doubt who know them; but how they could justify some of their means to their righteous aims and ends is beyond our knowledge. All we can do is to be generously charitable.

CHAPTER XLV

Changed Condition of the Colony at the Close of King Philip's War — Process of Recuperation — Erection of a New Meeting House — Evangelical Character of the Concord Church — Progress in Educational Affairs — Early Circulating Library — Donation of Land by Capt. Timothy Wheeler — Real Estate Transactions— Adjustment of Riparian Rights of the Bulkeley Mill Privilege — Settlement of the Controversy Concerning the Blood Farms — Historical Sketch of the Blood Family — Indian Deeds in Confirmation of Old Titles.

AFTER the close of King Philip's war the colonial towns were not slow in engaging in the work of reconstruction and soon there was once more seen upon the hillsides and along the glades safe and pleasant homesteads and plenteous harvest fields. After the waging of the terrible conflict a sense of security came over society and there was fresh inducement to effort. The local Indian question it was believed had been settled. There was no longer the possibility of a sudden uprising by which all progress might be impeded and any enterprise that had been undertaken destroyed. It had become safe now to invest in new lands to further clear away the forest, and to erect bridges and make passable roads.

It was now considered comparatively safe to live in any portion of central or southern New England. The traveler could make his journey through the wood without danger of an interruption or signs of an enemy. The settler's wife could build a fire for the evening meal and her husband in the distant field could smile at the sight of the cheerful chimney smoke and the thought of supper that would await him as he left his hard day's work without having his happiness interfered with by a consciousness that the rising smoke might attract savages. The children could gather fresh flowers in the meadows; women could venture alone by the countryside and cattle could be allowed to browse at will in the brushwood with only the merry tinkle of the cow bell to disclose their whereabouts, so great had become the security almost immediately after the war had fully ended.

The town of Concord in common with others of the colony early felt the welcome impetus and was not backward in taking advantage of the brightening prospect and in accepting of the invitation of new circumstances to develop her resources. Centrally situated as she was among the townships of the county her territory was both convenient and attractive and from time to time new names were added to her list of inhabitants.

With the changed conditions came new sights and sounds which formed a contrast with what had just preceded them which was very marked. Instead of the hurrying footsteps of forest messengers coming with tidings of the near approach of war parties and the sight of new levies of soldiers sent by the Council to rendezvous at Concord and perhaps be billeted upon the inhabitants, and of clumsy carts loaded with the goods of fleeing refugees whose homes were menaced and guarded by a convoy of grim troops, there was heard the rattle of the hay-rigging coming from the meadow loaded with sedge or from the field with corn, or the load of wood from the forest or there might have been seen jogging to the grist mill, the farmer from some remote district or from the border of some adjacent town; or the teamster from "up country" going to market with his produce and that of his neighbor to be exchanged in barter for such commodities as they could not produce or make for themselves.

To a small extent the townships that had suffered the most severely in the war were assisted by the colony in a temporary abatement of taxes. In 1676 valuable assistance was rendered from a fund sent to America from Ireland called the "Irish Charity Donation or Fund." The gift was designed for the people of Massachusetts, Plymouth, and Connecticut colonies and was made "by divers Christians in Ireland for the relieffe of such as are Impoverished Distressed and in Nessesitie by the late Indian Wars." It came to this country by the "Good ship called the Kathrine of Dublin." The fund is supposed to have been procured by Rev. Nathaniel Mather a brother of Increase.

The tax abatement for the town in 1676 was £50. The amount allowed Concord people from the charity fund was £$o. Eighteen families consisting of seventy-two persons received benefits from the fund.

The goods contributed consisted of oat meal, wheat, malt, butter, and cheese. The appraised value of these was as follows: malt "18s per ball, butter 6d, cheese 4d.

During the entire colonial period we conclude that the regular routine of town business went on without much essential variation. There were about the same officials to be chosen from year to year the same objects for which to appropriate money and the same ways and means to be employed for meeting these things.

There was a careful surveillance by the town of all its officials and of its affairs in general, and but little if anything was left at loose ends which appertained to the public interest.

The following copy of instructions given to the Concord selectmen in the year 1672 shows the nature of subjects to be looked after.

"Instructions given to the Selectmen of Concord for the year, 1672.

1 To see that the ministers Rates be discharged according to time

2 To ascamen whether the meting house, be finised according to agreement, & if not, that it may be; but if the agreement be fulfiled, then to take cear that somthing be done to keep the water out, and that the pulpet be altred.

4 That spedy kere be taken to mend or denudes, the foote bridg over the Riv' at the Iron Works:

5 To treat with Capt. Thomas Wheler about his leese of the Townes farme & if it may be upon Resonable termes to alter that perriculer wherein the Towne is Jn Jnoiyned to send such a nomber cattle yearly to be herded by him;

6 To let out the land & housing where now John Law dweles; for the benefet of the towne,

7 To take order that all Corn filds be sufficently fenced in seson, the Crane fild & bricke keld field especially;

8 And that incorigment be given for the destroing of blackburds & Jaies;

9 That speciall cear be taken to preuent damiag by swine in come fieldes & medows

10 That shepe & lames be keept from doing damiag in cornefields;

11 To make a Record of all the habitationes, that are priviledged with liberty at Comones;

12 To take account of the laste yeares selectmen for what is don, [due?] to the Towne by Reent by John Law, or by givft by Joseph Meriam; or otherwise of wright dew to the Towne, not to Restraine the selectmen from lenity towards John Law;

13 To see that menes lands both Improved & unimproved be truly broth, [brought in]

14 To take care that vndesiarable persones be not entertained; so as to become inhabitants

15 To take cere that psones doe not ouer Charg ther Comones with Cattle,

16 That all psones that have taken the oath of fidellity be Recorded,

17 That cere be taken that Cattle be herded, as much as may be, with convenence

These perticolers were agreed vpon by vs whose names are vnderwriten nehamia. hunt; John fflint; John miles; Will dated 4: 1. mo. £jj heartwell; Tho; Wheler Joshuah brooke Joseph; heaward; Gershom. Brooke, Humpry barit John Billings"

But while public proceedings usually moved on uninterruptedly and with only here and there a ripple of change or excitement in 1689 the rule was broken in upon by an event which disturbed the whole town. This was an order by the colonial authorities to compel all who would participate in home government to become freemen or in other words to qualify themselves by taking the following "freeman's oath."

"'I, A. B., being by God's providence an inhabitant and freeman within the jurisdiction of this commonwealth, do freely acknowledge myself to be subject to the government thereof, and therefore do swear, by the great and dreadful name of the everlasting God, that I will be true and faithful to the same, and will accordingly yield assistance and support thereunto with my person and estate, as in equity I am bound, and also truly endeavor to maintain and preserve all the liberties and privileges thereof, submitting myself to the wholesome laws and orders made and established by the same; and, further, that I will not plot nor practice any evil against it, nor consent to any that shall do so, but will timely discover and reveal the same to lawful authority now here established, for the speedy prevention thereof; moreover, I do solemnly bind myself, in the sight of God, that when I shall be called to give my voice touching any such matter of this state wherein freemen are to deal, I will give my vote and suffrage, as I shall judge in my conscience, may best conduce and tend to the public weal of the body, without respect of persons, or favor of any man. So help me God, in the Lord Jesus Christ.'"

At an early stage of Colonial history only a freeman could vote or hold office or serve on a jury; and only church members could become freemen.

This rule which was formally in force till the close of the administration of Sir Edmund Andros worked to the exclusion of many substantial citizens. In process of time however the rule became so changed that by taking the oath of fealty to the Colony a person could vote in municipal and military matters and hold town office. By this change, whereby it was made possible for persons to be elected to office without being subjected to the process of becoming freemen, an active participation in town affairs became more general. After a while however the reform had a setback; and in 1689, a few years before the Colony passed into a Province, the old method was for a short period revived; and again no one could vote unless he had been made a freeman. The immediate result of this movement was to lead many citizens who were church members to apply to be made freemen.

The following is a list preserved among the State Archives Vol. 5 page 352, containing names of Concord citizens who having complied with the conditions were constituted freemen at the time of the revival of the old method of eligibility. That they were church members is evident from the fact that only church members could be made freemen.

"In Concord ye 3 of 1st munth 16.

An acount taken of the nonfrreemen which are free holders, whos housing and Lands do amount to the uallew of six rante by the year.

Mr. James Minerd
Nathanell Stow
Danell Dane
Nathaell Harwood
Thomas gobile S(enior)
Eliphelet fox
Robord Blood, S
John Ball
John wheler, S
Samuel fletcher
Nemiah hunt, S
Timithy Ries
Samuell Davis, S
Samuel Stratten
John Shaperd, S
Johnethen habord
Abraham Tempel
Joshua Wheler
Recherd Tempel
James Smadly
Isaac Tempel
Nathanell Buse
Simon Davis
John wood
Roberd Blood
Abraham wood
Simon Blood
Obadiah wheler
Josiah Blood
John Haward
Judath poter
Thomas Wheler
John Jones
Steuen Hosmer
John Hartwill
THOMAS: WHEELER:
HOMPHARY BARET
NATHANIEL BILLING SELECT MEN
STEUEN HOSMOR

276

ELIPHELET FFOX

21 March 1639. Voted by the Court to be ffremen

Ebenezer Prout, Clerk

Consent

Js' Addington Sec'

Besides the foregoing who are supposed to have given the Court satisfactory credentials of Church membership upon their application to be made freemen, we have the following names of citizens who also applied to be made freemen about the same time together with the requisite certificate for church membership.

"Concord March 12th

All whom ye knowledge of what is here exp'ssed doth concerne may please hereby to understand, that ye psons here named are members in the full comunion of the church; Leiften' Simon Davis, Leiften' Jonathan Prescot, Joseph firench, Thomas Pellot, Samuel Hunt; Eliezer fflag, Samuel Hartwell, Samuel Myriam, John Wheeler, Samuel How, Abraham Taylor, John Hayward, Nathaniel Ball, Samuel Wheate, Timothy Wheeler, John Myriam, Daniel Pellet; Wittnesses my hand; Edward Bulkely."

All above written (Except Daniel Pellet) voted to be frreemen.

his age being questioned.   Js'Addington Sec'.

Ebenezer Prout Clerk.

certificate of church membership.

These documents are interesting not only as illustrative of the working of the political system of the times, but they are also valuable as indicating how large a proportion of the town's population belonged to the church.

Among the more important events which occurred at Concord during the latter part of the Colonial period was the building of a new meeting house.

As stated in an early chapter of Part 1 the first meeting house was built soon after the settlement began and stood upon the little hill by the "strate strete" at the beginning of Lexington street. This which was undoubtedly built of logs had no successor upon its perched position on the hill top but was followed by a more imposing structure erected upon the plain by the brook. Agitation upon the subject of a new house of public worship began soon after the death of the first minister, and in 1667 a vote was taken in town meeting to erect one. The building was to stand "between the old edifice and Deacon Jams'," Jan. 27, 1668, a committee consisting of Capt. Timothy Wheeler, Joseph Wheeler, and John Smedly was chosen to plan and take charge of the business of construction, and in 1672, the selectmen were to see if the contract for completing the work had been fulfilled. The new house of worship in style closely resembled the old meeting house at Hingham, Mass., which was built in 1681. It had a peeked roof with four sides or slopes in which were dormer windows and was surmounted by a belfry. The main structure was nearly square and had a gallery. Along the walls were ranged a few pews, but the center was mostly filled with plain seats. A vane was on the spire inscribed with the date, 1673.

As no further reference will be made to ecclesiastical matters of the Colonial period we will observe in passing that the indications relative to the early church at Concord are that its creed and its ministers were evangelical, and that the religious traditions of the town are in substantial accord with those of the typical Pilgrim and Puritan. The light that shone in the wilderness was a gospel light and among the twinkling stars that glittered through their night of solicitude and sorrow none were as bright to the settler as that which arose and stood over the place where lay the Babe of Bethlehem. The Christ of that first Christmas was the Christ of the Concord colonist. It was to His word that he looked for guidance, by His sacrifice he believed he would be saved, and upon this rock he built his church.

One sign of progress after the close of Philip's war was an increased interest in education. In the early years of the township learning took a low place. The times were hard. To obtain a livelihood required the greatest effort, but straightened as its circumstances were, the town was early supplied in its several districts with those who were competent to teach the children and youth to read and write. In 1665 complaint was made against the town for its lack of a "Lattin Schoole Mr." It was also about this time repeatedly reminded of its laxity in providing educational privileges in general.

In the Mass. Archives Vol. 129, page 130 is a paper of indenture executed by the overseers of the poor of the town of Boston and Ebenezer Prout of Concord by which a child nine years of age was to be brought up. She was to "Be taught perfectly to read English, Sew, Spin, and Knit as she shall be capable;" she was to be supplied with "wholesome sufficient meat, drink, Apparel, washing, & Lodging;" and at the end of the term, she was to be dismissed with "two new Suits of Apparel throughout, one for Lord's days, the other for working days."

The date is 1688 and the term of indenture was until the subject became 11 years old or was married. This transaction between Ebenezer Prout and the Boston guardians of the poor corresponds in its substance to a report of the town constables to the Council of the state of education in Concord about 1680. In the report it is stated that they found "no children or youth not taught to read and know the Capital laws."

In addition to school privileges and the educational agency and influence of the pulpit, the town was early favored as has been stated in another part of this volume with a catechistical exercise on the Lord's day, a practice probably the first of its kind in this country, and if it may be considered a Sunday school then the pioneer Sunday school in America. The town early had a circulating library and this too perhaps was the first one in the country. In 1672, the town instructed the selectmen "That ceare be taken of the bookes of marters & other bookes, that belong to the Towne, that they be kept from abeuce uesage, & not to be lent to any person more then one month at one time."

At this distant day it is not easy to conceive of the exact methods of pronunciation in the everyday conversation. From the manner of spelling it is possible to suppose what may have been the style of pronouncing certain syllables. An occasional use of the letter a instead of e in such words as certain and clerk easily leads to the conjecture that they were pronounced as to the first syllable like a in far. In the use of the letter e for i in such words as district and little, the inference is that they were pronounced as they were spelled.

The writing of various words with a terminal e, which are written in modern times without it as in the words "poore" and "yeare" may suggest the possible prolongation or trilling of the letter r. So also where double consonants begin a word as "ffirst" for first, a natural conclusion may be that the sound of the syllable containing it was somewhat lengthened.

The absence of any elision of the letter h in words that begin with an aspirate lead to the inference that none of the English settlers at Concord elided the aspirate in their talk.

The cause of common schools received an impetus in 1687 by a gift of land as set forth in the following clause in the will of Capt. Timothy Wheeler who died in July of that year.

"I Give to the Towne of Concord my house that stands near Eliaz. Fleggs house with the Land thatitt stands upon and is joyned to itt; wch is about Three acres; be itt more or Lesse bounded by the Highway on the North East by my Land (viz') the Gutter and Eliazer Fleggs Land on the North West & South This I say I Give to the said Towne to be improved as followeth [viz']; That about halfe an acre of the said Lott be laid out to the training place the fence to Run from the Corner of the House to the brow of the Hill upon a straight Lyne; the Dwelling house with the rest of the Land w'h all that is upon itt I give to be Improved for the furtherance of Learning and the Support of a Schoole in the said Towne"

The more notable real estate transactions during the later years of the Colonial period consisted mainly in the adjustment of relations already existing or in minor transfers of original grants.

In 1667, an agreement was reached relative to a matter or controversy which had long been going on concerning the Bulkeley mill privilege. As has been stated in the story of the town's settlement a corn or grist mill was caused to be erected by Parson Peter Bulkeley on the mill brook the dam of which was near the present public square. When he died the property was conveyed to his widow Grace Chetwood Bulkeley and shortly after there arose the vexed question as to what were the exact rights of flowage, which were accorded to the mill proprietor when the town granted the mill privilege. The land about the mill pond was valuable on account of its near proximity to the public places and it might take but a slight elevation of the "splash boards" of the dam to cause the water of the pond to encroach upon it and occasion "wetness" about the new meeting house grounds, and the town pound and perhaps damage the tan pits. In several instances the town officials had been instructed to guard the immediate vicinity of the backyard of the meeting house against inundation from the water of the mill brook.

But the temptation to augment the mill power by increasing the fall at the flume was perhaps only a natural one, and hence in spite of expostulation on the part of the public the maximum height was adhered to until matters were settled by arbitrament of the court whose verdict was as follows:

"1. That the ounors of the sajd mill shall have liberty from tjme to time, & at all rjmes, to rajse the water fowre ffoote tenn inches perpendiccular ffrom the bottome of the mill troffe, as now it lieth at the head of the milne pond, but the wast or low shott not to be made narrower then now it is, or to be raysed higher then to rajse the water (at the head of the pond) to fower ffoote seuen inches ffrom the bottom of the milne troffe before the water runns ouer the wast.

2. What land lyeth vnder water, by reason of the milne pond, at such a head of water as aforesajd, shall be the propriety & propper right of the ounors of the sajd mill for euer, excepting alwayes land which the toune of Concord haue formerly granted to any of their inhabitants, all wch land each proprietor shall enjoy according to his toune grant after the mill is wholly disannulled.

3. The ounors of the sajd mill for euer shall not be iable to sattisfy any damage donn to any person or persons whatsoeuer, by such a head of water kept and majntejned as before sajd.

4. The ounors of the sajd mill foreuer shall enjoy the benefit of all that water wch may be obteyned by any menes formerly attempted i. e. to the higth of such a head of water as aforesajd, wch water shall not be diverted by any person or persons whatsoeuer.

5. Lastly. The ounors of the sajd mill foreuer shall enjoy priuiledge on the comons for clay & sand convenient for the repaire of the mill damage from tjme to tjme as formerly they haue enjoyed.

SYMON WILLARD
JNO FOUNELL,
& JOHNATHAN DANFORTH.

The Court approves of this return."

In 1686 there was an adjustment of the controversy relating to the Blood farms. These farms consisted of certain territory in and about the present town of Carlisle. A part of them was owned by Robert Blood as early as 1642.

Because situated outside the boundary line of any town the dwellers oil them were styled borderers. These farms being in no incorporated town were without civil or ecclesiastical status. The occupants paid their rates in Billerica but when the Indian war came they paid their rates in Concord, and had the protection of Concord's garrison houses.

Subsequently these rates by order of the Court were refunded to Billerica. The question of jurisdiction in this and similar instances was settled by the General Court Oct. 11, 1682. After citing facts in cases of a like nature that had occurred in different places it ordered that Borderers should pay the county treasurer two shillings for every two hundred acres of land; and towns were to "assess all country grants of lands & all belonging to peculiar persons that lye neerest to each toune or tounes."

Upon this authority the Concord constables went to the Blood farms with a tax warrant. They were roughly received by Robert and his son. The consequence was that Robert Blood Sr. was fined ten pounds for ill treatment of the officers and "vilifying his Majesty's authority."

The exact merits of the case at this distant day may not be known. The occupants of the Farms were obliged to pay rates whether they received benefits or not. Their roads were poor, they were remote from church privileges and were doubtless having a hard time enough in the distant wilderness. The matter was however settled March 17, 1686, Robert Blood with the assent in writing of his sons Robert and Simeon negotiated a treaty with Peter Bulkeley Esq, Henry Woodis and John Smedly Senior, acting for Concord, by which Robert Blood should thereafter pay to Concord all civil and ecclesiastical dues incumbent upon him, and a due proportion of whatever expense there might be in building and repairing the meeting house.

On the other hand Robert and his heirs were to be exempted from all town offices and their waste land was not to be reckoned in their minister's rates.

It was also agreed that convenient roads should be laid out for them at the town's expense, and no town rates were to be assessed to them except as above specified.

The adjustment of the civil relations of the "Blood farms" to the town of Concord ended a long controversy and one in which all the parties to it doubtless believed that they were in the right. By the terms of adjustment however the territory did not necessarily become a part of the township neither was it always considered a part of it.

For years after the discussion was ended the Concord selectmen before their triennial perambulation of the town boundary lines were accustomed to notify the proprietors of the Blood farms in accordance with the rule usually observed in such cases where the officials of one town notify those of another of their proposed examination of boundaries.

These farms became a part of Carlisle. The following is an outline sketch of the Blood family. The American ancestor was James, who went to Concord in 1639. James Blood is said to have been a brother of Col. James Blood known in English history in connection with the reign of Charles II. He died Nov. 17, 1683 leaving a large estate.

His wife Ellen died in 1674. James and Ellen Blood had five children Mary, Richard, John, James and Robert. Mary married Lieut. Simon Davis. Richard was one of the first settlers of the town of Groton and was one of its prominent land proprietors. He left a large family of children whose descendants have been quite numerous. John died in 1692. He and his brother Robert owned over two thousand acres of land in Concord including the Blood farms which were inherited by the children of Robert.

James married Hannah, a daughter of Oliver Purchis of Lynn, and lived at what has since been known as the "Old Manse" owning a tract of territory thereabouts. He was a deacon in the church and died Nov. 26, 1692. His wife died in 1677. They left only one child.

Robert married Elizabeth, a daughter of Major Simon Willard in 1653. They had twelve children. Robert Blood died Oct. 27, 1701. His wife Elizabeth died Aug. 29, 1690.

In 1684, many years after the purchase and transfer a confirmatory deed was obtained from the heirs or their representatives of the land in the new grant. The reason for obtaining these deeds was the preservation of evidence, and the importance of it was perhaps occasioned by the threats of Sir Edmund Andros to vitiate landed titles.

The following are copies.

"To all People to whom these presents may come, Greeting Know ye that We, Mary Neepanaum John Speen and Sarah Speen Dorothy Winnetow Peter Muckquamack of Natick and James Speen & Elizabeth Speen his wife of Waymasset Indians For and in Consideration of a valuable sum of money to us in hand paid by Capt. Timothy Wheeler Henry Woodis James Blood and John Flint The Receipt whereof we do hereby acknowledge and therewith to be fully satisfied and contented have sold and by these presents do sell aliene enfeoffe and confirm unto the said Capt. Timothy Wheeler Henry Woodis James Blood & John Flint of Concord in the County of Middlesex in the Massachusetts Colony in New England for the use and behoof of themselves and the rest of the Proprietors of the said Town of Concord a certain tract or parcel of Land containing by Estimation a Thousand acres be the same more or less and is situate lying and being within the last Grant of Land by the General Court to the said Town of Concord and is bounded Southeast by Sudbury & the Land of Stow alias [Pompasitticut] and Northwest by the said Stow running by them upon that Line about a Mile and a Quarter, near to a Hill by the Indians called Naaruhpanit and from thence by a strait Line to the North River at the old bounds of the said Town of Concord unto them the said Timothy Wheeler Henry Woodis James Blood & John Flint for themselves and for the use & behoof of the Rest of the Proprietors of the said Town of Concord to them their heirs assigns and successors forever and we the said Mary Neepanaum John Speen and Sarah Speen his wife Dorothy Winnetow Peter Muckquamuck and James Speen and Elizabeth his wife, do hereby covenant and Promise to and with the foresaid Timothy Wheeler Henry Woodis James Blood & John Flint and the rest of the Proprietors of the said Town of Concord that we are the true proprietors of and have good Right & full power to grant bargain & sell the above granted & bargained premises unto the said Timothy Wheeler Henry Woodis James Blood and John Flint and the Rest of the Proprietors of the said Town of Concord to them their heirs successors and assigns forever and that the said Timothy Wheeler Henry Woodis James Blood John Flint and the Rest of the Proprietors of the said Town of Concord them their heirs assigns and successors forever shall and may at all Times and from time to time forever hereafter peaceable have hold occupy possess and enjoy the above granted Premises in fee simple, be the same more or less without the Let denial or contradiction of us the said Mary Neepanaum John Speen, & Sarah Speen his wife Dorothy Winnetow Peter Muckquamuck and James Speen and Elizabeth his wife, or any of us or any of our heirs or any other person or persons whatsoever lawfully claiming & naveing any Right Title or Interest therein or to in any part or parcel thereof—

In acknowledgment of this our act & Deed we have hereto put our hands and seals this fifth Day of May in the year of our Lord one thousand six hundred eighty & four

Signed Sealed & Deld in the presence of
John Speen his mark and seal
Sarah Speen her mark and seal
Moses Parker James Speen and seal
Noah Brooks
Samuel Wheeler Junr
Elizabeth Speen her mark and seal
Benjamin Bohow his mark
Dorothy Winnetow her mark
Sarah Bohow her mark and seal
John Speen & Sarah his wife
James Speen and Elizabeth his wife and Dorothy alias Winnetow acknowledged the within written instreument to be their Act & Deed.

May 5. 1684. before Peter Bulkeley assist. The following deed purports to convey eight thousand acres:

"To People to whom These presents may come Greeting Know ye that We John Thomas and Naanonsquaw his wife Tasunsquaw The Relict of Wawbon decd and eldest Daughter to Tasattawan Sagamore decd Thomas Wawbon her son Solomon Thomas John Nasquaw James Casumpal Senr and Sarah his wife & Sarah the Relict widow of Peter Conoway Indians for and in Consideration of the sum of one and twenty pounds, fifteen of it long since paid to us [blank in record] and the Remainder which is six pounds is now paid to us by Capt. Timothy Wheeler Henry Woodis

James Blood and John Flint of Concord the Receipt whereof we do hereby acknowledge and therewith to be fully satisfied and contented have sold and by these presents do sell aliene enfeoffe and confirm unto the said Timothy Wheeler Henry Woodis James Blood and John Flint of Concord in the County of Middlesex in the Massachusetts Colony in New England for the use & behoof of themselves and the Rest of the Proprieters of the said Town of Concord a certain Tract or parcel of Land containing by Estimation Eight Thousand acres be he same more or less and is situate lying and being within the last Grants of Land by the General Court to the Towntof Concord and is bounded Southeast by the old bounds of the said town of Concord and is bounded Easterly partly by Billerica partly by a Farm formerly laid out by Major Willard tor himself and partly by Chelmsford till it meets with Nashoby Line and then Westerly by the said Nashoby to the Southeast Corner of the said Nashoby and [then northerly] by the said N[ashoby] till it meets with St[ow] and so bounded northwest by the said Stow till it comes Near to a Hill by the Indians called Naaruhpanit and then running upon a strait Line to the North River at the old bounds of the said Town of Concord unto them the said Timothy Wheeler Henry Woodis James Blood John Flint agents for the Town or Concord and to the rest of the Proprietors of the Town of Concord to them their Heirs and Successors and assigns forever and we the said John Thomas and Nasquaw James Casumpat and Sarah his wife and Sarah the Relict widow of Peter Conoway do hereby covenant and promise to and with the foresaid Timothy Wheeler Henry Woodis James Blood John Flint and the rest of the Proprietors of the Town of Concord that we are the true Proprietors of and have good Right & full power to grant bargain and sell the above granted and bargained premises unto the said Timothy Wheeler Henry Woodis James Blood & John Flint and the rest of the Proprietors of the Town of Concord to them their heirs Successors and assigns forever and that the said Timothy Wheeler Henry Woodis James Blood and John Flint &the rest of the proprietors of the said Town of Concord to them their Heirs Successors & assigns shall and may at all times & from time to time forever hereafter peaceably have hold occupy possess and enjoy the above granted premises in fee simple be the same more or less without the Let denial or contradiction of us the said John Thomas and Naaonsquaw his wife Tasunsquaw widow and eldest Daughter of Tasattawan Late Sagamore decd Thomas Wawbon Solomon Thomas John Nasquaw James Casumpat Senr & Sarah his wife and Sarah the Relict widow. Peter Conoway or any of us or any of our heirs or any other person or persons whatsoever lawfully claiming & having any Right Title or Interest therein or two or in any part or parcel thereof.

In acknowledgement of this our act & Deed we have hereto put our hands and seals this fourteenth Day of August in the year of our Lord one Thousand Six hundred Eighty and four.

Signed Sealed & Del'd, in the presence of
John Thomas his mark and seal
Naanunsquaw her mark and seal
Ebenezer Ingolds Tasunsquaw her mark and seal
Joseph Shambery his mark
Thomas Wabon and seal
Andrew Pittamey his mark
Solomon Thomas his mark and seal

James Casumpat Sen' his mark and seal
John Nasquaw his mark and seal
Sarah the widow of Peter Conoway her mark and seal
Sarah the wife of James Casumpat her mark and seal
Midd. ss. Concord August the 29 1730

before his Majesty's Court of General Sessions of the Peace appeared Mr. Joseph Woolley and made oath that he was present and saw John Thomas Naanonsquaw Tasunsquaw Thomas Wabun Solomon Thomas James Casumpat John Nasqua Sarah the widow of Peter Conaway and Sarah the wife of James Casumpat execute the within Instrument as their act & Deed and that he together with Ebenezer Ingolds Joseph Shamberry & Andrew Pittamey at the same time tet to their hands as Witnesses to the Execution thereof Att Saml Phipps Cler. Pads"

In 1671 Peter Bulkeley of London a son of Rev. Peter Bulkeley sold to Timothy Prout for the sum of £45, a tract of land of which it is said "the said Farm Lyeth upon and in the southerly part of the town of Concord. In 1683 and 84 it is asserted in a deposition that three separate families lived upon this land viz: Thomas Skinner, Thomas Pratt, Ephraim Ropes.

The following town record with date March 7, 1692, relates to the transfer of a small piece of land about the present public square.

"Eliazer Flagge of sd town did Request of the towne a peese of Grownd near to the meting house ye bredth of ye pownd all between the pownd & ye mill Brook ajoining to ye land yt was formerly Thomas Danes, and the Inhabitants did then freely Give the sayd litle plott of Ground unto the sayd Eliazer Flagge to set his tan pits upon it as his own land."

On May 14, 1692 the Massachusetts Bay Colony passed into a Province, and the old charter signed March 14, 1629, gave place to a new one signed by King William, which remained in force till the Revolution in 1775.

Before the going out of the old Charter and the coming in of the new, there was an interval of six years or more which has been styled the inter charter period. During this interval the affairs of state were administered by a commission which came to this country in the frigate Rose, and consisted of a council of which Joseph Dudley was the President. The remainder of the period governmental matters were managed by Sir Edmund Andros who arrived in this country Dec. 9, 1686, on the Kingfisher bearing with him authority to act as Governor of all New England.

The administration of Andros was an obnoxious one. There was oppressive taxation, increased expenditures by the rulers, and a threatened invalidating of all real estate titles. It is not improbable that because of this, Indian deeds were obtained about this time of lands bought many years before, the people doubtless thinking that a deed thus obtained of the aboriginal proprietors would stand the test of anything; but Andros Arrogantly informed the people that such papers were worth no more than the "scratch of a bear's paw."

After a short period of misrule during which the endurance of the people was terribly strained, and toleration of his tyranny was almost exhausted, a revolt came. The people arose in defense of their jeopardized rights, and with great unanimity began to take measures to defend their traditional liberties.

The administration of Andros was overthrown, and there was a reinstatement of the government which existed in 1686.

During the transition from a colony to a province, society was greatly disturbed and the people of the various townships met and discussed the existing condition of things. As a rule they were quite unanimous in their decisions and actions concerning their charter privileges. During this process of political change Concord was with the majority in an adherence to vested rights.

On April 19, 1689, Lieut. John Heald mustered the town's military company and started for Boston to assist in the expected revolt.

When the town met in convention on May 22, to consider the situation, their vote was cast for a reinstatement of the government which was in accordance with the charter of 1685, and to await orders from the new sovereign of Great Britain.

Before, however, the meeting of the Concord people in convention by their delegates, the inhabitants had defined their attitude as is expressed by the following copy of the selectmen's certificate.

"Att a meeting of the ffree-Holders of the Towne of Concord, wee do mutually desire that according as wee have declared ourselves by a writing sent by the Hands of our representatives, that our authority chosen & sworn in the year 1686 w'h the deputyes then chosen & sent to the court may reasume their places and if that cannot be attained, our desires is that that a councell of war may be chosen & settled by our representatives when met together art boston wth the rest of the representitives of the country."

It is a notable fact that three times upon the 19th of April with about a century between each, the town's militia have marched forth in the interest of American democracy. The first in 1689, to assert it, the second in 1775 to create it, and the third in 1861 to protect it.

At this period the "Clerk of Representatives" was Ebenezer Prout, a citizen of Concord, and when the order was issued for the removal of Andros for safe keeping till he could be returned to England, there to be tried for maleasance of office, the order was signed by Mr. Prout.

www.ingramcontent.com/pod-product-compliance
Lightning Source LLC
Chambersburg PA
CBHW051414090426
42737CB00014B/2665